WORLD
AFFAIRS

1900 to the present day

A British soldier stands guard on the roof of a building in Aden, during the troubles which preceded the granting of independence.

WORLD AFFAIRS

1900 to the present day

S. H. Wood, M.A.

Senior Lecturer in History,
Aberdeen College of Education

Oliver & Boyd

Oliver & Boyd
Croythorn House 23 Ravelston Terrace Edinburgh, EH4 3TJ
A division of Longman Group Ltd

ISBN 0 05 002065 X

Maps drawn by John Dugan.

Reprinted 1975, 1976, 1977 (updated)

Main text set in 10 on 12 Baskerville
headings set in Univers series
Printed in Hong Kong by
Yu Luen Offset Printing Factory Ltd

Contents

Preface

This book is intended to help students who are studying for one of the courses offered by examination boards in World History and General Studies, as well as those who are attempting to understand a little more of the world around them since such an understanding is probably more important today that at any other time in mankind's history.

Europeans still occupied a very powerful position in the world of 1900 and the text is arranged to try and show, firstly, how this dominant position was lost: it is then easier to see the emergence of new nations and the expansion of older, non-European ones to the important positions which they occupy today. Britain can no longer shut herself off from the rest of the world, confident in her power and security, assured that what happens around her is of minor importance. Her very existence is menaced by possible quarrels between distant nations armed with terrifying weapons that could wreck the future of the whole of humanity. The prosperity and stability of all nations are tightly bound up with the policies of each other.

A study of the events of the twentieth century can provide an understanding of the problems, fears and memories of past injustices that provide so powerful a motive for present behaviour, for while the technical skills that men command have reached a stage of astounding sophistication, the quarrelsome relations between different peoples make these skills a source of potential ruin. It is hoped that this survey will provide the student with a general picture of the major developments that make up the complete world situation of today.

Aberdeen. S. H. Wood.

1 | The Pre-War World

a) The Powerful Position of Europe

Although Europe is not a large continent in contrast to Asia, Africa and America, she occupied, in 1900, a position of power and importance out of all proportion to her size. Vast areas of Africa, India and South East Asia were owned by European states: in North America and Australasia European settlers had founded powerful countries of their own. Thus, in 1900, the most striking feature in world affairs was the power of Europe.

From the late fifteenth century, Europeans had travelled beyond their own continent seeking conquests overseas. Some traces of these early conquests could still be seen in 1900; in Africa, for example, Portugal still clung on to her conquests. The Portuguese and Spanish who in the 15th and 16th century had led the way in conquering lands and empires outside Europe, had been overtaken by the Dutch, French and British. These new colonisers fought not only the Portuguese and Spaniards, but also each other. Even relatively weak European states owned colonies, Belgium controlled the Congo, for example, and new European states like Germany and Italy struggled eagerly to win colonies too.

By 1900 the Dutch Empire was largely confined to the East Indies, while a vast French Empire extended across North and West Africa and parts of South East Asia, more than replacing the earlier French conquests in Canada and India which had been seized by the British in the eighteenth century. Above all the empires in 1900, towered the vast British Empire covering one fifth of the globe and including countries like Canada, Australia and New Zealand (largely inhabited by Europeans who managed their own affairs), India, Burma, East Africa, Malaya, Nigeria and the Gold Coast (where large native populations were ruled over by British officials) together with scores of island colonies and smaller settlements.

This European domination of so much of the world's surface had been a slow gradual process begun initially by winning areas on the coast and continued, for many years, to be largely confined to coastal areas. In the late nineteenth century however, a new violent forward surge of European conquest had resulted in Africa and South East Asia falling almost wholly into European hands, and had threatened the still un-conquered areas of China, Siam and Abyssinia.

1

Russia, straddling both Europe and Asia but deriving most of her strength from her western European regions, was busy copying the other European countries. She extended her frontiers across Central and Eastern Asia and, like Britain, France and Germany, was pushing the outdated and shaky Chinese Empire steadily closer to ruin.

Few countries seemed able to match the power of Europe. Japan was gaining in strength as a result of deliberately copying Western methods of industry and war, while the U.S.A. who was beginning to look beyond her own frontiers was a state founded by Europeans. Latin America consisted of states that had (with the exception of a few tiny areas) thrown off European control, but control had been in the hands of the less powerful European states of Spain and Portugal and in any case the countries of Latin America were, in 1900, weak and dependent on European and United States skill and money for any progress they could make. Persia and Siam escaped because the Europeans who ruled the nearby areas agreed not to make them colonies, and China eventually escaped, partly because her huge size made it difficult for Europeans to colonise and control her, and partly because Europeans turned upon each other in a terrible war.

The areas which had fallen into European hands varied from ancient civilised empires, like India, to more primitive tribal kingdoms, such as those of West Africa, and all suffered from the conquest. Eventually, some benefits did accrue; roads and railways were built for example, new industries were introduced and women gained more freedom, but the immediate result for areas that were conquered was catastrophic. The long term troubles which stemmed from conquest are visible even today.

The conquered peoples often tried to copy the European way of life and one idea they were quick to copy was nationalism which had a vigorous following in Europe in 1900. Nationalism means believing so strongly in your own nation that you are prepared to fight for it, conquer for it and seek to make it stronger, even at the expense of neighbouring peoples. Some of the European colonies were set up in countries where people lived in tribes, not nations, and colonial boundaries cut across tribal lands leaving areas which have subsequently proved very difficult to manage. The history of Nigeria since independence is a case in point. But independence has not always meant complete freedom for the original native population. In some areas, South Africa and Rhodesia for example, minorities of European settlers have refused to allow power to native majorities even when colonial rule ended.

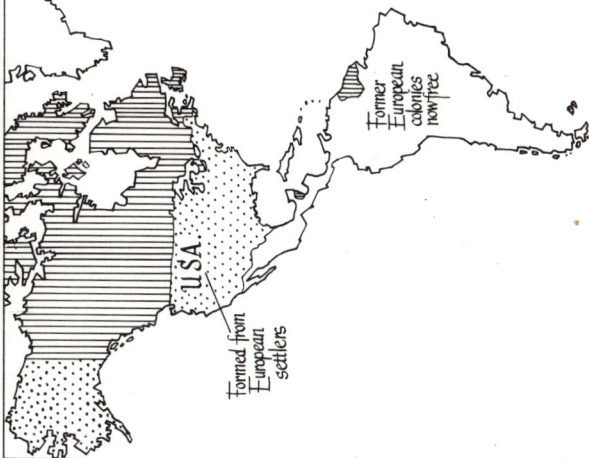

The World in 1900

European colonies, protectorates & dominions.

China & Persia dominated by European powers.

Siam tolerated as buffer state between different European powers

The Turkish Empire crumbling under European pressure.

Russia

Europe

Turkey

Persia

Arabia

Abyssinia

Tripoli taken 1911

Liberia

China

Siam.

Japan

U.S. Colonies

USA

formed from European settlers

Former European colonies now free

b) Why Europe was so Powerful

THE RICHES OF EUROPE: Europe had many advantages that helped to
offset her small size, for her climate and soil were favourable to the growing of many crops and a greater percentage of European land could be
usefully cultivated than in any other continent. Little of Europe was
barren desert or mountain in comparison with Africa or Latin America.
Europe had resources of timber and food supplies, many rivers to
provide fresh water and an easy means of travelling, all of which helped
her energetic peoples to grow in wealth and look outwards.

THE DESIRE TO TRAVEL: The search for knowledge, a love of adventure,
the desire to convert other peoples to Christianity and the desire to make
a fortune, all inspired Europeans to take great risks in travelling all over
the globe. Some Europeans deliberately left Europe in order to make a
permanent home abroad so that they could escape persecution at home
and arrange their lives according to their own beliefs. America provides
examples of all these reasons; the desire for knowledge helped inspire
Columbus, the desire for silver and gold encouraged Cortes to conquer
Mexico, Jesuits went out to South America to convert the people there
and farther north, in New England, English settlers arrived so that they
could escape persecution at home for being Puritans. In the nineteenth
century, as Europe's population rose, many thousands of Europeans
left for the U.S.A. in order to find for themselves a happier and more
prosperous life.

THE INDUSTRIAL REVOLUTION: Advances in industry and agriculture
in Europe gave her great advantages over other parts of the world and
stronger reasons than ever for wanting to dominate the rest of the world.
The growth of industries like coal, iron, textiles and chemicals, which
developed first in late 18th century Britain, had by 1900, strongly affected
France, Belgium and Germany and partly affected the rest of Europe.
Methods of mass production meant that Europeans could make goods in
greater numbers far more cheaply and they therefore looked eagerly for
markets for these goods and sources of necessary raw materials like
cotton, rubber and oil. These changes helped European nations to become much stronger and richer and widened the gap between Europe
and Africa, Asia and Latin America.

WARFARE: The revolution in industry also increased European superiority in warfare. Before the nineteenth century small European armies
had often overcome larger non-European ones simply as a result of better

discipline and tactics and the use of guns and cavalry. By 1900 Europeans had new weapons, in particular the steamship and the rapid firing gun, both of which were produced in large quantities.

PRESTIGE: Although some areas were made colonies because of their trading value others, conquered in the late nineteenth and early twentieth centuries, had little economic worth. The European colonists hoped that trade would eventually grow in places like French Indo-China but other areas were so obviously of little value that their acquisition can only be explained in terms of prestige. This is partially true of the parts of Africa colonised by Germany and especially true of the poor areas acquired with great difficulty by Italy. In 1900 the great powers had colonies, and these emergent states wished to prove that they, too, were great powers in every respect.

The Brief Life of European Colonies After 1900

In little over half a century control of much of the world was gone. This collapse had two major causes. Firstly, through the activities of the conquered peoples, who had become increasingly restless and resentful and learned to borrow European ideas and methods to use against their masters making them feel it was no longer worthwhile trying to stay in power. Secondly, Europe contributed to its own downfall, by two vast, costly and destructive wars. The wars of 1914–18 and 1939–45 exhausted Europe, ruined European prestige and distracted Europe from affairs in other continents. The wars fought between Europeans in the nineteenth century had not been very savage: the wars of the twentieth century were catastrophic. Out of this turmoil arose the present importance of the U.S.A. and Russia, states with very limited military power in 1900. But even these new powers owe their present position to Europe, the former being created by Europeans, the latter being partly European.

c) Tensions Inside European States

European countries in 1900 were ruled by governments which varied from despotism – as in Russia, where the Czar ruled alone and supreme, responsible to no-one – to republicanism, in France, where all citizens took a vigorous interest in politics. Systems of parliamentary government existed in Britain, Germany and Italy, though none were fully democratic. In Britain, many people still could not vote (women for example) while in Germany, the Emperor retained great powers, among them choosing the chief minister, the Chancellor. Politics in Italy were corrupt and government only seemed to work when a skilful man, like Giolitti, used threats and bribes to hold together a majority in parliament. Yet all these different kinds of government had a common fear of two powerful forces, Socialism and Anarchism. These seemed dangerous because they threatened violence and appealed to the poor, who formed the bulk of the population in Eastern Europe, Italy and Spain, and a large proportion in Britain, France and Germany. European governments did little or nothing to help the poor, and poverty was very real involving famine, sickness, and the probability of a miserable, dark and overworked life.

Socialism

For centuries, people had dreamed of ways in which to reorganise society so that wealth could be more fairly shared. The Socialists of 1900 followed a special version of these ideals which had been worked out by Karl Marx, a German forced to spend much of his life in exile in Britain. Many of Marx's ideas therefore came from studying conditions in Britain. He worked much of the time in the British Museum writing articles and pamphlets, the most famous being the *Communist Manifesto* of 1848. Marx's works contained studies on the state of society, how it came to reach its present state and what was likely to happen in the future. Many of his ideas were borrowed from others, from English economists, German philosophers and French revolutionaries, but Marx bound together these ideas in his own way to form what we now generally call Communism, though in 1900 the commonly used term was 'Socialism'.

Marx claimed to be a kind of scientist who had discovered the laws that decided how human society worked, as well as a prophet and revolutionary who appealed to people to change society. He believed that the way a country's economy was organised decided everything else, its government, its religion, even its art, music, and literature. Society had reached a point where capitalism was becoming the most important feature, that is where a small group of people, with much wealth, ran government and society for their own profit. But most of this wealth came from industry and industries needed workers. Marx foresaw a time when the workers would be so numerous they would sweep aside the capitalists and alter society so that industry and government worked for the benefit of all.

To workers living in misery, Marx's belief in their triumph was naturally attractive but Socialism also appealed to intellectuals. They were interested in Marx's discussion of the laws governing society's development, and ashamed of the squalor and misery in which many humans lived. All over Europe Social Democrat parties sprang up, formed from these two groups, while governments watched in fear, their fear manifested by persecution of party members. In countries like Russia, where persecution was particularly brutal, the Socialists became a secret organisation and often used extreme methods, whereas in more tolerant countries, like Germany, Socialists were more cautious and respectable and in less of a hurry to risk a revolution. Eventually a split, which was clear by 1920, came between the extreme and moderate Socialists. Today the term 'Communist' is used to describe the more extreme group, and 'Socialist' to describe the moderates.

Anarchism

Whereas Socialists were well organised, hoped to seize power and use government to carry out many reforms, anarchists hated all forms of government and wished to see them swept away. Anarchism was born in the mid-nineteenth century and its most eminent thinkers were a Frenchman named Proudhon and a Russian, Michael Bakunin. Anarchists believed that men were naturally good and ready to co-operate with each other, but that men who held great power and property became corrupt and selfish and, through governments, laws, police and armies, made life miserable for ordinary people. No reform of government was possible, it must simply be abolished, and though Proudhon hoped that this could be achieved peacefully as men saw the truth of Anarchism, Bakunin believed that violence was necessary.

Anarchism was especially strong in Russia and Spain and fear of Anarchist terrorism added a new violence to politics. Among the victims killed by Anarchists between 1894 and 1914 were no less than six heads of state, including two Spanish prime ministers, a French President, President McKinley of the U.S.A., King Humbert of Italy and the Empress Elizabeth of Austria. Like Socialism, Anarchism was international. It appealed to desperate men with nothing to lose as well as to more wealthy people who felt guilty about the wretched life endured by ordinary people.

Some governments simply tried to stamp out these forces, but many tried to reduce their appeal through reforms. The governments of Germany, Britain and France introduced many reforms, between 1870 and 1914, designed to improve life for ordinary people by bettering their conditions of work and education and reducing suffering during times of sickness and unemployment. Even these moderate reforms aroused bitter struggles, so great was the hostility of many of the well-to-do to increasing the power of the government and raising taxes.

Europe in 1914

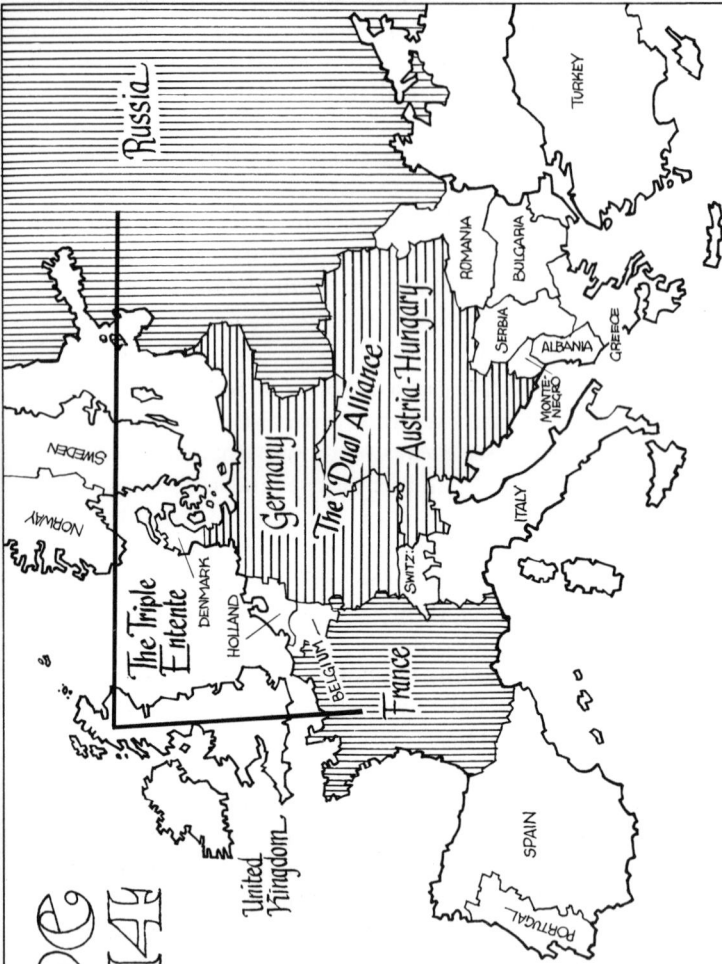

Russia

SWEDEN

NORWAY

The Triple Entente

DENMARK

HOLLAND

BELGIUM

Germany

The 'Dual Alliance'

Austria-Hungary

ROMANIA

BULGARIA

SERBIA

ALBANIA

MONTE-NEGRO

GREECE

TURKEY

SWITZ.

ITALY

France

United Kingdom

SPAIN

PORTUGAL

Franco-Russian Alliance

Against the ferment of Communism and Anarchism, other quarrels in European states seem small in comparison. The pressure for a share in power from the middle classes had succeeded in lands where they were numerous: and the Roman Catholic Church no longer seemed such a dangerous rival to politicians as it had in the 1870's when several governments feared the Pope was trying to increase his power and weaken the power of governments.

To the small number of well-to-do people who formed European 'society' however, even Socialism and Anarchism seemed remote. A rich and glittering group, shielded by their narrow life and education from fully understanding all the problems of ordinary people, they were, in 1900, still very powerful and confident. They could have had little awareness of the doom they were bringing down on themselves by leading their countries into war in 1914.

d) Tensions Between European States

The Europe that apparently dominated the world in 1914 was, in fact, bitterly divided within itself and split into two armed camps.

The German-Austrian Alliance

Germany had only emerged as a united, modern state in 1871 when a victory over France had joined Prussia, in the north, with the South German states to form the German Empire. At the head of the Empire stood the Kaiser (Emperor) who appointed Ministers and shared a little of his power with an assembly representing the different states, and also an elected assembly. Germany was rich and powerful, with booming industries which were rivalling and, in some fields, outstripping those of Britain. In addition, she had an army generally recognised as the finest in the world. But its Kaiser in 1900 was the vain and ambitious William II whose tactless policies and lack of real control over either government or army alarmed Germany's neighbours. William was supported by Germans eager to see their country as a powerful naval and colonial power; he allowed Tirpitz to develop a big German fleet that naturally alarmed Britain.

Germany's chief ally was Austria-Hungary, an unstable ramshackle empire that included people of many races, dominated by an alliance of Germans and the Magyars of Hungary. The Austrian Government, headed by the aged Emperor Francis Joseph, was fearful of any changes that might cause the empire to break up. They were afraid too, that the large numbers of Slavs in the empire would be attracted to the Slavs who

B

lived outside Austria-Hungary in the Balkans and in Russia. Austrian military power was declining and she needed German support, which Germany was ready to offer because she was afraid of becoming isolated.

The French and Russian Alliance

Opposed to this alliance was the curious combination of despotic Russia and republican France. France had never really forgiven Germany for the defeat in 1870–71 in which Alsace-Lorraine was seized from France, whilst Russia desperately needed money to improve her industries and French loans were forthcoming only at the price of French alliance. The fine French army and the huge Russian army seemed a formidable combination that worried Germany and made her people grumble that they were being encircled by enemies.

Italy's position

Italy was the ally of Germany and Austria as a result of a fit of resentment against France for seizing Tunis before Italy could. But Italy was not a powerful country and she was not enthusiastic about the alliance, refusing to be in any quarrel which involved Britain and still with ambitions to take land to the north and east that was held by Austria.

Britain's position

Britain was not tied to either side, indeed in 1900 she seemed on worse terms with France and Russia than with the countries she eventually fought in 1914. The chief reason for these quarrels lay overseas, in the shape of the colonial rivalry between Britain and France in Egypt and the Sudan, and between Britain and Russia in Persia, Afghanistan and China.

Thus an explosive situation was developing, a situation in which fear of German power, colonial rivalry, an arms race between the two sides and the rivalry of Austria and Russia in the Balkans, all contributed to the eventual outbreak of war.

e) Events Leading to the Outbreak of War

The Ententes

Attempts by Britain to form an alliance with Germany failed and fear of Germany's navy drove Britain closer to France and Russia. A new type of warship, called the *dreadnought*, outdated earlier types, made the large British fleet obsolete, and encouraged the Germans to build the new warships that promised to give her a real chance to rival

Britain. In Britain there was panic and in 1908 popular alarm forced the Liberal Government to double its dreadnought building programme. In France, concern about Russia's weaknesses and alarm at German policy encouraged a welcome to discussions for an end to quarrels between the two countries. In 1904 Britain and France signed an *entente*, which was not an alliance but a sorting out of colonial problems that nevertheless made the next stage easier: better relations with Russia.

In 1904 and 1905, Russia was defeated by Japan and this blow, plus persuasion by the French, led to talks with Britain which ended in an *entente* that worked out solutions to the colonial rivalries of Russia and Britain. Though still the ally of no-one in Europe, Britain's sympathies were clearly pulling her to one side and it was not long before military chiefs in France and Britain were holding secret discussions on what to do in the event of war with Germany. They drew up plans for Britain to defend the North Sea and Channel, and France, the Mediterranean. German fears of encirclement were increased by the policy adopted by the British, yet Britain's position was not sufficiently open and firm to really worry the Germans.

The Moroccan Crises

The German government at this time was not satisfied with the small empire it had so far gained and was immediately jealous of any other power trying to take control of any of the few remaining areas outside European domination. The French, who already held Algeria and Tunis, attempted to gain control of Morocco, and in 1905 and 1911 Germany made two attempts to halt this development, even going so far as to send a warship to Morocco. But though Germany forced European conferences on Morocco, she failed to stop French influence there from increasing, for Russia naturally backed France, and Britain, afraid of a German naval base being established in Morocco, did likewise. Even Italy would not back Germany.

The German War Plan

Although the German Army was huge and well equipped, the prospect of having to fight both France in the west and Russia in the east so alarmed the General Staff that they drew up a plan to cope with this problem. This plan, known as the Schlieffen Plan, was the only war plan Germany had in 1914 and came to be of overwhelming importance. To mobilise an army in 1914 took considerable time and planning; the carefully thought out German scheme enabled Germany to mobilise first so that

The Balkans 1908

1914

once war seemed probable there was always pressure on Germany to declare war quickly in order to gain an advantage. General Schlieffen believed that she needed this advantage to deal effectively with the two-front war problem. He hoped that a massive attack on France from the north through Belgium (to avoid strong French defences farther south) would win a quick victory. Belgium was neutral, Britain would be offended, but if a quick victory could be won in the west, Britain might well keep out of the war and Germany could then deal with Russia whose forces would be slower to mobilise. So any German clash with Russia also meant war with France. Both Russia and Austria suffered from this same problem of having only one plan, and that a plan for total, not limited, warfare.

The Balkan Crisis

In the troubled Balkans came just such a clash, which in normal circumstances would have been restricted to a petty squabble but in fact led to total war. The Balkans were no longer dominated by Turkey but consisted of a number of restless states of which the most important was Serbia. Austria had already offended Serbia and Russia, Serbia's ally, by seizing Bosnia and Herzegovina which had once been Turkish and which were inhabited by Serbs. In 1912 an alliance of Balkan States fought a successful war with Turkey, then in 1913 they began quarrelling amongst themselves.

From these Balkan wars emerged a stronger Serbia more hostile than ever to Austria. The war of 1912 led to Austria, backed by Germany, intervening to deny Serbia a port by insisting that a separate state of Albania be formed; it was this that led to Serbia's seeking compensation elsewhere, chiefly from Bulgaria, in the 1913 war.

The many Slavs in the Austrian Empire were drawn towards their fellow Slavs in Serbia and the feeling grew in Austria that Serbia must be dealt with. Moreover both Aehrenthal, Austria's Foreign Minister, and Hotzendorf, her Chief of Staff, were eager for a war to prove Austria was still a major power. But behind Serbia stood her ally Russia, already humiliated by defeat from Japan and by the disgrace of failing to get compensation for herself when Austria took Bosnia and Herzegovina, and failing to prevent Austria creating Albania. Russia was not going to be humiliated again and if Austria had to fight Russia too, then she needed to feel sure of German support. Both the Kaiser and Moltke, the Chief of Staff, were ready with promises of support to Austria if she faced such a crisis.

The Outbreak of War

On June 28th, 1914, Francis Ferdinand, Archduke of the Austrian Empire, was assassinated in the Bosnian town of Sarajevo by Slav extremists. Austria pinned the blame on Serbia and demanded humiliating terms for settlement; she declared war though Serbia was ready to agree to nearly all the terms. Austrian mobilisation meant Russian mobilisation in reply and Germany was thus forced to put her war plan into operation in support of Austria.

On August 1st Germany declared war on Russia, on August 3rd on France, and on the 4th, Britain declared war because Germany would not promise to respect Belgian neutrality. As the declaration for war was made, so politicians in Germany and Austria were elbowed aside, military men took over and made decisions regardless of their political consequences. No one realised how long and terrible the war would be, indeed most countries entered into the fray in a mood of light heartedness. In most capitals, large crowds gathered to cheer the news of war and volunteers rushed to enlist before it was all over.

The coming of war shattered the idealism of those who had thought that there would be no more major wars because they saw that even the victors would lose heavily. Even Socialists, who had supported the idea of an international brotherhood of workers, proved generally ready to forget this ideal and put nationalism first. Only small minorities opposed the war in 1914, and these minorities were fiercely persecuted, indeed persecuted far more severely in many states than were opponents of the Second World War.

f) Conclusion

In this confused manner, Europe rushed into a war in which all its energies were turned upon itself. Though for Europe this was sheer disaster, for much of the rest of the world the events of 1914–18 brought new opportunities and relief from relentless European pressure. It quickly became clear that the fierce grip with which Europe appeared to hold so much of the world was far from secure and might easily be broken. This naturally encouraged Europe's potential rivals, inspired the peoples of European colonies to hope that independence would soon be theirs, and gave those weak countries struggling to hold on to independence against European pressure, new hope that they could and would triumph.

The assassination of Archduke Francis Ferdinand of Austria in 1914 was one of the causes of the First World War. The Archduke, wearing a plumed hat, is seen here on a ceremonial occasion.

Europe's rivals

The U.S.A., even though formed from emigrants from Europe, had become, by 1914, a powerful independent state with clear ambitions of its own. Its size, its enormous resources, its large population and powerful industries clearly made it a force to be reckoned with, but the U.S.A. had tended to avoid world politics and had confined its military efforts to its own continent. The U.S. navy easily crushed the Spanish navy to establish its dominance over the Caribbean, but the U.S. army was very small and the U.S. federal government was strongly opposed to wars overseas. The Great War in Europe provided U.S. industry with an opportunity to grab markets from its European competitors which it was quick to seize; even though the U.S.A. eventually entered the war it was never as dramatically affected as the major European countries.

In the Far East, Japan, too, seized the opportunities that 1914–18 provided. By 1914 Japan had grown beyond the humiliating weakness that had allowed Europeans to bully her in the mid-nineteenth century. She had deliberately and cleverly copied European military methods and built up her industries, so that her Emperor, and the powerful landowners who surrounded him, had been able to defeat Russia in 1905.

Japan had big ambitions for her own expansion, and nearby in China lay splendid opportunities for conquest and control now that Britain, France and Germany were busy fighting one another. Whereas Japan successfully copied Western ideas, because her government was not too proud to learn from others, the rulers of China refused to learn from the West, despite repeated humiliations, and China in 1914 was backward, weak, and divided. Its armed forces were poorly trained and equipped and were divided into units serving rival warlords who struggled for mastery over their unfortunate land.

Europe's colonies

The areas of the world dominated by emigrants from Europe, areas like Canada and Australia, were still loyal to their European mother country and followed obediently into conflict. But they were so rudely shaken by the horror of the war that they insisted on a more independent status by 1918. Areas where small numbers of Europeans controlled large numbers of non-Europeans were, apparently, less suddenly affected. Yet it was these areas which were to experience the greatest changes.

In 1914 Europe appeared to have largely overcome local opposition to its rule in Africa, South East Asia and India: by 1918 it was clear that this control could only hope to be temporary. The British navy, so long free from rivals and able to roam the seas at will, had to face the existence of competitors like Japan, and had to concentrate its efforts more in European waters. The British Empire felt the effects of the shrinking of British power; from the huge empire of India, ruled, amazingly, by so few Europeans, to the states of West Africa only recently captured, the blow to British prestige and strength was felt. The German empire disappeared and French security in the parts of the world she controlled was opened to question. In 1914 the colonial peoples lacked the education, economic knowledge, skill and development of their masters, but the war so damaged Europe's strength and prestige that there was an upsurge of hope among those wishing to be free of outside control.

Yet for most peoples of the world the quarrels of Europeans were, in 1914, obscure and meaningless. For most people in South America, Asia, and Africa, life was a hard struggle to hold together a miserable existence: throughout these areas the majority of people obtained their living from poor methods of farming on inadequate patches of land. Outside Europe, the U.S.A. and Japan, well developed industries were rare and provided employment for only a tiny proportion of the world's population. In China, India, Egypt and Bolivia, the majority were ruled by masters they disliked. Whether they were foreigners or local people who were wealthy made little difference: few rulers felt obliged to think of their subjects as anything other than providers of labour and taxes: few people understood enough to organise themselves adequately to throw off their rulers. Foreigners might come to dig for minerals or gather crops, but the benefits of such work usually flowed to the foreigners and a small select group of the native population, never to the mass of the people. The world, for many in 1914, was a savage and brutal place.

New unity in the world

The Great War also emphasised how the world of the twentieth century was more united than ever before. Though different states battled and quarrelled with one another, new links between states had grown up making what happened in one part of the world of serious importance to other parts. These links can be seen in the way, by 1914, railways crossed continents, steamships crossed oceans with speed and efficient reliability, and more and more trade flowed between the different countries of the world. Thus, what happened in Europe or the U.S.A., in Japan or the U.S.S.R., affected the prosperity of all parts of the globe to a greater or lesser extent. This development increased with the passage of time, and so did the speed with which events in one part of the world could be passed on as news to other parts of the globe. To the postal service and telegraph, the twentieth century added radio, telephone and television as common methods of spreading knowledge. Booms and slumps, wars and treaties, riots and rebellions, all once the concern only of those immediately involved, in the twentieth century became, more and more, matters of interest and concern to the whole world.

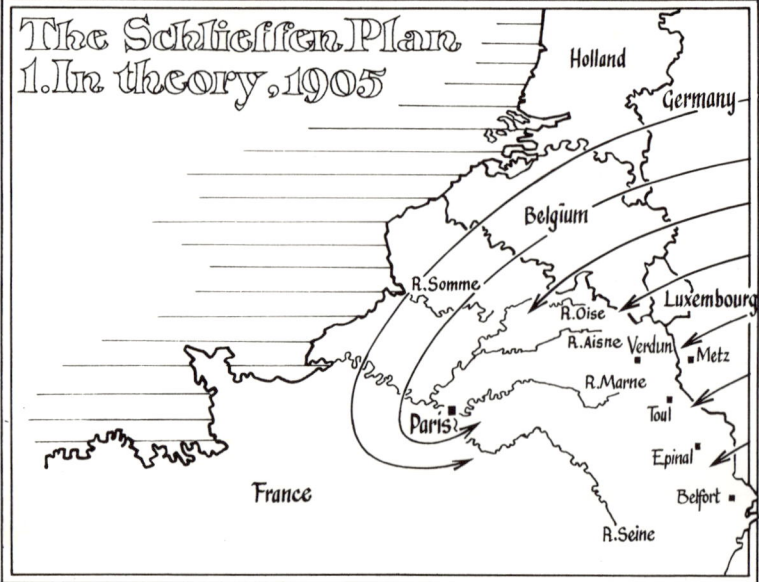

The Schlieffen Plan
1. In theory, 1905

Holland

Germany

Belgium

R.Somme

R.Oise

Luxembourg

R.Aisne Verdun

Metz

R.Marne

Paris

Toul

France

Epinal

Belfort

R.Seine

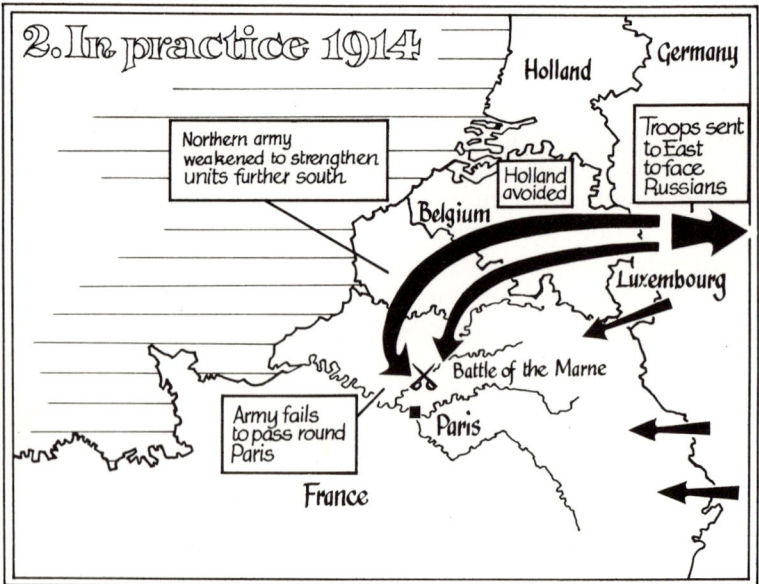

2. In practice 1914

Holland

Germany

Northern army
weakened to strengthen
units further south.

Holland
avoided

Troops sent
to East
to face
Russians

Belgium

Luxembourg

Battle of the Marne

Army fails
to pass round
Paris

Paris

France

2 | The First World War and its Aftermath

The events of the War

a) A New Kind of War

For a century Europe had been only briefly troubled by serious wars, and these wars (of which the most important was the Franco-Prussian War of 1870) did not prepare people for the nightmare that lay ahead. Wars had not generally been 'total', that is they had not involved the whole nation in serious suffering, and the armies fighting the wars had not been very large. But the many experts who expected another brief conflict, and the peoples who clamoured for quick victories, were all soon to realise that they were involved in a new kind of war in which suffering would be far more terrible than ever before.

New weapons

New inventions like the tank and the machine-gun totally altered the character of war. These new weapons were developed by the large business firms, like Krupps in Germany and Vickers in Britain which had grown up in the industrial revolution of the nineteenth century. The machine-gun was, perhaps, the most important invention; its rapid deadly fire made attacks difficult and costly and meant that troops who were well protected by trenches, sandbags and barbed wire could beat off all but the most overwhelming assaults. The cavalry, previously the most highly thought of section in most armies, was particularly vulnerable and was soon reduced to taking a negligible part in the war. This situation of having an extremely strong defence was not seriously upset until the later stages of the war when a British invention, the tank, once more strengthened the attack.

The howitzers, mortars, field guns and massive artillery developed by both sides made it possible for great damage to be inflicted by bombardment. So did the use of gas shells and 'creeping barrages', in which the artillery methodically bombarded enemy positions yard by yard as the infantry advanced behind the gunfire. At sea the torpedo and the submarine transformed naval warfare, making attacks on merchant shipping far easier and threatening the massive, expensive battleships of European navies. The torpedo and the mine put an end to the notion that British battleships could cruise safe from destruction unless faced with battleships of a similar size. Both sides soon found it unwise to risk their battlefleets at sea for long.

Civilians involved in the war

Nor were civilian populations as free from the effects of war as they had been in the past. The need for massive armies to batter their way through enemy defences, and the equal balance of the two sides on the Western Front, meant that before long men were being forced by conscription to join in the war. Women, compelled to fill jobs vacated by men called into war service, achieved a new importance as a result of their part in the war. Civilian populations were also open to attack from long range guns at sea and on land, and from airships and aircraft. These latter weapons of war, useful for scouting for the army and for searching for submarines, could also be used for bombing.

Count Zeppelin had given Germany a marked advantage in the development of airships, and Zeppelin raids on Britain caused great alarm and some destruction until Britain developed guns and fighter aircraft capable of dealing with the slow and vulnerable airships. Both sides gradually improved their aircraft, fitting machine-guns, increasing range and manoeuvrability, and both sides produced fighter 'aces' like the German Manfred Von Richthofen, with many successes to their credit. As the old, small professional armies were pushed aside and replaced by the new mass conscript armies, and as the war dragged on, in growing bitterness, ordinary people became far less tolerant of their leaders and thus the Great War changed governments too. Political, economic and social changes, even revolutions, were brought about by this conflict.

b) 1914

The German advance in the West

Germany and Austria-Hungary, known as the Central Powers because of their geographical situation, had a united position, good communication and, before long, unity of command because Austria's weakness led to increased German interference. To support France, British forces had to cross the Channel, while to lend support to Russia was very difficult indeed and in any case British forces were small in numbers in 1914. The rapidly mobilised and well-led German army was able to attack in the West, hopeful of gaining the quick victory that Schlieffen had seen as so necessary. The attack was supervised by Moltke and spearheaded by Von Kluck's army which was to sweep through Belgium and northern France, pass to the west of Paris and drive the French back on their own defences.

Moltke altered Schlieffen's plan to strengthen his forces farther south so that they could check the advance of large French forces gathering to try and recapture Alsace-Lorraine. The German advance was delayed by the brave resistance of the small Belgian army, especially at Liège where the fort held out for some time until finally hammered into the ground by the massive Krupp artillery. As the advance continued, the Germans also made contact with a small British Expeditionary Force of under 100,000 troops led by Sir John French which, like Joffre's French army, was hastily retreating. The French army had thought simply in terms of attack, not defence, but its rash attacks had been crushed and all the placid calm of Joffre was needed to avoid panic.

The Allied recovery

The pace of their advances wearied the German troops and the gaps opening up between their different armies alarmed their generals so

Kaiser Wilhelm II, accompanied by members of his general staff, inspecting German troops at the front during the First World War.

much that the Schlieffen Plan broke down short of Paris. On their own initiative the northern German armies turned inwards, short of Paris, and gave the French the chance to counter attack. It was Gallieni, governor of Paris, who saw this opportunity and convinced Joffre of the need to attack in the area of the River Marne, a plan that proved most successful for during September the Germans were pushed back several miles to the River Aisne. Both sides hastily extended their lines to the coast in a bid to seize the Channel ports, a race that was narrowly won by the Allies with the help of a determined fight by British forces at Ypres.

The war in the West settled down into a stalemate as both sides dug in and put up barbed wire defences. Till 1918 the war in the west consisted of attempts to break this deadlock in desperate battles that destroyed the countryside, turning it into a nightmare landscape where nothing grew.

The terrible conditions of war

From the end of 1914 until almost the very end of the conflict, the huge armies engaged in the war endured conditions which either crippled or sent out of their mind many of those who escaped death on the battlefield. Faced with trenches, barbed wire and machine guns the generals could find no solution except to throw even greater numbers of men in vain assaults against enemy lines. At best a few miles of dangerous ground would be captured at huge cost, yet the Germans still struggled for victory, and the British, French and Russians tried to throw back the invaders.

For ordinary soldiers all this meant an existence so terrible that it is hard to appreciate. Any order to attack brought the grim probability of death. Terrible bombardments from huge gatherings of artillery had to be endured. In winter, trenches and shell craters filled with mud and water, men might drown if they took a false step. The use of poison gas by both sides brought an added terror to war. Yet more and more men had to be found to replace those lost and to build up even bigger armies in the hope of overwhelming the enemy. Even the British, who for so long had opposed conscription, had to accept the need for it in 1916. Thus, the terrible war came to affect more and more families, involving whole peoples in a way no earlier war had done.

The Eastern Front

Moltke's forces in the West had also been weakened by the need to divert troops to the Eastern Front where the Russians had mobilised with surprising speed and had added to their original plan for an attack on

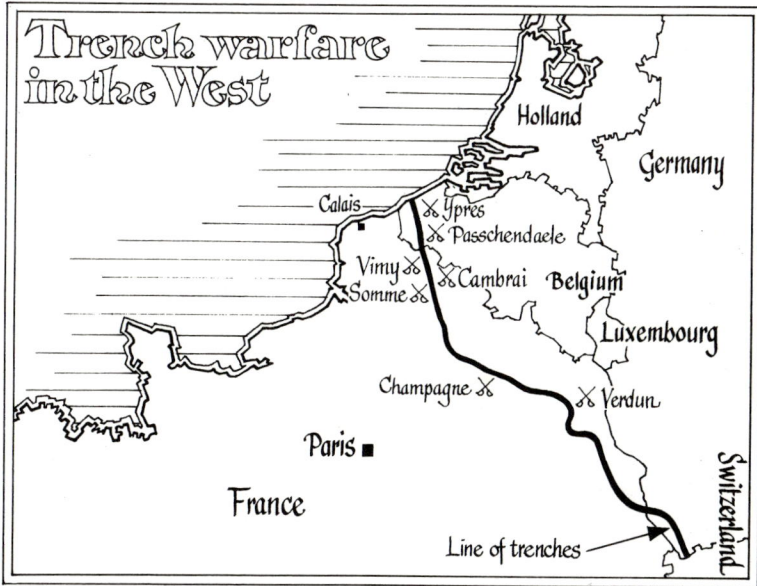

Trench warfare in the West

Holland

Germany

Calais

Ypres

Passchendaele

Vimy

Cambrai   Belgium

Somme

Luxembourg

Champagne   Verdun

Paris

France

Switzerland

Line of trenches

Austria, to save Serbia, an invasion of East Prussia to take the pressure off Joffre's forces. But the Russian armies were poorly trained and equipped and incompetently led by their generals, Samsonov and Rennenkamp (who were on bad terms with each other) and were easily defeated at Tannenberg and the Masurian lakes. These victories brought great prestige to the successful German generals, Hindenburg and Ludendorff, but the Russians had helped Joffre and their attack on Austria went well, eventually leading to victory at Lemberg.

The campaigns of 1914 showed up the defects in the impressive plans of the generals. Moltke was an intelligent man, worried by the weaknesses he knew were in the Schlieffen Plan, unable to offer any convincing alternative, and finally ruined by his failure to fulfil the scheme of the man who had drawn it up but who, in 1914, had been dead for several years. As the Germans marched across France, ever more weary, the French were able to use the railway system that spread out from Paris to move their troops rapidly to where they were needed. The masses of grey-clad German troops made excellent targets for the machine-guns and the 75s (the French field guns), as well as for the old fashioned rapid rifle-fire of the British. Moltke ended the year in despair, the British leader, Sir John French, was soon in a state of alarm and dismay, and the way was clear for calmer men. Joffre, large, solid, cheerful and placid seemed unshaken by disasters, a rock on which all could rely. Douglas Haig, soon to succeed French, was also a very confident calm soldier with a deep belief in himself. The Germans found a similar hero in Hindenburg, though whether he deserved their admiration is doubtful since he had few ideas of his own and depended heavily on his brilliant assistant, General Erich Ludendorff.

c) 1915

The Eastern Front

The Austrians had failed to defeat even Serbia and the new German commander in chief, Falkenhayn, agreed to Hindenburg and Ludendorff's demands for more German troops in the east. Under Mackensen, these new German forces chased the Russians out of the Austrian Empire and defeated them at Gorlice.

The Western Front

On the Western Front the Germans stood on the defensive in 1915, beating off repeated allied attacks both by the British army, strengthened through vigorous recruiting by Lord Kitchener and under their new chief, Douglas Haig, and by the French.

Historians still quarrel about the qualities and skills of Haig and Kitchener. Haig had certainly risen to the top very rapidly, and his confidence in using his men against strong defences is difficult to find sympathetic. Yet he was also ready to listen to some new ideas (he was too eager to use the tank and wasted it at first) and it is, perhaps, unfair to remember him simply in relation to the terrible losses suffered by his men whilst forgetting his success in the 1918 campaigns and the inability of any senior officer to find a way to victory that was not very expensive. Kitchener, the Secretary for War, has been criticised for distrusting tanks and machine-guns, for refusing to share any of his power, and for his lack of experience of European Warfare. But Kitchener had to work with an ignorant and unhelpful cabinet that expected too much of him, and at least he, like Haig, sensed that the war would be lengthy. Joffre continued in serene command of the French forces, though his failure to drive back the Germans was beginning to shake his reputation.

The Gallipoli Expedition

New ways of achieving victory were therefore sought and the British ministers, Churchill and Lloyd George, pressed their scheme to switch the attack to Turkey. The Turks had joined the Central Powers in November 1914, they controlled the best Allied supply route to Russia, helped by two German warships, the *Goeben* and the *Breslau*. The first attack on the narrow entry to the Black Sea, the Dardanelles, was naval and led by Admiral de Robeck, but was halted when three vessels struck mines and sank (March, 1915). In April, troops under Sir Ian Hamilton landed nearby on the Gallipoli peninsula only to meet vigorous Turkish resistance that prevented them from moving inland. After suffering heavy losses from disease and frost, as well as battle, the Allied army (which included many Australians and New Zealanders) was forced to retire, defeated. This encouraged Bulgaria to join the Central Powers and their forces proved too much for Serbia who was now defeated. An Allied plan to help the Serbs was ruined by the Greeks, who insisted on remaining neutral, so that all the Allies now held in the area was a small bridge head at Salonika.

The whole campaign was a most depressing experience for all who had hoped for a speedy end to the war. It showed up all too clearly the poor planning of the British government which was confused about whether the attack should be purely a naval one, and then despatched Hamilton without even an adequate map. The frequent delays gave the Turks a chance to strengthen their defences with German help, and Hamilton's clumsy handling of the attacks meant heavier losses than were necessary and the missing of a possible chance of success. The episode strengthened the arguments of generals like Haig who insisted that the war must be fought and won on the Western Front and that all other schemes were a waste of manpower.

The Entry of Italy

However, 1915 also saw a new ally join Britain and France. Italy had been the ally of the Central Powers, but had failed to declare war in 1914; in 1915, ambitious to capture land from Austria, she signed the Treaty of London with Britain and France. But the war did not go well for Italy, for a harsh and difficult battle in the Alps brought no gains.

d) The War at Sea

Early Naval Clashes

The conflict at sea opened with a series of minor battles including two battle cruiser victories won by the bold and dashing Admiral Beatty, in 1914 in the Heligoland Bight, and in 1915 off the Dogger Bank. The Germans bombarded Hartlepool, Yarmouth and Scarborough in 1914, and won the battle of Coronel in the South Seas too. This latter German force was eventually defeated off the Falkland Islands by Admiral

c

German submarine (U-boat) U.35 holding up a British merchant ship in the Mediterranean, May 1917. While U-boats became a serious threat to Allied shipping during 1916 and 1917, they also led to the U.S.A. entering the War.

Sturdee's squadron. Other early German efforts concentrated on damaging British trade and included attacks by surface raiders like the *Emden* which did great damage to British vessels in the Indian Ocean, as well as by U-boats which were far more difficult to catch. With the fall of Germany's colonies to Allied forces the German surface raiders found places to coal and refit hard to obtain and the U-boats therefore became more important than ever. But an all-out campaign by the U-boats was risky, for the U.S.A., with its vast trade with Europe, was neutral and irritated by the British blockade of Germany; heavy U-boat sinkings of American shipping would turn U.S. anger against Germany. U-boat attacks caused loss of life, the British blockade didn't. In 1915 Germany received warning of this danger; a U-boat sank the *Lusitania*, a liner carrying a hundred Americans among its passengers, and vigorous American protests were directed at Germany. The German Chancellor, Bethman Hollweg, restrained the military leaders and halted the U-boat campaign so that the U.S.A. remained, for the moment, neutral.

The Battle of Jutland

The only serious naval battle came in 1916 when Von Scheer's High Seas Fleet, preceded by Hipper's battle cruisers, put to sea ignorant of the fact that the British had the key to the code used by the Germans and that Jellicoe's Grand Fleet was sailing from Rosyth and Scapa Flow to intercept. Beatty's battle cruisers made the first contact with the Germans and though Beatty's force suffered heavy damage, he managed to draw the High Seas Fleet on to Jellicoe's guns. Twice the Grand Fleet was able to pound the Germans before the end of daylight and the fear of torpedo attack caused the action to be broken off. During the night the Germans broke through the British fleet in a successful dash for port. Both sides claimed victory, for on the one hand the Germans had fled, steaming hastily back to Kiel, whilst on the other hand they had inflicted far heavier damage on the British than they had suffered themselves. Jellicoe was criticised for his cautious handling of the battle, but he realised the superior quality of many of the German ships and he was very much aware of the disastrous results for Britain of defeat. The sea was Britain's life-line bringing food and raw materials, and carrying away goods to be sold, as well as the route to France to reinforce British troops.

Renewed U-Boat Warfare

After 1916 the Germans concentrated on U-boat warfare. From the 31st January, 1917, U-boats were allowed to sink on sight vessels trading with Britain in a bid to starve Britain into surrender despite the effect of this policy on the U.S.A. This campaign waged by over 100 U-boats did huge damage until the use of convoys, depth charges, hydrophones to detect the presence of U-boats, and a daring raid on U-boat bases at Zeebrugge and Ostend cut losses from 335 ships sunk in April down to only 103 in November.

e) 1916

Verdun

The character of the war seemed to alternate with the years; whereas Germany advanced in the east in 1915 and 1917, in 1916, and in 1914 and 1918, there was strong German pressure on the Western Front. Falkenhayn decided to attack Verdun, a French fortress town in a prominent and exposed position; he hoped that France would be so determined to hold the city that she would pour more and more men into a narrow area where they could be destroyed by German artillery. The attacks were commanded by the Imperial Crown Prince and, at first, seemed a complete success, for outer rings of forts were captured and the French driven back. But a desperate defence was organised by

Pétain, Verdun was held, and it was the Germans who now began pouring in men in a bid to win final success. The total losses in this terrible battle numbered over half a million and after it, Falkenhayn was replaced by Hindenburg and Ludendorff.

The Somme

By 1916 the British army had grown to a vast size and was able to launch an attack on the line of the River Somme. Haig opened up his attack with a huge artillery bombardment which lasted a week yet failed to clear the ground sufficiently for the infantry advance. Thirty useless miles of ground were all that the Allies gained from the battle that lasted from July until November and cost the Allies 600,000 lives. Both Britain and France were shaken by Verdun and the Somme and changes followed in order to try and gain victory by more determined efforts. Asquith, the cautious well-meaning Liberal P.M., was pushed out of office and replaced by the much more active Lloyd George, whilst Joffre, the stolid and comfortable French commander, was replaced by the dashing and optimistic Nivelle who had a new and attractive scheme for winning the war.

The Eastern Front

The war in the West encouraged the Russians to try a new attack in the East in 1916. Brusilov's Russian troops did well in an advance into Galicia, and Romania was encouraged by this to join the Allies. But the Germans checked Brusilov's advance and easily dealt with Romania so that at the close of 1916 no end to the war was yet in sight.

f) 1917

The Entry of the U.S.A.

By this time the politicians in Germany had lost control to military leaders and these leaders were determined to win victory by any means, whatever the cost. This meant total U-boat warfare and led to the entry of the United States into the war on the side of the Allies. Thomas Woodrow Wilson, the U.S. President, had been elected to office as an opponent of war, but the U-boat sinkings and the discovery that Germany had tried to bribe Mexico to attack the U.S.A. shocked Wilson (and American opinion) into supporting entry into the war. The Czar of Russia had been forced to abdicate in March 1917 by the Russian people made desperate by the miseries caused by the war; Russia seemed now to have a democratic government so that the U.S.A. felt it was joining

The Eastern Front

Baltic Sea

Germany

Russian advance into Germany halted 1914

The Masurian Lakes

Tannenberg

Russia

The Central Powers

Russian advance into Austria halted 1915

Gorlice

Austria - Hungary

Serbia
Conquered
1916

Montenegro

Albania

Adriatic Sea

Romania

Black Sea

Bulgaria

Greece

Turkey

The Dardanelles.
Allied Gallipoli
Expedition
defeated

Neutral
for most
of the war

a war for democracy. American business men had loaned considerable sums of money to the Allies and were naturally more sympathetic to their cause. But the U.S.A. was not really prepared for war and the build up of her forces after she had declared war in March was slow; German hopes could still rest on winning a quick victory before the Americans arrived in force.

German successes against Russia and Italy

German hopes of overcoming British and French resistance were encouraged by the collapse of Russia and a victory over Italy in 1917. Russia was partly distracted by upheavals in domestic affairs which resulted in the downfall of the Czar and then the downfall of the Provisional Government that replaced the Czar. The Communists, who emerged victorious from this struggle, ended the war with Germany and began negotiations that led, eventually, to the signing of the Treaty of Brest Litovsk by which Russia lost much land. The peace in the East enabled Central Power forces to concentrate on the West and the first signs of this came in Italy where an Austro-German army won the battle of Caporetto and forced the Italians to retreat rapidly until they reached the River Piave where they turned and put up a stern resistance, encouraged by the arrival of British and French reinforcements.

The Failure of new Allied offensives in the west

In early 1917 the Germans had withdrawn to a shorter and more easily defended line in the west whilst they concentrated on winning the war in the east, and against this line, near Rheims and Arras, Nivelle launched a huge series of French and British attacks designed to break through and win the war. But once more the defence was too strong and attacks broke down before withering machine-gun fire, and a large part of the embittered French army mutinied. The disgraced Nivelle was replaced by Pétain, but for some time, the brunt of the fighting fell on the British army. Haig responded with a new offensive: the Third battle of Ypres. But Haig's lengthy preparations delayed the attack and rain turned the battlefield into a sea of treacherous mud in which wounded men drowned.

There were limited successes like the use of tanks farther south at Cambrai in large enough numbers to win success and the capture of Messines Ridge by General Plumer's troops, but in general the attack was very costly and by the end of the year had ground to an ignominious halt.

The tank solved the problem of how to overcome trenches and barbed wire, yet most generals were very suspicious of it at first. It seemed slow and liable to break down and the German leaders decided not to give it serious attention. So, although Haig failed to use tanks properly at first, when he received enough of them and learned how to handle them in large units, he had the means for securing that final victory of 1918 in which the British played the leading role. However, this hope lay in the future; for the moment there seemed great danger. By their offensive efforts in 1917 the allies seemed to have exhausted themselves and exposed themselves to the counter-stroke Ludendorff was preparing, with the growing numbers of troops from the Eastern Front. It needed all the fire and spirit of Clemenceau (the new French Prime Minister) and Lloyd George, to cope with the disaster of early 1918.

The Middle East

In the Middle East, allied forces achieved much better results than their larger counterparts in France. At first the Turks had been quite successful in their campaigns against British forces, but, by 1917, both General Maude in Mesopotamia and General Allenby in Palestine were advancing

This photograph, taken by an Allied war photographer at Chateau Wood near Ypres in 1917, gives an impression of the utter desolation of a battle strafed wood. The troops are Australian.

through these areas, driving back the Turks. In Palestine efforts were aided by an Arab revolt against Turkish rule which was helped by an Englishman, T. E. Lawrence.

g) 1918

The German attack

To face the new onslaught the British and French at last placed their armies under a joint supreme commander, Marshal Foch. But since General Pershing's American troops were still few in numbers the Allies could only retreat before Ludendorff's skilfully organised attack in which the Germans advanced in small groups, by-passing pockets of resistance that were dealt with by following companies. By July the Germans were once more at the Marne, but, once more, their attack broke down from a combination of exhaustion and the opposition of Allied forces growing rapidly in size and using tanks in large numbers. Even so the Germans were pushed back very slowly, and it was not they who collapsed first, but their allies.

The Defeat of Germany's Allies

Allied pressure on Greece at last persuaded her to enter the war and the Allied forces in Salonika were able to advance, knock Bulgaria out of the war and help Serbia and Romania to recover. At the end of October, Turkey was forced to admit defeat and early in the following month the Austro-Hungarian Empire withdrew from the war. Austria withdrew partly because of defeats – at Vittorio Veneto the Italians gained their revenge for Caporetto – but also because their whole empire simply crumbled apart as the separate nationalities clamoured for freedom and even Hungary declared itself to be independent.

German defeat

By now Ludendorff was convinced that the war must be ended before fighting entered Germany and the German army was totally destroyed. Popular discontent in Germany because of defeat which seemed to have come very suddenly, and at the harshness of life caused by the Allied blockade, showed itself in restlessness in the army, the mutiny of the navy at Kiel, and the establishment of a Socialist government under Eisner in Bavaria. In November the Kaiser abdicated and fled to Holland, a Socialist, Ebert, became Chancellor, and on the 11th November, 1918 an armistice on the Western Front was finally signed.

The Great War had ruined the Russian, Austrian and German Empires, it had caused vast losses of life and destruction of property and had led to a great growth in the power of governments as they increasingly extended their control in order to wage war more successfully. In some people the Great War left a bitterness against all warfare, but in others it produced resentment at defeat and a determination to wage war again, and this time more successfully. Whilst war raged in Europe the U.S.A. and Japan had been able to greatly increase their strength, and many European colonies had obtained chances of greater freedom whilst their masters were so busy elsewhere.

The Peace Treaties

a) The Peacemakers

The Peace of Paris, which ended the Great War, was negotiated as a series of separate treaties (named after places near Paris) by a group of senior politicians assisted by committees of experts. The dominant figures were the heads of government from France, the U.S.A. and Britain, namely Clemenceau, Wilson and Lloyd George (for Orlando, the Italian P.M., left the Congress in anger at the treatment received by Italy's claims). The defeated powers were not seriously consulted. Germany, especially, was to hold this against the settlement – that it was a *diktat* in which she had not been properly consulted.

WILSON: Wilson seemed in the strongest position; he was head of a vast and wealthy state and not immediately subject to the pressures of an electorate; but in fact his work was rejected by Americans who chose a Congress hostile to Wilson that eventually refused to agree to the settlements he had negotiated. Some of Wilson's idealism had faded as America fought the war, but he was still determined, above all, to create a League of Nations to prevent another major war. He had outlined his aims at the beginning of 1918 in the 'Fourteen Points' which the Germans regarded as the basis for settlement so that they felt resentment whenever the terms varied from the Points. The Fourteen Points included proposals for building Europe on a basis of nationalism – the Balkans, the Austrian Empire, the Turkish Empire, Belgium and Poland would all be treated on the basis of control of their own affairs. France was promised Alsace-Lorraine, Poland was promised access to the sea, Italy was promised national frontiers, and there were a number of general declarations of idealism such as those in favour of open treaties not secret ones, the reduction of armaments, and the free navigation of the seas.

Peace treaties
1. Germany

German frontiers 1914.

Areas lost.

Denmark

N. Slesvig

The Polish Corridor
[West Prussia & Posen]

Lithuania
Memel

East Prussia

Holland

Germany

Weimar

Poland

Belgium

Eupen-Malmedy

Saar

Parts of Silesia

Alsace Lorraine

France

Demilitarized area

Austria
[Germany forbidden unity with Austria]

LLOYD GEORGE AND CLEMENCEAU: Wilson was not a European and could afford to be idealistic; Clemenceau and Lloyd George – though both had been radicals at home – had to think of the feelings of the electorates after the bitter war. Lloyd George had just won an election on promises to treat Germany harshly and make her pay for the war and Clemenceau was, naturally, concerned above all for the security of his country from further aggression. Clemenceau pressed for harsh terms, he was more interested in positive safeguards than vague American assurances. Lloyd George was more moderate, yet his ministry had made promises to the electorate and dared not be too generous. The whole settlement was negotiated hastily at a time when immediate memories of the war still made men bitter, but though the terms were harsh, they were less severe than those that Germany had inflicted on Russia at Brest Litovsk.

b) The Treaty of Versailles

The Treaty of Versailles which was negotiated with Germany proved to be the source of much post war trouble. German resentment was already growing as a result of the maintenance by the Allies of a blockade of Germany through the winter of 1918; the Treaty of Versailles greatly increased this resentment.

Territorial Terms

Germany lost land in Europe that reduced her size and split her into two separate areas; she also lost all her colonies.

    i)   Alsace-Lorraine was recovered by France.

    ii)   Denmark gained North Slesvig, after the local population had voted in a plebiscite to decide their own future.

    iii)   Belgium gained Moresnet and Eupen-Malmedy.

    iv)   The Saar was to be run by the League of Nations until 1935 when its inhabitants would vote to decide whether to join France or Germany. Until 1935 its coal mines would be run by the French.

    v)   Memel was to be administered by the League. (In fact Lithuania seized it in 1923 and the League eventually accepted this situation.)

    vi)   Poland gained West Prussia, Posen, and the richest part of upper Silesia. Danzig, the chief port in the area, was to be a free city.

vii) German colonies were handed over to the victorious powers who, however, agreed to run them as mandates on behalf of the inhabitants of the area. There were different kinds of mandates (and in some very little attention was paid to the idea of reporting regularly to the League and encouraging the native peoples to manage their own affairs), but the general principle was that colonies were not to be simply seized by the victorious; some care for the local inhabitants should be shown.

German Military Power

In various ways the Allies tried to restrict German military power to prevent her from ever being able to wage war again.

i) Her fleet was handed over to the British and eventually scuttled itself at Scapa Flow.

ii) Her army was limited to 100,000 men.

iii) Germany was not to have tanks, aircraft, submarines, surface vessels of over 10,000 tons or a system of conscription.

iv) The Rhineland was to be occupied by the Allies for 15 years and a 30-mile wide zone on the east of the Rhine was to be a permanently de-militarised area.

The War Guilt Question

By Article 231 of the peace terms, Germany was held to be responsible for the war and though the Allies could not punish the Kaiser who had sought refuge with the Dutch, they used this clause to demand from Germany compensation for the damage caused by the war. These reparations were, in Wilson's view, only to cover the cost of the actual war damage, but the British and French successfully demanded compensation for the cost of fighting the war. The Germans had to hand over ships, coal and other materials as payment whilst a Commission worked out how large a sum the reparation should be. In 1921 a figure of £6,600 millions was put forward, but it seemed so vast an amount that the Germans made only a very feeble effort to pay it off.

c) The Break Up of the Austrian Empire

Before the actual Treaties of St. Germain and Trianon were signed with Austria and Hungary in 1919 and 1920, the Austrian Empire had already collapsed so that, in granting independence in the way they did, the Allies were only confirming what was already a fact.

i) Austria became a small, independent Republic which was forbidden to unite with Germany.

Representing the Allies at the Peace Conference in Paris were, from left to right, Italian Prime Minister Vittorio Orlando, British Prime Minister David Lloyd George, French Prime Minister Georges Clemenceau and American President Woodrow Wilson. Orlando later left the Conference in anger.

ii) Italy gained Istria, Trentino, the South Tyrol, Trieste, Zara and Lagosta.

iii) Czechoslovakia became an independent state, formed from the former provinces of Bohemia, Moravia and Slovakia.

iv) Yugoslavia was created from Serbia to which were added Bosnia, Montenegro, Dalmatia and Slovenia.

v) Poland gained Galicia.

Thus Yugoslavia dominated the Balkans, for Bulgaria was punished by the Treaty of Neuilly, 1919, by the loss of lands to Greece, Romania and Yugoslavia.

d) The Turkish Empire

In 1920, by the Treaty of Sèvres, the Allies agreed to deprive Turkey of her Arab possessions and a part of Asia Minor, the former became mandates of Britain and France and the latter passed to Greece. The Sultan of Turkey accepted the terms of the Treaty but many Turks felt that they were being too harshly dealt with, and, under the leadership of Mustapha Kemal, the hero of Gallipoli, they formed the Nationalist

Party, defeated the Greeks and and overthrew the Sultan. A new treaty had to be signed at Lausanne in 1923 as a result of this *coup d'état* and the triumphant Mustapha Kemal was able to carry out many reforms modernising Turkey.

e) Comments on the Treaties

President Wilson hoped that by setting up national states, war in Europe would become unnecessary. Unfortunately it proved so difficult to draw clear boundaries between nations which were acceptable to all, that, after the treaties, many states contained within their frontiers peoples whose ties of language, tradition, race or religion lay elsewhere. Czechoslovakia, for example, included three million Germans living in the Sudetenland, there were Germans in Poland, Slavs in Italy's Istria and Austrians in Italy's Tyrol. Not even the victorious powers felt fully satisfied by the treaties, Italy resented her failure to obtain Fiume, which had gone to Yugoslavia, and France felt insecure in spite of Wilson's promises of support should Germany ever attack her again.

The defeated powers naturally felt indignation. Compensations and the division of their land were particularly resented whilst Russia, defeated in 1917, had been virtually ignored in the treaties and had lost a massive belt of east European territory. The Germans resented the

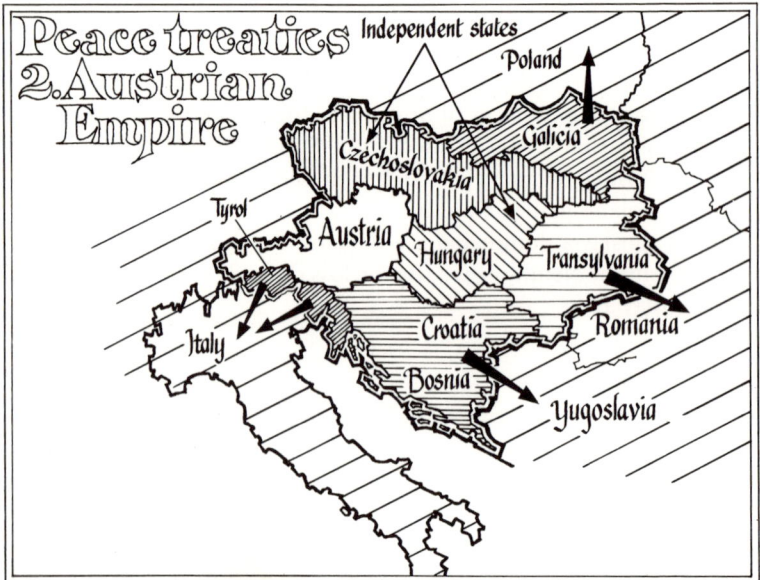

Peace treaties 2. Austrian Empire

'Polish Corridor' which split their state, but even the Poles were not wholly satisfied, for they had wanted to own Danzig and, having failed, began to build a new port nearby at Gdynia. The reparations bill was, as the eminent English economist J. M. Keynes argued in *The Economic Consequences of the Peace*, too vast to be reasonable. The break up of the Austrian Empire, he argued, was also economically harmful for it split up a natural economic unit based on the Danube, though it is hard to see what the Allies could have done about this since Austria's Empire collapsed without aid from the peacemakers.

The treaties left Germany resentful and yet they were not fierce enough to crush her permanently; since Germany had simply had a peace dictated to her she felt no loyalty to it, particularly since the Germans argued that they had signed the armistice in the expectation of a peace based on the Fourteen Points, only to meet with far harsher punishment. The hopes of a better and more peaceful future which were expressed in the establishment of the League of Nations were soon to be shaken too, for Wilson, the chief peacemaker, the inspiration behind the League and the guarantor of French security, could not even persuade the American Congress to pass the peace treaties.

The League of Nations

a) The Establishment of the League

The Organisation of the League

The League of Nations was established at Geneva in a mood of hope for the future when men felt that never again must a conflict as terrible as the Great War be permitted to happen. The League consisted of an Assembly that met annually, where every member had one vote, and a Council on which there were four permanent members, Britain, France, Italy and Japan, and four non-permanent members (later six). The League was served by a number of permanent officials, the Secretariat, and by a series of special commissions to deal with particular problems. Every member agreed to the Covenant, promising to bring his quarrel to the League before resorting to force. But not only did the League hope to prevent war, it also hoped to reduce disease, poverty and injustice in the world. In addition, an International Court of Justice was set up at the Hague to deal with legal disputes between Nations.

SANCTIONS: The main difficulty was what to do about states who were unwilling to allow the League to settle their disputes and this was a problem that was never satisfactorily solved. It was not easy for the League to act since Assembly decisions had to be unanimous, but, provided a decision could be reached, the League could punish an offending state by applying sanctions which might mean economic blockade, or even military action.

The League's problems were increased by the refusal of the United States Congress to ratify Wilson's personal presidential support of the League which meant that the U.S.A. did not become a member. Communist Russia lay outside the League; Japan took little interest; the League was therefore very much a European affair and especially dependent upon Britain and France. The resentment felt by Italy and Germany towards the peace treaties meant that it would be difficult for them to co-operate in the League, for the League seemed, all too easily, an organisation for preserving the Peace of Paris.

b) The League's Successes

The League was really only successful when tackling the disputes of small countries who could be bullied. A dispute between Lithuania and Poland over Vilna was settled in 1920 in Poland's favour; a clash between Sweden and Finland over the Aaland Islands was decided in Finland's favour. The League settled the question of where the frontier between Poland and Germany should be in Silesia; it sorted out a quarrel between Turkey and Iraq over the Mosul area in favour of Iraq; it brought solutions to quarrels between Greece and Bulgaria, Peru and Colombia and Bolivia and Paraguay. The League also administered the Saar, and its Commissions to deal with problems like drugs and health, and its International Labour Office to improve working conditions, all had a number of successes.

Until 1929 the personalities of some of the leading statesmen also helped the League to prosper, for Ramsay Macdonald and Austen Chamberlain in Britain, Briand in France and Stresemann in Germany, all made an effort to make the League work. This spirit of co-operation can be seen in the Dawes Plan of 1924 which re-assessed Germany's ability to pay reparations and provided Germany with a U.S. loan. A British plan in 1924 to make arbitration between quarrelling states compulsory (the Geneva Protocol) failed, but a more moderate scheme in 1925 succeeded. In that year the Locarno Pact was signed between Germany and her Western neighbours to guarantee the existing frontiers and

French Prime Minister Georges Clemenceau chats with Field Marshal Earl Haig, Commander of the British forces in France, at Cambrai in October, 1918.

to ban the waging of war between them. However Germany's eastern frontier, which was her major source of grievance, did not receive similar treatment.

In 1926 Germany joined the League as a permanent member of the Council; in 1934 even the U.S.S.R. joined the League. In 1927 the League passed a Polish resolution prohibiting wars of aggression and in 1928 the Kellogg Pact, renouncing war, was signed by most states. Finally in 1929 the Young Plan cut down German reparations still further and the army of occupation was removed from Western Germany.

c) The Failure of the League

After 1929 the League was increasingly ignored and states sought for security in the more usual way by increasing their armed forces and signing separate treaties with each other. Economic troubles played a big part in the League's decline, as was foreshadowed in 1923 when the French occupied the Ruhr, one of the richest parts of Germany, in order to obtain the compensations Germany had been failing to pay. In Germany this caused economic hardship and, immediately, left and

D

right-wing parties opposed to the League made political gains. A period of greater prosperity followed this trouble but in 1929 the collapse of an economic boom in the U.S.A. ended U.S. loans to Europe and soon affected Europe itself.

As unemployment rose and savings became worthless, so Communists and Fascists, who disliked the League, made big political gains and in some states even won power with their offers of vigorous action. Mussolini in Italy and Hitler in Germany both turned away from the League and began to break its rules. In 1923 Britain and France had given way before Mussolini's bullying of Greece (when she was blamed for the murder of an Italian general) and in 1935 they failed to deal firmly with Mussolini's aggression in Abyssinia, just as they had failed in 1931 to deal with Japanese aggression in Manchuria. Both Italy and Germany left the League. Germany occupied the demilitarised Rhineland, equipped her army with forbidden weapons, merged Austria into Germany and bullied Czechoslovakia into handing over the Sudetenland.

In the face of this defiance, unsupported by the U.S.A. and too suspicious of Stalin to co-operate with Russia, Britain and France began hastily to rearm and to try and avoid war by giving way to the demands of Hitler. In any case, by the 1930's the British in particular felt guilty about parts of the Versailles settlement and did not feel able to stand up to Hitler when he declared that he only wished Germany to be as other states and to have the weapons they had. Indeed, it was Britain herself who broke the disarmament restrictions on Germany by negotiating a separate special naval agreement with Hitler.

The League could be no stronger than its members and the failure of disarmament conferences shows that states were not really willing to trust their affairs to the League. Many of the League's troubles grew out of the Paris Settlement which it was supposed to respect, yet which contained provisions bound to make the flourishing of a moderate democratic government in Germany very difficult. Increasingly the League was ignored and with the Second World War it finally vanished; its few assets were eventually transferred to the United Nations. Several features of U.N. organisation and several incidents in its history prove the desire of some members, at least, to avoid repeating the mistakes of the League.

3 | The Russian Revolution

Events leading up to the Revolution

a) Nicholas II and his Empire

The Government of Russia

In 1894 Nicholas II succeeded Alexander III to the apparently all-powerful position of Czar. There were no legal limits to his authority which extended over an enormous state in which peoples of many races lived; his vast army was feared throughout Europe and his secret police searched out his enemies. Ostensibly to help the Czar rule Russia, there was a Senate, a Council of State and a Council of Ministers, but all these bodies could only offer suggestions and the Czar could dismiss them if he wished. Supporting the Czar were the nobles, the Russian Orthodox Church and a system of local government in which the few assemblies that existed were carefully watched over by the Czar's agents.

THE CZAR AND HIS ADVISERS: In fact this imposing system was decaying. One of its weakest points was at the very top – the Czar himself. Nicholas was a man of a very limited and narrow ability, ignorant of his people's needs, yet refusing to share power with more able people. There were capable men available to serve him, men like Sergius Witte and Peter Stolypin, but Nicholas soon became jealous of competent ministers and dismissed them. The few people he did trust were quite unfitted to help Nicholas rule. His wife Alexandra, a German princess, was even more stupid and ignorant than her husband whilst Gregory Rasputin, the strange Siberian 'holy man' who came to be so important, was interested only in selfish short-term schemes.

The Weakness of the Government

Though the army was huge, it was very short of equipment, training, supplies and proper leadership. The secret police were corrupt and some of their number were revolutionaries. The local elected assemblies, the *Zemstvos*, which tried to improve health, education and roads, were watched suspiciously and even hampered if they seemed to be doing too

43

Czar Nicholas II, 1868–1918, despotic ruler of Russia from 1894 until his abdication in March, 1917.

well. The nobility's power had been dwindling for some time and the Orthodox Church had become so narrow that educated Russians had lost all respect for it. The very size of Russia made government difficult for communications were very poor indeed.

b) The Russian Economy

The Peasantry

Russia was a poor and backward country at the turn of the century, in comparison with Britain or Germany, and five-sixths of her population were peasants. Primitive farming methods and a poor soil made scraping a living from the earth very difficult. The three field system was common and farming implements were crude. A minority of peasants, the *kulaks*, prospered, it is true, but they were a very small minority and were often hated by poorer peasants. A heavy burden of taxation bore down on the peasantry. They alone paid a poll tax, they alone could suffer the legal punishment of being flogged, they were not even free to travel where they wished and they were still having to struggle to try and buy their land after serfdom had been ended in Russia in 1864. There were too few jobs in the towns, and too few opportunities to move to other areas to reduce the pressure towards an explosive situation in the countryside.

Industry

Russia lacked large scale heavy industries, and those that existed were usually short of capital. Coal, iron, oil and textile industries all existed but the working class employed in this way cannot have numbered more than ten per cent. of the population. Most of these workers lived in wretched poverty, inhabiting poor homes and working long hours with very little sympathetic attention from the government. The best the government could manage was to try and see that when workers joined workers' organisations the government could still watch over them and to this end the police helped form trade unions in the hope that workers would join these and not more troublesome political organisations.

The growth of Russian industry owed much to Sergius Witte who served as Minister of Communications and then Minister of Finance. Witte encouraged the building of railways, though he found it very difficult to raise the money for improvements and his taxes made him very unpopular.

c) Nicholas II's Non-socialist Opponents

For centuries Czars had been troubled by revolts by desperate peasantry and, in the nineteenth century, by members of the educated upper classes too; but their poor leadership and lack of discipline and military skill meant that such rebels were usually easily defeated. Nicholas II's enemies were numerous, but they were as hostile to each other as they were to the Czar for much of the time.

The Liberals

Russia had such a small middle class that it was difficult to find support for a cautious moderate Liberal Party to change Russia without a revolution. To poor peasants and workers, more extreme parties demanding the destruction of the government were more attractive than the Liberal Party which hoped for a gradual change in Russian Government towards a system like Britain's in which the ruler shared power with an elected assembly. The small Russian Liberal Party consisted of teachers, lawyers, doctors, and other members of the educated classes who were concerned about the way their country was run, but it was faced by a huge obstacle – Nicholas II flatly refused to even consider sharing power.

The Social Revolutionaries

These revolutionaries hoped to destroy the existing government and build a new government based on the peasantry. However the bulk of the peasantry took no notice of the S.R. leaders and the S.R. organisation was full of police spies. Even the head of its fighting organisation, Azev, who was involved in several murder plots to kill S.R. enemies, was both a terrorist and a police spy.

d) The Social Democrats

The small S.D. party was the one which eventually triumphed in Russia, yet no-one in 1900 would have thought this at all likely. It was founded by Georgi Plekhanov, an able writer who lived most of his life in exile preaching the Marxist idea that a real revolution could only come from workers.

Lenin

Plekhanov attracted several Russian Socialists to his place of exile, and among them was Vladimir Ilyich Ulyanov, better known as Lenin. Lenin, the son of a school inspector, was expelled from university for being involved in student politics and went on to work on a Russian Socialist newspaper *Iskra*. Associated with him on the paper was Julius Martov, but the different ideas about Socialism held by Lenin and Martov led to a quarrel and a permanent split in Russian Socialism. In 1903, at a Congress held first in Brussels and then in London, the Russian Social-ists split into those following Lenin (the *Bolsheviks* i.e. majority) and those following Martov (the *Mensheviks* or minority) on the question of party organisation. Martov believed the party should be as widely based as possible, but Lenin held that it should consist of a small group of professional revolutionaries and it was Lenin who, in 1903, triumphed. But his triumph was short-lived, because he tried to follow up his victory with such ruthless attacks on the Mensheviks that many moderates deserted him and he even lost control of *Iskra*.

Trotsky

One of Lenin's most able opponents was Leon Bronstein, better known as Trotsky, a Ukrainian Jew who was a brilliant speaker and writer. But though Trotsky vigorously attacked Lenin, the Mensheviks never really regarded him as one of their number for he was too awkward and

Much of the original Russian Communist doctrines were based on the ideas of Karl Marx. Born at Trier, in Prussia on May 5th, 1818, Marx published his famous *Communist Manifesto* in 1848.

individualistic. Trotsky developed his own ideas of how the revolution in Russia should be planned and decided it would only work if it spread over the rest of Europe too.

Stalin

During these early years, Joseph Stalin was a very insignificant figure. Most Socialist leaders in Russia came from the middle class; Stalin was one of the few who came from lower down the social scale for his father was a poor peasant shoemaker. Great family sacrifices were made to send Stalin to a theological seminary, but it was not long before he was expelled for the interest that he showed in Marxism. He turned to organising revolutionary plots only to be caught and sent to Siberia.

Thus Nicholas II's opponents were divided – indeed the Bolsheviks and Mensheviks devoted nearly all their energy to attacking each other and none of them had really massive support. It needed a major catastrophe to develop which the Czar's opponents could exploit if they were to have any chance of success. In 1904 Nicholas proceeded to provide such an opportunity by blundering, unprepared, into a war with the formidable forces of Japan.

e) The Russo-Japanese War

The Causes of the War

Wenzel von Plehve, Russia's Minister of the Interior, urged on Nicholas the idea of a successful war to take attention away from domestic troubles. Japan was an obvious enemy for the two were rivals in the Far East and Nicholas had hated the Japanese ever since an attempt had been made on his life during a visit to Japan.

Japan was alarmed by the extension of Russian power in the Far East, as indicated by the building of the Trans-Siberian Railway, one of Witte's favourite schemes. The Japanese armed forces had been modernised and in 1894 they defeated Chinese forces and forced China to hand over certain areas. Russia objected to this Treaty of Shimonoseki and, backed by France and Germany, forced Japan to hand back to China part of her gains, notably the Liaotung Peninsula which included the important centre of Port Arthur; Russia then, herself, obtained a 25-year lease on Port Arthur and linked it up to the Trans-Siberian Railway which she had already extended across Manchuria to Vladivostok. The Japanese were extremely alarmed; they tried to negotiate with the Czar, only to find their offers rejected and, indeed, the Russians offered further provocation by starting to interfere in Korea in which Japan was especially interested. Japan decided war was inevitable and having secured themselves from the danger of fighting France as well as Russia by signing a treaty of alliance with Britain, the Japanese launched a surprise torpedo attack on the Russian Far East Fleet.

Events of the War

The first attack, followed shortly by a second, frightened the Russians into withdrawing their fleet into Port Arthur and mining the entrance to it. This left the Japanese in full control of the sea and they were able to ship over their formidable army to besiege Port Arthur. The Czar had allowed a dangerous situation to develop without his forces being prepared; the Russian general in the Far East, Kuropatkin, found his troops badly equipped and very short of artillery, whilst the Trans-Siberian Railway was in such a primitive state of development that only a trickle of supplies and reinforcements could reach him. The Japanese army was brave, disciplined, well equipped and well led and able to defeat bigger Russian forces first at the Sha River and then at Mukden.

The Russian Far East Fleet finally ventured out to sea only to be destroyed by Admiral Togo's fleet; Port Arthur surrendered, and in a final desperate bid to save the war Nicholas ordered the Baltic Fleet to sail east. Rozhdestvensky's aged and undermanned force limped eastwards, so terrified of torpedo attack that it fired on Hull and Grimsby trawlers by mistake and nearly brought Britain into the war, and the Baltic Fleet finally met its doom in less than an hour in the Straits of Tsushima as Togo blocked its way to Vladivostok. This defeat at sea finally ruined the Czar's hopes, for though Kuropatkin's army was now in much better shape, there was so much trouble inside Russia that he had to negotiate an end to the war.

The Treaty of Portsmouth 1905 (U.S.A.)

Witte was called back to office to help save the Czar: his skill – plus U.S. support and the fact that the war had cost Japan dearly too – meant that the peace treaty was less severe than Russian defeats might have indicated was likely. Russia lost Port Arthur and the Liaotung Peninsula, half the island of Sakhalin and all claims to Korea. Defeated in the East, Russian foreign policy turned back to the West and began to take a much greater interest in the Balkans, thus helping to generate the friction which caused the First World War.

f) The Revolution of 1905

Far from fulfilling Plehve's hopes that war would prevent trouble inside Russia, the news of defeats increased political unrest. The war made little sense to most Russians, and Plehve himself became one of the first victims of increasing terrorist activity. Nicholas tried to prevent further disturbances by making a moderate man, Sviatopolk-Mirsky, Minister of the Interior. But his small and feeble reforms only irritated the Czar's opponents who demanded a democratic system of government – which Nicholas still would not grant.

Bloody Sunday

The Czar's hand was forced by the growing violence in Russia and the clumsiness of his police in trying to check it. News of Port Arthur's fall reached St. Petersburg at a time when one of the police sponsored unions, the Association of Factory and Mill workers, was organising a strike. The Association now went on to plan a demonstration that would present a petition to the Czar asking for an end to the war and reforms in Russia. The demonstrations, on Sunday, 22nd January, were led by Father George Gapon, a priest who was very interested in social reforms. But though it was a peaceful demonstration, the police were alarmed by its size, opened fire, and killed many of the marchers.

This tragedy aroused a furious upsurge of popular anger. Terrorists killed many eminent people, the universities closed, a general strike developed, and the crew of the newest battleship in the Black Sea Fleet, the *Potemkin*, mutinied. Nicholas had, once more, to turn to Sergius Witte for help.

The October Manifesto

Nicholas needed Witte not only for his reputation as a reformer, but also his financial skill to obtain loans to restore the shattered economy. By this time workers in St. Petersburg had taken matters into their own hands by forming a workers' council (or *Soviet*). Although the Soviet eventually failed and was broken up by police, its example was copied in 1917 and its president, Trotsky, gained prestige. But for the moment Witte divided the Czar's enemies by producing a programme of reforms, the October Manifesto, that helped the activities of the moderate reformers by offering the hope that, at last, the government of Russia would really be improved. The Manifesto promised that a *Duma* (a nationally elected assembly with power to make laws) would be called and that Russians would, in future, be free from arrest without proper reason being shown, and free to meet and speak as they wished. The Liberals organised a political party, the Cadets, to fight the forthcoming election, so did right wingers, who backed up their campaign with terrorism. Thus the 1905 revolution collapsed before the promise of reforms. A few minor incidents continued – the cruiser *Ochakov* mutinied, there was a strike in St. Petersburg and an armed rising in Moscow – but most Russians waited for the Duma to meet in the hope of real reforms to reduce the misery of their lives.

g) The Dumas

Nicholas' hostile attitude towards reformers soon became clear. He appointed a new and brutal Minister of the Interior, dismissed Witte (who had raised a massive French loan) and put in his place the elderly and lazy Goremykin who was ready to do as he was told. The Duma was not elected on the simple principle of 'one man one vote' but instead there were arrangements to try and make sure that the people the Czar thought he could trust, such as landlords, should have great influence. Furthermore, the Czar was to rule by decree when the Duma did not meet and the ministers were to be appointed by the Czar and responsible to him, not to the Duma.

The Cadet Party dominated the first Duma; the more extreme politicians of the left, and especially the Bolsheviks, had been caught unprepared by the 1905 Revolution and were not clear as to the best policy to follow. The Duma drew up a programme of reforms, but it was simply wasted effort, for the Czar ignored the programme, dismissed the Duma, and called for new elections which were carefully managed to weaken the Cadet Party. Even so, there were too many reformers in the second Duma for the Czar's liking; he dismissed it and savagely altered the electoral laws with the result that in the third Duma there were far more Right Wingers and Octobrists (cautious reformers eager to co-operate with the Czar).

The Czar felt more confidence now, because he had a new and able Minister of the Interior, Peter Stolypin, who dealt successfully and vigorously with trouble makers. The third Duma lasted until 1912 and yet further changes in electoral procedure followed before the fourth Duma met. The Czar seemed to have triumphed for the Bolsheviks and Mensheviks were as divided as ever, the Social Revolutionary Party had just discovered Azev was a police spy and was suitably shaken, and the Liberals shrank from using violence.

Gregory Rasputin, nick-named the 'mad monk', rose to power through his influence over the Czarina. In the picture above he is seen, seated left, at a party held in his honour.

h) Stolypin and Rasputin

During the period between the 1905 Revolution and the Great War the Czar relied chiefly on two men, on Peter Stolypin, an able and hard-working minister, and on Gregory Rasputin. As long as the Czar did not feel secure he allowed Stolypin power, but when Nicholas felt safer so he turned increasingly against his chief Minister and trusted more and more in Rasputin. The two men disliked each other – they well repre-sented the possibilities open to the Czar – Stolypin offered good govern-ment and cautious reforms to make Nicholas less unpopular, whilst Rasputin offered nothing except his own powerful personality and ridi-culous religious beliefs.

Stolypin's Reforms

As well as dealing sternly with trouble-makers, Stolypin also tried to win the support of the richer peasants, the kulaks, by giving them much more freedom to build up large and prosperous farms. He cut away power from the village communes which, until now, had possessed authority to control peasants' lives, and encouraged peasants who were able to afford it to gather together land in large blocks (instead of in scattered strips). The policy did nothing for the vast majority of the peasants who were not kulaks, yet it seemed to be doing so well that revolutionary leaders became very alarmed. In 1911 Stolypin was murdered whilst attending an opera in Kiev by a revolutionary who also took money from the police. In this suspicious way the revolutionaries were rid of a dangerous enemy and Nicholas was rid of a man whose success was making him jealous.

Rasputin's Career

Rasputin was coarse, illiterate and a peasant, an odd man indeed to influence the Russian court. But he was shrewd, had a magnetic personality and managed to convince the Czar that he had the skill to help stop his sickly, haemophilic son from continual bleeding. The Czarina, unbalanced and extremely superstitious, was convinced by Rasputin's skill that he was indeed the 'Man of God' he claimed to be. Rasputin finally became so powerful that he was virtually able to dismiss ministers who disliked him and have them replaced by others more amenable, with the result that at the very moment when Russia was approaching the crisis of 1914, it was Goremykin who became Chief Minister. During the war, Rasputin's influence did not dwindle, more and more ministries were filled with men he could trust, until even right wingers came to hate him for the disastrous effects he was having on the government and the shame that he brought to the Czar.

Documented evidence of Rasputin's immorality was collected and presented to the Czarina but she refused to believe it. Eventually Prince Yussopov and a number of other prominent men decided Rasputin would have to be killed. But his death proved more difficult than his murderers anticipated, neither poisoned cakes and wine nor a bullet succeeded in hastening his end. It finally took a beating and several bullets to terminate his extraordinary life; then his body was dumped in the River Neva.

i) The Collapse of Czarist Rule

The War Defeats

Nicholas had become involved in another war for which he was as ill-prepared as he had been for the war against Japan. The Russians had large armies it was true, but size alone could not bring an assurance of victory. Good leadership, discipline and modern weapons were needed – and Russia lacked all of these. Soon German armies were penetrating deep into Russian territory, depriving her of valuable industries and farmland and heaping humiliation on the Czar who had taken personal command of the war. The Czar attempted to stifle criticisms of his mismanagement of the war which inevitably increased. He ignored too, appeals to reform his methods of government so that the only course to take for those shamed by defeat and those whose lives had increased in suffering because of the war, was revolution.

The February Revolution

The Revolution began on the 18th March, 1917, but as Russia was using an old calendar system at the time which differed from the one in use in the rest of Europe, the date in Russia was February 23rd and the event has since been known as the 'February Revolution'. It was not a carefully planned revolution guided by skilful leaders but a mass display of discontent. It was confused and chaotic but so widespread that Nicholas could not find sufficient reliable troops to crush it. The Revolution began in Petrograd (as the capital had been renamed) where there had already been trouble in connection with food distribution. Workers, angry at

A militant-looking Lenin strides across Red Square in Moscow while inspecting troops in May, 1919.

being told there was no bread for them, began attacking the houses of people they suspected of hoarding bread and were soon joined by sympathisers and then by most of the garrison of 200,000 recently recruited peasant soldiers. Within the capital, which was soon under rebel control, there reappeared the Soviet led by Mensheviks like Chkheidze, and Trudoviks like Kerensky. Soviets sprang up in other cities but the Petrograd Soviet led the way, issuing its famous 'Order Number One' calling on troops to form committees and refuse to obey orders not consistent with the orders of the Soviet.

The Czar's Abdication

Nicholas tried in vain to form a new government led by Liberals and finally, at Pskov, headquarters of the Northern Army, he abdicated. Since his son was so ill Nicholas offered the throne to his brother Michael, but Michael would not accept it and power, therefore, slipped to a Provisional Government led by Prince Lvov which sprang from the Duma.

How the Bolsheviks seized and secured power

a) The failure of the Provisional Government

Prince Lvov's government was dominated by Liberals with the aggressive Paul Milyukov as Foreign Minister but was surrounded by numerous difficulties. Some were of its own making, for instance it never acted boldly or ruthlessly though there was an extreme crisis in both domestic and foreign policy, it failed to carry out reforms, it insisted on continuing with a hopeless war policy. The Soviet in Petrograd was not plotting revolt, for its Menshevik leaders did not think a Marxist revolt was possible since most Russians were peasants, yet it had great prestige, it was very unco-operative and a persistent nuisance to the Provisional Government.

Land reforms were desperately needed and some peasants were already seizing landlords' estates helped by soldiers who deserted to return home ('voting for peace with their legs' as Lenin described it). But the government did nothing effective about the land problem and seemed more concerned with pursuing the war. Its repeated failures caused the resignation or downfall of several of its ministers until Lvov himself resigned. As Liberal power declined, so the power of Alexander Kerensky increased. He rose from being Minister of Justice to be Minister of War and eventually Prime Minister. With him rose a group of S.R.s and Mensheviks who took over various ministries. Though Kerensky proclaimed more democratic war aims than Nicholas had done, he still persisted with it and when a new offensive led by Brusilov failed, it helped discredit the Prime Minister and the political groups helping him.

b) The October Revolution

The Bolsheviks had played a very small part in the February Revolution and had quarrelled among themselves as to what to do. Minor Bolsheviks like Wacheslav Molotov, who were in Russia, denounced the Provisional Government; but Lev Kamenev, a more important leader, returned to Russia and supported the Government's war policy. In April Lenin himself returned, crossing Germany in a sealed train, for the Germans hoped that he would upset the Russian war effort. He was welcomed at the Finland Station by Menshevik leaders of the Soviet but he soon offended them, and indeed, some of his own party, by bluntly stating his own policy. In his 'April theses' Lenin denounced the Provisional Government and the war and demanded a government formed from the Soviets as well as peace, and the nationalisation of land. He eventually triumphed within his own party at least and it soon adopted his slogans of 'All power to the Soviets' and 'Bread, peace, and land'. Lenin was greatly helped by the fact that Trotsky, who had a number of able followers and great influence in the naval base of Kronstadt, decided to join the Bolsheviks.

The July Rising

But in July 1917, the Bolsheviks suffered a serious setback when a rising by a pro-Bolshevik machine gun regiment and by the Kronstadt sailors forced the Bolshevik leaders to join in to try and keep control. But they were not really ready, they were defeated; their newspaper, *Pravda*, was closed and Lenin and Zinoviev fled into hiding whilst Kamenev was arrested. All their hopes seemed ruined.

The Kornilov Rebellion

The Bolsheviks were rescued by Kerensky himself, for Kerensky suddenly found himself faced by a new enemy in General Kornilov. Kerensky needed all the allies he could find to deal with him, even if it meant arming his recent enemies. General Kornilov, who had succeeded Brusilov as Commander-in-Chief, attempted to seize power and his troops began a march on Petrograd but he was defeated by loyal troops

One of the leading architects of the Communist régime which followed the Russian Revolution was Leon Trotsky. He held several important government posts until he was finally edged from power by Stalin.

and workers. The Bolsheviks not only won prestige for the part they played but were also able to organise the Red Guards, all-important if Kerensky was to be overthrown.

The Revolt

Not all Bolsheviks agreed with Lenin that Kerensky should be overthrown, certainly Kamenev and Zinoviev were not enthusiastic but Lenin found a supporter in Trotsky and it was Trotsky who played the major role in planning the revolt. By now he had won a powerful position for himself in the Petrograd Soviet and he used this to organise the revolt. The city was divided into sectors and Bolshevik agents were sent out to win over factory workers whilst Trotsky himself undertook the difficult task of persuading the local garrison to give an oath of loyalty to the Soviet. His success meant that the 20,000 Red Guards met with little opposition on November 7th (October 25th by the old calendar) when they seized key points in Petrograd. A little later Moscow, too, fell to the Bolsheviks after more serious fighting. The Provisional Government was threatened by the Bolshevik cruiser *Aurora*, anchored in nearby Petrograd harbour, and Kerensky fled. He found help difficult to obtain for most generals hated him just as much as the Bolsheviks and the small force he eventually scraped together was easily defeated by the Red Guards.

E

A wave of drunkenness celebrated the Bolshevik triumph, though it seemed risky for them to celebrate so soon as few would have given much for their chances of staying long in power. They were a tiny minority who had succeeded through determination and organisation, whilst their enemies were divided, confused, far less ruthless, and disgraced by the failure of their policies. It seemed odd that Marxists should triumph first in an industrially backward country and not in Britain or Germany where workers formed the majority of the population, but Lenin never let pure Marxist theory stand in his way. In any case Marx's writings were confused, not always consistent and at one point he spoke of a country moving towards socialism by means of a small group of socialist workers seizing power and ruling as dictators until their country was sufficiently advanced to become truly socialist.

c) Early Bolshevik Reforms

Kerensky had promised to call a new elected assembly, but when the assembly finally met, the Bolsheviks and the allies they had found in the left wing of the S.R. party abused it and dismissed it. A series of decrees abolished the rights of landlords (in the hope of pleasing peasants and the S.R.'s) and the old secret police was scrapped—though a new and more efficient body, the *Cheka* was set up in its place. Hostile newspapers were shut down, church schools closed and a new legal system set up.

Economic changes

The war and the changes in government had done nothing but harm to Russia's economy. The new government began by nationalising many industries and setting up a government body called *Vesenkha* to supervise the economy's workings. The trade unions found that the Bolshevik victory did nothing to help them as the Bolsheviks declared that now a workers' government was in power it was unnecessary for unions to do anything but accept government orders.

A new system of government

In March 1918 the Bolsheviks adopted the name 'Communists' and began work on a new system of Government to keep Communists safely in power, a system which turned Russia (officially in 1924) into the Union of Soviet Socialist Republics: Soviets were set up all over Russia; local Soviets elected regional ones, regional ones elected state Soviets until finally the All Russian Congress of Soviets with over 1,000 delegates, was elected. This was far too large a body to rule Russia and real power

lay with the Council of People's Commissars who could make laws by
passing decrees.

The Treaty of Brest Litovsk

The most important of the early acts of the Communists was to give
Russia peace. Trotsky was now Commissar for Foreign Affairs and it was
he who arranged an armistice with the Germans in December, 1917 and
led the Russian delegation which worked with the Germans in drawing
up a treaty. The German terms, however, were so harsh that Trotsky and
several other leading Communists did not wish to accept them. They
hoped that by prolonging talks they could delay signing the Treaty long
enough for the Russian example to affect other parts of Europe and for
a much more widespread Communist Revolution to come to Russia's
aid. The more realistic Lenin saw that peace, however hard the terms,
was necessary and a treaty would have to be signed. As the German
Army marched on the capital, quite unaffected by Trotsky's appeal to
the German soldiers not to fight their fellow workers, Lenin had his way.
Trotsky resigned rather than sign the treaty and Chicherin inherited his
difficult task. Meanwhile the Left-Wing S.R.s became so angry that they
rebelled. The peace treaty was finally signed at Brest Litovsk in March
1918 and deprived Russia of Poland, Finland, Latvia, Lithuania, Estonia,
the Ukraine, Bessarabia and parts of White Russia and Transcaucasia.
Russia lost at one blow one third of her population and many valuable
industries.

d) The Civil War

Trotsky now became Commissar for War and worked to reform and
increase the Red Army in order to meet the inevitable attack by anti-
Communists. The Red Army was formed from the Red Guard, conscripted soldiers and non-Communist officers who had to be carefully
watched by Communist agents and threatened by all sorts of punishments. But the 'Whites', i.e. the Red Army's opponents, though
numerous and in control of much of Russia, were divided, poorly led and
their different groups never co-operated with each other. It was hard
for S.R.s, Mensheviks, Liberals and Right Wingers to find a policy they
could agree on in the areas they controlled. Although they received help
from several foreign countries, it was very half-hearted and rapidly
dried up when the Great War ended and the Allies no longer needed to
try and overthrow the new anti-war government of Russia to keep open
the Eastern front against Germany.

The Treaty of Brest-Litovsk

Norway

Sweden

Finland

Estonia

Petrograd

Latvia

Russia

Germany

Poland

Brest-Litovsk

Treaty Frontier

Kiev

1914 frontier

Austria-Hungary

Ukraine

Romania

Serbia

Bulgaria

Albania

Batum

Greece

Kars

Turkey

The Siberian Revolt

The war began in earnest when the 45,000 members of the Czech Legion (soldiers who had deserted from the Austrian Army) became suspicious of Communist attempts to move them and seized part of the Trans-Siberian Railway. The Czechs provided a shield behind which anti-Bolshevik Russians could organise and their success so alarmed the Communist Commissar in charge of the imprisoned Czar and his family at Ekaterinburg that he had all his captives executed. American and Japanese forces arrived, in theory to help the Czechs, but in fact the Americans did little that was useful and the Japanese never left the parts of Far Eastern Russia they wanted to control. The Czech advance was halted by the Red Army and weakened by quarrels between the S.R.s and Right Wingers in the White forces. Soon most of the Czechs abandoned the war and returned home. This left the former Black Sea commander, Admiral Kolchak, in charge. Kolchak, however, proved a poor leader for not only did he lose battles, but his cruelty angered the local people in the areas he controlled and eventually he was seized and handed over to the Bolsheviks.

North Russia

In North Russia, Murmansk and Archangel were the chief centres of anti-Communism. Britain intervened here partly, at first, to try and change the Russian government in the hope of bringing Russia back into the war with Germany, and partly because some British politicians hated Communism and wished to ruin it regardless of the war with Germany. But as the Red Army became stronger so the British were faced with the choice of withdrawing or greatly increasing their war efforts. Too many British people were opposed to this war (including the whole Labour Party) for it to continue and in Autumn 1919 the British withdrew taking a few Russian allies with them but leaving the remainder to the Red Army. Shortly afterwards came a new threat from the North. Yudenich led 20,000 troops in a desperate dash to seize Petrograd, only to fail 30 miles short of his target.

South Russia

The third area of White activity lay in the South where a series of commanders led forces in the area until, eventually, a moderate republican, Anton Denikin, emerged as permanent commander. Some foreign aid came from the French and British, but Denikin was a poor general and his advance on Moscow did not begin until Kolchak was already beaten and the Red Army was therefore able to mass against him. He was forced to retreat and, in despair, abandoned command to Baron Wrangel, a cavalry officer who proved a capable commander and the only White leader to really try and improve conditions in the area he controlled. But his forces were too small to cope with the massive advance of Frunze's Red Army and in 1920 he was forced to abandon the war.

e) The Polish War

Although Poland had only recently re-emerged as an independent country after over a century under Russian, German, and Austrian control, it soon showed itself to be a very determined state and, under Pilsudski, tried to conquer the Ukraine which the U.S.S.R. also hoped to gain.

The first Polish advance was halted by a Red Army led by the brilliant 26-year-old general Tukhachevsky and the Communists themselves began to move forward. The problem then emerged as to where the frontier between Russia and Poland should be drawn. The Russians, eager for victory, rejected the British suggestion of the 'Curzon Line'. But with French help the Poles were able to counter-attack and, after a period of heavy fighting, the Treaty of Riga was signed in March 1921 leaving Russia much of the Ukraine.

So, by 1920, the Communists had beaten down enemies outside and inside their country and were able to concentrate on making sure all areas were loyal. Georgia was one of the most unreliable areas and Stalin was allowed to bring the state to heel, a task in which he used very brutal methods. The Communist triumph sprang from the advantage of having a central position in a land of poor communications from which they could strike at the various enemy forces around the fringes of Russia. They were able to stress the dangers of returning to the old Czarist system of government which many who were not Communists thought would be even worse than Lenin's government.

f) War Communism

The many years of war had done so much damage to Russia's economy that, from sheer necessity, the government was forced to interfere more and more and money was used less and less (as it became worthless). Some Communists welcomed this development as being a big step towards establishing true Communism but it involved some very harsh methods of government. This was especially true in agriculture, there was a desperate shortage of food so the government declared grain a state monopoly. It was further proclaimed that people found hoarding grain would be severely punished and that anyone who informed on hoarders would be rewarded. Poor peasants were organised against the kulaks who were suspected of not handing food over, and were backed by military units sent out by Trotsky.

Not unnaturally this harsh policy was not a success, it caused a tremendous amount of resentment and even led to a mutiny in Red Army units at Saratov. Food remained so scarce that people began leaving the towns in large numbers to search for something to eat till by 1920, there were thirty per cent. fewer people in the towns than in 1917. The government had neither the power nor the skill to manage the enormous task of running all parts of the economy. It could not stop the huge black market in food, it could not make many factories obey its orders and it even had to appoint inspectors to check on the inspectors already checking on factory managers. Only Stalin gained anything from this muddle for he managed to make the *Rabkrin* (the inspectorate) into a kind of private police force. The government at first tried to solve the problem by giving priority to certain industries, but when this did not work, Lenin decided that economic policy would have to be changed. A revolt in the supposedly loyal city of Kronstadt shook the Communist Party into agreeing with Lenin that a new way must be found to manage the economy.

g) The New Economic Policy

This change of policy, the N.E.P., meant abandoning the chief ideas behind the War Communism, that the state could supervise the whole economy in detail and that there would be no private profits. Something more like the existence of a normal market was allowed to return to Russia. The peasants now had to pay a fixed tax in produce to the state, not surrender the whole of their produce, and state control of industry was also reduced. The state ceased to be the sole supplier and distributor of goods and the use of money was encouraged instead of the direct exchange of goods. Industries were divided into those considered to be essential to the state, which continued to be directly controlled by the state, and less essential industries, which were to be supervised in general by a government department. Industries were grouped into trusts, each trust having a board which appointed managers to run the separate factories within it and each factory was given a production target set by the government. However Russian industries continued to be hampered by lack of capital; capital was needed to improve plant and increase capacity, yet capital was what foreign governments were reluctant to lend to Communist Russia.

The economic situation began to improve, but production still ran at below the 1914 figure and the 'scissors' crisis persistently troubled the government. This crisis obtained its name from the appearance of graphs that showed industrial and agricultural prices in relation to each other. At first agricultural prices were high since food was desperately short, whilst industrial prices were low as few could afford to buy manufactured goods. But in 1923 agricultural prices fell as a result of peace and recovery, and industrial prices shot up as demand increased. The government never really managed to close the 'scissors' and bring industrial and agricultural prices into some sort of harmony.

h) The Treaty of Rapallo

The shift in economic policy away from harsh extreme methods was matched by a similar shift in foreign policy. At first the *Comintern* (Communist International) led by Zinoviev, an organisation of all the world's Communist Parties now dominated by Russia, lived in daily hope of Communist revolutions in many other countries. But revolutions did not come or, when they did (as in Germany) they were crushed. It became obvious that Russia needed better relations with her neighbours in order that trade could flow again and a first step in this direction was marked by the Treaty of Rapallo, signed with Germany in 1922; its terms were not very important but it caused a great stir in Europe simply because it was between Communist Russia and a non-Communist state.

Throughout this period, Lenin had worked very hard to build up his Communist Utopia, but a wound sustained in a murder plot troubled him and then in May 1922, he suffered a stroke which meant that he could no longer effectively lead the government, and the Party. The problem of who was to succeed him became more and more important, but of all the possible candidates, few would have guessed, in 1922, that the eventual victor would be Joseph Stalin.

The Rise of Stalin

a) The Growth of his Power up to 1924

To many Communists, Stalin seemed a man of common sense steadily devoted to Marx's ideas and Lenin's leadership. By never thrusting himself forward and taking risks he did not attract the dislike that fell on his

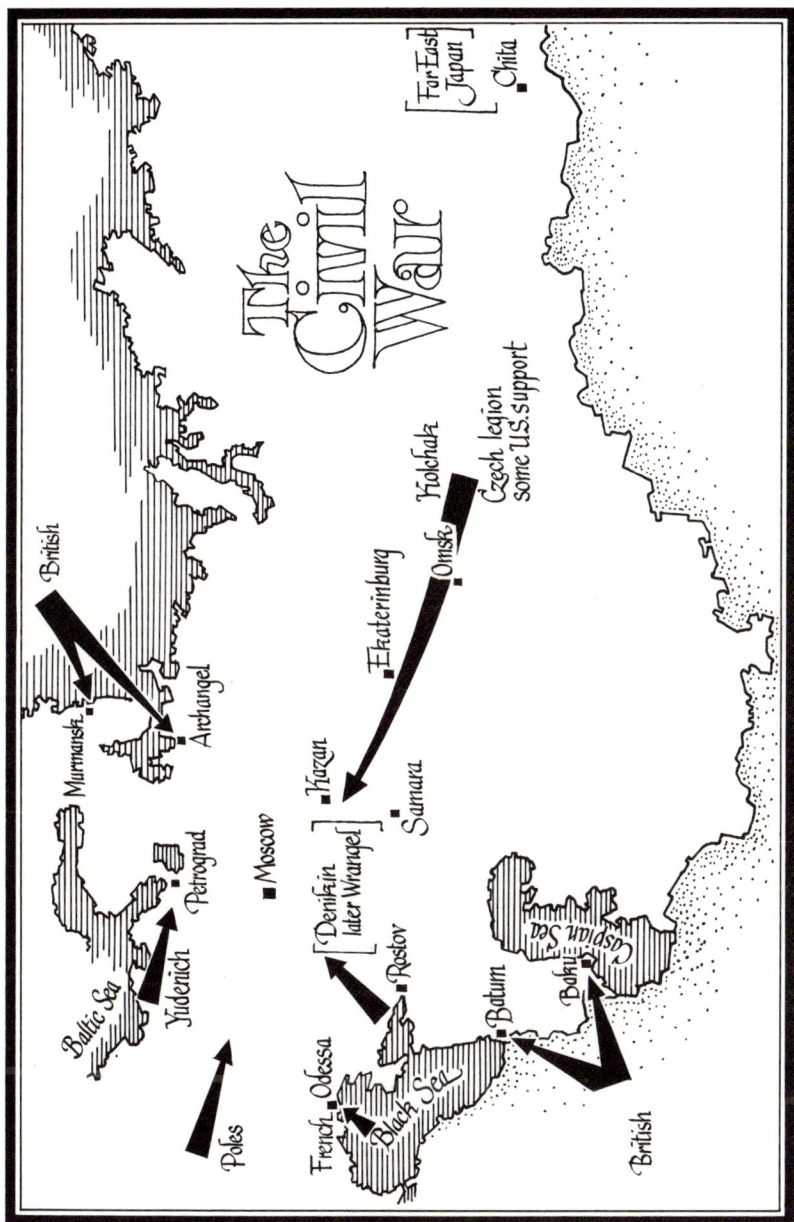

The Civil War

Far East
Japan
Chita

British

Czech legion
some U.S. support

Kolchak
Omsk

Ekaterinburg

Murmansk
Archangel

Kazan
Samara

Moscow
Petrograd

[Denikin later Wrangel]

Yudenich

Baltic Sea

Rostov

Poles

French Odessa

Black Sea

Batum
Baku

Caspian Sea

British

chief rival, Trotsky. Yet by the time Lenin died on 21st January, 1924, Stalin had already built up a most powerful position for himself. Lenin eventually realised the danger he could be to the party and added a section to his will warning the Party of Stalin's harshness and greed for power.

General Secretary

For a time Stalin served as Commissar of Nationalities, dealing with the non-Russian sections of the population and building up his contacts with Communists in these regions. In April 1922 he became General Secretary of the Party and it was this position which made him so powerful. Stalin ran his *Orgburo* which controlled party administration with ruthless efficiency, putting his supporters in all the key posts. His Department carried out detailed administration, managed propaganda and carried out the work of assigning people to jobs. It gathered and sorted out information before presenting it to the *Politburo*, where Party leaders met to make important decisions, and it also helped check on the loyalty of Party members and remove the disloyal. Its work seemed dull to the other Party leaders; Trotsky and Bukharin were both members of the Orgburo but they never attended any of its meetings. In this way Stalin was able to influence the series of elections out of which the Supreme Congress of Soviets was chosen, yet his methods were so silent and self-effacing that they passed largely unnoticed.

Stalin's rivals

Most Communists feared Trotsky much more than Stalin, for Trotsky was a recent convert to Bolshevism and in earlier days had said many bitter things about Lenin. Many of his ideas seemed extreme and risky and Trotsky did not help his own cause by his apparent indifference to the cultivation of support. Zinoviev, like Trotsky, a Jew, was another possible candidate for the succession to Lenin. But he had damaged his chances by differing with Lenin about important policy decisions – chiefly about the wisdom of the October Revolution. However he was an able orator, head of Comintern, and supported by his inseparable friend, Kamenev. Other party leaders included Bukharin, the party's leading theorist, but a poor politican, and Rykov and Tomsky who were practical administrators and not serious candidates.

Trotsky's isolation

Even before Lenin's death, Kamenev, Zinoviev, and Stalin had begun to work together against Trotsky, whilst Trotsky's counter attacks proved inadequate and spasmodic. In particular he failed to exploit his influence in the army and outside the party, hampered by his belief that 'the party in the last analysis is always right because the party is the single historic instrument given to the proletariat for the solution of its fundamental problems'. Since Stalin ensured that the party, as represented at its congresses, was dominated by his followers, Trotsky was doomed to failure.

b) Stalin's victory over his rivals

The most serious crisis facing Stalin's ambitions came when Lenin's will was read and his attack on Stalin was made known to the Central Committee. Zinoviev saved Stalin by arguing that Lenin's fears had proved groundless, Kamenev supported him and Lenin's widow protested in vain. The will was not published. The three allies opened a vigorous campaign against Trotsky, during which Stalin formulated his views on 'socialism within one country' developed as an attack on Trotsky's theory of permanent revolution, but later used as the basis for Stalin's own policies. As a slogan, it proved popular with a war-weary country and with party officials who were beginning to enjoy running the country.

Stalin strengthened his position by contriving the addition of three of his supporters to the existing seven members of the Central Committee. He also sent Kirov to dislodge Zinoviev from his strong grip over Leningrad (formerly Petrograd). Having edged Trotsky out of all important posts, Stalin felt safe enough to turn on Zinoviev and Kamenev, inducing them to work with Trotsky – a spectacle that did not impress those who remembered the recent violent abuse that had passed between them. Stalin expelled them from the Politburo, removed Zinoviev from the Presidency of the Comintern, and finally expelled them, and their followers, from the party. Trotsky lived in exile, finding an eventual home in Mexico, but even here he was not safe. Stalin resented the stream of hostile literature which poured from Trotsky's pen and in 1940 Trotsky was hacked to death with an axe by one of Stalin's agents. Kamenev and Zinoviev preferred to submit humble apologies and were allowed back into the party.

c) The Purges

Stalin's policy of assuring himself of complete power reached a peak in the purges by which he succeeded in eliminating most of the old Bolsheviks and replacing them with men like Mikoyan who owed their promotion to Stalin. The event which triggered off the purges was the murder of Sergei Kirov, on the 1st December, 1934, by a young Communist associated with the more liberal minded whom Stalin had seemed to favour. A purge began in Leningrad and, under Yagoda, head of the

N.K.V.D. (the recently re-organised and re-named secret police) a series of purges of the party were organised. Thousands were deported to Siberia, others confessed their guilt in 'show trials' and were executed. Kamenev, Zinoviev, Bukharin, Rykov and Tukhachevsky were only the more eminent of the many who perished between 1935 and 1939. Yagoda himself 'confessed' to murdering his predecessor and was replaced by the more violent Yezhov. The defendants were usually charged with trying to assassinate Stalin, wreck Russia's military and economic power and restore capitalism, but many were condemned unheard and others only tried in secret. The purges destroyed much of the leadership of the party, the army, the diplomatic service, the Comintern, the Trade Unions and the *Komsomol* (the Communist Youth Organisation). One of the last victims was Yezhov; his successor was the sinister Beria.

One of the most amazing features of the purges was that many of those actually tried in public confessed to the crimes with which they were accused. Yagoda even admitted to being guilty of the preposterous charge of conniving at the death of Kirov. Their motives in confessing are not clear. Perhaps loyalty to the party drove them to it, for most of the victims still clung to the belief that the party could do no wrong. Perhaps some form of torture produced confessions, possibly it was a hope that each crime they confessed to would be the last, but at all events Stalin had succeeded, by this ferocious blood letting, in eliminating any alternative government.

d) Economic Policy

The most striking feature of Stalin's pre-war rule was the extent to which he succeeded in developing Russian industry. This was done at considerable cost, particularly to the peasantry; yet when the burden inherited from wars, the lack of capital, the losses of territory, and the suspicion with which other states viewed Russia are remembered, it was an impressive achievement. Stalin did not work to a detailed, overall plan, rather his measures tended to be short term, to be abandoned unfinished or, like the Five Year Plans, to have values and motives that were psychological.

The Five Year Plans

The first Five Year Plan, announced in 1928, marked a break with the N.E.P. policy of coping first with agriculture and tolerating the kulaks in order to ensure food supplies. Stalin reversed the process and demanded huge sacrifices in order to build up heavy industry. Since the kulaks persisted in being unco-operative, Stalin aimed to find the

Iosif V. Dzhugashvili, the son of a Georgian shoemaker, who as Joseph Stalin ('man of steel') became virtual ruler of the U.S.S.R. in 1924.

necessary food by a policy of forced collectivisation of agriculture. Only the poor peasants welcomed this policy and the result was a civil war in which rebellious villages were surrounded by troops with machine-guns and kulaks were deported to Siberia. The wealthier peasants retaliated by destroying crops, livestock and property as an act of deliberate sabotage. Agriculture suffered; in 1929, for instance, there had been 34 million horses in Russia, by 1933 there were only half that number and too few tractors to make good the loss.

Yet the Five Year Plan provided a psychological stimulus, a promise of better things to come, a promise to which many people willingly responded. Stalin was no economist, and when he realised his policy of collectivisation was far from a complete success he tried to appease the peasants. He made concessions to peasant individualism, allowing them private plots of land, poultry and cattle of their own and angered the Politburo and Central Committee by trying to shift blame for suffering on to them. Indirect inducements to collectivisation were now used, such as the setting up of Machine Tractor Stations which controlled valuable machinery and gave preference in its use to collective farms.

The targets for production were formulated by *Gosplan* (the State Planning Commission) and they were so optimistic that their attainment was most unlikely – an increase of 179 per cent. in production by large-scale industries, for example. The targets were never reached, but money for investment was scraped together and the volume of production rose at a time when capitalist countries were hit by depression. Immediately the Five Years were over, a second Five Year Plan was proclaimed and clear signs of economic growth could now be seen. The necessary tractors and combine-harvesters began to appear; between 1928 and 1938 the output of electricity rose from 6 to 40 billion kWh; coal production increased from 30 to 133 million tons; 31.5 million children attended schools in 1938 whereas only 12 million had attended in 1928.

Because skilled workers remained in short supply 'shock brigades' of specialists were organised and every possible stimulus employed to persuade the people to make greater efforts. Competitions were organised between factories and greater rewards were made to the more successful. In 1935 a new device emerged, named after Stakhanov, a Donets miner, who greatly exceeded the average production of coal per man. 'Stakhanovites' sought to copy his success, but not all workers were impressed – because work norms were liable to be raised if a Stakhanovite showed that production could be increased even more.

e) The 1936 Constitution

The publication of this document was preceded by all the appearances of serious study. At first glance the constitution seemed both generous and democratic, likely to impress France and Britain with whom Russia was, at the time, seeking to align herself against Fascism. Instead of the series of indirect elections that culminated in the Congress of Soviets, the supreme legislative body was to be chosen by direct, equal, universal secret suffrage for all over the age of eighteen.

In fact this outward form meant little since Article 141 provided that only the Communist Party and its subordinate organisations had the right to nominate candidates for election. The apparently generous treatment of the various regions was equally deceptive. Although there was a Supreme Council meeting in two divisions, one to represent the Union, the other the Nationalities, the real power still lay with the Council of Commissars. Lenin had promised the non-Russian in Russia self-determination, but in fact as Communist rule grew in strength so regional rights were reduced. Stalin justified the constitution on the grounds that it simply reflected the reality that Russia had not yet achieved true Communism and that the dictatorship of the party was therefore necessary since it represented the true interests of the workers. Party warfare, on the West European pattern, he denounced as simply a kind of class struggle which Russia must be spared.

f) Stalin's Foreign Policy

Although many Communists placed great faith in the Comintern in its early days, Stalin tended to view it with contempt. As he established his power in Russia, so he extended his grip over the Comintern, squeezing out radicals and rebels and contriving that the Russian delegation should completely dominate Comintern affairs. His task was made easier by the tendency of foreign Communists to closely identify their cause with the cause of Russian Communism despite the fact that it soon became clear that Stalin did not believe a, world revolution would come soon and was not prepared to risk the Russian Revolution in an attempt to bring about world revolution.

Stalin's first attempts at moderation failed. He assisted the Kuomintang in China, helping to build up the prestige of Chiang Kai-shek, only to see Chiang turn on the Chinese Communist Party and massacre many of its members. The Anglo-Russian trade union council of 1925 –an attempt to bridge the gap between Communist and non-Communist unions – likewise failed. Stalin, then, tended to veer to a more extreme line, urging foreign Communists not to co-operate with other left-wing groups (thus, indirectly, helping Hitler to power).

The Policy of better relations with the West

However Hitler's success by 1935 and his vigorous opposition to Communism stimulated Stalin to seek security through better relations with the Western democracies. Russia joined the League of Nations and occupied the permanent seat on the Council of the League vacated by Germany. Litvinov, the Commissar for Foreign Affairs, became the strongest advocate in the League of a policy of collective security. Co-operation with other left wing groups in 'Popular Fronts' against Fascism became the policy of the Comintern and the Communists were soon the loudest advocates of national defence in most countries.

But although both Laval and Eden visited Moscow, Stalin found it impossible to obtain definite pacts with Britain and France and thus suspected that they secretly approved of Germany's military revival in the hope of seeing Germany attack Russia. The Popular Front governments which, briefly, ruled in France and Spain only seemed to increase capitalist distrust of Russia. This presented particular difficulties in Spain where, in the civil war that began in 1936, Stalin had no desire to see Franco win, yet felt that if the Popular Front triumphed then Russia's chances of obtaining definite agreements with Britain and France would be even more remote. Russia sent aid to Spain to counter German and Italian aid to France, though some of this aid was turned against

Leading members of the Russian government which came to power on the death of Stalin. Left to right in the front row are Nikita Khrushchev, Marshal Zhukov, Marshal Bulganin and Mikhailovich Molotov. Andrei Gromyko shades his eyes with his hand just behind Khrushchev.

the Communists' allies, the Anarchists and the semi-Trotskyist P.O.U.M. At all events Stalin was well rewarded, for most of Spain's gold reserve was sent to Russia to pay for aid.

Stalin's fears of isolation were increased by British and French behaviour at the Munich conference when they allowed Hitler to take the Sudetenland from Czechoslovakia, with whom both Russia and France had pacts. Litvinov pledged Russian aid to the Czechs if the French would do the same, but it is difficult to know what would have happened if the French had agreed, for the Romanian and Polish governments denied the Russians passage for the Red Army to cross to Czechoslovakia. Stalin was inclined to suspect that Czechoslovakia was a bribe to Hitler to use the Anti-Comintern Pact against Russia.

Stalin's Pact with Hitler

Only after he had committed Britain to support Poland did the British Prime Minister, Neville Chamberlain, begin making lethargic approaches to Stalin which seemed to assume that Britain could use Russia if it suited her. Stalin attempted to reach an understanding with Hitler and, as an indication of this, dismissed the Jewish Litvinov and replaced him with the silent and obedient Wacheslav Molotov. Perhaps, if British and French negotiations had been conducted with vigour and realism, Stalin might have co-operated with them but it was instead the German representative, Ribbentrop, who finally signed a pact with Russia on the 23rd August 1939. In return for neutrality, Russia was to be allowed parts of Poland, Finland, Estonia and Latvia as her sphere of influence. When Hitler attacked Poland on September 1, Russian troops moved in to occupy the areas they had been allocated, meeting determined resistance only in Finland. It took nearly four months for the Russians to finally crush the small Finnish army. This campaign encouraged Hitler to feel contempt for the Red Army which had lost most of its senior officers in the purges.

Stalin had expected the Poles and French to put up a serious fight against invasion and when both countries fell he became concerned for Russia's safety. He sought to increase his security by incorporating his 'sphere of influence' into Russia and by taking Bessarabia and North Bukovina from Romania. But mounting German pressure squeezed Russia out of the Balkans. Stalin's only success was a pact of neutrality with Japan. Yet Stalin refused to believe the warnings he received of 'Barbarossa', the German plan for the invasion of Russia; he even ignored a warning from Churchill that gave almost the exact date of attack. Stalin seems to have expected a German invasion to be preceded by increasingly harsh demands from Hitler (as had been the case with Czechoslovakia and Poland) and was taken wholly unawares by the sudden opening of the German offensive on 21st June, 1941.

F

4 | Fascism

Introduction

Fascism was a peculiar development of the post-war period following 1918, which differed from the left-wing movements of Socialism and Communism and the right-wing movements of monarchy and despotism. Fascism is not easy to define, since it was never clearly and fully expressed, but it owed something to the ideas of both left and right, and a great deal to the consequences of the Great War. The word 'fascism' had its origin in Italy where it was used to describe the political party led by Benito Mussolini which used as one of its symbols the *fasces*, or bundle of rods which was the symbol of authority held by magistrates in Ancient Rome. Fascism tried to appeal to the people, to be a mass movement, and to promise reforms: but it also offered right-wing policies of

THE CLASH OF FASCISM AND COMMUNISM, 1917–39

FASCISM

Fascism triumphant   Fascism tolerated

Germany   Italy   Spain   Britain & France   Russia

Communism defeated   Communism tolerated   Communism triumphant

COMMUNISM

dictatorship and aggressive foreign policies. It therefore flourished in countries where there was great popular discontent with the existing situation and a desire for more national glory. Fascism varied in Italy, Germany, Spain and Portugal in many details, but in all cases great stress was placed on the leader, the great man who would lead his people to prosperity and success and who had to be obeyed.

Fascism in Italy

a) Conditions favouring the rise of Fascism

The failure of parliamentary democracy

Most Italians had little reason to feel affection towards the system of government with which they had been ruled since unification. Politics had been corrupt, many small parties squabbled for office and governments were built more from bribes than from beliefs. The system had not produced great successes, either, there was widespread poverty still, especially in the South, and attempts to win an empire had resulted in defeat at Adowa at the hands of the Abyssinians. During the war the system had been altered slightly, proportional representation was introduced and the party bosses found this more difficult to control. But the largest parties, the Socialists and the Catholic Popular Party, were inexperienced and failed to co-operate.

The effects of the war

Few Italians had been enthusiastic about the war, both the Catholics and Socialists had disliked it, it caused the death of half a million Italians, left a large war debt and a twenty-five per cent. drop in industrial production. There were also humiliating memories of Caporetto and resentment at the lack of interest in Italy's claims at the peace conference.

Post-War confusion:

Resentful Nationalists, led by the poet D'Annunzio, in 1919 seized Fiume, which they claimed should be Italy's. The nationalists were supported by ex-soldiers and by many wealthy and influential people, but opposed by Socialists and Communists. Violence between these groups increased and there seemed little the government could do about it. Conditions in Italy thus provided a real opportunity to someone who could offer order, economic recovery and a revival of national self-confidence. Mussolini offered all these things.

b) The rise of Mussolini

Early career

Though Benito Mussolini had been brought up by his blacksmith father to be a Socialist and had, for a time, edited the Socialist paper *Avanti*, the war caused him to break with the party and become a firm supporter of Italian intervention. He served in the war on the Isonzo front, was wounded, and after the war was one of the many resentful Nationalists who clashed with the left-wing groups. Mussolini showed a gift for oratory and journalism and qualities of personal charm.

Fascism

In 1919 he began forming combat groups (*fasci di combattimento*) from ex-soldiers which he organised on military lines to resist the Socialists and Communists. Backed by upper class people who feared Communism, the Fascist 'black shirts' used force to break up socialist groups, employing mobility to off-set their lack of numbers. They launched attacks on the unions that the socialists were building in the countryside, and then on municipal councils run by socialists. They had some support from Giovanni Giolitti, a leading politician, and in 1921 fought in the general election winning 30 seats. By then they had 2,300 squads, had control of Milan and Genoa, and their tactics of beating up opponents, burning opponents' offices, and administering doses of castor oil to unfortunate victims became increasingly effective.

The march on Rome

In 1922 Mussolini felt sufficiently confident to attempt to seize power. In fact the disorderly progress of the Fascists could have been easily halted by the army; but the army, like the king and the politicians, had no desire to resist Mussolini. The leader arrived by train to accept King Victor Emmanuel III's offer of the position of Prime Minister.

c) The Fascist Organisation of Power

The battle with opponents

At first Mussolini co-operated with other parties, his cabinet contained four Liberals and two Populists, and he proceeded cautiously. But the election of 1924, which gave him a majority in the Chamber of Deputies, was a time of great Fascist brutality against their opponents and led to a brave speech against this terrorism by Giacomo Matteotti, the Socialist leader. Matteotti was murdered, most non-Fascist deputies

THE FOUNDATIONS OF FASCISM

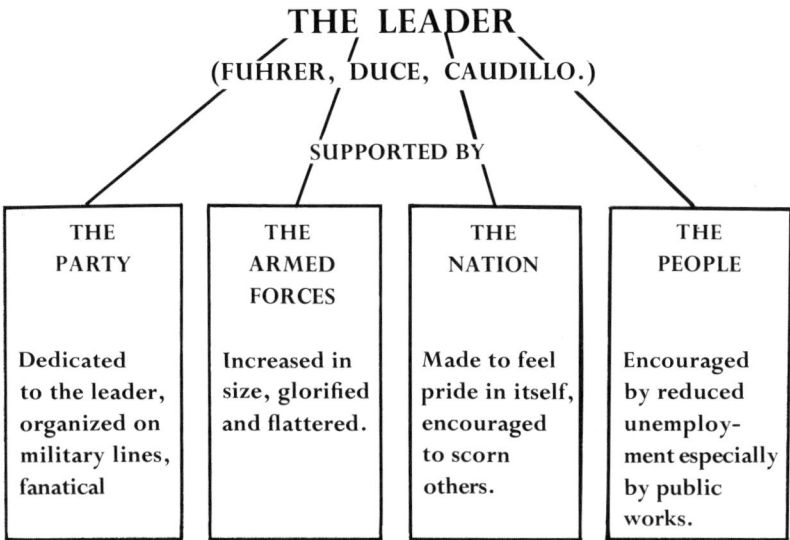

THE LEADER
(FUHRER, DUCE, CAUDILLO.)

SUPPORTED BY

THE PARTY	THE ARMED FORCES	THE NATION	THE PEOPLE
Dedicated to the leader, organized on military lines, fanatical	Increased in size, glorified and flattered.	Made to feel pride in itself, encouraged to scorn others.	Encouraged by reduced unemployment especially by public works.

left the Chamber, and it seemed Mussolini was in danger. But the *Duce* (leader) blamed others for the murder, rode out the storm, and by 1926 felt sufficiently confident to deprive the deputies who had left the Chamber of their seats and dissolve their political parties. Mussolini was now able to pass laws by decree, to build up support by forming a Fascist Youth Movement, and to constantly impress Italians with his determination to re-create for them the glory of Ancient Rome. Even the Fascist salute was modelled on that used in Ancient Rome.

The Corporate State

Mussolini had frequently spoken scornfully of the ordinary parliamentary system, and he proceeded to replace it with a new kind of organisation. In 1925 Mussolini had negotiated an agreement with Italian businessmen, and had ordered that only Fascist trade unions could negotiate for the workers. In 1926 he brought the two sides of industry together in a series of corporations representing employers and unions with powers to settle wages and conditions of work. These corporations were organised into thirteen national confederations and in 1928 the confederations were allowed to select candidates for the Chamber of Deputies. The Fascist Grand Council sorted out these candidates and presented a final list to the electorate for approval. Eventually, in 1938, Mussolini abolished the Chamber of Deputies and replaced it with the Chamber of Fasces and Corporations representing the Fascist party and the new corporations.

This imposing structure of power suited the employers, for strikes were forbidden and the Fascist-dominated corporations did not greatly benefit workers. But, despite the use of propaganda, youth movements and impressive displays, Mussolini was not an absolute despot loyally followed by party and people. By many he was simply tolerated; the Fascist Grand Council seldom met; within the party there was graft and corruption, and Mussolini felt it necessary to bow before the authority of the Church.

d) Mussolini's religious policy

Mussolini made great efforts to please the Roman Catholic Church, which at this time was in a peculiar position for Popes had refused to recognise the state of Italy which had been created in 1870. However Pius XI and many Catholics were afraid of the spread of Communism and were willing to negotiate with Mussolini, who had saved Italy from Communism. Lengthy discussions resulted, in 1929, in the signing of two agreements, the Lateran Treaty and the Concordat.

THE LATERAN TREATY: The Vatican City, where the Pope lived, was recognised as a separate sovereign state. In return the Pope recognised the kingdom of Italy.

THE CONCORDAT: Roman Catholicism was declared to be the religion of the state, there was to be a Catholic University in Milan and Roman Catholicism was made compulsory in schools.

There is no doubt that Mussolini's success was very popular, for the division of Church and State had been embarrassing to many Italians.

e) Economic Policy

PUBLIC WORKS: As a sign of the power and greatness of Fascism, an expensive programme of public works was begun that provided many fine roads, blocks of flats and sports stadiums. This also reduced unemployment – Italy was not as badly hit by the depression of 1929–30 as some other European states.

ECONOMIC IMPROVEMENTS: Industries were encouraged, iron and

steel production rose, and a rise in wheat production reduced Italy's dependence on imported food. Sick industries were developed, hydro-electric schemes encouraged, and land drainage schemes undertaken – especially at the Pontine Marshes near Rome.

f) Early Foreign Policy 1922–35

AIMS: Mussolini intended to show that Italy was not a state to be treated with contempt, but much of his activity was bluster and for many years his actual policy was cautious and designed not to offend Britain or France. He regarded Hitler with suspicion at first, fearing an over-mighty neighbour on his frontiers if Hitler seized Austria. He eventually secured Fiume for Italy and held up this acquisition as a great triumph.

CORFU: In 1923 Italian members of a commission trying to settle the Greek frontier were murdered and Mussolini promptly demanded an apology and an indemnity, and when both failed to come he sent the Italian fleet to bombard and occupy the Greek island of Corfu. He would not let the League act in this matter and eventually it was settled in Italy's favour by a conference of ambassadors.

OPPOSITION TO HITLER: By signing the Kellogg Pact and the Locarno Pact, Mussolini demonstrated his willingness to co-operate, despite his increasing irritation with Britain and France, whose empires were so much larger than Italy's. Italy tried to build better relations with the Balkan states, especially Albania, which received much Italian aid. Such a cautious policy was sensible in view of the very limited size of Italian resources, and, when faced at first with Hitler in Germany, Mussolini maintained his early policy. In 1934 it seemed likely that Austria would be absorbed into Germany, for the Austrian Chancellor, Dollfuss, was murdered by Austrian Nazis. Mussolini rushed troops up to the Brenner Pass on the frontier and forced Hitler to draw back and allow the Austrian government to recover control. When Hitler re-introduced conscription, Italy joined with France and Britain in forming the Stresa Front to condemn Hitler's action. It was Britain, not Italy, that broke the unity of this Front.

g) Later Foreign Policy 1935–40

ABYSSINIA: In 1935 Mussolini used the excuse of border incidents at Wal-Wal on the Abyssinian-Italian Somaliland frontier to attack

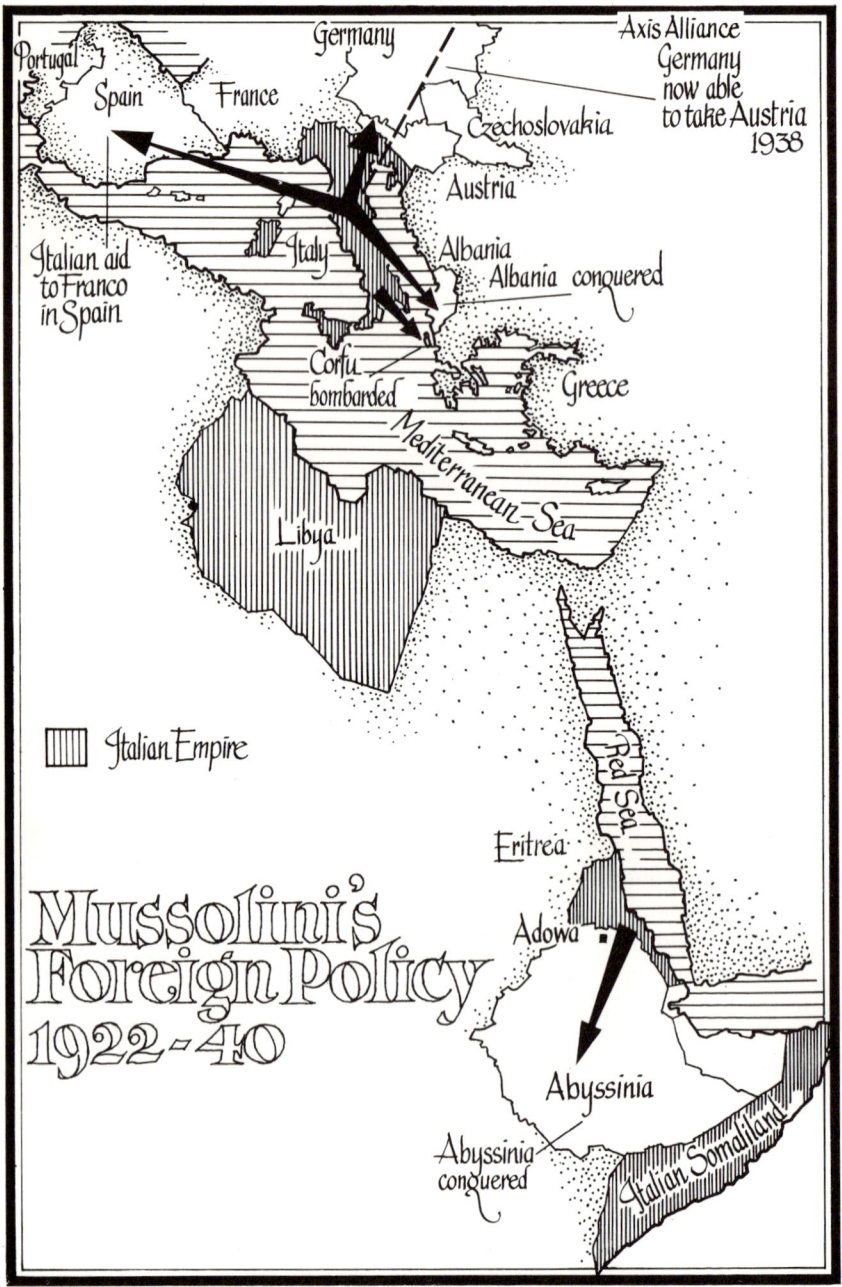

Mussolini's Foreign Policy 1922–40

- Portugal
- Spain
- France
- Germany
- Czechoslovakia
- Austria
- Axis Alliance Germany now able to take Austria 1938
- Italian aid to Franco in Spain
- Italy
- Albania
- Albania conquered
- Corfu bombarded
- Greece
- Mediterranean Sea
- Libya
- Italian Empire
- Red Sea
- Eritrea
- Adowa
- Abyssinia
- Abyssinia conquered
- Italian Somaliland

Haile Selassie's state. This marked a turning point in Italian foreign policy for it led to growing hostility between Italy and France and Britain and pushed Mussolini closer to Germany. The attack was designed to avenge Adowa, was further glory for Mussolini and added to Italy's empire. The Abyssinians were not equipped with modern weapons and found the task of stopping Mussolini's modern army and airforce impossible. But Mussolini's troops, led by De Bono and Badoglio, needed supplies, especially oil, and an application of economic sanctions by the League was demanded by Abyssinia. Though the League condemned Mussolini and banned arms shipments, there was no ban on oil, coal, iron and steel. Mussolini felt anger at Britain and France, the chief League powers, for criticising his actions in view of their own huge empires and contempt for them because they did not act vigorously. Pierre Laval for France, and Sir Samuel Hoare, for Britain, suggested that Italy should keep part of Abyssinia and have a protectorate over the rest. This merely caused a delay giving the Italians time to complete their conquest and declare the area part of the Italian Empire by May 1936. After the victory the limited sanctions on Italy were abandoned, the League had suffered a blow from which it never recovered, and Mussolini was drawn closer to Hitler who had sympathised with him during the crisis.

THE SPANISH CIVIL WAR: Italy and Germany were pulled closer together by their joint support of the rebellion of the army leaders and of Fascists against the Spanish Republican Government. Encouraged by Galeazzo Ciano, his foreign minister, Mussolini poured troops into Spain to help Franco: they failed to win the striking successes he hoped for and he had to increase Italian intervention. Eventually Franco won, but by then yet more serious problems had emerged.

THE AXIS ALLIANCE: Hitler took care to flatter Mussolini and in 1936 Mussolini spoke grandly, if vaguely, about a Rome-Berlin axis around which important politics would turn. In 1937 Italy withdrew from the League and the following year Mussolini introduced laws against Jews in Italy, in imitation of Hitler. He even ordered his troops to start marching with the Prussian goose step. Their alliance was linked with Japan, in the Anti-Comintern Pact, which clearly proclaimed their intention to fight Socialism and Communism.

AUSTRIA: The alliance meant Mussolini was badly placed to resist Hitler when, once more, the Nazis sought to merge Austria in Germany.

This time, in 1938, the Germans were successful and Mussolini was not made more popular in his country by the arrival on the frontier of the mighty German state. Increasingly Hitler dominated Mussolini both through his skill and fanaticism, and through the superior strength of the state he ruled. In 1938, when Hitler was campaigning for part of Czechoslovakia, Mussolini encouraged Britain and France to negotiate with Hitler at Munich, but his sympathies were with the triumphant Hitler who, he felt, was by far the strongest leader in Europe.

ALBANIA: Italian economic aid had made Albania into a near-Protectorate of Italy, but Mussolini was not satisfied and in 1939 he seized the country driving out King Zog, in an attempt to win a success that would equal Hitler's triumphs.

Entry into the Second World War

In 1939 Italy and Germany signed an alliance, the Pact of Steel, yet Hitler still went his own way in preparing for war, negotiating with Russia, and finally attacking Poland. This attack brought Britain and France into the war, but Mussolini remained neutral, alarmed at these develop-

Benito Mussolini, in characteristic pose, speaking in Rome prior to the Second World War. Unlike Hitler, Mussolini never won full popular support and his declaration of war on the Allies in 1940 met with little enthusiasm.

ments and feeling that Italian forces were not ready for major conflict. Germany's successes in 1940 convinced him it was worth taking a risk and in June he declared war on France and Britain. There was little enthusiasm in Italy, Italian forces were not well prepared and proved unable even to conquer Greece. The war was to prove Mussolini's ruin, he had not made Italy the powerful military machine that he had boasted he would create. Fascism in Italy had not gone deep, it remained rather superficial and far less disturbing than Fascism in Germany.

Fascism in Germany

a) Conditions favouring the rise of Fascism

The Weimar Constitution

When the Kaiser abdicated, Germany became a republic, the Weimar Republic. This republic was based on elaborate rules to provide for a parliamentary democracy and guarantees for freedom of speech, religion, assembly etc.; it represented the German people in one assembly (the *Reichstag*) and the different states of Germany in another. At the head stood the President, chosen nationally, in special elections. Women were given the vote, trade unions were freed from restrictions and, on paper, it seemed as if Britain and France would have a co-operative partner, like themselves a Parliamentary democracy. But the Weimar constitution also allowed the President to rule by decree in case of emergency, and emergencies were likely in view of the hostility of left and right-wing groups to the Weimar Republic and the peace treaties for which it was blamed.

Left and right-wing violence

This lack of stability was shown by armed risings which the Republic found hard to control. In 1919 the Communists, led by Rosa Luxemburg and Karl Liebknecht, tried to seize power and were only thwarted by the free corps (right-wing groups of ex-soldiers) upon whom Noske, the Minister of the Interior, had to call. But rightist groups were no more loyal than the left and in 1920 Dr. Kapp led army units due to be demobilised to seize control of Berlin. Right-wing feeling, infuriated by the terms of the Treaty of Versailles, was already encouraging the legend of 'the stab in the back', i.e. that Germany was betrayed by politicians who signed the armistice. The Kapp rising was defeated by a general strike, but it inspired a similar movement in Bavaria which ejected the socialist government and let in right-wing rulers who, henceforward, sheltered right-wing nationalists hostile to the Weimar government. Both incidents showed the Republic's weakness – its need to call on one group of enemies in order to defeat the other.

The Army

The German Army held a high position of prestige in the nation's eyes, and had not been totally defeated in 1918, though total defeat would have come if the war had continued. The Army resented the restrictions imposed on it by the Treaty of Versailles and many former members of it helped form the extreme nationalist political parties like the Nazis, and the groups of militants called the free corps. Among those remaining within the army, there was sympathy with these nationalist groups and pleasure in seeing the treaty restrictions by-passed by the irregular forces of troops built up by Nationalists. Ludendorff himself lent his great prestige to the Nazis in 1923. By means of secret agreements with Russia, the Army were able to experiment with new weapons inside Russia, in return the Germans trained Russian officers, and were thus breaking the treaties long before Hitler came to power.

Economic instability

The war, the blockade, the reparations, and the French occupation of the Ruhr, all hurt the German economy and in 1923 there was a slump. The German currency collapsed in value and middle class people saw their savings become worthless almost overnight. Right and left-wing groups increased their membership rapidly, a sign that the Republic would be tolerated only as long as there was reasonable prosperity. Germany recovered from her setback with reorganised reparations (the Dawes Plan), the skilful leadership of Gustav Stresemann who became Chancellor for a few months in 1923, the determination to deal with disorder expressed by General Seeckt and the reorganisation of finance by Dr. Schacht. With the added prestige of Hindenburg as President (1925) and the valuable aid of American loans, Stresemann achieved stable government for six years. A much more serious slump in 1929, and the death of Stresemann, repeated the crisis of 1923 in a far more serious manner. The consequent rise in unemployment, and loss of savings, fanned the resentment of Germans. Once more they looked to the left and right for leadership, not to Heinrich Bruning, the moderate Centre Party chancellor, who was struggling to enforce sensible but unpopular economic policies by means of Presidential decree. This was the opportunity for which the Nazi Party was waiting.

b) The Rise of the Nazi Party

Hitler's early career

Unlike Mussolini, Adolf Hitler experienced little but failure in his early life. He was born in 1889, in the Austrian town of Braunau, the son of a minor customs official. His progress at school was not very successful and his ambitions to be an artist remained unfulfilled. He was rescued from a poor, frustrated, and shiftless life by the war when he volunteered for service with a Bavarian regiment. In the army, he found companionship and a purpose in life; he served bravely, was promoted corporal, and decorated for his courage. After the war he joined the many discontented ex-soldiers who formed various groups and eventually in 1919 attached himself to one such group, the National Socialist German Workers' Party. His skill as a speaker, and his burning fanaticism, soon made him their leader – *führer* – and helped him build up the strength of the party.

Hitler's ideas

Hitler had spent part of his early life in Vienna, and there he had picked up many of his ideas, especially hatred of the Jews, who were blamed for all Germany's failings and were portrayed as evil, corrupt and sinister people. Hitler could speak with a wild, magnetic and terrifying oratory, but his ideas were not very complex nor always very clear. He believed in a crude kind of racial theory that held that the Aryan Nordic, or German people were a superior race who should be freed from Jewish contamination and allowed to assume their rightful role in dominating Europe. Hitler's ideas tended to change according to circumstances; at first there was considerable emphasis on changes to suit ordinary people, he stressed 'Socialist' as well as 'Nationalist'. Later, he modified these views in order to win the favour of rich industrialists. But his ideas, vigorously expressed, and backed by the violence of the brownshirted stormtroopers, the S.A., led by Captain Röhm, could prove very appealing at a time of economic crisis and a national sense of humiliation.

The 1923 bid for power

By 1923 Hitler (who had been joined by Ludendorff, the war hero) and his movement were sufficiently well organised to attempt to seize power in Munich. The attempt, the famous Beer Hall Putsch, was a total failure. In the face of police bullets only Ludendorff showed courage, and Hitler himself was tried and imprisoned, though his sentence of five years was reduced to nine months, a very lenient punishment for an attempted revolution. During his imprisonment he dictated *Mein Kampf (My Struggle)* to Rudolf Hess. The work was a curious mixture of autobiography, twisted historical fact, and prophecies of future success. In the early years that followed, the Nazi Movement found it a struggle to hold their membership but there was consolation in seeing many of the rival right-wing groups killed off.

The growth of the party

Hitler decided that the way to power lay not through revolt, but through legal means. He attempted to make his party more acceptable to the army and the wealthy, much to the annoyance of Otto and Gregor Strasser and Joseph Goebbels and their supporters who wanted to attack capitalists. The Nazis objected to the Young Plan to scale down reparations since they believed Germany should not pay anything, and here Hitler was fortunate. Hugenberg, leader of the Nationalists and owner of several newspapers and cinemas, allied with Hitler and helped him campaign and gain publicity. But it was the slump which really benefited Hitler. By 1932 there were 400,000 in the S.A., attracted by the excitement and the employment. The Nazis gained the backing of the unemployed and the discontented well-to-do: it was the money of rich businessmen that enabled Hitler to pay the S.A., and mount an expensive publicity campaign.

c) Hitler's entry into power

In 1930 the Nazis gained 107 seats in the Reichstag and were second in size to the Socialists; in 1932 Hitler stood against Hindenburg in the Presidential elections and, though defeated, received over 13 million votes. As Germans turned more to Nazis and Communists, stable government became difficult, Bruning lost power and Hindenburg had to use his power to rule by decree. There followed a complicated battle for position between conservative politicians like Franz von Papen, and General Schleicher, an ambitious soldier favoured by Hindenburg. All protagonists had however one thing in common, a hatred for Socialists and Communists and a hope of using the Nazis, whom they thought they could control, towards their own ends. In 1932 there were two elections, in the first 230 Nazis were elected to the Reichstag whose total membership was 608, but in November they lost thirty-four seats and, to the alarm of conservative Germans, the Communists were the ones who gained. In January, 1933, Papen, who had lost the position of Chancellor to Schleicher, allied with Hitler and Hugenberg and persuaded Hindenburg to accept their coalition ministry by which Hitler

The Reichstag building in Berlin at the height of the fire which destroyed it in March, 1933. A Dutchman, Van der Lubbe, was accused of the act.

became Chancellor, Papen Vice Chancellor and Hugenberg Minister for the Economy.

A new election in March 1933, in which S.A. violence reached new heights in terrorising opponents, resulted in 288 Nazis and fifty-two Nationalists being elected. Since many Germans also voted Communist, it was clear that most Germans had rejected the moderate Parliamentary way. Thus Hitler, unlike Lenin or Mussolini, gained power quite legally. Those who thought they could control him were pleased that Wilhelm Frick (Minister of the Interior) and Hermann Göring (Minister without portfolio) were the only Nazis in the Cabinet, but were soon sadly shaken by the violent turn of events.

d) How Hitler strengthened his position

The Reichstag Fire

Just before the election, the Reichstag Building had been burned down by a fire started by an eccentric Dutchman, Van der Lubbe. Hitler blamed the Communists, used the crisis to suspend the guarantees of personal liberty in the constitution and empowered the government to take over the government of the separate states. He used these powers to the full and had soon brought all the states under the control of all-powerful Nazi governors. The Communists were clearly innocent of causing the fire and, for long, the Nazis themselves have been blamed for staging the incident, but possibly Van der Lubbe was right in claiming it was a single-handed act of protest.

The Enabling Law

On the 23rd March, 1933, the Nazis used the crisis, and the support of the Centre Party, to pass the Enabling Law giving the government power to rule by decree for four years, to depart from the constitution and to conclude foreign treaties. This law formed the basis of the Nazi dictatorship which enabled Hitler to sweep aside rivals, reduce Papen and those who had hoped to use Hitler to mere servants, and dissolve all parties except the National Socialists.

The Gestapo

In addition to the S.A. and the S.S. (the *Schutzstaffeln* or security force, a special elite of Nazis devoted to Hitler) the Nazis established a political police force called the Gestapo (an abbreviation of *Geheime Staatpolizei* or secret state police). Both Gestapo and S.S. were supervised by Himmler, a serious believer in Nazi ideas, and a narrow-minded fanatic who was responsible for some of the worst Nazi cruelty. Himmler's men were soon in control of the police, were free of all legal restraints and were helped by the use of Special 'People's Courts' in which the judges were Party officials. Thousands of people were interned in concentration camps run by the Death's Head S.S. in which they were terrorised.

Trade Unions

The unions, with their strong organisation and their working class sympathies were broken up, much to the satisfaction of Hitler's wealthy supporters. Instead Hitler established a Labour Front, organised by Dr. Ley, which fixed wages and hours and did not permit proper free bargaining by the workers.

Control over the Army

The Army resented the S.A., for Röhm, the S.A. leader, had made it clear that he wanted to abolish the army and replace it with the S.A. But Hitler needed Army support too much to allow this to happen, and his efforts to satisfy Röhm by giving him a place in the cabinet did not work. Röhm remained a possible rival and a leader of the left-wing Nazis who disliked Hitler's alliance with the wealthy. On June 30th, 1934, Hitler savagely dealt with this problem in a series of murders carried out by the S.S. known as 'the Night of the Long Knives'. Schleicher, Röhm and Gregor Strasser were the more eminent of the many who died and the danger from the S.A. vanished. Hitler also dismissed both the Army Minister and the Commander in Chief so that he could appoint Keitel and Brauchitsch whom he could trust to do as they were told. The Army was pleased by an increase in its size and by improvements in its weapons. It was also impressed by the skilful judgement shown by Hitler in his foreign policy. By building up S.S. army units (the Waffen S.S.) and by letting the Nazi leader Göring control the new air force, Hitler made sure of loyalty in at least some parts of the armed forces.

The Führer

In August, 1934, Hindenburg died and Hitler took his position as President, as well as retaining his own as Chancellor. In a plebiscite, 38 million Germans declared their support and only five million showed disapproval. Hitler was clearly the leader of Germany and the Army itself was ready to swear an oath of loyalty to the Führer.

e) The War for People's Minds

The Young

Nazi policy aimed at recruiting the support of the younger generation. The educational system was supervised closely, school books were re-written to glorify Germany and Hitler, and about a quarter of all university teachers lost their posts as the Nazis dismissed those they regarded as disloyal. A Nazi Youth Movement was built up, in 1938 membership of it became compulsory.

The Churches

The Nazis had closed nearly all the Church-run schools by 1937, but their policy towards the Churches never risked total persecution. In 1933 Hitler negotiated a concordat with the Catholic Church which seemed to promise mutual toleration, but he was soon breaking his agreements as much as he dared. Against Protestants, the Nazis were more savage. Hitler reorganised the churches into a National Church, with his own choice, Muller, as Reichbishop but numerous Protestant ministers defied Muller who soon resigned. Several hundred of these

G

men, led by Martin Niemöller, were sent to concentration camps as punishment for their defiance.

Propaganda

Hitler had won over Joseph Goebbels, a former supporter of the Strassers and a very clever man, and installed him as Minister of Public Enlightenment and Propaganda. Nazi propaganda was poured out, in newspapers, on the radio, and in cinemas; but the most impressive events were the huge and carefully stage-managed rallies where Nazis shouted their support for their Führer and Hitler responded with violently emotional speeches.

f) The Nazi Jewish Policy

Hatred of the Jews was a major theme in Hitler's speeches. The half million Jews in Germany were denounced as traitors, Jews were held to be behind Communism, and were sneered at as loathsome and evil persons who should be punished and even eliminated. German Jews were quite prominent in the professions, in intellectual life and in small-

The Power of Hitler

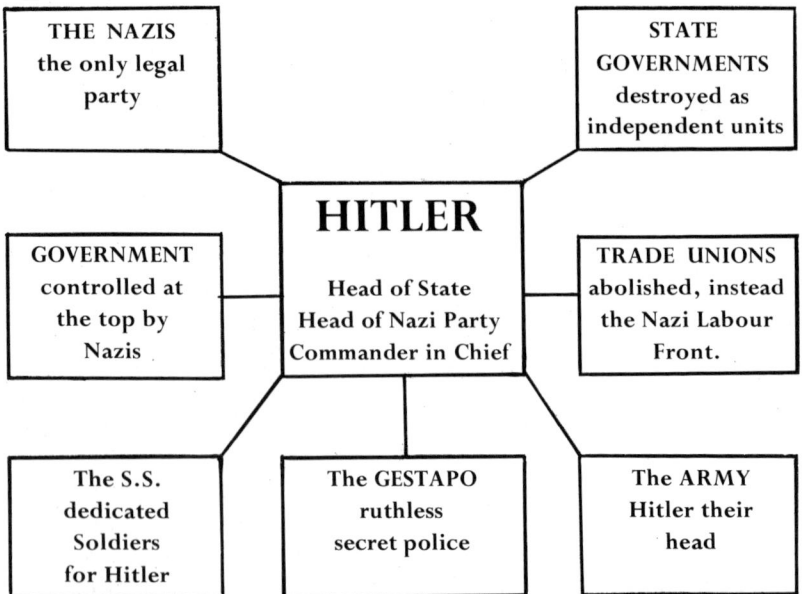

THE NAZIS the only legal party		STATE GOVERNMENTS destroyed as independent units
GOVERNMENT controlled at the top by Nazis	**HITLER** Head of State Head of Nazi Party Commander in Chief	TRADE UNIONS abolished, instead the Nazi Labour Front.
The S.S. dedicated Soldiers for Hitler	The GESTAPO ruthless secret police	The ARMY Hitler their head

scale trading; their real patriotism was unquestioned, yet they were made the victims of attacks which were an ominous sign of what the Nazis would do to the Jews of other lands when they conquered them.

The Nuremberg Laws, 1935

These laws deprived German Jews of all rights of citizenship, all rights of public employment, farming and positions on the stock exchange, and forbade them to marry Aryans. In 1938 they were compelled to carry special papers and their homes and business premises were frequently the object of attacks. In November of that year more violent persecution developed, Jews were rounded up, banned from business, law and medicine, made to pay fines, and imprisoned in increasing numbers. Hitler's last decision was to decide on the 'final solution' of the Jewish question, which meant a deliberate policy of exterminating Jews in special concentration camps, such as Auschwitz and Buchenwald. Six million Jews were slaughtered in this nightmare episode; the greatest crime in modern history.

g) Economic Policy

Agricultural Policy

Hitler showed only limited interest in economic policy, preferring to leave the details to others. Agriculture was organised by Darré who tried to increase production and stabilise prices in farming, with state aid. He planned the 'hereditary homesteads' or small properties, capable of supporting a family, that could not be split up into smaller units. Yet even here racial policy played a part for the homesteads could only be held by 'pure' Germans with no Jewish connections.

Industrial Policy

Early Nazi policy had been full of vague promises of reform, even of the nationalisation of large industries and the abolition of unearned incomes. These promises had served their purpose in attracting the lower class support he needed then Hitler dropped them and, in the Night of the Long Knives, eliminated those Nazis who still believed in them. Partly because much of his support came from wealthy businessmen, and partly because Hitler believed in struggle and the survival of the fittest, Hitler left business alone as a free enterprise system. Dr. Schacht helped the German economy by his attempts to make Germany self-sufficient. Synthetic substitutes were developed for products Germany lacked, like rubber and wool, while exports were boosted at the expense of imports.

Hitler had promised he would deal with unemployment and, within five years of coming to power, he had kept this promise. Full employment was achieved by a programme of public works (like the magnificent motorways, the autobahns) by rapid rearmament, and by increases in the armed forces.

h) Foreign Policy

Aims

Hitler was an openly declared opponent of the Peace Treaties of 1919–20, but he was not foolish enough to take sudden great risks. Instead he proceeded cautiously, a step at a time. He was helped by a feeling prevalent at the time, especially in Britain, that Germany had been harshly treated by the Treaty of Versailles. Anyway the British were reluctant to use force and the French were determined there would not be a repetition of 1914 and concentrated in future on defensive wars. Probably Hitler had no overall plan, but seized opportunities as they came along, using them skilfully, and repeatedly showing the German generals that his judgement of what could be risked was far better than theirs.

THE POLISH PACT: Alarmed by the fear of the growing friendship between France and Russia, their chief enemy, Poland signed a ten year peace pact with Germany in 1934.

1934, Failure in Austria

The murder of the Austrian Chancellor Engelbert Dollfuss by Austrian Nazis eager to unite their country with Germany so alarmed Italy that she moved troops to the frontier and Hitler had to hastily disown the Austrian Nazis. The friendship of Italy was clearly worth cultivating and Hitler devoted his energies to charming Mussolini.

Rearmament

Germany withdrew from the League of Nations in 1933 and from the Geneva Disarmament Conference in protest against the refusal of the other powers to grant her equality at once. Encouraged by the plebiscite in the Saar (1935) which voted for a re-union with Germany, Hitler introduced conscription and began building aircraft and submarines. Italy, France and Britain had drawn together in the Stresa Front to face Nazi Germany, but in 1935 Britain broke this agreement by negotiating a special naval treaty with Germany allowing the latter a surface fleet thirty-five per cent. the size of the Royal Navy, and a submarine fleet.

THE AXIS ALLIANCE: Hitler won the gratitude of Mussolini by his
sympathy during the Abyssinian crisis and their joint co-operation
during the Spanish Civil War drew them closer together. They were
linked to Japan in the Anti-Comintern Pact to resist Communism all over
the world and in the Pact of Steel became firm allies. Hitler was soon
the dominant partner in this alliance.

THE RHINELAND 1936:   Hitler correctly guessed that the French army,
though larger, would not offer resistance if Germany re-occupied the
de-militarised Rhineland and so, despite the fears of the Generals,
German troops moved in to an enthusiastic welcome and no opposition
of any kind.

THE ANSCHLUSS: Early in 1938 Hitler bullied the Austrian Chancellor,
Dr. Kurt von Schuschnigg, into accepting Nazis into his government.
Probably Hitler was content to leave things like this, but the Austrian
Nazis became so aggressive and troublesome that they provoked
Schuschnigg into standing up to them and preparing a plebiscite so that
Austrians could vote on whether they wished to join Germany. Hitler
was furious at this act of independence and ordered his troops to the
frontier with Austria whilst sending new bullying orders to Schuschnigg.
The Chancellor resigned; a Nazi, Seyss-Inquart, took his place, and

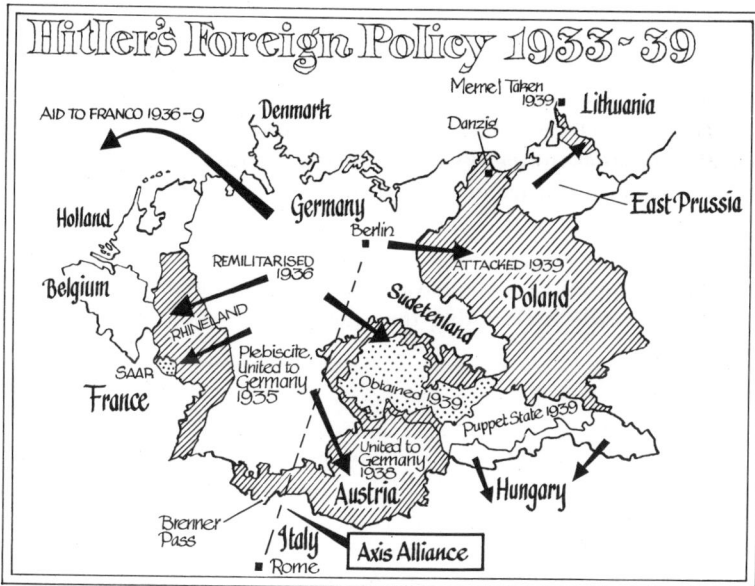

Hitler's Foreign Policy 1933~39

AID TO FRANCO 1936-9
Denmark
Memel Taken 1939
Lithuania
Danzig
Holland
Germany
Berlin
East Prussia
Belgium
REMILITARISED 1936
RHINELAND
ATTACKED 1939
Sudetenland
Poland
SAAR
Plebiscite, United to Germany 1935
Obtained 1939
France
Puppet State 1939
United to Germany 1938
Austria
Hungary
Brenner Pass
Italy
Rome
Axis Alliance

invited German assistance, thus making possible the *Anschluss* (union with Germany). This time Mussolini did not act. He was too dependent on Hitler by now.

The Czechoslovakian crisis

Czechoslovakia was a prosperous, strong, and well populated state. Its government was democratic and wisely led by Eduard Benes; its army was efficient and well equipped from the great Czech Skoda factories. Within its frontiers however, chiefly in the Sudetenland, lived three million Germans and among them had grown up a troublesome Nazi party led by Konrad Henlein who demanded that the Sudetenland should be joined to Germany, not Czechoslovakia. The Czechs had the alliance of France and Russia and felt confident in rejecting the impossible demands put forward by Henlein. Britain was not committed to Czechoslovakia but her Prime Minister Chamberlain, who was hoping to develop better relations with Italy and Germany, felt Germany had been badly treated and expected she would behave reasonably if granted concessions. Three times Chamberlain visited Hitler to discuss a compromise settlement, whilst in the background the German army prepared to attack Czechoslovakia. The last meeting in September 1938 was held at Munich between Hitler, Mussolini, Chamberlain and Daladier and it led to the destruction of Czechoslovakia. In their eagerness to avoid war and in the mistaken belief that Hitler spoke the truth when he said the Sudetenland was his last demand, Britain and France agreed to the partitioning of Czechoslovakia, allowed Hitler to take the Sudetenland, and allowed parts of the state to go to Poland and Hungary. The rest of Czechoslovakia was now an easy prey and in March 1939, after stories of Germans being ill-treated in Czechoslovakia the German army moved in; Britain and France, who had welcomed the Munich settlement with huge relief, were now forced to face up to Hitler's ambitions which had caused him to seize non-German lands. Hitler's denunciation of the naval treaty with Britain and of the Polish Pact finally made it clear that the western allies would have to take a firm stand.

The Polish crisis

The ease with which he had won encouraged Hitler to put forward new demands. Lithuania was easily bullied into handing over Memel, but Hitler's main target was the Polish corridor that separated East Prussia from the rest of Germany. With Britain hastily building up her forces, and offering unconditional guarantees to Poland (and to Romania and

Adolf Hitler declares war on Poland to the acclamation of the Reichstag. Seated behind Hitler is the President of the Reichstag, Herman Göring.

Greece) Hitler realised that it was vital to come to terms with Russia. Russia could most easily help Poland, and a war in the east, plus fighting against Britain and France in the west, was more than Hitler was ready to face. The Russians disliked Poland, felt no faith in Britain and France because of the Munich episode, and were, anyway, pleased at the prospect of western capitalist countries tearing each other to pieces whilst Communist Russia stood aside. British and French efforts to win Russia's alliance were so feeble that in August, 1939, Ribbentrop, Germany's Foreign Minister, and Molotov, for Russia, signed a non-aggression pact from which Russia was to gain her 'former Baltic lands' and part of Poland. With this security Hitler felt able to attack the Poles (who had rejected all his demands) after a series of faked border incidents. On September 3rd, two days after the German onslaught on Poland, Britain and France declared war on Germany. In six years Hitler had undone all the work of the Peace of Paris and wrecked all attempts to build in Germany a moderate parliamentary system. Germany had large and splendidly equipped armed forces, and at their head stood a fanatic dedicated to German supremacy in Europe through a system of calculated cruelty and sadism which was unique in history.

The Spanish Civil War

a) Introduction

In Spain and Portugal (and, indeed, in Austria under Dolfuss and Schuschnigg) a quite different kind of Fascism developed. In Italy Fascism appeared to be in control of the state, and in Germany it certainly was; but in Portugal and Spain Fascism was only one element in the forces which supported the strong leaders (*caudillos*) who emerged – Franco in Spain, and Salazar in Portugal. In Portugal the republic established in 1910 suffered an unhappy history until Dr. António Salazar, a professional economist, was allowed power in 1928 and, because of his success, given increasing authority until by 1936 he was very powerful indeed. He continued in office until the autumn of 1968, when illness compelled him to retire. Only one party – the National Union – was permitted, but Salazar avoided the foreign and imperial adventures of Mussolini and Hitler and relied on the Church and the upper class, not on wild efforts to whip up popular support. Salazar was a devout Catholic who increased the power of the church, giving it a monopoly of education for example, in contrast to Hitler, who hated the Churches. Spain eventually produced a state more like

Salazar's than Hitler's but Spain did contain a Fascist Party and the battle between Franco's Nationalists and the Republic Government was seen, at the time, as a real clash between left and right. Spain became a battle ground for Fascists and Communists from other lands.

b) The Background of Discontent

The Carlist Wars

Spain was occupied by the French in 1808 and, for a time, was ruled by Napoleon's brother Joseph. With the intervention of the British, the French were driven out and the Spanish Bourbons restored to power in 1815. They proved an unsuccessful line of rulers, were sometimes inefficient and occasionally cruel. A rival sector of the ruling family, the Carlists (named after Carlos, their first leader) several times plunged Spain into civil war in their attempts to seize power. At the dawn of the twentieth century, there was still an important Carlist group in Spain.

The Failure of the Monarchy

Alphonso XIII succeeded his father to the Spanish throne in 1886 and reigned until 1931. His reign was marked by a number of adversities, in spite of Spain's neutrality during the First World War. In 1898 Spain was easily defeated by the U.S.A. and deprived of the remnant of her former American colonies, whilst in Morocco, which she had partitioned with France in 1911, the Spanish were unable to defeat the Riff leader, Abd el-Krum and were forced to seek French aid. These setbacks helped General Primo de Rivera to seize power with the promise of more successful government. He succeeded in bringing the war to an end in Morocco and improved government, but he offended sections of the army, mismanaged finance and in January 1930 was dismissed by the King. Resentment against Primo de Rivera was now directed against the King and when the local elections, permitted in 1931, showed a majority in favour of a republic, Alphonso abdicated.

Regional troubles

Spanish government had long been troubled by the resentment shown by some areas of Spain towards the central government. This feeling was strongest in the Basque provinces and in Catalonia, both near the French frontier, and any government attempting to destroy the traditions and privileges of these areas was bound to meet with trouble.

The Spanish Civil War

Ovieda

Asturias

France

Catalonia

Barcelona

Portugal

Madrid

New Castile

Valencia

Murcia

Cordoba

Seville

Granada

Rebel [Nationalist] areas at the outbreak of war, July 1936

Government [republican] areas

c) The failure of the Republic

Spanish politics were conducted on extreme lines and with a tradition of army interference. There were too many groups which hated each other, and too much readiness to resort to violence for the new Republic's history to be smooth. The Republican Party, backed by intellectuals and some middle class people, was not, itself, sufficiently strong to deal with the other parties and, indeed, needed the help of some of them. Of the few outstanding leaders the Republicans produced, the most notable was Azana, who attempted to reduce army influence, reform agriculture and education and at the same time please Catalonia and the Basque provinces by granting them self-government. Four of the other major groups were the Socialists, the Anarchists, the Catholic Action and the Falange.

The Socialists were a large group, led by Largo Caballero, and controlling a powerful trade union organisation, the U.G.T. The Communist section of the Socialist Party was very small before the outbreak of war. Spain was one of the few countries in Europe where Anarchists were numerous. Their chief stronghold was Catalonia, especially the thriving port of Barcelona, and they too had a trade union organisation, the C.N.T. The Anarchists were restless and violent and clashed in frequent battles with the U.G.T.; one Anarchist group, the F.A.I., was dedicated to violence.

The Catholic Church in Spain was very powerful and resented the attacks on it by the Republican government. A party called Catholic Action, led by Gil Robles, was formed to defend the Catholic interest and was soon a large and important movement.

Finally, the Spanish Fascist Party, led by Primo de Rivera's son, José Antonio, was known as the Falange. It copied Mussolini's organisation and urged Spaniards to fight the menace of Socialism.

So many warring groups made effective government difficult. The Army would only tolerate the Republic as long as it maintained law and order, and this it failed to do. Thus the different right-wing groups – Army, Church, Falange, Monarchists and Carlists – drew closer together and in response, pushed the left-wing groups into forming an alliance, the Popular Front. This uneasy alliance of Socialists, Anarchists and Republicans triumphed in the 1936 elections, installed Azana as President, and frightened the right wing into revolution. Violence became more common; among the victims of murder plots was Calvo Sotelo, a leading right-wing politician, killed by Assault Guards who resented the murder, by Fascists, of one of their comrades.

d) The events of the Civil War

The Rising of the Nationalists

In the summer of 1936 a carefully planned Army plot succeeded in winning control of much of the country, though failing to take the Basque provinces, Catalonia, and Madrid together with much of southern and eastern Spain. The rebels had the advantage of the support of the bulk of the army, especially the colonial troops in Morocco who were led by General Franco. With Italian help, Franco was able to transfer his troops to the mainland where, led by Yague, they threatened to take Madrid.

THE INTERNATIONAL BRIGADES: Volunteers from many countries poured into Spain to help save the Republic from right wingers. Real idealism inspired these men; many were Communists, but all believed they were fighting to halt Fascism. The brigades were rushed to the front at Madrid and brought Franco's army to a standstill. The war now settled down into what might have been a conflict neither Franco's forces, nor the troops serving Largo Caballero's government, could win.

Foreign intervention

It was the intervention of Italy and Germany together with Portuguese sympathy for Franco which helped ruin the Republic. First, Italian troops led by General Roatta arrived, organised into units with impressive names like the 'Black Flames' or the 'Black Arrows', but much less impressive when in action. Italian equipment for Franco's troops poured in too, and so did German support. Hitler sent far fewer men than Mussolini but the aircraft unit he sent, the Condor Legion, played a vital part in helping Franco win the war. Italian and German intervention meant that the Republic lost control of sea and air, and on land the Nationalists were able to resume their attack. Britain and France were badly divided over what to do in this situation. That a British Conservative Government should be reluctant to help rescue a Spanish Government of Socialists, Communists and Anarchists is not, perhaps, surprising, but France had a Popular Front Government led by a Socialist, Leon Blum, and might have been expected to be more helpful. Instead, Britain and France tried to organise a Non-Intervention Committee. The Italians and Germans co-operated in principle with this but betrayed it in practice. It was left to Russia to aid the Republic and Russian supplies and experts, paid for in Spanish gold, began to

THE TWO SIDES IN THE SPANISH CIVIL WAR

THE GOVERNMENT		THE REBELS
THE SOCIALISTS		ARMY LEADERS
THE COMMUNISTS	VERSUS	SPANISH FASCISTS
THE ANARCHISTS		CHURCH
THE REPUBLICANS		THE UPPER CLASSES
		COLONIAL TROOPS
RUSSIAN SUPPLIES AND EXPERTS	FOREIGN AID	GERMAN SUPPLIES AND EXPERTS, ESPECIALLY AIRCRAFT.
VOLUNTEERS FROM MANY COUNTRIES		ITALIAN AID, EXPERTS AND TROOPS.

pour in and, not surprisingly, to greatly help the growth of the Spanish Communist Party. The Communists became so powerful that they were able to remove Caballero as Prime Minister and replace him with Negrin; they also devoted some of their strength to crushing left-wing rivals, as well as fighting Franco.

Franco's victory

By 1938 Soviet aid to Spain was dwindling, whereas Fascist aid was not. General Mola's troops were able to conquer the Basque provinces, easily breaking through their famous defence 'the ring of iron' and backed by German aircraft who, at Guernica, experimented with the effects of bombing a civilian population. The Republicans counter-attacked at Teruel, and, though at first successful, eventually exhausted themselves with the result that Franco's forces were able to advance east to the coast, cutting off Catalonia from Madrid. Another Republican counter attack on the line of the River Ebro began well, but Republican supplies were running low whereas Franco received yet more German aid in return for Spanish iron. In January 1939 Catalonia was captured and finally Madrid fell in March, following an overwhelming attack during which the defenders were weakened by quarrels among themselves.

The war had been both cruel and brutal. Within the areas they controlled, each side had persecuted people it suspected of supporting the other. Franco insisted on unconditional surrender and many Republicans were, in 1939, driven into exile or put in prison. He emerged as the successful leader through his skill as a soldier, his control over the Army of Morocco, which was the backbone of the effort, and through the foreign aid he received in such generous quantities from Germany and Italy. The policy of non-intervention was shown to be a pitiful failure and provided Hitler with yet further evidence that Britain and France were declining military powers.

Franco ruled Spain until his death in November 1975. A small number of Spanish troops were sent to help Hitler, otherwise Spain was not seriously hurt by the second world war. Post '45 Spain grew slowly in wealth, helped especially by a booming tourist trade. Franco's death was followed by the restoration of the monarchy in the person of King Juan Carlos, and by a slight relaxation of rules preventing normal political activity.

5 | European Democracy between the Wars

Introduction

Parliamentary democracies had won the Great War and, for a time, this system of government seemed triumphant. But the triumph was short-lived, for democracy was threatened from the left by Communism, with its base in Russia, and from the right by various forms of despotism, but notably Fascism. Upon Britain and France rested the burden of defending the parliamentary system in which many parties were permitted while the armed forces kept out of politics, but Britain and France were both experiencing troubles of their own. The Great War had left damage, debts and bitterness and the post-war economic crises, particularly of 1929–32, aggravated these problems (especially since Germany paid so little in reparations, while the U.S.A. insisted that Britain and France pay back the debts they had run up during the war).

In Eastern Europe, democracy certainly failed to flourish, except in Czechoslovakia. Hungary was dominated by Admiral Horthy, Poland by Marshal Pilsudski. In the Balkans monarchists dominated Yugoslavia, the army controlled Bulgaria, General Metaxas was Greece's strong man behind the king, and Prince Carol controlled Romania.

Farther west, democracy did better in small lands like Switzerland and the Scandinavian countries of Norway, Sweden, and Denmark. These were lands which had escaped the ruinous Great War, had moderate political parties and capable governments. They rode out the depression well and even developed quite advanced systems of sickness benefits and old age insurance. But these were small countries unable to exercise a decisive influence on world affairs, Switzerland and Sweden in particular were more attracted by neutrality than by intervention to aid democracy. Thus, with the U.S.A. not participating in European affairs as had been expected, and with the League discredited after 1935, it fell, above all, on Britain and France to justify the parliamentary system.

France 1918–40

a) Background, the problems of the period

The French Republic had emerged from the war victorious and played a major role in the peace settlement which not only humiliated her rival, but compelled Germany to hand back land she had seized in 1871. With the withdrawal from Europe of the U.S.A., the civil war in Russia, and British uncertainty as to her future policy, France's large army appeared to dominate Europe. But in fact, France was beset by difficulties which led to a worsening political situation at home and an increasingly defensive and futile foreign policy. The Third Republic had never been very popular and the problems of the pre-war period – frequent changes of government and scandals connected with it – continued after the war. Those who supported the Republic were menaced by extremists to left and right who had little patience with the democratic system.

The Left

Pre-war France had seen a rise in membership of the Socialist Party, strikes, and aggressive trade unionism. With the example of the U.S.S.R. to inspire them, the more extreme Socialists under Thorez broke away to form the Communist Party. Lenin insisted that other European Communist Parties must obey Russia's orders which were that Communists were not to co-operate with other reformist parties, but were to seek to overcome them. The rest of the Socialists, led by Leon Blum, dared not go too far in support of the Republic for fear of losing working class support to the Communists.

The Right

The Republic also continued to be plagued with the hostility of groups who wanted strong nationalist government. On one side was the Church, opposed to the Republic's anti-clerical attitude and, at its worst extreme, influenced by the anti-Jewish movement led by Charles Maurras, the *Action Française*; while on the other, were the growing numbers of people who admired Mussolini, and even Hitler. These groups, which included the ex-servicemen's *Croix de Feu* organisation, either wanted Fascism in France or were afraid of Communism and Socialism. They also won sympathy among the upper ranks of the administration and officers in the army.

The Legacy of the War

The war had cost the lives of well over a million servicemen and many more wounded, parts of the country had been completely devastated and huge debts run up to pay for the war effort. The French government had had difficulty in raising finance for the war at home and resorted to heavy borrowing abroad. Thus France was deeply indebted to the U.S.A. and desperately needed reparations from Germany to cope with these debts. Nor did the population recover easily from the war, the birth rate remained low, and fear of the populous and increasingly powerful Germany made some politicians, for instance Laval, eventually decide that France could only survive by collaboration with Germany.

Economic difficulties

French industry, generally, remained inefficient in comparison with the industries of the U.S.A. and Britain. A few manufacturers like Citroën were introducing American methods, but most units of production were small and inefficient. Similarly in farming there were too many small units. Finance was poorly handled by successive governments faced with real dilemmas; extra cash could have come from a general rise in taxation – to which the Left were violently opposed – or from taxes on the wealthy – to which the Right were opposed. Fiddling with the currency, devaluation and further debts, took the place of bold but risky measures to raise production and increase efficiency.

The Army

The victorious French Army drew the wrong conclusions from its success. The strongest influence in it was Marshal Pétain who believed the supreme strategy was defence and the whole Army fell under his spell. There were a few who, like de Gaulle, realised the importance of the tank as an offensive weapon, but no one would listen to them. The Army preferred to erect its massive steel and concrete Maginot Line and hide behind it.

Political opinion in the country remained badly divided between 1918 and 1940. The changes in government between Left and Right were caused by very small swings in votes. Neither side could produce stable governments, both sides were coalitions that easily split up, and the unhappy Radicals, caught between the two extremes, were never strong enough to manage alone.

H

Raymond Poincaré was born at Bar-le-Duc in 1860 and studied law before being elected a deputy in 1887. He was invited to form a national government in 1926.

b) The Bloc National's victory

The Fall of Clemenceau

The 'Tiger', who had led France to victory and had represented her at the peace conference was determined to use his prestige to smash his rivals. In the elections of November 1919, his right wing coalition, the *Bloc National*, swept the electoral board winning 433 seats to the 86 Radicals and 104 Socialists. There were so many ex-servicemen now in the Chamber of Deputies that it came to be known as the 'Horizon-Bleu' Chamber after the uniforms of the men. But Clemenceau did not reap the rewards of victory. Some Frenchmen blamed Clemenceau because France had not imposed harder terms on Germany, whilst many disliked him for treading on their toes during his stormy career and now took the chance of revenge. He failed in his bid to be elected President, instead it was the ex-Socialist Alexander Millerand who emerged, temporarily, as the dominant politician.

The failure of the Bloc National

Millerand sent General Weygand to help the Poles halt the Red Army but he was less successful in finding ministers who could manage home affairs. The Americans demanded repayment of loans and the French in turn attempted to extract reparations from the reluctant Germans. In March 1921 the French occupied three industrial cities in the Ruhr to put pressure on Germany; then in January 1923, the P.M., Raymond Poincaré, extended this into occupation of the whole Ruhr. This attempt to be tough failed, because the German population was uncooperative and the French were unable to run the industries profitably themselves.

c) The failure of the Left-Wing Coalition

An alliance of Socialists and Radicals, therefore, had plenty to attack and in the 1924 elections succeeded in winning a majority over the Bloc National. But though the Socialists helped win the election, they would not accept the responsibilities of office and it was left to the Radical Edouard Herriot to form a government. Yet the Radicals did not really offer the kind of programme favoured by Socialists. On the whole, the Radicals represented peasant proprietors, shopkeepers and small-scale businessmen who disliked government interference, whereas the Socialists wanted greater interference in order to raise wages and improve working conditions. The Radicals really only dominated because the Socialists and Communists were engaged in violent conflict.

THE RADICAL FAILURE: Herriot found himself faced with economic problems which he could not solve, and the French mandate, Syria, was in revolt against French rule. General Sarrail was pushed out of his capital, Damascus, and reduced to the humiliation of bombarding it in order to recover control. Between 1921–6 a campaign to gain control of Morocco dragged on. The Radicals mismanaged the provinces of Alsace-Lorraine, offending the inhabitants by introducing stricter forms of government and by attempting to reduce the power of the Catholic Church.

Poincaré's return

By 1926 the situation was so desperate that one of the few strong politicians the Republic possessed, Raymond Poincaré, was called into power to form a national government and deal with the economic crisis. Poincaré's answer was to tighten up administration, increase taxation and cut expenditure until, by 1928, he had managed to stabilize the franc. Then, in 1929, he retired at the very moment when a new economic crisis hit France.

BRIAND'S FOREIGN POLICY: A tough policy towards Germany had failed, the allies France had acquired in East Europe – Poland, Czechoslovakia, Romania and Yugoslavia – were not yet really of much military value and the Foreign Minister, Aristide Briand, altered policy into one of co-operation with Germany. The Dawes Plan reconstructed reparations, the Young Plan continued this process. Briand helped achieve the Locarno Pact to settle Germany's western frontiers by mutual agreement and he also played a big part in the Kellogg Pact denouncing war. Briand worked hard to make the League function properly yet failed to achieve his very praiseworthy ambitions. With the brief exception of the 1924 Labour Government, the British were most unco-operative in following a similar policy whilst the slump of 1929–31 and the rise of the Nazi Party finally disillusioned Briand. In 1932 he lost power and died soon after his fall from office.

d) The Temporary Revival of the Left

The Right Wing found Poincaré difficult to replace and in the elections of 1932 the revived Radical-Socialist alliance once more recovered power and Herriot found himself back in office. Once again the left achieved power at the very moment when there was a major crisis. The world depression had not hit France, at first, as badly as other powers, but by 1932 its effects were beginning to be felt, there was unemployment and financial difficulties. Herriot clung on to power for a mere six months, then four other Prime Ministers succeeded him rapidly, all equally unable to cope with affairs of state.

The Stavisky Affair 1934

The last of these Radical P.M.'s, Edouard Daladier, was discredited by another of the financial scandals for which the Third Republic was famous. The government tried to hush up a most suspicious episode in which a dubious financier, Serge Stavisky, had been involved in floating large loans with, apparently, help from some ministers. Stavisky eventually committed suicide while the Right Wing clamoured for the downfall of the government.

THE RIGHT-WING UPRISING: In February, Right-Wing groups, like the Action Française and the Croix de Feu, filled with hatred for the government and for Jewish financiers whom they imagined they saw everywhere, attempted to attack the Chamber of Deputies. The police opened fire and repelled the attackers, killing several of them. The episode was enough to finally bring about the downfall of Daladier.

Laval's rise

Men more sympathetic to the Right – first Doumergue, then Laval, attempted to lead the government until new elections in 1936. The only notable minister during this period was Louis Barthou, the Foreign Minister, who introduced new vigour into French foreign policy in an attempt to revive France's alliances with other European powers to face the new Nazi Germany. Unfortunately Barthou was assassinated, in October 1939, in Yugoslavia, and France returned to her more feeble attitude, expressed particularly by Laval. When Hitler re-occupied the Rhineland in March 1936 the much larger French Army made no attempt to oppose him; France was once more badly divided, the Right Wingers even sympathizing with Hitler who, like them, opposed Jews and Communists. Laval's policy of appeasement was also seen in Abyssinia when he suggested to the British Foreign Secretary, Sir Samuel Hoare, that Mussolini should be allowed to keep two-thirds of Abyssinia. Laval, like Hoare, was discredited by the exposure of news of this offer, but the French, like the British, had failed to take a firm stand towards Fascism and France's eastern allies began to desert her whilst Belgium proclaimed her neutrality.

e) The Popular Front

The Formation of the Front

The Right-Wing attack on the Chamber of Deputies alarmed the Radicals and Socialists into making efforts to patch up their crumbling alliance. But the real change on the Left was brought about by the Communist Party abandoning the lonely hostility which had brought it so little success and, in obedience to Moscow, switching to a policy of alliance with the Socialists. Stalin's alarm at the growth of Fascism accounts for this change of heart which brought Thorez to the fore as the leading spokesman for Left-Wing unity. In 1934 the Socialists and Communists allied together as the Popular Front and were soon joined by the Radicals, a combination powerful enough to win the 1936 elections.

The Matignon Agreements

Leon Blum, the Socialist leader, now became Prime Minister with the support of the Communists, though none of the latter would accept ministries. A wave of strikes followed the elections as the workers celebrated; Blum succeeded in calling union and employers' representatives together to work out better conditions. The Matignon Agreements settled a twelve per cent. wage increase, the nationalisation of arms factories, a forty-hour week, holidays with pay, minimum wage rates and collective bargaining to settle future disputes.

Blum's failures

High unemployment and a poor rate of productivity made financing these reforms difficult; big business and Right Wing groups hated Blum and his Socialists, but his allies, too, gave him trouble. Strikes broke out, the Communists attempted to take over trade unions controlled by the Socialists and Blum was discredited by his feeble policy towards the Spanish Civil War. Although he allowed supplies to cross the frontier, Blum was too well aware of the deep divisions in France to risk any further intervention. In June 1937 he resigned and by 1938 the Popular Front had crumbled.

f) Vichy France

The defeat of France

With so much sympathy for Fascism in preference to Communism, French foreign policy became feeble and followed Britain's lead wherever it went. Edouard Daladier led the ministry which permitted Hitler's success at Munich, made promises to Poland and thus became involved in the war. He dared not take positive measures because few Frenchmen cared enough to stand up to Hitler; the most vigorous opponents were the Communists and they were soon discredited by Hitler's pact with Stalin. In March 1940, Paul Reynaud, hitherto in charge of yet another attempt to improve the economy, became Prime Minister, called Weygand back from Syria and made Phillippe Pétain his vice premier. In May, Germany attacked Belgium and Holland and broke through into France. The hopeless military situation led to an armistice with the Germans in June and the resignation of Reynaud from the Premiership, making way for Pétain to take his place.

Pétain's rule

Defeated France was divided into occupied and unoccupied zones. Pétain and his government settled in Vichy to rule their zone and keep as much independence as possible, but the Germans occupied the best areas and burdened the French with demands for money. Some French leaders believed in wholehearted collaboration with Hitler, and Laval, the leader of these, was the most prominent minister in Vichy France. Democracy vanished as the government was remodelled by Pétain, and laws against

Marshal Henri Pétain, General in Chief of the French Armies in 1917 and Prime Minister of Vichy France during the Second World War.

the Jews and in favour of the Roman Catholic Church were features of Vichy rule. Soon little remained of the independence for which Pétain had struggled; in November 1942 the Germans occupied the rest of France and the Vichy regime became a puppet government.

Resistance to Nazi rule

In the mood of defeatism and pacifism, few Frenchmen followed General de Gaulle, whom Churchill had put in charge of the Free French forces in Britain, at first. As Britain and the U.S.A. recovered however and Nazi rule became more brutal, resistance in France increased. The entry of the U.S.S.R. into the war marked a turning point, for now the French Communists with their efficient underground organization and fanatical zeal began to sabotage the German war effort and conduct guerrilla attacks. Despite harsh German replies these Resistance fighters greatly helped the war effort of the Allies, welcomed de Gaulle and wreaked revenge on those who had collaborated with the Nazis in a brief reign of terror to celebrate victory.

Conclusion

Democracy in France had not been a success, for its very inability to secure stable government and economic progress, plus its uncertain foreign policy, encouraged many Frenchmen to despair and turn instead to other solutions. Many became Communists; some came to feel that pacifism was the only sensible foreign policy; many became Fascist in sympathy, hostile to Communism – preferring Hitler to Blum. No determined stand against Hitler was possible in these circumstances, and the difficulty was aggravated by the poor support France received from Britain. Britain opposed Poincaré's toughness in 1923, only briefly tried to make the League work, broke the Stresa Front against Hitler, insisted on non-intervention in the Spanish Civil War, and preferred to give way to Hitler over the Rhineland and Czech questions. British democracy too, must bear much of the blame for Fascism's easy successes.

Britain 1918–40

a) The changing position of Britain and her people

Britain was the centre of a vast empire; she emerged from the war with her armed forces greatly enlarged by conscription; she had played a major part in the military campaigns and, at the peace conference which followed won further colonies and terms which were designed to prevent Germany from ever rivalling her at sea. Her allies, the U.S.A. and France, were also democracies and democracy was adopted as a form of government by many other states. Britain had pioneered the industrial revolution and had a most impressively advanced economy. Yet, between the two wars, Britain was troubled by strikes, economic depression and colonial difficulties she could not solve; her foreign policy was depressingly feeble and in 1940 she stood alone, and very vulnerable, before a largely hostile Europe. It is easy to blame the inter-war government, yet in many ways their muddle and caution represented people's wishes, and Britain's imperial and economic position was clearly shown to be weakening long before the troubles commonly thought to be those of modern Britain. Britain changed, too, in other ways, moving towards becoming a modern welfare state whose benefits were financed by high taxation and managed by a large civil service.

Increased democracy

In 1918 the vote was extended to include all men over the age of twenty-one and all women over thirty who were ratepayers or the wives of rate-payers. The extension of the franchise to women was in recognition of the valuable role they had played in winning the war, rather than the result of the success of the suffragettes. Even so, women had to wait until 1928 before they were given the vote on the same terms as men. The rapid rise of the Labour Party indicated that the wishes of ordinary people must be taken into account as never before. Some Labour sympathisers were intellectuals, supporters of periodicals like the *New Statesman* and the *Left Review*, but the strength of working people can be seen in that the leaders of the Labour Government of 1924 were from poor families. The Liberal Party, already split by the quarrel of Lloyd George and Asquith, became progressively weaker.

Mass Entertainments

The popular press flourished between the wars, battling for readers with all sorts of cut-price offers of goods, and was occasionally attacked as irresponsible by staid politicians. Stanley Baldwin, in particular, grumbled that the press barons exercised power without responsibility, but the need for alarm about this was diminished by the availability of other sources of news. The British Broadcasting Company was formed in 1922 and on 1st January 1927 became the British Broadcasting Corporation. Under the high-minded Lord Reith it provided news and entertainment to be picked up by thousands of receivers, for the B.B.C. had no commercial competitors. The cinema industry boomed, as a wave of splendid picture palaces with impressive names like 'Granada' were built and showed films which were no longer silent, but were 'talkies'. Football, dog-racing and outings to the seaside were all indications of the ways in which working people could get away from their cramped houses and factories. Governments had to take account of popular feeling as never before, as some of their policies show.

Social improvements

Many of the improvements of the period pointed the way towards the present welfare state by providing state intervention to aid the needy. Some of these reforms were the work of Socialists, but the bulk were not, for the Labour Party like the left in France, generally received power and a crisis together. It was Neville Chamberlain, a Conservative, who probably did most for social improvements. State aid to improve housing and increase and extend unemployment benefits are two of the outstanding achievements of the period.

THE ECONOMY: Improvements were possible because the high level of taxation necessitated by the war (income tax rose from 9d. to 6s.) continued afterwards and helped provide the necessary revenue despite Britain's trading, financial and unemployment difficulties. There were particular moments of crises, such as 1929–31, but in general the signs of Britain's economic troubles were already clear. Britain depended too heavily on her old industries of coal, textiles and shipbuilding, which had been crucial to her early success but were now meeting fierce American, Japanese and German competition. It was in areas connected with these industries that unemployment was most persistent.

The Commonwealth and Empire

Further signs of Britain's dwindling world authority could be detected in her overseas possessions. The dominions of Canada, Australia, New Zealand and South Africa clearly emerged as independent states. This was officially recognized by the Statute of Westminster in 1931, but it was already clear as these states had been represented separately in the Peace of Paris and were given mandates to look after. In the areas which Britain still controlled, she was faced with the growing problem of nationalism. Ireland posed the greatest problem, but there was also unrest in India where Mahatma Gandhi's Congress Party sought to bring an end to British rule. The Arabs in the British mandates and protectorates of the Middle East, encouraged, as they thought, by the British, also began thinking in terms of nationalism. It came as a bitter shock however, when the British government agreed to the setting up of a Zionist State in Palestine in 1918. Almost immediately, thousands of Jews poured into the country, driving out the Arabs. Hostility flared, there were riots and finally a full scale civil war.

BRITISH GOVERNMENTS 1918–40

DATE	PRIME MINISTER	GOVERNMENT
1919–22	D. Lloyd George	Coalition
1922–3	A. Bonar Law S. Baldwin	Conservative
1924	J. Ramsay McDonald	Labour
1924–9	S. Baldwin	Conservative
1929–31	J. Ramsay McDonald	Labour
1931–9	J. Ramsay McDonald S. Baldwin [1935] N. Chamberlain [1937]	National Party Chiefly Conservative
1940–45	W. S. Churchill.	Coalition

Faced with so many economic and imperial problems, and at the same time struggling to cope with the conditions of a new democracy, most British Governments in the inter-war period erred on the side of caution and orthodoxy, avoiding either bold solutions to domestic problems or vigorous answers to foreign ones. Yet the electorate's votes indicate its preference for this caution, so no single person or small group of people can be blamed for the crisis in which Britain found herself in 1940.

b) The Lloyd George Coalition

Until 1922 Lloyd George's coalition government remained in power, but 'the Welsh Wizard' was chiefly dependent on Conservative votes. The Labour Party was re-united as those members, like Henderson, who had supported the war rejoined their fellow Labourites in Opposition, assisted by a group of Liberals who still followed Asquith.

The coupon election

Lloyd George and his ministers won the 1918 election on the strength of their success in the war and on promises to make Germany pay the cost of the war. Nearly three quarters of the coalition members were Conservatives. Conservatives held several key offices including the Foreign Office (Balfour) and the Exchequer (Austen Chamberlain) so that Lloyd George was heavily dependent on the Conservatives continuing to support him now that the national emergency was over. In fact a series of troubles caused the Conservatives to decide that their Liberal P.M. was a liability and the 'coupon' – as Asquith scornfully called the letter signed by Lloyd George and Balfour jointly backing coalition candidates, was not repeated.

The weakening of Loyd George's position

Resentment grew against Lloyd George, firstly because he failed to be as tough with Germany as he had promised, and secondly because he had failed to be as moderate and idealistic as the great economist, Keynes, demanded in his very successful book *The Economic Consequences of the Peace*. The Government dropped many of the war time controls introduced to manage the economy, but became very unpopular for its handling of demobilization and was soon faced with working class hostility as the brief post war economic boom collapsed and unemployment rose. Two reforms aimed to help working people were introduced, the Housing Act of 1919 provided state aid to provide houses at low rents and the Unemployment Insurance System was extended to cover all workers earning up to £250 p.a., except agricultural workers and domestic workers, with an unemployment benefit of 15s. a week for men and 12s. for women. But strikes became increasingly serious, the miners were especially restless following the ending of State Control and the handing back of the mines to private ownership. The owners, troubled by foreign competition, sought to cut wages and extend hours. Lloyd George delayed the trouble by appointing the Sankey Commission to look into the mining industry, but the Commission was ineffectual, the Government announced its intention of ignoring its report and the miners struck. They failed because the National Union of Railwaymen and the Transport Workers' Federation, with whom they had a Triple Alliance, failed to support them on what became known as 'Black Friday'. Various attempts to bring together leaders of the two sides in industry failed and an acute housing shortage made nonsense of Lloyd George's promises of providing homes fit for heroes. All the hopes aroused by the end of the war that a new and better age was beginning rapidly faded, and, to make matters worse, a terrible influenza epidemic in 1918–19 killed 150,000 people. Lloyd George's foreign policy suffered a blow when his support to the Greeks came to nothing. The Greeks were defeated and driven from Asia Minor by the Turks and, for a moment at Chanak, British troops seemed likely to fight the Turks they were facing. In Palestine British troops vainly attempted to stop the conflict of Arabs and Jews whilst in India, 1919 was the year of the Amritsar Massacre in which 379 of the peaceful Indian demonstrators were shot by British troops.

Ireland

Ireland had remained a problem which seemed to have no solution. In 1916 Irish extremists had staged the unsuccessful Easter Rebellion in Dublin, but their failure, far from checking extremism, seemed to encourage it. Lloyd George was faced with a new hazard when the Irish members chosen in the 1918 election were overwhelmingly from the Sinn Fein movement which wanted to break with Britain. These members refused to come to Westminster, gathered in Dublin and declared, in January 1919, that they were the parliament of an independent Ireland. Lloyd George had been a prominent member of the pre-war Liberal Government which favoured Home Rule, yet he proceeded to treat the Irish rebels harshly. The Royal Irish Constabulary was reinforced by the 'Black and Tans' (ex-soldiers who wore R.I.C. cap badges and black belts on their khaki uniforms) and a savage war

The burned out shell of a car used as a street barricade during the Easter Rebellion in Dublin, in April 1916, draws a grim parallel with the Belfast disturbances of 1969.

was conducted with the Irish Republican Army in which tortures, murders and great cruelty were enacted on both sides. In December 1920 Lloyd George offered home rule, with one parliament for Southern Ireland and another for Ulster: the Sinn Fein leaders Arthur Griffiths, De Valera, and Michael Collins refused, but Ulster accepted and obtained its own parliament. As the guerrilla war dragged on, with money from the American Irish to aid the I.R.A., feeling in Britain turned increasingly against this policy and in July 1921, a truce was arranged to enable discussions to take place. In December Collins and Griffiths agreed to Lloyd George's terms, called off the war and the Irish Free State was established as a Dominion in the Commonwealth. But Sinn Fein split over these terms: De Valera led those who refused to accept them and till April 1922 a civil war raged between the two sides in Ireland, during which Michael Collins was shot. Eventually, and reluctantly, the extremists called off their campaign and on December 6th, 1922, the Irish Free State came officially into existence, though occasional acts of I.R.A. violence against Ulster continued for many years.

c) The First Labour Government 1924

The End of the Coalition

This series of misfortunes was more than the Conservatives could tolerate: led by Andrew Bonar Law and Stanley Baldwin, they decided to break with Lloyd George's Liberals. Lloyd George was forced to resign, an election was held in November 1922 and the Conservatives were elected back to power with Bonar Law as P.M. The Liberal Party remained disunited, the Asquith and Lloyd George factions watching each other suspiciously from opposite sides of the fence, a situation which greatly helped the Labour Party.

BALDWIN'S MINISTRY 1923: Bonar Law was forced to resign in May 1923 through ill-health and his place was taken by Stanley Baldwin, a shrewd but cautious politician with a gift for presenting himself to the public as a man of great common sense and reliable soundness. Baldwin decided that the answer to Britain's economic difficulties lay in protecting British agriculture and industry from foreign competition by introducing duties and tariffs on imports and on this issue he fought an election at the end of 1923. The Conservatives failed to win a clear majority; their 258 seats were outnumbered by the combined strength of the 158 Liberals and 191 Labour M.P.s.

MacDonald's Government

Some Labour M.P.s thought that it was wrong for Labour to accept power when they would have to depend on Liberal support and would therefore not be able to introduce vigorous Socialist policies, but Ramsay MacDonald thought otherwise, accepted the leadership of the government, and installed Philip Snowden as Chancellor of the Exchequer. Only a few reforms were possible, the most successful being Wheatley's Housing Act of 1924 which provided for the building of far more homes, but money was tight and Snowden did not help with his rigid, over cautious attitude to spending public money. MacDonald put new life into the League of Nations by his enthusiasm for it – the Dawes Plan and the Geneva Protocol and better relations with France and Russia were features of this period. The government established diplomatic relations and signed trade agreements with the U.S.S.R., but found itself in an impossible position without a clear majority. New elections were held in October 1924.

THE DEFEAT OF MACDONALD: The Labour Party was abused by its Conservative enemies as semi-Communist and so it was quite serious that, four days before the election, the Zinoviev Letter was released by the Foreign Office. This letter was published by the *Daily Mail* and purported to be advice from the Russian Communist leader to British Communists to organize a revolution. Although its authenticity was very doubtful and the Labour Party had quite clearly refused to have anything to do with the Communists, it was enough to worsen the already difficult position of MacDonald's ministry. A small swing against the Liberals resulted in the Conservatives being returned with a clear majority. The first Labour government had proved such a great disappointment to its supporters that the I.L.P. decided to break away in protest at the feebleness of MacDonald's policies.

d) Baldwin's Government, 1924–29

Stanley Baldwin was an intelligent man and his cabinet contained men of real ability, notably Neville Chamberlain the Minister of Health, Austen Chamberlain the Foreign Secretary and Winston Churchill the Chancellor of the Exchequer. Reforms were introduced including Neville Chamberlain's overhaul of local government (the Local Government Act 1929) which gave County Councils responsibility for caring for the poor, exempted farms from rates and reduced rates in factories. It also brought the different aspects of insurance, health and welfare work into one large and more extended scheme. Austen Chamberlain co-operated with Briand and Stresemann in achieving the Locarno Pact and the period of better international relations which lasted until 1929.

Yet the administration tends to be remembered for its troubles and failures, and its tendency to drift rather than offer a vigorous lead. In 1925 Churchill decided that Britain should return to the gold standard; this pleased financiers but raised the price of British goods abroad which aggravated the unemployment problem and increased the desire of employers to cut wages. It was these economic troubles which led the government to be involved in the most notable event of this period.

The General Strike, 1926

The Miners' Federation continued to be the most restless of the unions and when employers requested discussions about wage cuts, the miners' leaders H. Smith and A. J. Cook flatly refused. Baldwin delayed a crisis by a government subsidy while Sir Herbert Samuel led an enquiry (by

Troops escort lorries carrying foodstuffs through the streets of London during the General Strike of 1926.

men who knew nothing of the coal industry) into the mines question. The report of the enquiry included short term recommendations for wage cuts and this was enough to make the miners appeal to the other unions and go on strike. The T.U.C. gave its support and on 3rd May the strike spread to transport, gas, electricity, printing and building workers. But the government had used the delay given by the enquiry to organise for just such an emergency whilst the unions had given little thought to what they would do. Troops and volunteers ran essential services, and in nine days the general strike had collapsed. The miners, deserted by the other unions, struggled on for six months, but were eventually forced to admit defeat and accept increased hours of work and reduced wages. Unfortunately Baldwin's government then exploited its success rather vindictively. The strike was a blow to unions, whose membership dropped after 1926, so there was little need for the Trade Disputes Act of 1927. This act made strikes designed to coerce the government, and strikes in sympathy with other unions, illegal. Union funds were henceforth not to be used for political purposes (i.e., financing the Labour Party) unless members clearly stated their wish for this. This was the system of 'contracting in' as opposed to the previous system of 'contracting out', and was a blow to Labour Party finances. In May 1929 a general election was held, with Baldwin proclaiming the need for caution and good sense, for 'Safety First', but it was insufficient to secure him victory, for 288 Labour M.P.s, 260 Conservatives, and 59 Liberals were elected.

e) MacDonald's Second Term in Office

The second Labour Government once more included Snowden; Henderson was Foreign Secretary and, for the first time, there was a woman in the cabinet, Margaret Bondfield, Minister of Labour. Yet again the party idealists felt thwarted, little was achieved and the cabinet split, for Britain was hit, like the rest of Europe, by the Great Depression.

THE SLUMP: Unemployment and out of date industries had been persistent problems since the war and were now aggravated by Britain's heavy dependence on overseas trade at a time when many countries lacked purchasing power, there were growing numbers of riots, and the Russian market was cut off. Britain had lost many of her overseas investments during the war and had become very vulnerable to changes in world trade. The collapse of the American financial boom in 1929 spread rapidly to Britain, caused massive unemployment and the withdrawal of foreign capital from Britain. There were some benefits in that prices were low so the cost of living fell, but generally the atmosphere was one of panic.

The Forming of a National Government

MacDonald agreed to head an all-party ministry to cope with this crisis, even though the bulk of the Labour Party considered this wrong. Led by Lansbury, Attlee and Cripps, they broke with their leader, and Snowden and Thomas, eventually expelling them from the party. Conservatives like Baldwin, Hoare, and Neville Chamberlain entered the Cabinet, as did two Liberals, Sir Herbert Samuel and Lord Reading. Once more the Labour Party was split, but only a dozen Labour M.P.s supported the National Government and Labour provided the strongest opposition to the government's efforts to tackle the crisis.

Economic Measures

J. M. Keynes suggested a programme of large scale public works to deal with the situation but the Cabinet shied away from such boldness and preferred the advice of the May Economic Committee that there should be cuts in expenditure. Reduced salaries for the armed forces and the teachers were among the proposals; the services took particular exception to this, there was a non-violent mutiny by the fleet at Invergordon and their cuts in pay were modified. Even the teachers, although they did not strike, eventually lost only ten instead of fifteen per cent. of their wages. Very limited public works were begun, Snowden would not release the money for more. Britain went off the gold standard and Neville Chamberlain imposed a ten per cent. duty on most imported goods other than those from the empire. These measures offended the Liberal element, who left the Cabinet, and the New Party, which had been formed by the ex-Labourite, Oswald Mosley, who was indignant that his suggested economic reforms should have been ignored. Both of these groups did badly, for the Liberal decline continued and the New Party became a British Fascist movement which was never large and was totally disgraced by the scandalous behaviour of the Nazis they admired.

Changes in leadership

An election in October 1931 had given the National Government overwhelming power, but it was now heavily Conservative and when MacDonald retired in 1935 it was Baldwin who took his place. In May 1937, Baldwin made way for Neville Chamberlain, but not before he had skilfully handled a minor crisis in 1936 when Edward VIII, the new king, had been pushed into abdication by resolving to marry Mrs. Simpson, a twice divorced American. The pattern of serious respectability set by George V had come to be expected in the monarchy and Edward had to make way for his brother George, then Duke of York.

f) Britain on the eve of war

Britain was recovering from the depression by the time Chamberlain succeeded Baldwin, and her difficult relations with Ireland were at last improving. In 1932 De Valera had become P.M. of Southern Ireland and had proceeded to cut as many connections with Britain as possible culminating in a declaration in 1937 that Southern Ireland (now named Eire) was wholly outside the Commonwealth. Chamberlain accepted the situation in 1938, handed over the three ports in Eire used by the British Navy and must take much of the credit for the better relations between the two countries which began to develop. But the policy of appeasement, of trying to win the friendship of other governments, worked far less well in relation to the Fascist states.

On his arrival back from the Munich Conference, Neville Chamberlain holds aloft the 'No war' pact document he signed with Hitler in September, 1938.

Baldwin, MacDonald and Chamberlain held power from 1930–40 during the time when the Nazi party obtained control of Germany and forced concessions which broke the Peace of Paris; when Italian Fascism became more aggressive and broke League agreements; and when Japan, too, found aggression easy and profitable. Some people in Britain, like George Lansbury, were pacifists; others, like Churchill, believed in aggressive national foreign policy: British governments muddled along, following a half-hearted policy of backing the League, yet attempting to secure national interests where it was convenient. It was Britain who broke the Stresa Front against Germany by negotiating a separate naval agreement with Hitler, and it was a British minister, Hoare, who helped encourage Mussolini's attack on Abyssinia by an offer of two-thirds of Abyssinia to the Italians. Britain failed to fully apply sanctions against Italy, and abandoned them altogether in 1938. Hoare was disgraced by the news of his offer to Mussolini, but Anthony Eden, who replaced him at the Foreign Office and favoured a more energetic policy, was responsible for the ineffective non-intervention policy over the Spanish Civil War which in fact allowed foreign aid to flow easily into Spain.

Eden's successor, Lord Halifax, deluded into believing that Hitler's demands were limited and could be easily satisfied, felt, like Chamberlain, that appeasement was the way to deal with him. On the whole, most people seem to have agreed with Chamberlain, for his return from Munich was welcomed with great enthusiasm. Britain had no appetite for war and there was a fear of the harm which a new war would do now that bombing of civilians seemed so easy. In the year following Munich, the government began to rearm and build up the squadrons of Spitfires and Hurricanes which were to become so vital in 1940. The navy was also improved, but the army was neglected and so was a real effort to win Stalin's alliance. Hitler's new attacks between 1939–40 made it clear that appeasement, far from working, only encouraged aggression. Essentially, Chamberlain was a very hard working and able, though rather intolerant administrator and financier. In foreign affairs he proved no better than Baldwin and finally had to step down in favour of Winston Churchill who for years had seemed a dangerous warlike extremist, but was now shown to have been right about the need to take a strong stand against Nazism. The Labour Party had dropped its earlier pacifist sympathies and joined Churchill in a coalition government to win the war; with Attlee as deputy P.M. and Eden as Foreign Secretary. The British people were more united than ever they had been in 1914 in their determination to win a war that had been forced upon them.

6 | The Second World War and its Aftermath

The Events of the War

a) Blitzkrieg

The closing stages of the Great War had shown that changes were taking place in the art of warfare which reduced the strength of defences to meet attack. Tanks and aircraft gave armies not only mobility but also the opportunity to strike behind the main enemy lines either by means of rapid advances by columns of tanks, or by parachute and glider-borne forces landing behind enemy lines or by attacks from the air including the terror-bombing of civilians. The Italian general, Douhet, was a leading thinker in the belief of the supremacy of air power in future wars, he believed that the bomber would always be able to break through defences. In fact air power proved not to be so decisive as had been first thought and although fighter defences did well, bombing was not as ruinous (until atom bombs were used) as expected. Command of the air did not automatically mean victory, as the Second War and later the Korean and Vietnamese Wars confirmed.

The British and French, although they had used tanks in the Great World War far more than the Germans, were slow to follow this up in the Second World War and it was German generals, especially Guderian, who best grasped the technique of the blitzkrieg (lightning war). The Germans did not have a great superiority in quantity of weapons, but they used what they had with great skill. Their splendid Tiger and Panther tank divisions, massed in columns, raced through enemy defences, and turned inwards in a pincer movement, cutting off large pockets of defenders who could be mopped up by following units of motorized infantry and artillery. This technique worked in France and in Russia, reinforced by the terrifying Stuka divebombers, who pounded the opposition troops, and by well placed parachutists who created disorder behind enemy lines. The British and French tanks were both inferior to the German, it was the Russian T34 which first proved a match for the enemy. Thus the allies, prepared for defence and with their First War thinking, were no match for the German army.

German offensives 1939·41

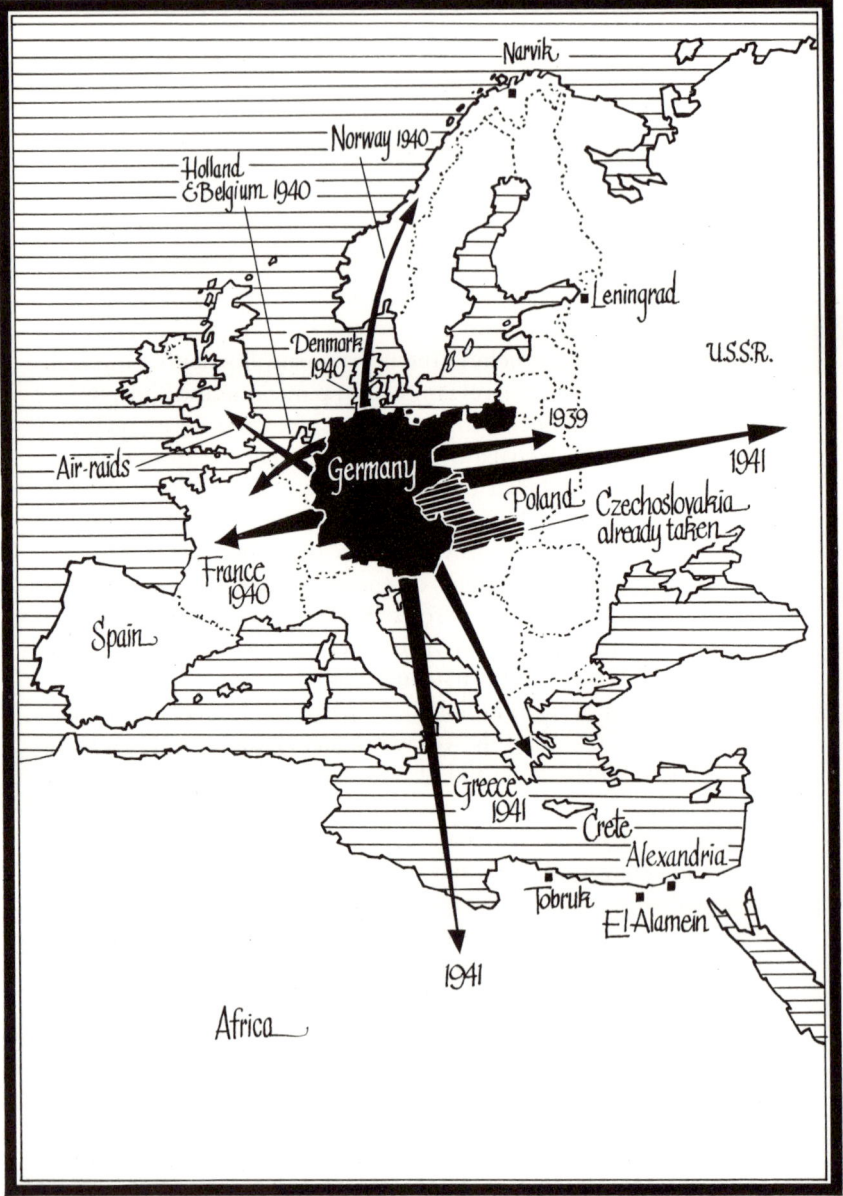

Narvik

Norway 1940

Holland
& Belgium 1940

Denmark
1940

Leningrad

U.S.S.R.

Air-raids

Germany

1939

1941

France
1940

Poland

Czechoslovakia
already taken

Spain

Greece
1941

Crete

Alexandria

Tobruk

El-Alamein

1941

Africa

b) The German Victories, 1939–40

Poland

The Polish army was brave, but quite unable to cope with the German blitzkrieg. Without the help of Britain and France, and menaced by Soviet forces determined to grab East Poland, the Polish army was overwhelmed in three weeks, its cavalry easily smashed, and Poland's cities bombed. The Polish force had been spread out, with no reserves; its air force was destroyed on the ground, and a last desperate resistance by the citizens of Warsaw flickered out in gallant defeat.

Russia's War with Finland

Stalin rapidly seized the Baltic states: only Finland resisted, yet this was one of the most important areas for Russia to gain if Leningrad was to be made more defensible. The Finnish troops exploited the wooded, lake-studded land very skilfully and held off the massive Russian forces until March 1940. Then weight of numbers crushed their resistance and much of their southern territory was added to Russia.

Denmark and Norway

Hitler was determined to control the Baltic to secure various vital supplies, and his forces overran Denmark in a day. Norway put up greater opposition, with British and French aid, but though the Germans suffered losses at sea, on land they broke the final resistance around Narvik and established a puppet government under the pro-Nazi Norwegian Vidkun Quisling. Thus Hitler secured Swedish iron ore (which was shipped down the fjords to Germany from Narvik) and obtained excellent bases for his submarines which proved especially useful when Russia entered the war and Britain attempted to send supplies there by sea. These disasters shook the Allied governments; in England Chamberlain was forced to resign and was replaced by a coalition government led by Winston Churchill with Attlee, the Labour Leader, as Deputy P.M.; in France Reynaud replaced Daladier.

The Netherlands and Belgium

These two states attempted to remain neutral, but neutrality was no deterrent to Hitler and in May, 1940 they were rapidly overrun by the familiar blitzkrieg tactics, during which Rotterdam was heavily bombed. The Netherlands fell easily, but Belgium had a large army and strong defences. Unfortunately the Belgians did not co-ordinate their operations with the British and French, and their surrender placed the allied forces moving to their aid in a dangerous position.

The Invasion of France

Whilst Poland had fallen, the allies had done nothing to attack Germany. The French manned the powerful forts of the Maginot Line and the British army under Lord Gort landed in Northern France; but neither considered attacking Germany, their commanders convinced that strong defence was the best tactic. Nor did they attempt bombing attacks, for Germany had yet to bomb them and the Allied leaders were reluctant to take the first step. This was the period of the 'phony war', a demoralizing time when nothing happened on the Western Front. Then Manstein's plan for assault on France hit the unprepared defenders. The Ardennes region was heavily wooded and thought to be an unlikely area of attack hence the defences here were weak, but it was here in fact that Von Rundstedt's armoured columns broke through, racing north to the sea and cutting off the British and French forces who had gone to help Belgium.

Dunkirk

The trapped forces were not however pressed, since Hitler ordered the main attack to be directed against Paris, which fell on June 14th, despite General Weygand's attempts to form a new defensive line. Göring's Luftwaffe promised to deal with the Anglo-French forces massing near Dunkirk, but though its attacks did damage, Admiral Ramsay's hastily improvised rescue fleet of nearly 900 craft (some were small pleasure boats) managed to evacuate 340,000 men (200,000 of them British) between 26th May–4th June. Equipment had to be left behind and the withdrawal hastened France's defeat, but Hitler had missed a great opportunity.

The Fall of France

Mussolini declared war on the Allies on June 10th and attacked Southern France, whilst Guderian's German armoured columns also invaded southern France, advanced north, and trapped the half million men in the Maginot Line. The French government fled to Bordeaux and recalled the veteran hero Pétain to head the government. On June 22nd an armistice was signed between France and Germany in the very railway carriage where Marshal Foch had received the German surrender in 1918. Northern France was occupied by Germany, but the rest of the country remained unoccupied and for the time being was administered from Vichy by the French under Pétain, Darlon and Laval. Vichy France possessed a navy, a considerable army and colonies; it also represented the feeling of some French who thought that something must be salvaged from defeat.

c) The Attack on Britain, 1940

Naval Clashes

German attacks on British forces were at first limited to naval efforts. U-boats and magnetic mines destroyed several British vessels including a carrier, the *Courageous*, and the battleship *Royal Oak*. But Britain had her successes too. In December 1939 the pocket battleship *Graf Spee* which had destroyed nine British ships in its attacks on Atlantic trade was trapped by three cruisers, the *Ajax*, *Exeter*, and *Achilles*, and scuttled itself in the River Plate.

Operation Sea Lion

The quick victory over France took Hitler by surprise and he had to improvise a hasty plan to invade Britain. But first Germany had to win supremacy in the air by eliminating the Royal Air Force and so, from August to October, a desperate struggle for air control took place. During the Battle of Britain, as it was called, the smaller numbers of the R.A.F. were offset by the use of radar, which pinpointed the attackers and made it easier for enemy planes to be located and shot down. The advanced design of the Spitfires and Hurricanes which poured off Beaverbrook's production lines, also helped, with Britain reaping the benefit of having started to mass-produce aircraft two years later than Germany. Göring switched his attacks from radar stations and airfields to night bombing of London and other cities, to terrorise the inhabitants. But this, too, helped the R.A.F. avoid defeat because it allowed Fighter Command a respite during the day. Operation Sea Lion had to be postponed, Britain suffered air raids and heavy shipping losses from U-boat attacks, but was not in danger of invasion. Nor did air raids by either side (for the R.A.F. under Arthur Harris began replying in kind with area bombing) wreak the havoc which had been expected, civilian populations stood up well to attack and industrial production was not ruinously affected. Anti-aircraft guns, barrage balloons, fighter defences, and radar all reduced the offensive power of the bomber. At sea, the German battleship *Bismarck* sank the *Hood*, a new British warship, before she was herself cornered and battered to destruction.

d) The Mediterranean War

Mussolini's offensives

Italy entered the war once German victory seemed certain in the hope of easy pickings. In fact she was far from prepared, her people far from enthusiastic, and the war rapidly ruined the Duce. Italian troops in Albania attacked Greece only to be promptly chased out again by the Greek Army. In North Africa the Italians were no match for Wavell's British troops who soon freed Abyssinia (restoring Haile Selassie) and, led by General Connor, trapped a large Italian army in Libya. At Taranto, in November 1940, the Italian navy was badly damaged by Cunningham's British fleet and effectively immobilized.

German Intervention in the Balkans

With the war in France over, Hitler came to his ally's aid and rapidly reversed the situation. Romania, Hungary and Bulgaria were easily bullied into becoming Germany's allies, but an attempt to do the same in Yugoslavia failed when the army overthrew the pro-German Regent. In eleven days however the Germans had crushed Yugoslavian resistance and were soon in control of Greece too. The whole Balkan area was now under Hitler's control; the British, who attempted to help the Greeks, had been swept aside, and suffered further humiliation at Crete where the defenders were overwhelmed by German paratroop and glider forces. Only Malta remained as a mid-Mediterranean stronghold, and Malta was under heavy pressure, pounded by Axis air attacks.

Rommel in North Africa

The German Afrika Corps under General Rommel, which had come to the aid of the Italians in North Africa, used their tanks to great advantage in the desert. A first advance in 1941 drove the British back across Libya until only the port of Tobruk was left outside their Egyptian base. A second thrust by Rommel seized Tobruk (1942) and entered Egypt, threatening Alexandria itself. Sir Claude Auchinleck succeeded in checking the advance at El Alamein, but the situation was very grave. Churchill now intervened, he appointed General Harold Alexander as Middle East commander and General Bernard Montgomery as commander of the Eighth Army. With the help of American tanks and supplies the British were able to plan a counter attack.

The British aircraft carrier squadron in line ahead on the Malta Convoy. An aircraft takes off from H.M.S. Indomitable.

e) The Invasion of Russia

Hitler had on many occasions voiced his desire to spread his conquests into Eastern Europe and crush Communism; on June 22nd, 1941, he put his words into effect by launching 'Barbarossa', the invasion of Soviet Russia.

Rapid German Success

Hitler insisted on a three-pronged attack and not the single concentrated thrust his generals advised. In the north, Leeb advanced on Leningrad, in the centre Bock attacked Moscow, and in the south Rundstedt's troops rushed into the Ukraine. Initially all advances did well, using the successful blitzkrieg tactics and large numbers of Russians were trapped and forced to surrender. In spite of Allied warnings, Stalin was wholly unprepared and had no serious plans to meet the crisis. By the end of 1941, both Leningrad and Moscow were in danger, the Crimea had fallen, Finland had seized the opportunity to recover the land taken from her by Stalin, and Russia's richest lands were in German hands.

Russian Recovery

Only the Russian winter halted the German advance and gave Stalin a chance to recover his nerve. Troops from Siberia, well clad and used to winter warfare, were rushed to the front and were skilfully used by the great Russian general, Zhukov. Large numbers of Russian T34 tanks began to appear and prove they were a match for the German tanks. The German generals wanted to retreat, but Hitler insisted that they stand firm and prepare for new offensives in the summer. The winter was severe, German troops suffered from frostbite and a shortage of food, whilst their tanks froze up without constant warming and care.

Stalingrad

Once more, as summer came, the German tanks rolled forward and Von Paulus, in the south, reached Stalingrad, an important industrial and communications centre which the Russians were determined to hold. Chuikov's troops in the city defended every building and the Germans found their advances very costly. This was one of the most bitter clashes in a war notorious for its barbarity, for Hitler was contemptuous of the Slavs and allowed the S.S. to be particularly brutal towards them; this in turn encouraged Russian reprisals. Once more winter caught the Germans inadequately prepared, the Russians counter-attacked and Zhukov trapped the Germans in Stalingrad, subjecting them to furious attacks until in January 1943, 90,000 Germans surrendered.

The last German attack

In the summer of 1943 Hitler launched a final desperate attack, from which the Russians quickly recovered and, helped by the fact that Hitler could not spare reinforcements from other campaigns, began a relentless advance.

The whole of the eastern conflict was marred by German savagery which bred great resentment in the minds of the nations who suffered. In Warsaw in 1942 the Germans herded together 400,000 Jews in a walled ghetto, took away many to be slaughtered, and massacred the rest on the spot. In Czechoslovakia the murder of S.S. leader Heydrich by Czechs prompted the Germans to destroy the villages of Lidice and Lezaky, killing the male inhabitants and sending the women to concentration camps.

HITLER'S EUROPE 1942

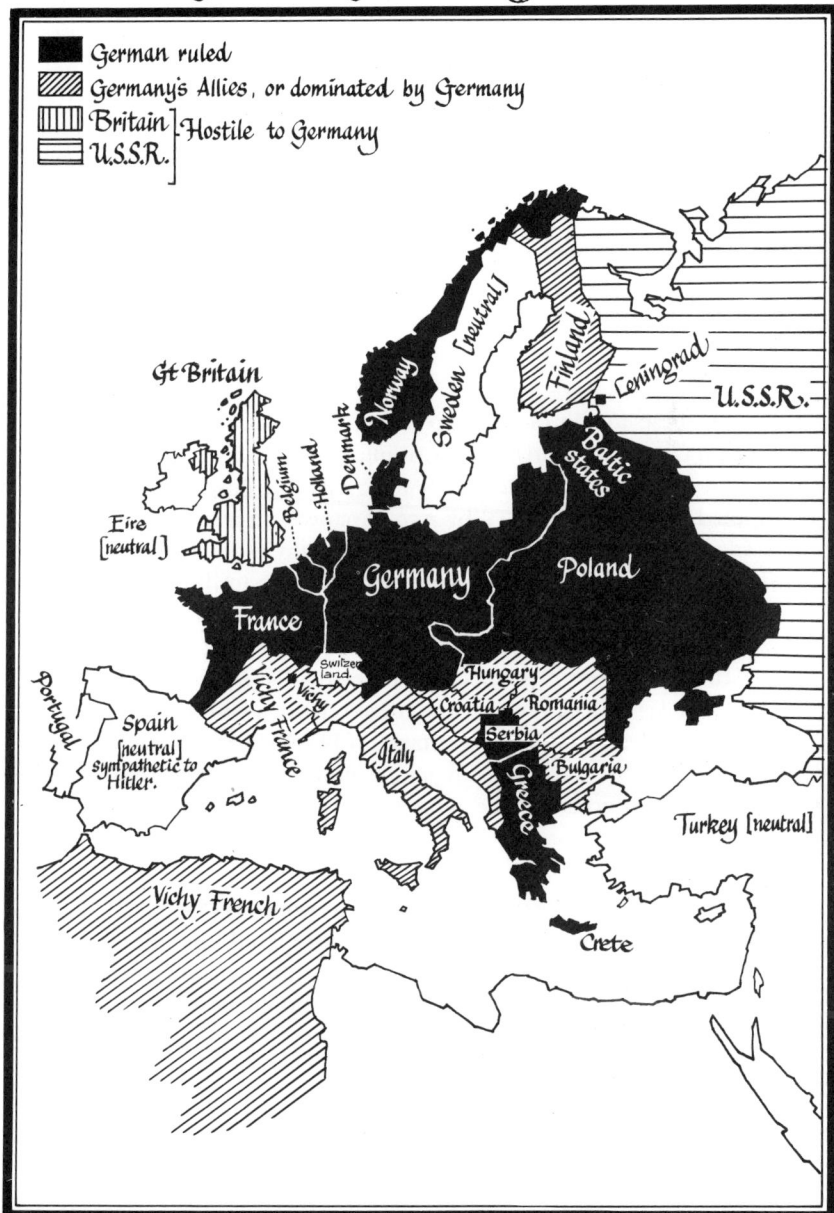

German ruled

Germany's Allies, or dominated by Germany

Britain] Hostile to Germany

U.S.S.R.

Gt Britain

Eire
[neutral]

Norway

Sweden [neutral]

Denmark

Holland

Belgium

Finland

Leningrad

Baltic states

U.S.S.R.

Germany

Poland

France

Portugal

Spain
[neutral]
sympathetic to
Hitler.

Vichy France

Switzerland.

Vichy

Italy

Hungary

Croatia

Serbia

Romania

Greece

Bulgaria

Turkey [neutral]

Vichy French

Crete

f) The Widening of the War

Roosevelt's pro-British attitude

Though the U.S. President, Franklin D. Roosevelt, strongly sympathised with Britain, the bulk of Americans were against entry into the war. Roosevelt did however provide Churchill first with fifty old destroyers in return for the use of bases in the West Indies, and later with growing quantities of war materials on a 'lend lease' basis under which Britain was not required to make immediate payment. In August, 1941, Churchill visited Roosevelt and, on board the *Prince of Wales*, the two leaders worked out and signed their 'Atlantic Charter'. The Charter declared conquests should not be made from the war and that freedom for nations and for individuals should be preserved.

Pearl Harbour

But even these measures were stretching the isolationist sectors of the American Government to breaking point, when Japan solved Roosevelt's difficulties by attacking the U.S. Pacific Fleet in Pearl Harbour. The raid on December 7th 1941 by 350 Japanese aircraft had not been preceded by a declaration of war. Since Germany and Italy also promptly declared war on the U.S.A., Roosevelt was able to directly intervene in the European conflict to which he agreed to give precedence. In 1941 Japanese politicians had lost control to the militarists who could not resist the temptation to ape the successful German defeats of the British and French in Europe. Japanese relations with the U.S.A. had been steadily deteriorating. The attack on Pearl Harbour, and the destruction of MacArthur's aircraft in the Philippines, were regarded as necessary precautions for the Japanese advance into South East Asia.

The Fall of S.E. Asia

In ten weeks General Yamashito's Japanese troops had reached Singapore. European forces were virtually unprepared, in addition the Japanese had air and sea superiority and superb troops, whilst the local populations saw no reason why they should resist the Asian invaders for the sake of their colonial masters. Singapore's defences faced seaward, but the Japanese attack came from landward so that the Japanese not only captured 60,000 British troops, they also sank two British warships, the *Prince of Wales* and the *Repulse*. The conquest of south east Asia, the Philippines, the Dutch East Indies and Burma brought Japan control of many valuable raw materials including tin, oil, rubber and bauxite. The Japanese victory had been suprisingly easy;

Japanese advances in 1942

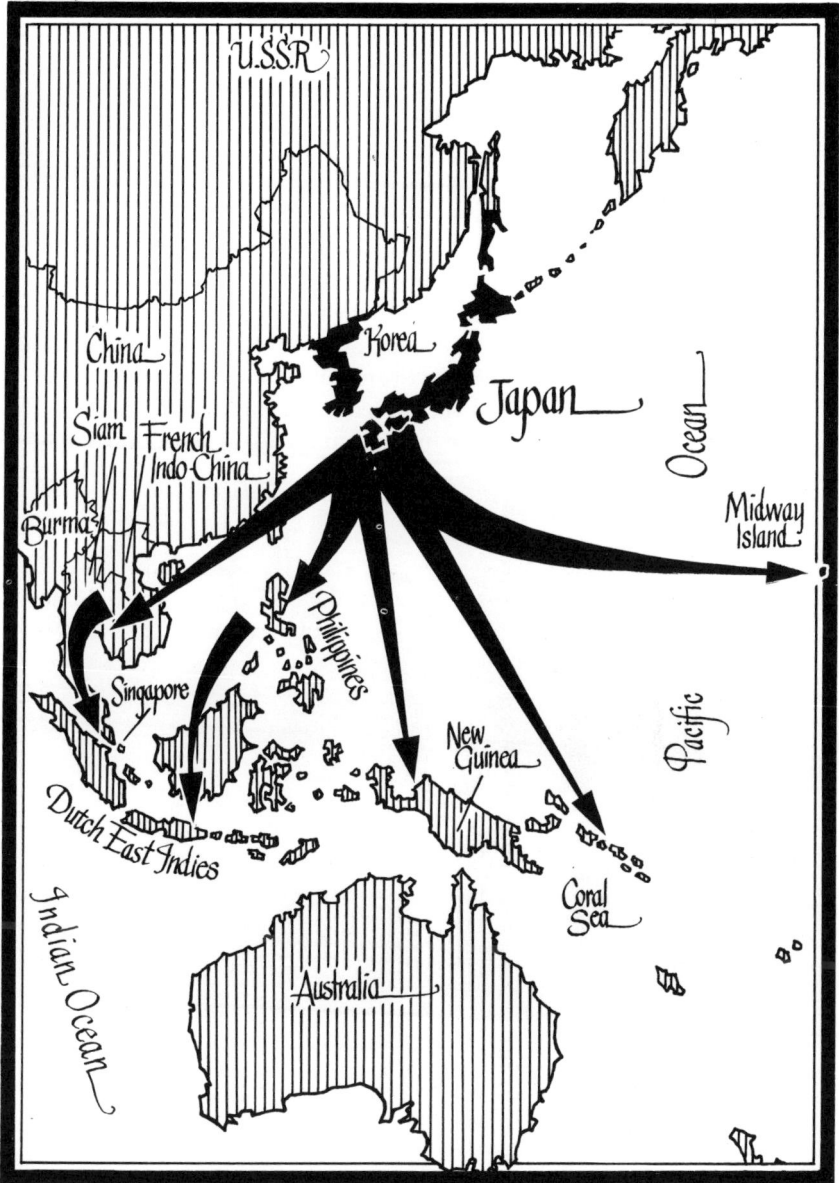

by April 1942 Admiral Nagumo's warships were roaming over the Bay of Bengal and even threatening northern Australia.

g) Allied Successes in the Mediterranean

The Conquest of North Africa

Though many American leaders wanted to concentrate on defeating Japan, Roosevelt agreed with Churchill that Hitler must be defeated first. Stalin had been demanding for some time that a second front be opened by Allied landings in France but the Allied leaders felt this was too difficult. Instead, they decided to concentrate on North Africa and Italy. This was a combined operation between General Dwight D. Eisenhower's forces, which landed in French North Africa in November, and Montgomery's Eighth Army. The Vichy French remembered resentfully that their fleet at Oran had been attacked earlier in the war by British warships, and when the Americans landed they resisted for some time. Eventually, under Giraud, the French capitulated to the Americans, meanwhile the Germans used the invasion as an excuse to occupy Vichy

This historic picture, taken at Allied Force Headquarters in Cairo during an Allied Planning Conference, shows from left to right, Anthony Eden, General Sir Alan Brooke, Air Chief Marshal Sir Arthur Tedder, Admiral Sir Andrew Cunningham, General Sir Harold Alexander, General George C. Marshall, U.S.A., General Dwight D. Eisenhower, U.S.A., and General Sir Bernard Montgomery. The Prime Minister, Winston Churchill, presided and is seen seated, centre.

France. General de Gaulle, who had escaped to Britain where he had formed a Free French Committee, now arrived in the area and began to assert his authority in a manner so arrogant that he irritated the Americans, just as he had already irritated Churchill. Montgomery, having built up much greater resources than Rommel, had already defeated him (23 October 1942) in the very hard fought second battle of Alamein and begun pushing the Axis westwards across North Africa.

The invasion of Italy

The remnant of the Axis troops – 160,000 of them – were soon cornered in North Africa and many forced to surrender. The Allies could now plan the invasion of Sicily. British and American troops invaded Sicily in July 1943 and within six weeks the island had been conquered. This was the last straw for the Italians who had long wearied of the war; they overthrew Mussolini and replaced him by Marshal Badoglio. In September Allied landings were made on the toe of Italy where the German forces fought hard to hold back the Allies. Skorzeny's Germans managed to rescue Mussolini and install him in control of Northern Italy. Weakened by the need for troops to be available for the invasion of Normandy, General Alexander's army was held south of Rome.

The Allied barrage during the Battle of Egypt in October, 1942, lights up the night sky.

K

The invasion of France

THE TEHERAN CONFERENCE: Stalin, Roosevelt and Churchill met in Persia in November 1943 to discuss future strategy. Stalin once more pressed for a second front, playing on Roosevelt's sympathies declaring that Russia was doing most of the fighting and that the war should be considered simply in military terms. Churchill, with his life-long hatred of Communism, was however thinking in political terms and favoured invasions of Southern Europe, especially the Balkans, which he hoped would give Britain and the U.S.A. control of these areas and not Russia. But Roosevelt believed Stalin would respond to generous treatment and the decision was made for a landing in France.

The Normandy Landings

The assembling of Eisenhower's invasion force in Southern England could hardly be concealed from the Germans, who gave Rommel command of the defences which the Germans hoped would throw back the invaders. The Germans constructed the 'Atlantic Wall', a defensive network of minefields, barbed wire and pill boxes, but they were wholly deceived by the Allies into expecting the invaders to land near Calais. In fact, despite bad weather, the Allies, led in the field by General Montgomery, landed on a sixty mile wide front in Normandy on June 5th and 6th. With the aid of landing craft, amphibious tanks and para-troops and using flail tanks to clear minefields, the Allies established a bridgehead at the cost of 2,500 lives. More men poured ashore until Montgomery, and the American Commanders Bradley and Patton, had a million men at their disposal. But difficulties in keeping such a force supplied had to be overcome. 'Mulberries', artificial harbours towed into strategic positions and PLUTO, the oil pipe-line-under-the-ocean were among the methods used.

Attempts to murder Hitler

During the last two years of the war, there were a number of attempts on Hitler's life, but they all failed. The Führer was well guarded, frequently changed his plans and appeared to lead a charmed life. A bomb left on his aircraft in March 1943 would have killed him had it not failed to detonate. In another attempt a bomb, concealed in a brief-case, was placed close to Hitler at a conference by Colonel Von Stauffenberg and only narrowly missed its objective through an officer, quite innocently, moving the brief-case from its position close to Hitler. In the purge which

British troops come ashore under heavy fire near Hermanville sur Mer from landing craft on 'D' Day (June 6th, 1944). Red Cross men can be seen giving assistance to casualties.

followed the 'July Plot', thousands of Germans were tortured and put to death. Even Rommel was not above suspicion; in October 1944 he was arrested and given the alternative of trial before a people's court or suicide by poison. Rommel chose suicide and in order not to shock military morale, was given a State Funeral.

Hitler's 'secret weapons'

Bomber Command's area bombing and American precision bombing failed to wreck German industries, but Germany had by 1943 lost air superiority and could not hit back in the conventional way. Then in 1944, Hitler launched his new secret weapons. The first of these was the 'doodle-bug' or V1, a jet aircraft loaded with explosive. Britain's defences quickly and successfully began to destroy these flying bombs but the Germans replaced them with a new menace – the V2, a rocket bomb launched from sites in the Netherlands which did great damage in England and led to strong pressure for an Allied advance along the northern coast of France. It was thus very important that the Normandy troops should break out of the circle of German forces attempting to hold them back.

h) The defeat of Hitler

The Normandy breakout

The British at Caen were tied down by heavy fighting, but Patton's American troops were able to break out and a German counter attack at Falaise was held and turned into an American victory. Now the advance was possible, the problem was whether to advance on all fronts or whether to go for a single strong thrust along the north into the Ruhr as Montgomery recommended. Since over half the troops were American, Eisenhower insisted that Patton and Bradley should be allowed to go forward too. Not all the glory should fall to Montgomery in the north.

The fall of Paris

An Allied landing in southern France linked up with the Normandy landings and made the German position in Paris hopeless. General de Gaulle and his Free French forces were given the honour of reoccupying their capital on 25th August and went on to play an important part in the advance on Germany.

The fall of Italy

At last Alexander's British, Commonwealth, French African and Polish troops were able to break the stubborn German resistance at Monte Cassino, push on into Rome and press against new German defences, the Gothic Line. By now Italians were openly opposing the Germans and their Resistance fighters greatly helped Alexander – Mussolini himself was caught by Resistance fighters and promptly executed. With the strong pressure on German troops in France, Alexander's troops were able to clear Italy of the Germans.

The Ardennes Push

The Allies continued to advance on Germany with one brief setback. An attempt to leap across the Rhine in September by landing paratroops at Arnhem, who would hold the bridges for Montgomery's main army, proved a disaster. Hitler decided on one last desperate counter attack and recalled von Rundstedt to command an attack through the Ardennes to reach the vital supply base of Antwerp. At first the Americans on whom this blow fell were caught by surprise and the Germans advanced rapidly. But the forces at St. Vith and Bastogne held on, more forces were rushed to the area to repel the enemy, and the German counter attack of December 1944 had failed.

Allied attacks on ITALY & GERMANY 1943-5

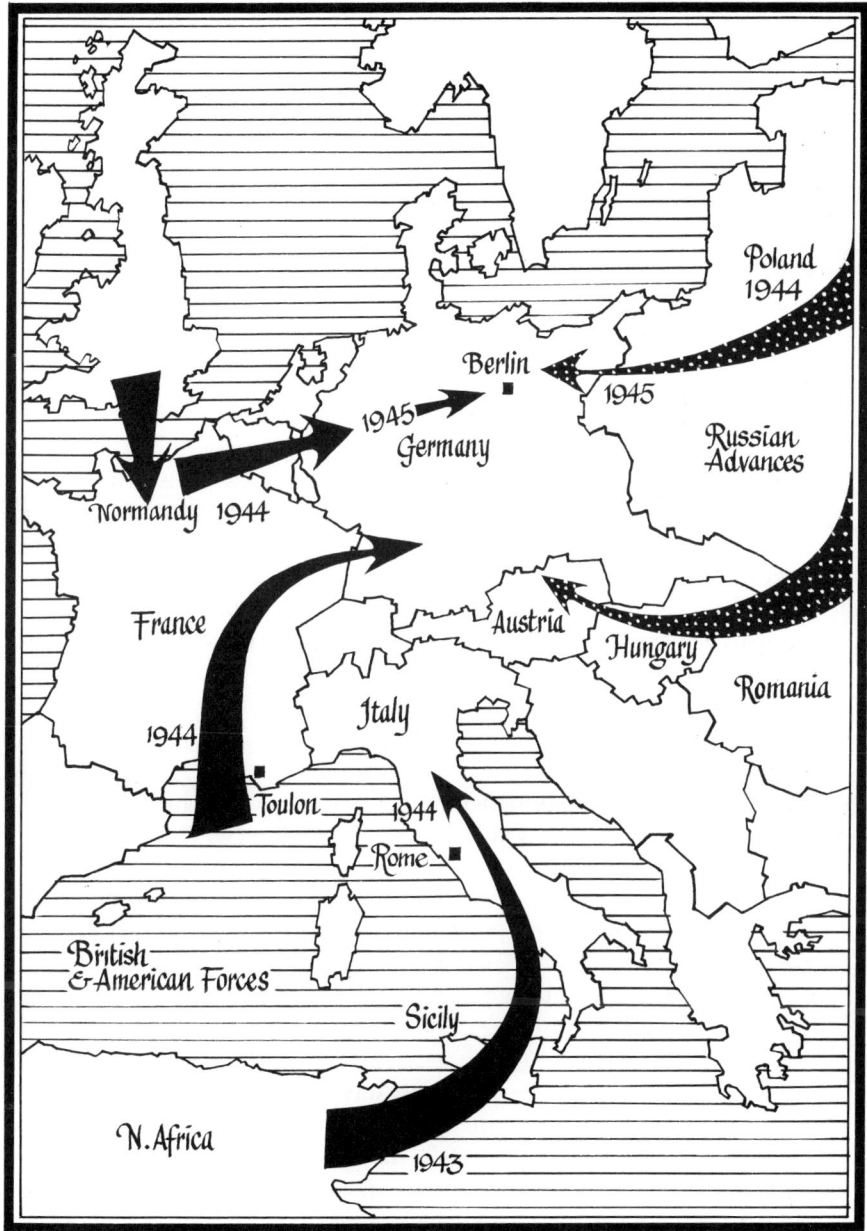

Poland 1944

Berlin

1945
Germany

1945

Russian Advances

Normandy 1944

France

Austria

Hungary

Romania

1944

Italy

Toulon

1944

Rome

British & American Forces

Sicily

N. Africa

1943

The Invasion of Germany

By now Hitler was directing the war from an underground bunker in
Berlin. On all sides his state was menaced as Zhukov's Russians cleared
Poland and Hitler's allies in the Balkans hastily changed sides. The
Americans crossed the Rhine, shortly followed by the British, whilst the
Russians penetrated East Germany, a vast invasion which the Germans
could not stem. Air raids became more intensive and included the
destruction of Dresden in February 1945. Dresden was an ancient and
beautiful city of no great industrial importance, but it was devastated
by Allied bombers in one of the most terrible examples of area bombing.
Finally, Americans and Russians linked up in Berlin to find that Hitler,
Eva Braun (whom he had just married) and all the Goebbels family had
committed suicide on April 30th among the ruins of their defences. On
May 8th the war in the west was over.

i) The defeat of Japan

British recovery

In 1942 Japanese forces held south east Asia and advanced on India,
which was already in a state of restlessness under British rule. But the
British adapted rapidly to suit the conditions and under Slim and
Mountbatten, held the Japanese offensive in the battle of Kohima
Imphal. General Wingate's Chindits became particularly renowned for
their skill in fighting the Japanese forces. A British invasion of Burma
was begun against stubborn Japanese resistance.

The American Recovery

The main burden of fighting fell on MacArthur's Americans and in the
battle of the Coral Sea they at last checked the Japanese. This battle was
primarily between carrier-borne aircraft, a feature of the war which
was of great importance. In June 1942 in the battle of Midway the
Japanese were once more defeated, losing four carriers and two heavy
cruisers, whilst the Australians blocked the Japanese in New Guinea
and eventually pushed them out of the island.

The harshness of Japanese rule

Japanese soldiers fought fiercely, rarely surrendered and were contemptuous of their enemies whom they captured and often treated with
extreme brutality. Their harsh rule in the areas they conquered soon lost
them local sympathy and local resistance groups, often Communist
inspired, added to Japan's problems.

THE JAPANESE RETREAT : The Americans gradually built up superiority in sea and air and were able to destroy large quantities of Japanese shipping. In October, 1944, the Americans landed on Leyte in the Philippines and another furious air and naval battle took place in which, eventually, the Japanese were defeated. The American advance was slow and costly, for the Japanese army was far from defeated. It took the Americans a month's fighting and cost 20,000 lives to take the eight square mile island of Iwo Jima alone.

The defeat of Japan

From their advanced positions American aircraft were able to bomb Japanese cities, for Japan had lost all her air superiority and resorted to the desperate device of using suicide pilots, men who flew their machines, loaded with explosives, directly into American vessels. The knowledge of the cost of conventional advance led to the decision by the U.S.A. and Britain to drop an atomic bomb on a Japanese city. The atomic bomb had been developed at Los Alamos by an Anglo-U.S. team under Oppenheimer and its destructive power was demonstrated when dropped by

R.A.F. Bomber Command played an important role in bringing the war into the Germans' own back yard. Here, the industrial and dock area of Mulheim, in North East Cologne, is seen under attack by Lancasters.

A scene in the courtroom during the war trials held at Nuremberg from November 1945 to September 1946.

a Superfortress on 6th August, 1945, on Hiroshima. On the 8th August the U.S.S.R. declared war on Japan and on the 9th another atomic bomb destroyed Nagasaki. A vast, conventional air raid pounded Tokyo on the 13th August and the following day total surrender was admitted by Japan.

Conclusion

Unlike the First World War, the Second appeared quite clearly as a war for democracy. No negotiated armistice was permitted by the Allies who demanded total surrender from governments they regarded as wholly wicked. The war saw the real rise in importance of aircraft, for German Junkers, British Lancasters and American Flying Fortresses were outstanding examples of bombers built to wreck enemy industry and morale. In this they failed, defences were stronger than had been anticipated, morale did not crack, and industries recovered. At sea the submarine dominated warfare, especially until the end of 1943 when the Allies finally mastered Donitz's 'wolf packs' of U boats. But the day of the big battleship was over. It was too costly and vulnerable, fast frigates and aircraft carriers were far more useful. The war brought total victory to Britain, the U.S.A. and the U.S.S.R., but the alliance was an uneasy one; it soon cracked under the strain of the post-war settlement, and former allies were, before long, squaring up to one another as enemies.

The Post-War Settlement

a) The Background

There could be no rapid and tidy solution to the problems left by the war; the U.S.S.R. and the U.S.A. had quite different views on how Europe should be reorganised. The immediate problems of devastation, ruin and refugees were met by relief measures out of which later United Nations' organisations grew, but the punishment of Nazi leaders was something which could be agreed upon.

The Nuremberg Trials

By the time the Nazi leaders came to trial, Hitler, Goebbels and Himmler had committed suicide, and another, Martin Bormann had disappeared. Otherwise the Nazi leadership was accused of crimes against humanity and of waging aggressive war in trials held at Nuremberg from November 1945 to September 1946. A few – for instance Von Papen – were acquitted, some like Hess and Speer were imprisoned, (Speer was released in 1967, only Hess remains) and others were executed. Göring was sentenced to death but took poison on the eve of his execution. Laval and Quisling were condemned and executed and Pétain given life imprisonment, but the punishment of the guilty did not end there. A number of leading Nazis disappeared and Jewish organisations set to work to find them and bring them to book. Their most notable success was the finding of Adolf Eichmann who had been responsible for the death of thousands of Jews. He was traced to South America, abducted and brought to Israel in 1960 where he was tried, found guilty and executed. But only on such negative matters could the Allies agree, indeed their differences appeared well before the war ended.

The Yalta Conference

Roosevelt had not accepted Churchill's demands for plans for the settlement of post-war Europe when the two leaders met Stalin at Teheran in

1943. But by February 1945, with the war nearly over, the harsh attitude of Stalin became clear in further meetings held at Yalta in the Crimea. Useful discussions on the U.N. were held, and Stalin agreed to admit France as an equal in the control of post-war Germany, but on the question of Poland serious differences emerged. Stalin planned to absorb part of pre-war eastern Poland into Russia and give Poland compensation from Germany, including Pomerania and Silesia, along frontiers marked by the Oder-Neisse rivers. Roosevelt thought this excessive, but the question was not finally settled and indeed it still awaits formal settlement, the present frontier is in fact the Oder-Neisse line but West Germany will not accept this as permanent. The question of who was to rule Poland also provoked argument. There were few Communists in Poland, but their position was greatly strengthened by the advance of the Red Army and by the death of many non-Communist Polish leaders in the Warsaw Rising of Polish resistance fighters awaiting the Red Army. Stalin held back his troops whilst the Germans crushed the rising, and though he had other excuses, there seems little doubt that he wished to see rivals to the Polish Communists destroyed. Stalin insisted at Yalta that the Communist Committee at Lublin was the Polish government and the Allies reluctantly agreed in return for Soviet promises that non-Communist leaders would be admitted to the government and free elections held within a month (it was two years before the elections were eventually held). At Yalta Stalin also agreed to declare war on Japan in return for territorial gains, for U.S.S.R. sovereignty being recognised over Outer Mongolia, and for privileges granted in Manchuria.

b) Territorial Arrangements

The settlement of frontiers was worked out over a period of years, not in one conference and was sometimes the result of the pressure of one great power, not the consequence of decisions reached by all the powers.

Japan

The conquests made by Japan before 1941, as well as those made after her entry into the war, were taken away, her armed forces were severely limited, and an allied occupation force controlled Japan itself. Her conquests of British and French lands reverted to their former owners: her conquests in China were returned to the Chinese government (though Korea was not merged into China) and Russia took South Sakhalin and the Kurile islands.

Germany

The future of Germany was discussed at Potsdam (16 July – 1 August 1945) by another great power conference. Roosevelt had by this time died and been replaced by Harry S. Truman, and during the conference Churchill was defeated in a general election and replaced by Clement Attlee. The powers agreed that Germany must be occupied and once more turned into a democracy, further that Germany should be divided into four zones of occupation and that they should share control of Berlin (which was in the Russian sector). The four powers would also work together in a Control Commission to solve common problems of transport and finance. Germany lost all her gains under Hitler, including the Sudetenland, and in fact her frontiers were reduced even beyond those of 1920 by the addition of parts of east Germany to Poland. Austria was to be a separate state, supervised by the powers. Russia also demanded very heavy reparation though the Western powers refused to find from their zones as much as Russia demanded.

Other powers

In February, 1947, terms were signed with Italy, Bulgaria, Romania, Hungary and Finland. Italy lost frontier land to France and Yugoslavia,

The 'Big Three' meet at Yalta in 1945. In this photograph, taken in the grounds of Livadia Palace where the conference was held, are Winston Churchill, President Franklin D. Roosevelt of the U.S., and Soviet Marshal Joseph Stalin.

the Dodecanese to Greece, Trieste to the U.N., and her colonies were made either U.N. trust territories or, in Abyssinia's case, independent. Russia took Bessarabia and North Bukovina from Romania and part of southern Finland, whilst Hungary lost Transylvania to Romania, and Romania gave up South Dobruja to Bulgaria. Reparations were also imposed on Finland, Bulgaria and Hungary from which Russia, Greece, Yugoslavia and Czechoslovakia variously benefited.

c) Political Arrangements

The future of the countries defeated or freed in the war depended greatly upon whoever was the dominant military force in the region. The Second World War was followed by a longer military occupation of Germany than the Great War had been, but Europe did not experience the wave of political unrest which burst out after the First World War. Most countries were heartily sick of war, there were too many refugees, too much suffering, and too many armies of occupation for revolts to succeed. Where however dramatic changes did take place it was usually because they were organised by the U.S.S.R., determined to create a belt of satellite states in East Europe and keep Germany weak and divided. Areas controlled by the West returned more rapidly to their pre-fascist democratic state and thus there grew up in Europe a clear split between Russian-supported Communist states and Western democracies. Berlin remained an awkward problem, it was partially controlled by the Western powers, yet was in the Russian sector of Germany. Churchill later described the division between these two camps in Europe as the 'iron curtain'. Only in Yugoslavia could the Communists behind the iron curtain claim to have popular backing and Yugoslavia was soon quarrelling with the U.S.S.R.

Eastern Europe

Stalin was determined that Russia should never suffer an attack by Germany again. He was also suspicious of Britain and the U.S.A. (with their atomic weapons) and determined to bargain from strength. Thus, as the Red Army moved into Poland, East Germany, Czechoslovakia, Romania and Bulgaria it encouraged local Communist Parties to seize power. This did not usually happen immediately, but the lack of any powerful non-Communist leaders and the hatred of fascism helped Stalin. By early 1948, the 'People's Governments' in which non-Communists shared power with Communists had largely disappeared and the non-Communist leaders had either fled, like Mikolajczyk of

Poland and Nagy of Hungary, or been imprisoned, a fate suffered by Cardinal Mindszenty in Hungary. Russia turned its zone of Germany into an independent state, the G.D.R., led by Walter Ulbricht, a state the west refused to recognise. But Yugoslavia went its own way, free of Red Army domination, led by a popular capable and sensible Communist, Marshal Tito, who was renowned for the success of his partisans in fighting the Germans. Tito refused to be bullied by Stalin and was duly punished in June 1948, by being expelled from the Communist Camp. Thus Russia backed minority parties and established Communist dictatorships in Eastern Europe.

Areas controlled by the West

Britain, France, and the U.S.A. encouraged local government in the areas of Germany they controlled and welcomed the emergence in local government of moderate democratic leaders. In late December 1946 the British and Americans joined together their zones, later the French sector joined too and thus West Germany was created, with an outpost in the Western-controlled areas of Berlin. France soon began to recover from the war and Italy, which had finally turned against Hitler, was operating as an independent democracy by 1947. Greece was a more serious problem: the Communist E.A.M. resistance movement was more powerful than the non-Communist E.D.E.S. British troops had invaded Greece during the last stages of the war and Stalin had agreed to Churchill's demand that Greece be recognized as an area of British, not Soviet, influence. When the Germans left Greece and the Greek Communists attempted to seize control, British and Greek regular troops attacked them and between 1944–5, fought a savage war which angered the Americans, who resented seeing British troops fighting Greeks whilst Hitler was still in control of Germany. It left a bitterness between Greek left-wing politicians and the Army which still exists.

The United Nations

a) Background

Whereas the League of Nations was founded in a mood of idealism, the U.N. grew up in a much more cautious and less optimistic time. Yet, for all this, the U.N. has probably been more successful. Whereas the League suffered from being expected to do too much, the U.N.'s limited achievements are more likely to reap praise. Obviously both organisations have faced the same problems of how to alter the policies of major powers and have not solved them, but in more limited fields the U.N. has achieved much.

Early Plans for the U.N.

The general statements in the Atlantic Charter were accepted, in January 1942, by twenty-six nations. In October of the same year four major allies, Britain, China, the U.S.A. and the U.S.S.R. signed an agreement to continue their co-operation after the war. Thus the first signs of the U.N. emerged – a general organisation for nations, aiming at worthy objects, but within which the major states would exercise great power. In 1943 in the discussions held at Teheran, Roosevelt suggested a U.N. of two committees (one of the four great powers) and at Dunbarton Oaks near Washington, in 1944, a more detailed scheme was worked out. The 1945 Yalta Conference also included discussions about the U.N. and it was here it was agreed to give the great powers the right to veto U.N. decisions whilst Stalin at last dropped his demand that all sixteen U.S.S.R. republics should have separate representatives.

The Establishment of the U.N.

The U.N. Charter was finally drafted in June 1945 at San Francisco, and the U.N.'s first meeting was held in January of the following year. Fifty nations signed the Charter, which laid down the U.N.'s aims and objects. The Charter was a separate agreement from the peace treaties, whereas the League of Nations' Covenant had been part of the treaties after the First World War.

b) The Organisation of the U.N.

AIMS: The general aims of the U.N. are all concerned with preserving peace and improving the conditions in which people live and work. Members agreed to work for peaceful solutions to problems, greater international co-operation, the preservation of human rights and economic and social improvements.

THE GENERAL ASSEMBLY: All member nations are entitled to one vote in the General Assembly and, by 1969, few countries lacked this right. Communist China is the most notable absentee, since the U.S.A. insists the U.N. is an organisation of peace loving nations and that China therefore does not qualify. China's place is occupied by the representative of Taiwan. General Assembly decisions do not have to be unanimous but the Assembly's power is limited because of the power of the Security Council. The Assembly usually meets for a few months every year, approves the budget and makes recommendations, but in November, 1950, it gained an additional right from a resolution declaring that if the Security Council fails to solve a threat to peace, the Assembly can consider the matter and take action into its own hands if two-thirds of the members so desire. This is an alteration to the constitution and strictly speaking is not a fully legal amendment to the Charter. It was used in 1956 when Britain and France were involved in war with Egypt and used their votes on the Security Council.

THE SECURITY COUNCIL: This body consists of five permanent members, Britain, France, the U.S.A., the U.S.S.R. and Nationalist China and six non-permanent members elected by the Assembly. In January 1966, non-permanent representation was increased to ten on the basis of five Afro-Asian States, two Latin American, one East European, two West European and other states. In fact the greater number of non-permanent members (who serve for two years each) does not give them control, for the permanent members enjoy the right of veto over all matters except the actual holding of a discussion and the summoning of the Assembly. The U.S.S.R. has made good use of its veto, in fact it was only her temporary absence which enabled the U.N. to act in the Korean War. The Security Council can make decisions for the U.N., this makes for greater speed and recognises plainly the strength of the U.S.A. and the U.S.S.R., without whose backing little is possible.

OTHER ORGANISATIONS: As with the League, the U.N. has many commissions to consider special problems. The Trusteeship Council has taken over the work of the Mandates' Commission, with increased power. Regular visits are paid to trust territories to ensure they are being administered in the interests of their inhabitants. The I.L.O. has continued to fight for better working conditions, U.N.E.S.C.O. deals with educational and scientific matters, F.A.O. with food and agriculture, W.H.O. with health, U.N.I.C.E.F. with the welfare of children and I.C.A.O. with civil aviation. U.N. agencies have struggled with problems of diseases, pests (like locusts), irrigation and the refugee question. The International Court, which is basically as it was under the League, continues to function at the Hague, made up of fifteen judges elected by the Assembly and the Security Council. Connected with the U.N., though not under it, is G.A.T.T., an organisation to deal with tariffs and trade in which members discuss means of lowering trade barriers.

In this aerial view of the city of New York, the United Nations building can be seen in the left foreground.

THE SECRETARIAT: A body of permanent civil servants carry out the day to day work of the U.N.; over 4,000 work in New York where the headquarters are housed in a thirty-nine storeyed glass and marble fronted building and there are over 1,000 in Geneva. At their head is the Secretary-General, who is elected for a five year term of office. The first Secretary-General was Trygve Lie of Norway, who was succeeded, in 1953, by Dag Hammarskjold, a quiet but determined Swede. Hammarskjöld was killed in an air crash in the Congo in 1961 while on a peace mission: his successor was U Thant of Burma. The position involves a great deal of hard work for little reward, though it carries considerable power. The Secretary-General can, for instance, bring before the Security Council any matter he feels threatens world peace.

c) The U.N. in Action

Its difficulties

It was suggested at San Francisco in 1945 that a U.N. army and air force should be established on a permanent basis with a General Staff. The suggestion was not, however, taken up and no genuine U.N. army emerged until 1956. Obviously, forces have to be raised by member countries sending contingents to trouble spots, but unless the members concerned are clearly neutral the Security Council is not likely to agree to this. Troops cost money and this has been a permanent problem because some members – notably the U.S.S.R. – have not paid adequate contributions and have reduced the Secretary-General to desperate appeals for funds to allow the U.N. to continue to do its work adequately.

Its interventions

A small U.N. force was sent to Egypt in 1956 after the war between Britain, France, Israel and Egypt. A U.N. resolution helped persuade Britain and France to drop their attack on Egypt and the U.N. force proceeded to take up a position on the border between Israel and Egypt. But a fresh crisis, coupled with Egyptian demands forced the U.N. force to leave in May 1967. A U.N. force helped restore order in the Congo between 1960–67 and end Katanga's separation before lack of money compelled it to leave. The U.N. also attempted to mediate between India and Pakistan over Kashmir, whilst its investigations into the Arab-Israeli differences have already brought one tragedy – the murder in 1948 of Count Bernadotte, the chief U.N. official.

The U.N. intervention in Korea is in a rather different category. Large numbers of troops were involved, but most were American and the U.S.A. had a heavy interest in one side of the quarrel, whereas other U.N. actions have been by small forces from neutral nations.

In many specialised fields, such as health and food, the U.N. has done much good, but, basically, it has failed to solve military problems from lack of military might. Weak nations have put much faith in the U.N., knowing their own vulnerability, but without the willingness of powerful nations to abide by U.N. decisions, little can be done. In disarmament the only progress has been an atomic test ban treaty in 1963 which France and China did not sign. China remains outside the U.N., for a time Indonesia, too, joined her. Yet the U.N. does hold out hope for the future as the rush of new African and Asian nations to join it shows.

Other activities

The peacekeeping role of the U.N. tends to attract most notice, but in fact the bulk of the work of the U.N. is in the hands of the various U.N. organisations which strive to cure disease, and end poverty and ignorance throughout the world. There are many obstacles to its work, including the immense size of the problems facing it, the constant shortage of

L

money, the ignorance and prejudice of many people and the suspicion and even hostility of some governments. Yet the very limited scale of success of the U.N. special organisations should not blind us to the very real success it has achieved.

The Economic and Social Council, composed of eighteen members elected by the Assembly, supervises the work of commissions that study special regions of the world. The Commission for Europe did much to help Europe recover from the war by means of programmes of research and investigation. Through the International Bank, loans can be made to help those in need: such loans have helped Mexico to build dams, and Brazil to develop electricity supplies.

In post-war Europe, the U.N. Relief and Rehabilitation Administration helped the many victims of the war until 1947 when its work was handed over to the International Refugee Organisation, which in turn struggled with these enormous problems with some success until 1951. Some measure of this success can be gauged in that over one million people were helped to settle in new homes and 73,000 were helped to return to their former homelands. The problem has never been permanently solved for new wars are constantly creating more refugees. The Food and Agricultural Organisation has sent out experts to help develop more successful farming methods in regions as widespread as India (where rice growing was improved) and Greece and Thailand (where more efficient fishing methods were taught to the local inhabitants). Diseases have been tackled by the World Health Organisation—a cholera epidemic in Egypt, for instance, was controlled and prevented from spreading through the Middle East. The malaria problem in Italy, Greece, and the Middle East has been attacked, and a world influenza centre has been set up to carry out research and spread around the globe information on the best ways to tackle this common illness. Centres have been set up in a number of areas by U.N.E.S.C.O. in an attempt to show local people the best ways of teaching illiterates reading and writing by simple methods.

Through its Programme of Technical Assistance, the U.N. has brought together experts from different bodies like F.A.O., W.H.O., and U.N.E.S.C.O. in order that, together, they can launch a combined attack on the problem of underdeveloped lands. This programme depended on voluntary contributions: like so much of the U.N.'s work it is dogged by a shortage of cash. Its work gives a glimpse of what could be done in a world free of war and the constant need to be prepared for war. Because the rich nations of the world spend so little on helping poor countries (and often their own poor, for that matter) and so much on their military machines, the problems of the poor cannot, at the moment, be solved. But it is wrong to entirely blame the apparently mean attitude of wealthy nations, for poorer nations are equally capable of a very grasping, grudging attitude to their own poor. Nations like Egypt and Indonesia for example have spent much of their revenue on soldiers and weapons. Like the League of Nations, the United Nations is not capable of doing more than the majority of governments and peoples will allow it to do, and this, in the second half of the twentieth century, really amounts to very little.

A picture of house-to-house fighting in Rostov during the German invasion.

7 | Post-War Europe

Introduction

The war had left behind in Europe great destruction of life, homes, savings, industry and communications; the first urgent task for governments was to rebuild. But the war also left a divided Europe, for the areas conquered by the Red Army were, by 1948, all under Communist control. Thus an iron curtain descended across Europe, cutting off East from West. The history of post-war Europe is a history of recovery from ruin, of tensions between east and west, and of the gradual but suspicious relaxing of these tensions. At the hub lay Germany, divided between Communist and non-Communist governments and therefore a source of trouble because many Germans wished for unification, whilst Germany's neighbours retained memories of a recent past too vividly to permit Germany to re-emerge as a dominant power. Germany is of considerable importance, because of its central position in Europe and because of its potential strength if allowed to reunite. In 1945, and for many years afterwards, Germany occupied a most significant position in view of the recent war; Germany had played the major role in causing the war so how could a strong and reunited Germany be allowed to re-emerge as a trustworthy neighbour? The diminished importance of post-war Europe is shown firstly by the rapid disappearance, after 1945, of most of Europe's colonies and secondly by the dependence of western Europe on the U.S.A., originally for economic aid, and later for defence, whilst eastern Europe is dominated by the U.S.S.R., a partly Asiatic power.

Behind the Iron Curtain

a) Post-war Russia

War damage

Since much of the fighting had taken place inside the Soviet Union, industry, agriculture and transport had all suffered in spite of Stalin's efforts to build up industries farther east, safe from German attack. This economic damage, plus human suffering brought about by the war, meant life in Russia in 1945 was harsh and grim. Stalin endeavoured to grab all the land he could from eastern Europe to help the Russian position but the problem was not so easily solved as the areas controlled by the Red Army were, generally, not the most advanced industrially. Nevertheless, the Russians took what they could, obtained ships from Italy and, for a while took reparations from West Germany in addition to continuing to exact a percentage on current production in those formerly hostile states now dominated by Russia.

'Stalinism' returns

The war had caused Stalin to relax his harsh grip on Russia so that he could win maximum support, and, for a time, he was popular as the leader of a triumphant people. But once the war was over, the old pre-war system of Stalinism returned with all its narrowness, cruelty and misery. Beria's secret police made sure Stalin was secure. Zhdanov supervised culture and made sure writers and artists produced nothing which was critical of Stalin, whilst repeated purges kept the Party in a constant state of fear. Labour camps were located in grim areas of Siberia and run brutally as near-slave centres: to them were sent people thought to be dangerous to Stalin.

Economic Policy

Russia once more returned to the pattern of Five Year Plans designed to build up heavy industry, but which brought little of benefit to the ordinary consumer. Like the earlier Plans, the Plans of 1946 and 1951 did much to strengthen heavy industry, even though they fell short of the targets which Stalin set. Agriculture again posed the most difficult problems, peasants worked reluctantly on the collective farms, food prices were high and there was a shortage of capital to bring farming methods up-to-date since money was being heavily spent on industry and defence. Many of the peasants had used the opportunity of the chaotic conditions caused by the war to seize larger plots of land for themselves, but the Government tried to bring agriculture under control through the M.T.S., the Machine Tractor Stations, which were run by dedicated Communists and which hired out farm machinery only to the obedient. Stalin also attempted to shape the economies of the East European countries in order that their production would benefit Russia; even though many had scarcely traded with Russia in the past, they now found themselves forced to do business with the U.S.S.R.

b) Post-war Eastern Europe

Titoism

By 1948 Stalin appeared to have triumphed in Eastern Europe: not only had he placed local Communists in charge of governments and ended the period during which Communists co-operated with other factions, he had also established the *Cominform* (as the renewed Comintern was called) to spread Russian influence over other Communist parties. Yet in the same year came the first serious split ... Yugoslavia became very reluctant to obey Stalin's orders and her leaders were expelled from the Communist camp.

Unlike other Communist leaders such as Ulbricht of East Germany, Tito had not been dependent on the Red Army; he had stayed in his own country during the war, helped liberate it, and was a national, as well as a Communist, leader. He had his own ideas about running his country and it was his ambitious plans to organise a federation of Balkan States which so angered Stalin that it led to a break between the two states. The break only served to increase Tito's popularity in his own land; his army and Party supported him, and though he lost Russian aid he turned instead to the West, stopped helping Communists in Greece (leading to the latter's defeat) and, far from being harmed by Stalin's hostility, seemed to thrive on it. Stalin made a grave error of judgment in his handling of the situation, he completely over-rated Russia's ability to frighten the Yugoslav Communist Party into obedience and was hampered somewhat by the fact that the U.S.S.R. had no common frontier with Yugoslavia. Moreover the Yugoslav Communist Party seemed, surprisingly to Stalin, quite content to believe that they could be genuine Communists and disobedient to Stalin at the same time. One odd consequence did follow, Albania, a poor small Communist state, resented her stronger neighbour, defied Tito, and clung to its Stalinist ways, continuing to do so even after Stalin was dead. However, even Titoism has its limits as Milovan Djilas found in 1954 when he was imprisoned for trying to start a socialist movement as a rival to the Communist Party.

The battle with the Church

The Communists in east Europe had by 1948 broken down all opposition by rival politicians (usually the leaders of Peasant Parties) either by killing, imprisonment or exile. Strong centres of possible hostility, however, remained in the shape of the Churches. The Orthodox Church was less of a problem than the Catholic Church, as it had no leadership

outside east Europe, whereas Catholics could seek guidance from the
Pope and the millions of Catholics in other parts of the world. The
Catholic Church of Poland the Communists found the most difficult
to bully. General Communist policy was to imprison a leading clergyman
on some pretext as a warning to the rest, thus Cardinal Mindszenty of
Hungary and Archbishop Stepinac of Yugoslavia were imprisoned. This
policy had little success in Poland and generally it was resented, while
Stalin, as he aged, seemed to become more and more suspicious of any
kind of opposition.

Policy in the satellites

With the exception of Yugoslavia the other east European states settled
down to becoming dependencies of the U.S.S.R., too weak to resist the
Red Army which stood behind the local Communist bosses. Only Finland
escaped the harsh bullying which had to be endured by the other states
of Eastern Europe.

Stalin was determined there should be no more Titos and during the
purges which followed in 1948 Communist leaders like Rajk, Minister
of the Interior in Hungary, and Kostov, Deputy P.M. in Bulgaria were
executed. Others, like Gomulka in Poland, were imprisoned while
Czechoslovakia was torn from the hands of President Benes who had
wanted to follow moderate policies which would keep his country on
friendly terms with both Stalin and the West. The supporters of Benes
were forced from power, among them Jan Masaryk, a popular leader
who died as the result of a fall from a window, a fall which many Czechs
believe was no accident. In place of these men came Stalinist Communists
headed by Klement Gottwald. Although Stalin had reacted to Tito, the
Marshall Plan and the failure of his blockade of Berlin by harshly stamp-
ing on the little freedom that his satellite states possessed, he stopped
short of merging them into the U.S.S.R. Stalin was a cautious man who
had no desire to offend the West excessively, thus he insisted that his
satellites were separate and independent 'people's democracies'. But
the west found these claims of independence particularly hard to swallow
in view of Stalin's actions. In Poland for example, he appointed a
Russian, Marshal Rokossovski, as the Minister of Defence.

Stalin's main object was to surround himself with satellite leaders who
were little more than 'yes-men' who visited him to receive their orders,
and rarely met each other. The equivalent of the Russian secret police
now appeared in east European countries too, to become as hated as the
N.K.V.D. in Russia. The satellite states were forced to copy Russia's
economic methods, produce Five Year Plans, collectivise agriculture,

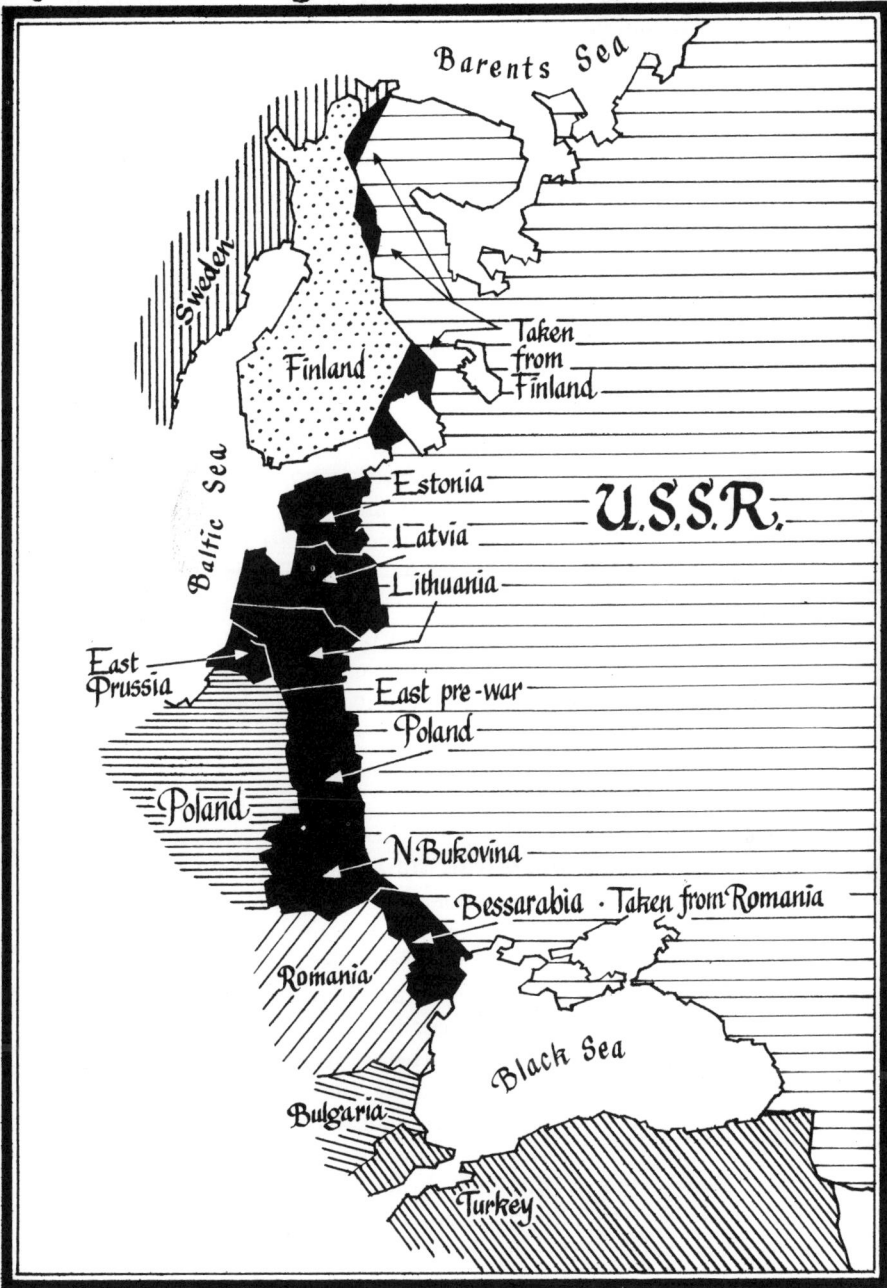

RUSSIAN GAINS IN 1945

Barents Sea

Sweden

Finland

Taken from Finland

Baltic Sea

U.S.S.R.

Estonia

Latvia

Lithuania

East Prussia

East pre-war Poland

Poland

N. Bukovina

Bessarabia · Taken from Romania

Romania

Black Sea

Bulgaria

Turkey

and provide goods needed by the Soviet Union. Most of these lands had been agrarian, not industrial and it was hard for many of them to change, especially when money for investment was short and the *Comecon* or Council for Mutual Economic Aid, formed in 1949, so feeble. Comecon was useful as a piece of propaganda with which the U.S.S.R. could answer the U.S.A.'s Marshall Plan, it also helped in the work of binding the satellites' economies more closely with Russia. In fact apart from carrying out some research and exchange of technical information, it was not really equipped to do much for its staff were few in number and it did not even have a constitution. American aid offered to Europe under the Marshall Plan had been offered to East Europe too, but Stalin forbade any of his satellites to accept it.

c) Foreign Policy

The victorious Red Army was large and well equipped and remained so, whilst Western armies were reduced after the war. Stalin was as suspicious as ever of the countries which had so recently been his allies and his foreign minister, Molotov, achieved fame at the U.N. for the regularity with which he said 'No' to all suggestions for new policies. A grudging amount of aid was sent to the Chinese Communists, but they felt little gratitude, while the policy of harsh opposition which Stalin insisted the Communists in western Europe should adopt did not bring them any great successes.

The Berlin Crisis

Germany remained the focal point of trouble. The West was ready to agree to re-unification on the basis of free elections, but Stalin, fearful for his Communist allies, would not agree and demanded terms involving neutrality, German disarmament, and profits for Russia from Germany as reparation. In June 1948, he tried to put pressure on the West by cutting road and rail access to Berlin, where the British, French and Americans all controlled zones, but the Allied response was to organise an air-lift, skilfully run by General Clay, which even managed to provide the Berliners with coal during the winter of 1948–9 and compelled Stalin to relax the pressure. Stalin meanwhile, had decreasing need to feel afraid of the Allies; in 1949 Russia exploded her own atomic bomb, followed shortly afterwards by an 'H' bomb; her conventional forces were huge. In addition, helped by captured German scientists, the Russians had developed rockets capable of delivering these terrible weapons of destruction.

d) The Death of Stalin

Stalin remained in absolute control of the Russian Communist Party and of Government and the Forces. Possible rivals were dealt with in various ways, even the great Marshal Zhukov was relegated to an obscure command at the end of the war. Not that struggles for the possible succession to Stalin did not take place; Andrei Zhdanov, one of Stalin's assistants, seemed the strongest candidate, but after his death in 1948, it was Malenkov who seemed most likely to triumph. These struggles for supremacy were often waged over the carrying out of different policies. Malenkov had to watch with alarm the rise of Nikita Krushchev who strongly supported a new way of increasing agricultural production by opening up unused areas – the virgin lands – and reducing the number of collective farms by making them larger. In his last months Stalin aroused terrible fears of a new purge by his criticisms, suspicions and accusations: he blamed Zhdanov's death on a plot and many of the Party must have been relieved when Stalin suffered a stroke and, on 5th March, 1953, finally died. Stalin had ruled Russia for almost twenty-five years and during that time was responsible for many changes. Industry was already developing in Russia at the beginning of the century and it has been widely argued whether the emergence of Russia as a modern industrial state owes a great deal to Communism or not, although certainly Stalin was responsible for the strong emphasis on heavy industry. His early leadership in the war with Hitler can be criticised: he made many errors, yet Russia did emerge triumphant and some credit must go to Stalin. Against this must be set his greed for power and suspicion of rivals which caused the death, exile, or imprisonment of thousands of his fellow countrymen and imposed a drab, narrow way of life in which almost all art was dull, no impartial historical studies were permitted and even scientific research had sometimes to be angled to suit Stalin's ideas. Communist rule in Russia was bound to be a dictatorship, since the Party was so small, but it need not have been the mean and fearful thing which Stalin made it.

e) The Khrushchev Era

Collective Leadership

Stalin's followers seem to have been fearful of the future following their master's death; they immediately proclaimed their unity as a group and relaxed some of the harshness of Stalin's rule, releasing some political prisoners. Malenkov became Prime Minister and First Secretary, but soon lost the latter post to Khrushchev, whilst Bulganin and

Zhukov were other notable figures in the government. But the chief of the secret police, Beria, was so feared by his fellow Communists that they turned on him and had him tried and executed. The solidarity of the group did not last long and Khrushchev was soon challenging Malenkov's leadership, criticising weaknesses in his policy of finding more consumer goods, attacking his failure to increase agricultural production, and offering policies of his own including reconciliation with Tito. In February 1955 Malenkov was forced to resign and in 1956 Khrushchev managed to push out the aged Molotov. Khruschev was a tough and adaptable man of great ambition whose chief strength lay in his control of the Party organisation; it was this strength that gave him victory and enabled him in 1957 to beat off counter-attacks aimed at dislodging him.

Foreign Policy

Khrushchev stressed the need to be more flexible in foreign policy, proved it by his visits to many other countries, (even the U.S.A.) and by his negotiations with Tito to end the break between the two nations, even to the extent of offering apologies to the Yugoslavs. In May 1955 Austria was freed from occupation and granted independence as a neutral state forbidden to re-unite with Germany. In reply to N.A.T.O., Russia organised the Warsaw Pact of East European states, though since the Red Army was already in these states it was only making legal what already existed. Khrushchev brought a bouncy boisterousness to foreign policy which contrasted with the grey, grim silence of Molotov. It sometimes gave offence, as in his aggressive speeches at the U.N.; it sometimes failed, as when he had to withdraw rockets from Cuba; and it offended the Chinese who hated seeing Khrushchev visiting capitalist lands, and who resented the readiness with which he gave aid to neutrals like Egypt and India and yet provided China with so little. Russia was forced into better terms with the U.S.A., partly through her growing quarrel with China, who had emerged as a rival in the leadership of the Communist world, claiming that hers was the true form of Communism, and partly because the terrible weapons of destruction now owned by the U.S.A. and the U.S.S.R. meant that these two powers had to tread cautiously to avoid total destruction. A 'hot line', a direct telephone link between Washington and Moscow, was established in 1963 and symbolised the need for the two states to keep in touch. Even though the Russians sent aid to many Communist parties, including those of North Vietnam with whom the Americans were engaged in battle, there was enough in common between them to enable a ban on nuclear tests above ground to be imposed.

Khrushchev's attack on Stalin

It was already clear, by 1956, that Khrushchev disagreed with several of Stalin's policies, and, at the Twentieth Party Congress held in that year, he chose to make a violent onslaught on Stalin, listing errors he had made and crimes he had committed. He attacked the 'cult of personality' by which people had been encouraged to believe Stalin was without fault, and suggested his own view that socialism could be reached in various ways. This was supposed to be secret, yet news of it leaked out and naturally caused a great stir. Statues and portraits of Stalin began to vanish, 'Stalingrad' was renamed Volgagrad, criticisms of Stalin's handling of the war were voiced and, above all, the satellite states became more restless.

f) Troubles in the Satellites

The example of Tito and the general misery of life caused restlessness in the satellite states, but the Red Army and the strong hand of rulers like Ulbricht in East Germany and Rakosi in Hungary, together with their secret police, prevented trouble. Khrushchev had seemed to favour a more lenient policy designed to win support in the satellite states, not simply rely on force to hold them down. In 1954 the Russians decided to sell to the satellite states Russia's share in the joint companies which had been created after the war to control their key industries and commercial enterprises. But Yugoslavia remained a risk because she continued to follow an independent path. In 1950 workers' management in industry was introduced and in 1953 Yugoslavia also abandoned collectivisation in the countryside. In 1963 Tito decided to reform the constitution, allowing elections in which candidates did not have to be Communists. It was always a worry to Russian leaders having to decide whether they ought to denounce Tito's policy, or whether they should attempt to retain his friendship at the risk of his independence affecting others. Some satellites showed their restlessness by bold open action, and even the more cautious, like Romania, dared to attack Russia's economic plans for East Europe, complaining of lack of consideration for their own economies.

The Berlin Uprising

The death of Stalin was followed by surprisingly little trouble except in East Germany where poor living standards, hatred of the government, wretched food and the raising of work norms caused a revolt in East Berlin in June 1953 which spread, but was crushed by Soviet troops.

Alexei Kosygin who succeeded Khrushchev as the Russian Premier in October, 1964. Unlike his predecessor, Kosygin did not also become Party Secretary.

There were riots in Czechoslovakia in the same month, but these too were dealt with. But the better relations between Russia and Yugoslavia alarmed the old Stalinist rulers in East Europe and encouraged national Communists like Gomulka, who was released from prison in 1954, and Imre Nagy who briefly held power in Hungary in 1954. The news of Khrushchev's attack on Stalin was enough to bring nationalist feelings and dislike of the Russians into the open, so that 1956 was a bad year for Khrushchev.

The Polish Rising

Early signs of trouble in Poland came in June in the form of a strike and demonstration at Poznan which although quickly suppressed, inspired other demonstrations and sufficient pressure to force the old Stalinist leaders out and bring Wladyslaw Gomulka to power. Gomulka was a Communist, but he was not prepared to give way to Russian threats, nor be bullied by Khrushchev and his fellow leaders who flew to see him; instead he achieved a compromise. Since Gomulka promised Poland would remain a member of the Warsaw Pact and Khrushchev was already in enough difficulties in Hungary without taking on the Polish Army (Gomulka had made it clear the Poles would fight) the Poles were allowed a greater control over their own affairs. Rokossovski left Poland but Gomulka made it clear he would not insist on full freedom of action for Poland, and he certainly would not share power with non-Communists. As a Polish Communist had emerged quickly enough to lead and control the movement, and had the backing of the Church led by Cardinal Wyszynski, a crisis was averted; but in Hungary things were different.

The Hungarian Rising

Rakosi and his A.V.O. (secret police) were loathed in Hungary and in July 1956, he resigned and was promptly replaced by Gero, another Stalinist. In October demonstrations inspired by events in Poland led to clashes with Russian troops and an explosion of anger against Russia and the A.V.O. which swept a Hungarian Communist, Imre Nagy into power and was so strong that even he could not control the movement. All the old apparatus of government was destroyed, Communist dictatorship ended, Hungary left the Warsaw Pact and asked Russian troops to leave. Janos Kadar, a supporter of Nagy at first, decided events were going too fast, left Budapest and was thus absent when Russian troops, led by tanks, attacked the ill-armed Hungarians and crushed their desperate resistance. Nagy fled to the Yugoslav embassy but was later given up and shot, and Kadar was invited to take on the difficult task of governing the country. Russia was helped in crushing this revolt by the fact that the rest of the world was partially distracted by the Suez Crisis; even so it horrified and angered many people and led to many Communists in Western Countries abandoning their party. As in Poland the Russian leaders had to decide whether a movement in East Europe was going too far and would endanger the Warsaw Pact. Gomulka could be trusted, but not so Nagy because he shared power with non-Communists and proposed turning Hungary into a neutral country. These events seemed to prove the truth of some Russian Communists' argument, that to allow the satellites too much freedom would lead to the collapse of Communist rule. The Russians were persistently and frequently faced with this problem throughout their empire. Intolerance meant that the Red Army would have to keep the satellites firmly under control; it also meant that the Russians would have little hope of pulling together other Communist states in Europe as real allies. A more relaxed rule involved risks, yet some Russian leaders still believed some relaxation of rule was necessary in the satellites: their standards of living rose as more effort was made to produce consumer goods. In East Germany however such relaxation was difficult.

The Berlin Wall

The Russians had turned East Germany into a German Democratic republic, but its ruler, Walter Ulbricht, was completely dependent on Russian aid and was so loathed that thousands of East Germans fled to Federal Germany each year. The main escape route lay across Berlin and, to block it, the East German Government built a huge wall across

Leonid Brezhnev took over the General Secretaryship of the Central Committee of the Communist Party of Russia on the fall of Khrushchev in 1964.

Berlin in 1961 along the East-West boundary. They cleared the ground nearby, and did not hesitate to have people attempting to escape shot. Ulbricht resigned in 1971 and died two years later. Expanding industries have increased East German prosperity in the 70s: great successes in the sporting world have also helped the state's reputation.

g) The Fall of Khrushchev

Under Khrushchev, Russia experienced a rise in living standards and some relaxation in tension. He evolved plans ranging over many fields, paying special attention to improving the country's economy and reviving the flagging Comecon which met more regularly with a proper constitution (1960) an international executive (1962) and much greater resources. After the Hungarian crisis of 1956 aid was sent through Comecon to help Kadar establish himself in power. Agricultural planning was also less tightly controlled from the centre and more incentives were offered to the collective farms. In industry Khrushchev tried to improve the overall management by bringing it closer to production and taking greater account of local needs. Russia's system of scientific and technical education began to pour out experts who produced successes of which the most spectacular were the sputniks (satellites which orbited the earth), and Yuri Gagarin's first manned orbit of the earth in 1961. But Khrushchev's boasts that the U.S.S.R. would soon catch up with U.S. living standards still seemed a very long way away, his concentration on peaceful competition with capitalism angered the Chinese, led to an open break with them, and to criticisms of Khrushchev for the aggressive way he pursued this clash. Nor had his policy of raising agricultural production by farming the virgin lands been a great success, whilst a drought in 1963 had diminished grain production to such an extent that imports were necessary. His climb down over Cuba in 1962 and love of power also caused opposition and on 13th October, 1964, he was outmanoeuvred, isolated and forced to resign. Though life in Russia improved under Khrushchev, the improvements should not be taken out of context; the dictatorship of the Communist Party remained, people were still barred from writing and speaking honestly (Boris Pasternak was threatened with expulsion from Russia for accepting the Nobel Prize for his novel *Dr. Zhivago*). Khrushchev now lives in retirement, a sign of one way Russia has improved since the days of Stalin: defeated men no longer suffer execution.

h) Russia since Khrushchev

The decline of harsh Russian rule in eastern Europe

Khrushchev was the last of the all powerful Communist leaders who combined the duties of Prime Minister with those of First Secretary of the Russian Communist Party. He was succeeded as Prime Minister by Alexei Kosygin and as party Secretary by Leonid Brezhnev. This divided leadership is a good illustration of the division of the Communist leaders between those who wish to concentrate in making Russia more prosperous while reducing quarrels with Western Europe and the U.S.A. and those who worried that a moderate policy would damage the power of the Russian leaders, encourage East European states to become more independent and even encourage people in Russia to criticise their leaders.

At first, it seemed as though the moderates had won. Kosygin continued the policy of meeting the leaders of the U.S.A. by going to see President Johnson in 1967, for discussions at Glassboro. Khrushchev had always made such occasions a moment for great showmanship, but Kosygin was quieter, more reticent. Like Khrushchev, the new Russian leaders were not on good terms with China; this split in the Communist world between two big powers, both of whom claimed that they were the true leaders of Communism, meant that smaller Communist powers had an opportunity to seize more independence for themselves by insisting that their support required something in return. The small state of Albania for example, which had a very poor relationship with its larger neighbour Yugoslavia, became a strong supporter of China chiefly to show her independence of Yugoslavia and the U.S.S.R. The states of Eastern Europe were growing more prosperous and their people less fearful of attack from Western Europe.

M

As their gratitude to Russia for rescuing them from the Nazis faded, so the small East European nations became more discontented with the way Russia controlled their affairs. They felt that Russian control was an insult to their own independence and a check on their hopes for greater prosperity. Only the East Germans could be relied upon to be obedient because their leaders were so unpopular they knew that should Russian protection be withdrawn they would automatically lose power. Romania was soon venturing to criticise the Russian dominated defence system, the Warsaw Pact, and refusing to follow Russia's policy of supporting the Arab states in the Middle East against Israel.

The Crisis in Czechoslavakia

As their Communist East European neighbours became bolder in moving towards greater independence from the U.S.S.R., so the Russian leaders became more worried by the problems this raised. If they allowed things to continue on these lines might not the Warsaw Pact collapse altogether, leaving the U.S.S.R. in a much weaker position to face the U.S.A. and N.A.T.O.? Might not the growing criticism of Russian leadership in East Europe encourage critics inside Russia itself? Yet if Russia dealt harshly with her critics would not this cause such anger that the East European countries (indeed Communists all over the world) would turn against Russia at the very time when she was trying to unite as many Communists as possible in order to isolate China?

The Russian leaders however made no concrete move until events in Czechoslovakia forced them to show their hand. The Russians had not experienced any difficulty with Czechoslovakia for many years after the Communists gained control. Its leader, Antonin Novotny, had been an obedient servant first to Stalin and then to Khrushchev. Novotny's police had dealt severely with people likely to cause trouble with Russia while the bulk of the Czech people had gone quietly about their own affairs. But in 1968 this peaceful situation collapsed.

A revolt against Novotny's leadership was made possible through the majority of his own Communist party deciding it was time to get rid of him and thus give Czechoslovaks greater freedom. Dubcek and Cernik were the leaders of this split from within the Party. Novotny struggled desperately to hold on to power but his supporters were so few and the outcry against him so great, that he was eventually forced to resign. The new leaders believed the Communist party should continue to rule Czechoslovakia, but that it should do so only because it deserved to be in power, and because it could show critics that it was fit to rule. Television, radio and newspapers were freed from the severe censorship

A Soviet tank rumbles through the streets of Prague during the Czechoslovak crisis of August, 1968.

which Novotny had imposed on them and searching enquiries were begun into his rule, people ill-treated by his regime gave evidence of their sufferings. Criticisms could not be kept under control and many Czechs objected to the way their country was dominated by Russia.

The Russian leaders were now faced with a direct threat to their position, at first they attempted to deal with it by cajolery and threats. Yet in spite of being joined by East German, Polish and Hungarian leaders in their attempts to make the Czech leaders toe the Party line, the Russians completely failed to either persuade or bully the Czech government. It seemed at first the Czechs had won the battle to decide the affairs of their own country, but in fact the Russian leaders were far too alarmed to allow the Czechs complete freedom. In August 1968, the Presidium finally accepted the arguments put forward by Brezhnev that Czechoslovakia's behaviour would damage the Warsaw Pact and even the security of the Russian leaders themselves. Russian armoured forces, with limited support from East Germany, Poland and Hungary, rumbled into Czechoslovakia. The leaders of non-Communist countries protested: Romania, Yugoslavia, and even China criticized the Russian action; but no one came to help the Czechs. The Czech army was far too small to stand up to the invaders, but this did not stop many Czech civilians trying to stop the Russian tanks by their own efforts, while the Czech press poured out repeated attacks on the Russian leaders. The Russians announced that the reason for their actions was that the Czechs were too weak to defend their border with the West, and that the Warsaw Pact was in danger. In reality their action was clearly caused through fear for their own position if criticism of Communist leaders had been allowed to flourish, rather than fear of an attack by N.A.T.O. The Czech leaders were seized, taken to Moscow and though later released, were harassed into agreeing to a settlement on Russian terms. Months of argument followed, because only a tiny minority of former Stalinist Czechs welcomed the Russians, and no alternative leadership to Dubcek could be found. Gradually, however, the Czech leaders were forced into making promises that they would restore censorship and stop criticisms of the U.S.S.R. They hoped that by so doing they would rid their land of the Red Army only to find that the Red Army was still inside their borders. The rest of the world were powerless to do anything but protest; when Brezhnev declared that Communist Eastern Europe was Russia's concern and that it would never be allowed to be anything other than Communist, he could feel confident that the Russian Army was able to enforce what he said. Romania and Yugoslavia began to fear for their own safety for it was clear that the leaders of the Russian Communist Party were too intoxicated by power and too afraid of criticism to allow freedom in the area of the world which they dominated. Eventually, in the spring of 1969, Russian pressure succeeded in levering the obstinate Dubcek out of his key office and in his place was installed the much more co-operative Husak. Before long other Czech reformers were forced out of influential positions too and Czechoslovakia's brief period of freedom seemed ended.

Western Europe

a) Introduction

While Eastern Europe suffered from Communist dictatorship, the policies of Stalin, and from Russian interference in their economies; the West benefited from the return of parliamentary democracy which proved more stable in France, Germany and Italy than it had before the war, and from generous American aid. Thus West Europe was able to recover more rapidly than East Europe from the effects of the war.

Prosperity increased, and co-operative schemes between different countries which linked up defence, economies and even political affairs met with a certain amount of success – in marked contrast to the failure of Comecon in East Europe. Of course some West European states – Sweden, Switzerland, Spain and Portugal – had not been involved in the war and had benefited accordingly; in Sweden and Switzerland, their own special systems of democracy continued to prosper, whilst in Spain and Portugal their dictators, Franco and Salazar, survived skilfully, till 1975 when Franco died and 1974 when Portugal had a revolution. Britain, after emerging from the war with her prestige higher than ever, suffered a serious decline in importance through her inability to afford the rapidly rising costs of being a great power, whilst her commitments in many parts of the world still meant that she had to spend vast sums on her armed forces. Suspicious of the movement for unity in Europe, Britain failed to take the opportunity of playing a leading part in it, and when she did finally act, it was in vain. Plagued with repeated financial troubles and with doubts as to her future role in the world, Britain's post-war years were not wholly happy ones.

b) Post-war Recovery

The devastation of war was particularly bad in Germany, though the Netherlands, Belgium, France, Italy and Britain also suffered heavily. In the immediate post-war period, the United Nations, through its Refugee and Relief Organisation, struggled with the problems of poverty, homelessness and even starvation. Homes had been destroyed, industries and transport disrupted, soldiers returned home and refugees fled, or were pushed, from Poland, East Germany and Czechoslovakia. One quarter of all houses in Germany had been destroyed or were so badly damaged that they were unfit to live in and roads, railways, harbours and bridges had all suffered very heavily from the impact of war. The war also seriously affected Europe's food production: the production of wheat, for instance, was down to thirty per cent. of the production of wheat in 1938. As in 1919 America provided Europe with aid to help her recover from disaster – disaster so great that it is hard to appreciate from a distance of twenty-five years.

Marshall Aid

Between 1948 and 1952 substantial American economic help flowed from America to Europe to aid post-war recovery and, since Stalin stopped any East European states from participating, the benefits went solely to the democracies of West Europe. The scheme derived its name from General Marshall, the U.S. Secretary of State who suggested it to President Truman and it proved of immense value in helping West Europe surmount the initial post-war difficulties. Participation in the Marshall Plan was offered by the U.S.A. on condition that the various governments which took part in the scheme accepted the task of administering the programme and would make a joint effort in helping to carry it out. A European organisation, therefore, had to be set up to discover the requirements of the various countries in the way of goods and finance. It was this which led to the setting up of a Committee for European Economic Co-operation – later changed to the Organisation for European Economic Co-operation. The sixteen European states in the scheme which included West Germany (represented until October, 1949, by the Allied Commanders of the occupational forces in Germany) were joined shortly afterwards by Yugoslavia and Spain as well. Thus funds from the U.S.A. not only helped to revive trade and production but also developed habits of co-operation and sharing which were a useful basis for the later growth of a movement for economic unity in Europe. The O.E.E.C. was finally wound up in 1960 to be replaced by the Organisation for Economic Co-operation and Development in which the U.S.A., Canada and Japan were full members. Marshall Aid was a very generous act by the U.S.A., but it should be seen in the light of American foreign policy of the time, of propping up West Europe against Stalinism. The Americans believed prosperity in West Europe would mean that Communism would lose its attraction to workers.

Recovery in West Germany

If the Russians had succeeded in having their way, the recovery of Germany would have been seriously delayed, for Russia, who had been especially badly hit by the German attack, asked for large-scale compensation. Molotov demanded from Germany 10,000 million dollars worth of goods, machinery and equipment to be supplied over a ten year period. At first, the U.S.A. seemed sympathetic towards the Russians, and an American official, Henry Morgenthau, declared that Germany was such a danger to world peace she should lose the industries, like Krupps, which made it possible for her to wage war. But as the Western powers and Russia became increasingly hostile to each other, so the former came to the conclusion that ruining Germany to benefit Russia was not in their own interests. Instead, a scheme was mounted to help Germany recover so she could join in the alliance to block Stalin's Eastern Europe. For four years, Germany was under the military rule of the four occupying allied powers, but the mounting cold war with Russia led to the three Western powers creating the West German Federal Republic with its capital at Bonn and an outlying fragment in West Berlin. The three Western powers did this by first reviving local government and then building up a federal government by joining the British and U.S. zones and later (April 1949) adding the French zone. The chief political parties which emerged following the setting up of the new Republic were the C.D.U. (Christian Democrats) and the S.P.D. (Social Democrats) and it was the leader of the former party, Konrad Adenauer, who in September 1949 was elected Federal Chancellor. The stability of the skilful rule of this elderly ex-mayor of Cologne, American aid, Dr. Erhard's management of the economy, and the energy and determination of the German people themselves, brought about a much more prosperous situation in Germany after 1948. It seems odd, indeed, that this revival should be led by a man who had been dismissed from his post as mayor of Cologne by a British officer because it was thought he did not have the energy to help Cologne recover from the war.

Revival in France

De Gaulle controlled the provisional government which ruled France, but he failed to secure the creation of a constitution for the Fourth Republic which was in line with his ideas of government and retired to make way for the old-style politicians, Communists, Radicals, Socialists and M.R.P., who brought back with them the frequent changes of government of pre-war France. Yet in spite of this, France recovered well from the war, chiefly through the skill of her civil servants and officials, in particular Jean Monnet, a brilliant economist who produced a series of plans for the French economy which first concentrated on key areas like steel, fuel, and transport, and then took in other branches of the economy too. A second plan in 1954, a third in 1958, and a fourth in 1962 provided for France planned investment, the growth of large numbers of technical and managerial experts and improved social services. Though governments changed in France, further stability was provided by Bidault and Schuman who controlled foreign affairs until 1954.

Italian Revival

War devastation in Italy was less serious than in either Germany or France and was limited largely to Rome and Florence. Recovery was rapid, thanks to American aid and the influence of a new leader, President Alcide de Gasperi. Like Adenauer in Germany, de Gasperi was a Christian Democrat. After his Party won a majority in the Italian Senate

One of the towns hardest hit by war damage outside London was Coventry. This
picture shows the damage to the city centre after an air raid in November, 1940.

in 1948 it came under heavy criticism from the Communists led by
Palmiro Togliatti but benefited from a split amongst the Socialists some
of whom followed Nenni and backed the Communists while others would
have nothing to do with the Communists. For eight years de Gasperi
presided over Italian recovery during which time her industries in
the north boomed, benefiting from the plentiful supply of labour
drawn from the poorer South, and produced high quality goods like cars,
motor cycles, scooters, and refrigerators which sold well throughout
the world.

Britain

Much to his indignation, Churchill, who had led Britain to victory, was
rejected by a majority of the electorate in July 1945 and a Labour Government, led by Clement Attlee, was swept into power by voters eager to see
real reforms to improve their country and prevent the return of the
unhappiness which had followed the previous war. The Labour Party
nationalised the coal mines, the railways and steel, set up a National

Health Service which provided free medical and dental care for all, provided increased and extended old age pensions and gave allowances for all children after the first. In 1944 the Butler Education Act had promised secondary education for all and the Labour Party proceeded to put this into effect, setting up grammar and secondary modern schools, raising the school leaving age to fifteen, abolishing fees in state schools and giving grants to enable pupils with ability to go on to university. All these reforms were costly – compensation had to be paid to the mine, steel and railway owners – but not only that, the mines and railways were in need of modernisation and reform and social reforms were obviously expensive. The Labour Party believed whole heartedly in reform and, when small charges for spectacles and dental care were imposed in 1950, Aneurin Bevan, one of the Party's chief architects of social reform, resigned. A severe winter in 1946, coupled with an acute housing shortage and the continuation of rationing made life in post-war Britain somewhat bleak. The Government attempted to tackle these problems, firstly by the rushed erection of thousands of pre-fabricated houses, secondly by designing and building bright 'new' towns like Stevenage and East Kilbride and thirdly by organising the Festival of Britain in 1951, an expensively arranged shop window to show off Britain's recovery to the world. But the continuing restrictions, represented by the stern figure-head of the Chancellor of the Exchequer, Sir Stafford Cripps, probably contributed to the drop in Labour's popularity in 1950 and their defeat in 1951. But at least the large-scale unemployment which followed the First World War was avoided.

c) Vanishing Empires

Europe's post-war divisions and her economic troubles clearly showed her reduced power. European states were too exhausted and weak to dominate the world and nothing indicated this more clearly than the speed with which their painfully acquired empires were lost. Spain and Portugal had not been involved in the Second World War and clung on to what was left of their empires, but Belgium hastened to part with the Congo, a Dutch attempt to cling on to the East Indies was in vain, and the huge French and British Empires disappeared rapidly. The few colonies left by 1969 had become more of a problem and burden to the colonialist powers than a source of pride and profit. In the Middle East, the British and French made no serious effort to recover control until 1956, when their attack on Egypt, who had just nationalised the Suez Canal, was a humiliating failure that had to be abandoned in the face of world wide anger. In Indo-China and Algeria, however, the

French fought hard to retain their empire, while in Malaya, Cyprus and Aden Britain became involved in costly wars. In Algeria and Rhodesia a large minority of white settlers plagued the home governments with their determination to avoid being swamped by independence on the terms of majority rule. Both countries found statesmen wise enough to see the folly of clinging on to empires. In France it was Mendès-France who ended the Indo-Chinese Empire and went a long way towards ending the North African Empire too, and both Labour and Conservative politicians played a part in freeing most of Britain's empire. Former colonies sometimes kept up contact with the mother country and gained aid in return, but the mother country could not dictate, and might even be bullied as Britain found in 1956 over Suez and when the expulsion of South Africa from the Commonwealth was successfully demanded. By 1969 the remaining fragments of the British Empire like Malta, Singapore and Gibraltar had become awkward, costly problems. Having advanced military power did not mean Britain could dominate people as events in Cyprus showed, for the movements against Britain, led by Grivas, triumphed and established Archbishop Makarios as P.M. To give independence was only to recognise the inevitable. Nor could the British Government continue to allow Commonwealth citizens to freely come and settle in Britain. An act in 1962 severely restricted their entry.

d) The Problem of Defence

The Truman Doctrine

Immediately the war was over, the Western powers began cutting their forces and U.S. troops began to leave Europe: not so the Red Army which continued to dominate Eastern Europe. One after another the East European states fell to Communists and alarm in West Europe naturally grew. In Greece the bitter struggle between Communists and non-Communists, supported by Britain, continued but soon the British were compelled to make it clear to the U.S. that they were unable to continue with the task of holding back Communism. In 1947 therefore President Truman issued a statement which came to be known as the Truman Doctrine in which he promised U.S. aid to help peoples stay free from the pressure of dictatorship of armed minorities and outsiders. This had world wide effects, but in Europe it meant American aid for Greece and the return of Americans in force to Europe (though, of course, they had not left their zones in Berlin and West Germany).

N.A.T.O.

In March 1948 Britain, France and the Benelux countries (Holland, Belgium and Luxembourg linked by a customs union in 1947) had signed a joint defence treaty, the Treaty of Brussels, and the fall of East Europe into Communist hands (Czechoslovakia fell in 1948) led the U.S. Government to decide that the U.S. should associate herself closely with this alliance. In April, 1949, the U.S.A., Canada, Iceland, Denmark, Norway, Portugal and Italy joined the original allies to form the North Atlantic Treaty Organisation whose members would come to the aid of any of their number who was attacked. It was in reply to this that Russia organised the Warsaw Pact of East European states, but N.A.T.O. was slow to develop until the Korean War (1950) gave it impetus. Until the Korean war, N.A.T.O. was very much an alliance by which the U.S.A. was committed to protecting Western Europe; the drain of U.S. troops to Korea however meant that it was necessary for Europe to do more to protect itself. A Supreme Commander (Eisenhower) was appointed to head a joint military command and a Secretary General led the official permanent organisation necessary to run N.A.T.O. The Americans were eager to bring the West Germans into N.A.T.O., but the prospect of a rearmed Germany greatly alarmed the French and lengthy discussions followed to find an acceptable solution.

The first solution was put forward by René Pleven, the French Minister of Defence, who suggested that the Germans supply troops to form part of a European Defence Community but that they should not have an independent national army of their own. Britain however, was not at all enthusiastic about this scheme and as a result the French themselves decided to reject it since they feared that, without British participation, the Germans would be too dominant in the Defence Community. The U.S.A. had hoped to strengthen the armies of the West and was angry at the French action, and the Germans too were offended. Britain's Anthony Eden played a large part in piecing together an agreement by which the Italians were brought in and Germany promised not to produce atomic, chemical, or bacteriological weapons, long range or guided missiles, bombers or warships. These restrictions could only be undone with the agreement of the Supreme Commander in Europe as well as two thirds of Germany's fellow allies in the West European Union. Not until 1955 was this difficulty finally resolved and West Germany permitted to have limited armed forces simply as part of a European army – whereas other countries retained national armies on loan to N.A.T.O. The Americans and British promised the French that they would keep large numbers of troops in Europe and the deal thus rounded off the question of German independence, for the occupation of West Germany ended and West Germany was thus recognised as an equal. N.A.T.O. was later joined by Greece and Turkey: its forces were not equal to the Russians in size, but its aim was to be strong enough to prevent a sudden swift attack, to be able to fight a delaying action during which the two sides could talk, with the threat that nuclear weapons would be used if necessary. In 1963 the U.S.A. attempted to solve the problems of Germany's wanting a share in nuclear weapons by putting forward a scheme for the provision of a force of twenty-five surface vessels, each with eight Polaris missiles, to be manned by crews made up of the Western allies – including Germans. This force, the M.L.F., pleased the Germans but the French were far less enthusiastic and the British began to suggest all kinds of alterations until finally the U.S.A.'s enthusiasm declined and the whole scheme was dropped.

The Weakening of N.A.T.O.

During the days of Stalin, West Europe felt constantly in need of military strength, but events in Russia following Stalin's death, plus the quarrel between Russia and China, made a war between N.A.T.O. and the Warsaw Pact Countries increasingly unlikely. Nuclear weapons now became a political hazard: some German leaders felt Germany should have them, while France busily set about developing her own nuclear weapons to prove she, too, was a great power. The Polish foreign minister, Adam Rapacki, suggested a nuclear free zone of Poland, Czechoslovakia and both Germanies, but this implied West Germany's leaving N.A.T.O. and was rejected. President Kennedy suggested a force with nuclear weapons should be created for N.A.T.O., manned by units from all nations (including Germans) but this scheme eventually failed and the whole future of N.A.T.O., in a Europe in which tension between East and West was decreasing was, by 1967, open to doubt. France was openly criticising N.A.T.O. and withdrawing her forces from its command. In addition she forced N.A.T.O. headquarters to shift from French soil and insisted that France should be allowed to develop her own defensive system since the Americans could not necessarily be trusted.

One result of Russia's invasion of Czechoslovakia in 1968 was to check this weakening of the forces of N.A.T.O., for the invasion aroused great alarm and dealt a hard blow to the French hopes that a European clash was ceasing to be likely. All the member states agreed that no further weakening of N.A.T.O. must be allowed to take place, and

Britain was able to offer the increase of her forces in Europe (especially naval units) as they withdrew from the distant parts of the world where Britain's large empire had once extended.

e) The Common Market

Systems of co-operation between European states grew up after the war. Apart from N.A.T.O. there was also the O.E.E.C. (Organisation for European Economic Co-operation) that administered Marshall Aid and the Council of Europe in Strasbourg where European Ministers held discussions. The two world wars had severely shaken the belief of Europeans in nationalism, they were more ready to co-operate than they had ever been before in order to defend themselves, prevent war and, increasingly, become more prosperous by reducing the trading restrictions between each other so that Europe could become eventually, one huge free market. The movement for unity, therefore, suited federalists (people who wanted to see old national boundaries destroyed and Europeans working together) those who disliked U.S. influence and hoped a united Europe might be more independent, and those who wanted to bring greater prosperity to Europe.

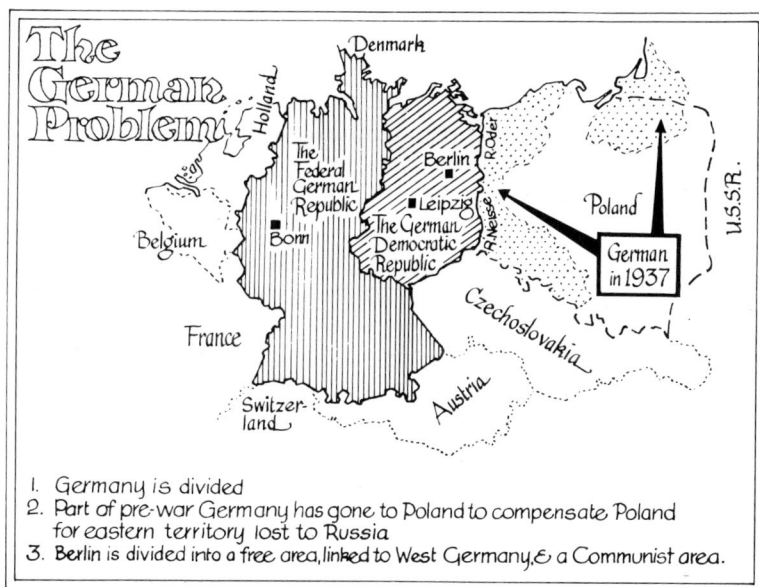

The German Problem

Denmark
Holland
The Federal German Republic
Bonn
Belgium
Berlin
Leipzig
The German Democratic Republic
R. Neisse
R. Oder
Poland
German in 1937
U.S.S.R.
France
Czechoslovakia
Switzerland
Austria

1. Germany is divided
2. Part of pre-war Germany has gone to Poland to compensate Poland for eastern territory lost to Russia
3. Berlin is divided into a free area, linked to West Germany, & a Communist area.

The Coal and Steel Community

Monnet, who had done so much for the post-war French economy, was soon thinking in terms of wider markets and won the alliance of Schuman, a prominent M.R.P. politician from Alsace-Lorraine who felt strongly about the need to end the clash of France and Germany. The Benelux countries had already begun breaking down trade barriers between themselves by 1951, and de Gasperi for Italy showed enthusiasm, too, for Monnet's plan to make a European free market for coal and steel. Finally, Adenauer and West Germany were won over, eager to free the Ruhr from Allied control as part of the plan and, like the others, ready to see vigorous changes in order to overcome the post-war difficulties of European coal and steel industries. In 1951 the European Coal and Steel Community came into being, ruled by a High Authority of nine and checked by a Court of Justice, a Council of Ministers and an Assembly which had power to force the High Authority to resign. Britain was invited to participate, too, but the post-war Labour Government felt suspicious of a movement in which non-Socialists were in charge and, like the Scandinavians, preferred not to be involved. Yet the Community was a great success, helped by a rise in steel prices, and the six who had created it were encouraged to go on to more ambitious schemes.

The forming of the E.E.C.

The experience gained in running the Coal and Steel Community could be applied to other fields and, once again, Monnet and Schuman were the driving force for a wider economic union, strongly backed by Speak the Belgian Foreign Minister. Lengthy negotiations begun in 1955 resulted in success when, on the 25th March, 1957, the Treaty of Rome, establishing the European Economic Community, was signed by the six countries who had formed the Coal and Steel Community. Once again Britain avoided becoming involved: her own suggestions for a much looser agreement, a free trade association, were turned down.

The six went on to establish a Commission, presided over by Hallstein, to govern the E.E.C., with a Court of Justice to check its actions, a Council of Ministers (from each state) to watch over it and an Assembly which met in Strasbourg, with Schuman as its first President, with power to dismiss the Commission. The scheme was that, by stages, the member states would reduce duties between themselves until, eventually, there would be free trade in goods, people would be able to travel freely from one state to another, and all would impose the same system of duties on trade with other lands. There were also vague promises that at some time in the future members would work out common commercial, economic and social policies. The plan was that the E.E.C. would move from a system by which one state could veto any proposal to a system of majority voting, but de Gaulle managed to delay the adoption of this development. To France, with her large farming community, it was very important that agricultural policy should be a part of the E.E.C., as well as industry, so it is not surprising that she had little time for the unsuccessful British plan.

Britain had suggested removing the barriers to the flow of industrial goods between member states but her plan made no provision for agriculture or the free movement, between states, of labour and capital, nor was there any attempt to adopt common economic and social policies. Finally, Britain hoped that members would each be free to decide their own tariffs with other countries; clearly Britain wanted a scheme to suit her own world trade, and especially her Commonwealth trade, and she could hardly expect the rest of Europe to agree to this. The E.E.C. scheme seemed a success as investment, production, trade and prosperity rose rapidly in all six nations, while the Investment Bank which was also set up was most helpful in providing money to improve economies – Italy especially benefited from this.

Difficulties

There were, of course, difficulties too, chiefly in agriculture. French policy here differed from that of her other partners because French farmers often had surplus produce to sell and the farmers of other lands were afraid this might affect their prosperity. As an example of this, in 1963 there were lengthy discussions over the establishing of Common agricultural prices which France wished kept low to suit the French farmers. De Gaulle was prepared to use all sorts of weapons to get his way, like the blocking of the M.L.F. nuclear force, and the holding up of general discussions between the E.E.C., E.F.T.A., and the U.S.A. Eventually a compromise was hammered out amid a certain amount of ill-feeling, but though there might be such differences, the members of the E.E.C. were all well aware that there was far more to be gained by staying together than by letting their quarrels go so far as to wreck the whole economic organisation of the six. A scheme for states to become associated with the Common Market was worked out, chiefly to benefit the former French colonies. But those, like Schuman, who hoped for political benefits, for the emergence of European government with increasing power to eventually create a federal state of

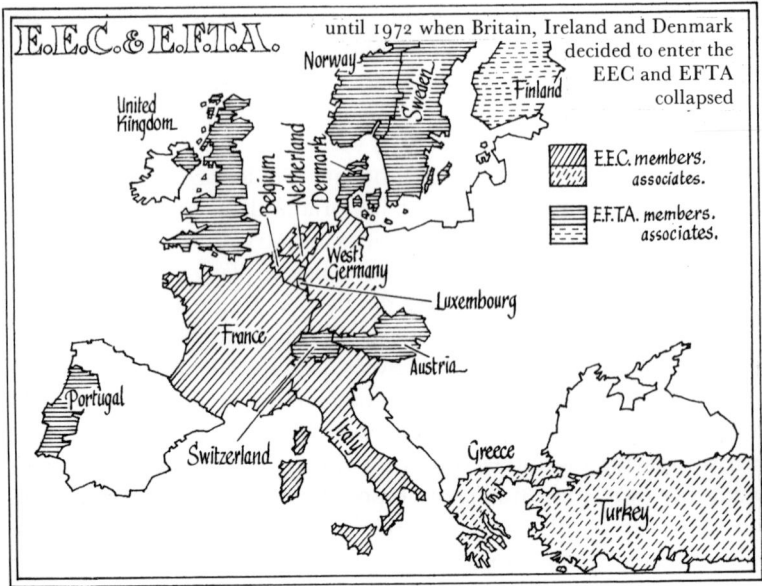

E.E.C. & E.F.T.A.   until 1972 when Britain, Ireland and Denmark decided to enter the EEC and EFTA collapsed

E.E.C. members, associates.

E.F.T.A. members, associates.

Europe, were disappointed by the hostility of France to this idea. De Gaulle preferred to think in terms of the six as forming a union of nation states; this annoyed men devoted to the ideal of European unity who believed that one of the eventual aims of the E.E.C. was to create a Europe that rose above nation states and caused their political separateness to fade away. In this respect, at any rate, de Gaulle was closer to Britain's attitude, for most British politicians (whether for or against joining the E.E.C.) feared the submerging of Britain in a united Europe.

f) de Gaulle

Both N.A.T.O. and the E.E.C. suffered setbacks consequent to the return to power of General de Gaulle in 1958. De Gaulle had ostensibly retired from politics in 1946, but made an unsuccessful bid to return in 1951. However, in 1958, he was swept back in triumph by a crisis which ruined the Fourth republic.

The downfall of the Fourth Republic

Though France's political climate changed frequently in the post-war years as Socialists, Radicals and M.R.P. battled for power and Communists made a nuisance of themselves, the failings of the Fourth Republic should not be overstressed. It helped create the prosperity of post-war France, it brought France into the E.E.C. and, under Mendès France, it began the very difficult task of cutting away the burden of the French empire. Tunisia and Morocco were granted independence without much difficulty but it was a different matter when Algeria demanded independence in 1954. For Algeria had a large European population and had always been considered a part of France. So strong were the feelings of the opposing factions – those who wanted independence and those against it – that a violent and bloody struggle ensued. The war dragged on, and all attempts to reach a satisfactory solution failed. In 1958, the colonists and army, afraid that Algeria was going to be abandoned by a weak French government, staged a revolution on the 13th May. They seized power in Algeria, took Corsica on the 23rd May, and soon had Paris trembling for its safety. To meet the crisis a great cry arose for the return of de Gaulle. Although de Gaulle had not voiced his own views over Algeria, the supporters of a French Algeria, led by Soustelle and General Massu, thought he favoured them, whilst the politicians considered de Gaulle preferable to a seizure of power by the paratroopers from Algeria.

The Fifth Republic

De Gaulle insisted that a new constitution must be drawn up to make strong government possible: for six months he was given authority to rule freely and then the constitution, which gave great power to the President enabling him to appoint Ministers, and weakened the Assembly, came into force. The followers of de Gaulle, the U.N.R., triumphed in the 1959 elections, as did de Gaulle in the elections for President.

ALGERIAN PROBLEM: At first de Gaulle's actions seemed to suggest that he supported the rebels in Algeria, but he moved cautiously towards negotiations for a free Algeria, knowing that most French people were weary of the war and that he had the prestige to carry people with him. Desperate attempts to stop this policy were tried, including risings in Algeria in 1960 and 1961, the forming of an anti-Gaullist secret army, the O.A.S., and plots and outrages including attempts on the General's life. All failed, Algeria became independent, rebel leaders were exiled or imprisoned and a popular vote showed overwhelming support for what de Gaulle had done.

DE GAULLE'S POLICIES: The benefits of post-war French economic recovery continued to flow in, though de Gaulle imposed increased burdens by his defence policy. He had always been very proud of French

N

General Charles de Gaulle held the office of President of France from 1959 until his retiral in 1969.

civilisation and culture, very hostile to Anglo-Saxon domination and was convinced that the U.S.A. could not be trusted to act always in conjunction with her allies. He developed nuclear weapons for France, he pulled away from N.A.T.O. and made visits and speeches which stressed the independence of France, he attacked U.S. policy in Vietnam and encouraged the French-originated settlers of Canada to assert themselves. Though elections reduced U.N.R. strength and de Gaulle had to face a serious contest to the Presidency in 1966 with Mitterand the Socialist Leader, repeated votes showed his skill in judging what most people wanted.

Early in 1968 discontent among students and workers led to demonstrations, riots and strikes which seemed likely to unseat de Gaulle. Yet elections showed that the stability and order he offered, as well as his promises of higher wages and a variety of reforms, appealed far more to the voters than the idealism of the student leader. Gaullists won a clear majority over their rivals and, with minor changes in his ministry, the General settled down once more to continue his rule.

But what should have been a further period of comfortable power for the General and his supporters before long turned into a situation in which the prosperity and independence he seemed to have provided for France were thrown into question. To end the troubles of May, 1968, and isolate the students, de Gaulle had been forced to promise big wage increases, whilst his determination to build up a nuclear force for France was very expensive. In November, 1968, cautious moves by the French government to try and make the franc stronger led to a belief among financiers that the French were going to devalue their currency, and caused a flutter in the International Money Market. Financiers rushed to get rid of their francs and buy instead the much stronger, safer, and more trustworthy German mark. De Gaulle was urged to devalue the franc, but he declared that such a solution would be absurd and a blow to French pride. Instead he preferred to announce severe cuts in government spending as a more satisfactory alternative. So the secure prosperity which he had promised seemed in doubt while the better relations between East and West Europe for which he had strived had been wrecked by the Czech crisis. Since he had dismissed Pompidou, who had built up a very impressive position for himself, from the Premiership and replaced him by Couve de Murville, de Gaulle was bound to feel that criticism must fall on himself alone. This worsening situation finally led to de Gaulle's fall from power. In the spring of 1969 he planned a reform of government which, when put to a popular vote, clearly did not meet with the support that de Gaulle expected and convinced the general that at last he must retire.

g) Britain

From 1951 until 1964 Conservative governments led by Churchill, Eden (1955-7) Macmillan (1957-63) and Douglas-Home (1963-4) struggled with the persistent problems of a dying British empire, the costly business of defence, money troubles, and a rate of economic growth slower than that of many other industrial lands. The Conservatives had come to power with promises of a better Britain: they abolished rationing and improved the housing situation, but the economic difficulties remained. Macmillan was convinced the solution lay in Britain joining the E.E.C.

The failure to join the E.E.C.

From 1961 to 1963 British negotiators, led by Edward Heath, worked hard to solve the problems of joining Britain, with her different system of agriculture, her responsibilities to the Commonwealth and E.F.T.A., to the Treaty of Rome. E.F.T.A. had been created in 1959 as a most unsatisfactory reply to the E.E.C.; it was smaller, less united and looser, and its members, the three Scandinavian countries, Britain, Portugal, Switzerland and Austria, were dominated by Britain. The E.F.T.A. countries planned to abolish tariffs between one another over a ten year period and trade within the area certainly increased. The chief

Commonwealth difficulties centred round food produced by Australia and New Zealand for the British market, yet even these difficulties seemed capable of solution until de Gaulle vetoed the British application to join on 14th July, 1963. Since the E.E.C. members had to be unanimous, this killed Britain's application, and de Gaulle explained at length that he felt Britain was not ready to join Europe, she had too many links with other parts of the world and was too closely tied to the U.S.A. Perhaps de Gaulle was angry at the refusal of Britain and the U.S.A. to share their secrets about nuclear weapons with France, and certainly he had reason to feel that British defence was heavily bound to the U.S.A. The scheme to build an independent British rocket, the 'Blue Streak' was abandoned in 1960. Britain then planned to buy 'Skybolt', a missile launched from bombers, from the U.S. but 'Skybolt' was scrapped in 1962. Then in December, 1962, without consulting de Gaulle, Harold Macmillan and President Kennedy had negotiated the Nassau agreements whereby Britain was to have Polaris submarines.

De Gaulle's suspicions of the U.S.A. were widely shared by many European politicians who feared U.S. control of European industry through her investments while others expected the U.S.A. to decide eventually that it did not need to maintain a military position in Europe as long range missiles made a foothold in Europe no longer essential. When Britain's hopes for 'Skybolt' missiles collapsed and de Gaulle expected her now to turn to Europe for her safety, Macmillan preferred to make a new agreement with the U.S.A. Germany's Chancellor Adenauer did not feel the need to exert himself overmuch for Britain; had not a British officer, in the past, declared him unfit to rule Cologne? Not only that, but Macmillan had tried to negotiate a European settlement with the U.S.S.R. and the U.S.A. without consulting Adenauer, although Germany's position in any European settlement was crucial.

The return to power of Labour

In October 1964, led by Harold Wilson, the Labour Party squeezed narrowly back into office with promises of reforms to cut defence down to size and carry out social and economic changes which would transform the country. In 1966 the Labour majority was greatly increased by a new election, but the party found sudden changes in policy very difficult to achieve. A huge debt was inherited which restricted reforms, it was not easy to cut defence commitments, for the U.S. was eager that Britain should stay in the Far East, and Malta furiously resented Britain's expressed desire to leave the island which depended on the British base for much of its employment. Reforms to improve social

Student demonstrators fight with the police on the Boulevard Saint Michel in the Latin Quarter of Paris in April, 1968.

security and education had therefore to be cautious. The continued slow rate of expansion of industry led Wilson and George Brown, his Foreign Secretary, to submit a new application in 1967 to join the E.E.C. This application, too, was thwarted by de Gaulle and the Government's problems continued to be so great that major social changes were prevented. Instead of greater prosperity, Britons were faced by higher taxes and in November 1967, the devaluation of the pound introduced by a new Chancellor of the Exchequer, Roy Jenkins.

Slowly, nevertheless, Britain was altering: more new towns were built, the railways were modernised by Dr. Beeching and the coal mines by Lord Robens, motorways began to cross the land, new industries boomed and automation increased. Edward Heath's Conservative Government, 1970–74, at last successfully negotiated British entry to the EEC.

h) Conclusion

By 1967 de Gaulle was one of the few important leaders of the war and the immediate post-war years to occupy still a prominent position. In 1963 Adenauer finally resigned from politics at the age of 87. His party had declined in strength and his successor, Erhard, depended on the support of the small Free Democrat Party to stay in power. This alliance proved his downfall for in December, 1966, the Free Democrats refused to agree to tax increases and Erhard lost office. After long negotiations, an alliance was formed of Christian Democrats, now led by Kiesinger, the new Chancellor, and Social Democrats led by Willy Brandt, former mayor of West Berlin and now Vice Chancellor and Foreign Minister. Under Brandt and (1974) Helmut Schmidt, the Social Democrats have carried West Germany cautiously forward to even greater prosperity.

De Gasperi no longer ruled Italy and Italian politics became less stable as a result: a variety of coalitions ruled the country, but Italy's new found prosperity in the North (between 1953–61 Italian industrial production doubled) and attempts to extend this to the South, denied power to the Communists (the largest C.P. in West Europe). In Spain, Franco continued to rule, but the problems of what would happen after his death loomed larger, although he seemed to be in favour of a return to monarchy. The Scandinavian democracies continued their prosperous and stable course, linked to Britain by E.F.T.A.; though somewhat annoyed by Wilson's disregard for E.F.T.A. by imposing a fifteen per cent. surcharge on imports to meet a financial crisis in 1964* they were ready to agree to Britain's new application to join the E.E.C., and, indeed, Denmark and Norway proceeded to submit applications of their own.

By 1967, then, Europe was experiencing greater prosperity than ever before, the movement to break down national boundaries was meeting with some success, tension with East Europe was reduced and the extremist parties which had so troubled Europe between the wars could make small impression on politics in the 1960's. The events of 1968 were, however, a warning against taking too optimistic a view of Europe's future. With Russia's invasion of Czechoslovakia the suspicions of West Europe were revived, a new determination to make N.A.T.O. effective appeared and hope for an early return to good relations with Eastern Europe was blocked by Russia's insistence on keeping her East European allies firmly under control. The financial troubles first of Britain, then of France, showed how vulnerable these countries were to economic pressures, how the affluence many Europeans were coming to take for granted was, in fact, far from secure. Economic troubles helped defeat first Labour (1970) then Conservative (1974) rule in Britain. From 1974 the Labour Government led by Wilson and (1976) Callaghan struggled with Britain's huge debts and weak currency, relying on oil from the North Sea to offset these troubles.

*Reduced to a ten per cent. surcharge on 27th April 1965.

Communism in Post 1945 E.Europe

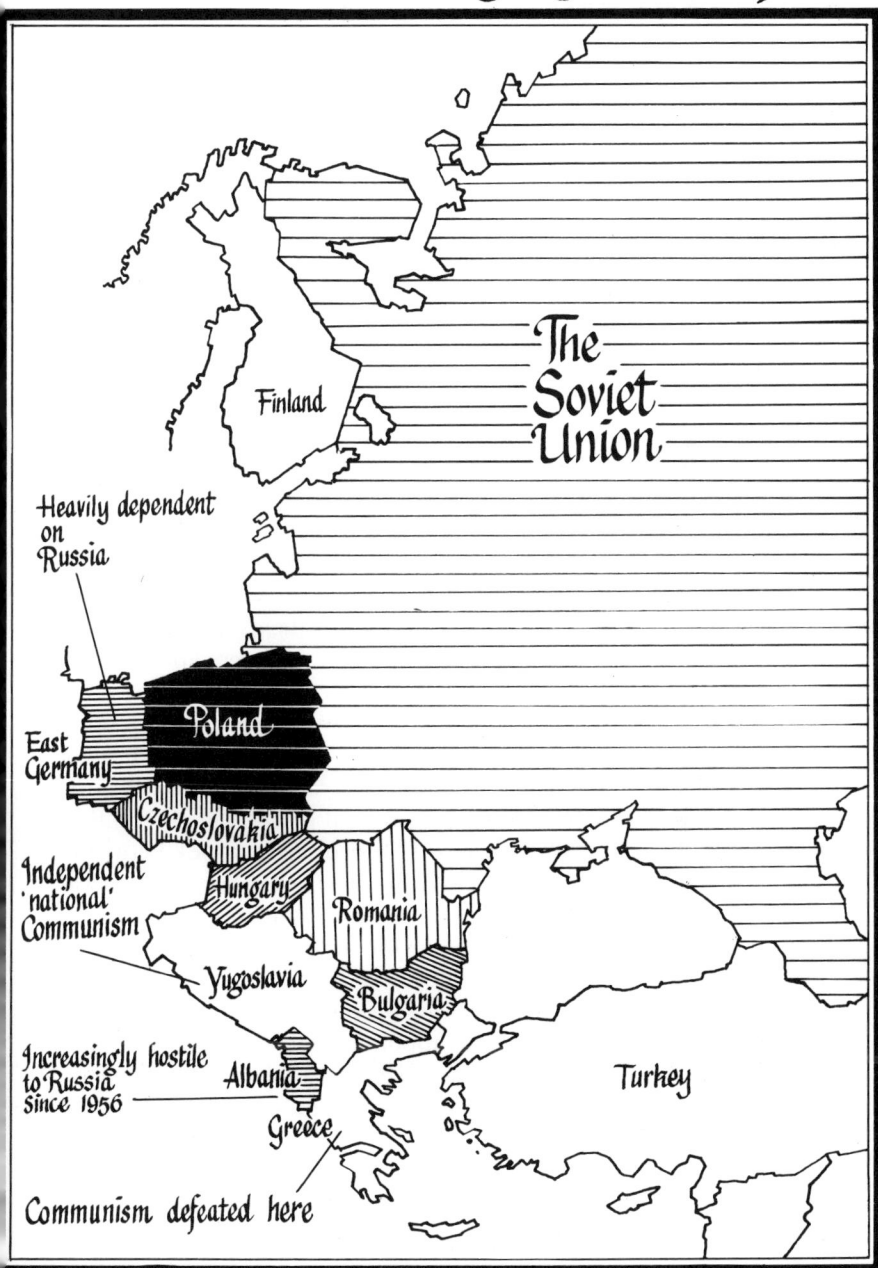

The
Soviet
Union

Finland

Heavily dependent on Russia

Poland

East Germany

Czechoslovakia

Independent 'national' Communism

Hungary

Romania

Yugoslavia

Bulgaria

Increasingly hostile to Russia since 1956

Albania

Greece

Turkey

Communism defeated here

8 | The Americans

Latin America

a) The Colonial Background

The Conquest of Latin America

Unlike Africa, South and Central America contained advanced civilisations when Europeans first arrived. The Mayas of Honduras, Guatemala and Yucatan, the Aztecs of Mexico and the Incas of Peru had developed well-organised societies with roads, massive buildings and fine pottery and metalwork. However, the Aztecs and Incas were not always popular with the peoples they had conquered, partly because of the savage religious rites they practised, so the Spanish and Portuguese invaders found many allies ready to help them overthrow the rulers of South and Central America. The conquest of Latin America was an astonishing achievement by small groups of men who used their superior weapons and skill as horsemen to such great effect that they were able to overthrow the mighty empires of the South American Indians.

Following the arrival of Columbus in the West Indies in 1492, other adventurers from Spain were attracted to this New World by stories of vast wealth to be found there, stories which were soon proved to be true by the discovery of gold and silver in several places, but especially in Peru. Cortes and his followers seized Mexico, Pizarro took Peru, and soon the riches of Latin America were flowing back to Spain. Brazil was captured by the Portuguese, and small British, French and Dutch settlements grew up in Central America. But it was the Spaniards who predominated, they took vast wealth from the area, and gave little in return other than their language, religion and way of life. Spain ruled strictly through a system of Viceroys appointed from the mother country; not only were the native Indians excluded from all share in government, so were Spaniards born in America (known as *creoles*) and men of mixed Spanish and Indian blood (the *mestizos*). However, Latin America was not united by Spain, despite the three centuries of peace which followed conquest, for the mountainous and often jungle-covered nature of the land made it difficult to have anything but a series of quite separate settlements.

The End of Spanish and Portuguese rule

In the early nineteenth century, colonial rule came to an abrupt and violent end in most of Latin America. The War of American Independence and the French Revolution were precedents for throwing off harsh governments which began to make the creoles restless. When Napoleon conquered Spain the link between Latin America and Spain was snapped and an attempt to recover Spain's former colonies by Ferdinand VII, the cruel and incompetent Spanish King restored after Napoleon's defeat, met with vigorous opposition. The people who had been managing their own affairs whilst the French ruled Spain would not accept the return of Spanish viceroys and rebelled. Their leaders were creoles like Simon Bolivar and San Martin and they were assisted by foreign volunteers, especially British seamen like Lord Cochrane. British trade with the area had been growing and Britain believed an independent Latin America would be a very valuable area with which to do business. Latin America was freed by the creole-led forces and by Britain's refusal to let Spain and her allies send more troops to the area, but it made little difference to ordinary people that their government had changed. The creoles were small in number and far richer than the Indians and they were not willing to share either wealth or power. All Simon Bolivar's hopes of linking the former Spanish Colonies together to form a federation were disappointed and Latin America remained a series of separate states ruled by dictators. Whereas Spanish Viceroys had been the dictators, now it was the creoles who provided the strong men (known as *caudillos*) to run governments. This focusing of government around a strong leader has remained one of the most striking features of Latin American politics, even though the leaders found it necessary to try and widen the areas from which they drew support. The rest of Spain's Empire also soon collapsed. The island of Santa Domingo broke out in slave riots and after years of upheaval emerged as a divided country in which the state of Haiti formed one part of the island and the Dominican Republic occupied the rest. Spain was left clinging on to Cuba, Puerto Rico, and the Philippines; in all of these areas government was corrupt and there was a constant fear of revolt.

Portugal parted from her massive colony of Brazil far more peacefully. In Brazil a separate empire developed following the exile there of the Portuguese royal family during the French occupation of their homeland. Brazil continued to be ruled by a separate branch of the Portuguese royal family until the death of Pedro II in 1889 when royal government disappeared, with little protest, and Brazil became a republic.

Latin America

USA

Mexico

Brit. Honduras

Atlantic Ocean

Cuba

Honduras

Dominica

Guatemala

Haiti

Puerto Rica

Salvador

Nicaragua

Costa Rica

Panama

Venezuela

Guyana

Surinam

Colombia

French Guiana

Ecuador

Peru

Brazil

Bolivia

Pacific Ocean

Paraguay

Chile

Uruguay

Argentina

Falkland Islands [Brit]

b) Latin America in 1900

In 1900 the states of Latin America were still run by caudillos and were still undemocratic. Because the mass of the people were poor and generally illiterate, and since there was a tradition of undemocratic rule, political troubles usually consisted of squabbles within the small group of the ruling class. Governments were still far from masters of their lands, for deserts, mountains and jungles divided up countries into scattered settlements. Some states had also suffered from foreign attack, notably Mexico, which had experienced a French attempt at conquest and had lost large areas of land to the U.S.A.

Economic problems

Economically, as well as politically, control of affairs lay with a small group of powerful men who had, by 1900, made some effort to develop their lands with the help of foreign capital. Spain had attempted to stifle industries in her colonies for fear of competition and had sought to use the colonies almost entirely as a source of precious metal. The creole rulers of the nineteenth century were landowners who were short of both skill and capital to develop industries. Foreign aid was necessary and it was now that Britain benefited from her support of the area in its bid for freedom as well as from her control of the seas. Britain had capital and skill to export and not even the U.S.A. was able to rival the economic power of Britain in Latin America during the nineteenth century. Foreigners sought from Latin America products which were profitable, they did not seek to develop sound economics based on several products, and they only invested in public utilities, like railways, if there was likely to be a profit here too. Latin American states tended to become too dependent on single products and were, as a result, very vulnerable to world trading conditions. Immigrants came from Europe to Latin America, especially Argentina where between 1857 and 1930 over six million immigrants, chiefly Italian, settled. By 1950 cities were growing rapidly as ports, centres of government and industry. Growing numbers of working and middle class people, dissatisfied with being ruled by small groups of landowners, were beginning to flourish in the cities. Argentina was soon the most prosperous state, its interior opened up by a network of railways so that meat could easily be transported to the coast and then shipped abroad in refrigerator ships. Chile's major export in the nineteenth century was nitrates, used as a fertiliser. This boom ('the Age of Manure') lasted till 1914 when there was a decline as substitute fertilisers were discovered, and copper became the economic mainstay instead. Brazil produced coffee, cotton and rubber; in 1900 it supplied over three-quarters of the world's coffee and nearly all the world's rubber. However, the Brazilians' dominance of the market had, by 1912 been undermined by their careless exploitation of wild rubber and by the development of carefully tended rubber plantations in the Far East, from seeds smuggled out of Brazil by an Englishman. Even in the field of coffee production, Brazil was beginning to meet serious competition by 1914.

In areas where trade and industry flourished, so did large cities like Buenos Aires and São Paulo. The caudillos who ruled Latin America were gradually forced to realise that landowners were no longer the only class to be considered, and that business interests also mattered. Social improvements were made very grudgingly for governments were most reluctant to tax the wealthy, and foreign concerns in Latin America cared only about political stability. Anyway, the mass of the population were still too ignorant and poorly organised to exert much pressure. Change became more rapid with the growth of industry, the mounting resentment of workers against their living conditions, and the grievances of the peasantry against their enforced poverty. To this was added a feeling that foreigners were draining Latin America of its wealth and giving little in return. This was what created a series of upheavals which racked the area in the twentieth century.

c) New Caudillos – Support from the Lower Classes

In several states, the increasing working class and the growing resentment of the peasantry encouraged the emergence of leaders who were willing to offer something to these people. The outstanding example of this type of new caudillo came in Argentina, but in other states, too, governments made more effort to win backing from lower class groups. Such a policy was risky, however, for if it went too far, the right wing, perhaps with army aid, or even with U.S. help, might intervene.

Argentina

The strong hold of foreigners on Argentina's economy, plus the political power of a small group of landowners, became increasingly a thorn in the flesh of the people of the cities – especially the huge population of Buenos Aires – and to those with strong nationalist feelings. These feelings were cautiously expressed in a Radical Party which managed to push its candidate, Irigoyen, into the position of President, in 1916. But Irigoyen proved both despotic and corrupt and despite the social reforms he introduced, was ejected from power by a right-wing coup. A much bolder bid for wider support began in 1943 when Colonel Juan Peron became head of the Labour Secretariat in a military government established in that year to modernise Argentina and free it from foreign dominance. Peron, aided by his wife Eva, used his position very skilfully to strengthen his prestige with workers. He patronised leading Argentina sportsmen, improved working conditions, encouraged trade unions over which he himself exercised control, and made the police into a kind of private army. His colleagues became envious of Peron's success and in 1945 they arrested him, but there was such an outcry (mobilised by Eva) that Peron had to be released. He formed a political party, the Labour Party, which triumphed in elections in 1946 winning majorities in the Senate and Chamber of Deputies and making Peron himself President.

Peron strengthened his position by attempting to suppress opposition, by purging the universities, by building hospitals and houses and by attacks on foreign influence in Argentina. He nationalised foreign utilities like the British-owned railways and interfered increasingly in the economy to secure minimum wages, shorter hours, and holidays with pay. His foreign policy offended other countries, including the U.S.A., for he openly sympathised with Italy and Germany during the Second World War. After 1950, the tide of popular opinion began to run against him. Peron had not broken up the large landowners' estates, but he had broken their monopoly of power and he had placed all the stress on industry, not agriculture. Eva's death was a serious blow, for her glamour, her lower class origins, and her zeal for social reform had done much to maintain her husband's popularity. Peron also found himself having to cope with an economic crisis stemming from drought and bad harvests and dislike aroused by the corruption and repression of his regime. He attempted to modify his policy both by trying to attract foreign investment and by paying attention to the interests of employers and professional men, but it was already too late and in 1955 he lost power to the army which had been alarmed by news that Peron was planning to distribute weapons to members of the trade unions he had organised.

Three years of military rule followed, then in an election in which Peronists were not allowed to stand, a Radical, Frondizi, was elected President with the help of Peronist votes only to be deposed in 1962 when he allowed Peronists to stand in elections. Peron's personal popularity had declined, as a vain attempt to return to power in 1964 demonstrated, but his period of office is an outstanding example of a

The former President of Argentina, Juan Peron, with his second wife Isabel, photographed during his exile in Spain.

break with the tradition of too much reliance on foreign capital and power vested in small groups of wealthy people. There has been a tremendous growth in city population in Argentina and there is a high standard of literacy yet democracy continues to find it very difficult to flourish in this prosperous land. After General Onganio's military rule, 1966–73, Peron at last returned. But he was now too old to be effective, died in 1975 and left a widow who ruled in his place under army supervision.

Mexico

A similar hostility to the influence of foreigners developed in Mexico plus resentment against the way the country was run by a small group of wealthy men. Diaz, a caudillo of the old school, was overthrown in 1911 partially by an alliance of people who thought dictatorship was wrong, and partially by ordinary Indian peasants who rebelled in protest against their wretched existence. A civil war of great savagery dragged on for many years during which many thousands died and the peasants established themselves as a force with which to be reckoned. They produced leaders like Zapata and demanded that they be given land from the estates of the wealthy landowers. Eventually fighting died down as a strong political party was organised, the Revolutionary Institutional Party, whose leaders carried out reforms. Instead of finding a new caudillo who would enforce changes, Mexico found a single party to control government and within which a series of leaders carried out reforms. The power of the Roman Catholic Church was reduced (despite a three year strike by priests), the property of British and American oil companies was seized in 1937, and some land was distributed among the peasants. Mexico is still a one party state in which the outgoing president strongly influences the choice of his successor and its economy has been developing with the help of the National Bank and the U.S.A. But more recently, under the leadership of Mateos, the pace of social and political reform has tended to slow down and be replaced by a desire simply to stay in office, even if this meant corruption and violence. Mexico's difficulties were highlighted when the Olympic Games were held in Mexico City in 1968. Just prior to the Games, Mexico's President, Diaz Ordaz, was faced with demonstrations by students and some sections of the working people critical of the way Mexico was being governed. He attempted to deal with this trouble by violent methods. The demonstrators, who claimed they wanted Mexico to be ruled according to its constitution, and not harshly bullied by a man who broke the constitution, were roughly man-handled by troops, trying to secure order before the Olympic Games began. With the Games over, Mexico faded from the world's headlines, but her people were left with the same problems as before.

Brazil

Although Brazil is a huge state with vast resources she has many problems including a persistently high rate of illiteracy and the concentration of most of her population in a relatively small coastal area. Her economic troubles, stemming from over-dependence on rubber and coffee, grew gradually worse until in 1930 there was a major crisis. As in Argentina and Mexico, a new type of caudillo, Getulio Vargas, emerged. Vargas saw the need to win support not just from a small group of rich land-owners but also industrialists and workers. He therefore carried out a number of reforms including a programme of public works and the development of textiles, steel, paper, and chemical industries. Vargas was finally compelled to resign in 1954, in his later years he had been increasingly unsuccessful and he eventually committed suicide. For a time, under first President Kubitschek and later President Goulart, Brazil had something more akin to a democratic system of government until, in 1964, Goulart was removed from power by the army, which thought him far too left-wing and not very capable. Thus, Brazil too became a military state, in this case under the leadership of General Costa e Silva. But the period of democracy had seen a bold experiment organised by President Kubitschek (1956–61) to open up the interior of the country by building an entirely new capital inland. The new capital, Brasilia, was designed by architects as one of the most striking modern cities in the world, though they could not prevent the inevitable huddle of poor dwellings from gathering around it, as around most Latin American cities. In Brazil, as in much of South America, great gulfs 'yawn' between rich and poor: less than two per cent. of the population own half of all agricultural land and coffee accounts for so much of Brazil's exports (over sixty per cent.) that any difficulty here hurts many workers.

Venezuela

After a costly and damaging struggle for independence, Venezuela remained unable to find a stable system of government until 1908. In that year, Juan Gomez seized power and ruled harshly for twenty-seven years. The discovery of oil was of immense benefit to the country's economy but, at first, the profits went either to the foreign oil companies or to the small ruling group in the country. This unsatisfactory situation helped the rise to power of politicians determined to change it and in 1945 Betancourt, leader of the *Accion Democratica* party, succeeded in winning office. He began a programme of redistributing land to help the poorer people, but his efforts to reduce the power of the army caused military leaders so much alarm that in 1950, led by Colonel Jimenez, they seized power. Until 1958 the army ruled, supported by businessmen and foreign oil companies, but Jimenez became very extravagant and the influence of foreigners offended even members of his own armed forces. In 1958, another revolt, led by young army and naval officers, restored a democratic system of government and allowed Betancourt to return to power. More reforms were introduced including programmes to improve education and health, money was raised by increasing the taxation on the oil companies' profits. In 1963 Betancourt had to resign the presidency as new elections were due and the constitution did not permit him another term of office. His successor, President Leoni, continued Betancourt's policies with the aim of making Venezuela one of the most prosperous and democratic countries in Latin America.

International Olympic teams circle the track at University Stadium during the official opening of the XIXth Olympic Games in Mexico City.

Uruguay

During the nineteenth century Uruguay was unable to find a stable government, yet it had many advantages over neighbouring territories for it was compact, free of mountain and jungle and inhabited by an almost wholly European population. Thus Uruguay was free from the problem of several peoples – European, Indian, negro and half-caste – living together, which made difficulties in some states. It was Batlle, President between 1903 and 1907 and again from 1911 to 1915, who set the pattern for the modern, democratic state of Uruguay which has the most advanced system of social security in Latin America. Uruguay was provided with benefits for people who were old, out of work or ill and her education system was improved. A new political system was organised with the deliberate aim of avoiding the emergence of a powerful man who might try and dominate the country. The army was kept so small that it could not be troublesome and the government was run by a national council of nine members, not by a single president. Yet despite all these benefits, Uruguay continued to be plagued by problems, but particularly from poor economic policies, from wasteful methods of government, and from inflation.

In all the Latin American states, the changes that have taken place have weakened the stranglehold on the government by the rich land-

o

owner class whose own fortunes have in turn diminished. Changes have come about without violent social revolutions, but huge problems still remain. Poverty and illiteracy continue, while the rise in population always threatens to outgrow the rise in industrial production.

d) Social Upheaval

Other Latin American states have not progressed so peacefully, but have suffered violent social and political upheavals that threaten to be far more drastic than the moderate policies of Betancourt or Goulart. In Bolivia, Guatemala and Cuba in particular, there have been great changes and much suffering, and it is the fear that Communism might obtain a firm hold in these areas that has led the U.S.A. to interfere more and more in the affairs of Latin American states.

Bolivia

There are great extremes of wealth in Bolivia, riches derived from tin and agriculture, and poverty among the peasants and mineworkers. Until 1932 its government was controlled by a small group of wealthy people who, although they sometimes squabbled among themselves, agreed not to share political power or economic wealth with the mass of the population. But in 1932 Bolivia became involved in the Chaco war with Paraguay and in this three year contest for control of a border area the Bolivians were defeated. The defeat brought disgrace to Bolivia's rulers and led to the emergence of the National Revolutionary Party, led by Victor Paz Estenssoro and backed by the workers from the tin mines. Between 1943 and 1946 the party shared power with the army, but the army leaders were very suspicious of its reforms and in 1946 pushed out the party members and replaced them by right-wing politicians. In 1951 elections were held and Paz appeared to be triumphant, but again the army intervened to block his path to power. This time, however, armed tin workers, students and peasants rose in rebellion and forced the army to allow Paz into power. Paz proceeded to nation-alise the tin mines, find land for the peasants from the big estates and bring the Indians (who formed half of Bolivia's population) into politics. Unfortunately tin prices fell, it was difficult to find enough food for the growing population and the party split between the moderates led by Paz and Hernan Siles who were ready to take U.S. help, and extremists led by Lechin who violently opposed foreign aid. Once more the army intervened, angry at the way Paz was arming the tin workers to try and protect his position, and in 1964 General Barrientos seized power and exiled Lechin. Bolivia remains one of the most unstable states in the world, troubled by hostility between miners and government and vulnerable because its economy is so dependent on tin exports and the farming land is of such poor quality.

Guatemala

Like so many of the other states, Guatemala's instability was, in part, due to its economic dependence on only a few exports—in this case, bananas and coffee. The rule of a series of caudillos lasted here until 1945 when Juan Jose Arevalo took office with the intention of carrying out reforms. There was much to be done in the way of reforms, for one thing Guatemala was a very backward country in which the vast majority of the population were very poor and owned little of the land. U.S. influence was great in both agriculture (where the U.S. United Fruit Company was the biggest single landowner) and in docks, railways, shipping and electricity. The desire for reform was, therefore, linked to a dislike of foreign influence and during the rule of Jacobo Arbenz, Arevalo's successor, this became particularly clear. Arbenz took land from the large estates and gave it to peasants, he allowed the Communist Party legal status and it grew rapidly in size. The U.S. Government became so alarmed that it backed exiles from Guatemala, who had been training in Honduras, when they invaded the country in 1950 to over-throw Arbenz. Led by Colonel Castillo Armas these invaders were successful in toppling the government. However, Arbenz's social revolution could not be wholly undone, and though Communism was outlawed and the political system purged, some agricultural reforms continued.

Cuba

Whereas the Bolivian and Guatemalan social revolutions were at least partially checked, the Cuban revolution, far from being halted, became more extreme. The corrupt rule of Spain in the island led in 1895 to the growth of a Cuban nationalist movement led by Marti, which sought to win freedom. The U.S.A. sympathising with the rebels as well as being interested in developing the sugar production of Cuba hastened to recognise Cuban independence. When a U.S. warship, the *Maine*, blew up in baffling circumstances in Havana harbour, the U.S.A. proceeded to wage war on Spain. After an easy victory the U.S.A. imposed the Platt Amendment (1901) on Cuba by which naval stations on Cuba were leased to the U.S.A. and Cuba recognised that the U.S.A. could intervene if there were danger to life, property, or freedom on the island.

Dr. Fidel Castro, Prime Minister of Cuba since 1959.

American influence grew through her control of the Cuban economy, both in the dominant sugar industry and in the service industries of railways, electricity and telephones.

There were many reasons for Cubans to feel resentment, and the island, with its high rate of illiteracy and its large city population was a very restless trouble spot. The great gulf between rich and poor, U.S. influence, unemployment resulting from the seasonal nature of work on the sugar crop (it only provided four months work a year) were all sources of grievance, to which was added the growing corruption and brutality of the ministry of Fulgencia Batista, who dominated government between 1933 and 1958. In the protests that this situation aroused, a Havana law student, Fidel Castro, was prominent. He spent two years in prison after an unsuccessful attack on a barracks in 1953, but was not discouraged and in 1956 led a new expedition that failed, at first, and was forced to retreat into the mountains. His band of dedicated guerrillas was never large, but it forced Batista to use harshness and terrorism to try and stamp it out; and these acts so increased Batista's unpopularity that, by January 1959, Castro had triumphed, for Batista's forces betrayed him.

Castro promised many popular changes including much more liberty and many social reforms, but he found it was not easy to keep his promises since vigorous social reform hurt American interests. This was demonstrated in May 1959, when the seizure of much property, including some which was American, aroused American hostility. This hostility strengthened Castro's desire for freedom from U.S. influence, but unfortunately Cuba depended too heavily on her sugar crop to be wholly independent and so Castro turned to Russia for help. When the U.S.A. suspended the sugar quota it usually took from Cuba in 1960, Castro replied by seizing American property on the island. The Communist Party in Cuba increased in importance and many non-Communists left Castro's ministry as he was drawn closer to Russia. Yet despite these difficulties, Castro managed to carry out some reforms and improved the position of the peasantry in particular. His prestige increased when his forces easily dealt with an invasion by American trained exiles in 1961, but in 1962 he suffered something of a setback when U.S. threats forced Russia to withdraw the missiles she had been sending to Cuba. Though many difficulties remain in Cuba, and her close association with Russia reduces her prestige in Latin America, Cuba remains a constant warning to the U.S.A. that the need for social and economic reforms in the countries of Latin America can easily turn into violent hostility to the U.S.A. Cuba offers a refuge for left-wing exiles from other states, it provides a place where they can train and from which they can then go out and try to bring about revolutions at home.

e) U.S. Influence in Latin America

The tendency of the U.S.A. to regard Latin America as an area in which she holds special province was shown as early as 1823 when President Monroe issued his Monroe Doctrine, warning Europeans not to interfere in any part of the Western hemisphere including Latin America. The U.S.'s military might and economic strength mean that she is easily tempted into intervening in South American politics. These interventions have naturally aroused great anger in the Latin American states, where the Monroe Doctrine has never been popular even though it sometimes brought benefits, as for example when the U.S.A. prevented Britain expanding her colony of Guiana (now the independent state of Guyana) at the expense of Venezuela.

U.S. intervention

One of the most notable examples of U.S. interference came at the beginning of the twentieth century when the U.S.A.'s desire for a

Two steam shovels take the last bite out of the isthmus of Panama to complete the channel for the Panama Canal on May 20th, 1913. The Canal was finally opened to traffic on August 15th, 1914.

canal* across central America led to a quarrel with Colombia. Colombia refused to lease to the U.S.A. the area she required so the U.S. replied by encouraging the people of the area to demand a separate state, and by promptly backing them to create the independent country of Panama. In 1903 the new republic granted the U.S.A. control of a ten mile wide strip through which to cut the canal in return for money and by 1914 the canal had been completed despite all the engineering difficulties and the deadly diseases, yellow fever and malaria, carried by the mosquitoes of the area. This intervention was the work of Theodore Roosevelt, who was also responsible for adding to the Monroe Doctrine the Roosevelt Corollary which allowed the U.S.A. to intervene in Latin American states to check disorder and cruelty. This law was one-sided, the Latin American states did not agree to it, yet it was used to justify U.S. intervention in the Dominican Republic in 1905, 1916, and, yet again, in 1965. Haiti was invaded in 1915 and Nicaragua in 1912 on similar grounds, yet the results of U.S. occupation were by no means beneficial to the

*The canal had been begun by a French company in the 1880's, but massive debt forced it into liquidation. In 1903 France sold the rights to the U.S.A.

areas they affected for the U.S.A. tended to train forces to keep order in the areas they occupied and these forces were able to take control of the government when the U.S. forces left. In Dominica, for instance, Trujillo used his U.S. trained troops to seize power in 1924 and to back his brutal rule until 1961 when the assassination of the dictator himself ended this despotism.

The 'Good Neighbour' Policy

U.S. policy was not always so selfish, however, and in 1933 President Franklin D. Roosevelt made it clear that he did not intend to follow earlier U.S. actions but would, instead, endeavour to make the U.S.A. a 'good neighbour' to the Latin American states. Although this meant that the U.S.A. withdrew from some of its interventions in Latin America (pulling out of Haiti for instance) the Latin American states themselves received little direct benefit other than the possibility of receiving loans. When the Second World War involved the U.S.A., Latin America clearly could not be counted on for support and U.S. leaders had to buy support by sending arms. Few Latin American forces fought in the war, instead the flow of U.S. weapons served to make stronger the armies in the various states of Latin America, so making it easier for them to control the politics of their own lands.

Even after 1945 when the U.S.A. made new efforts to build organisa-tions to help Latin America, the amount of help was very small. U.S. leaders were far more worried about the weakness of Europe and poured most of their aid across the Atlantic. So Latin American states continued to have little reason to feel affection for the U.S.A., and this suspicion was increased by U.S. policy in Guatemala in 1954. This country's poverty was in strong contrast to the profits made by the U.S. United Fruit Company which held a very powerful position in Guatemala. The Arbenz government attempted to reduce the United Fruit Company's power; in reply the U.S.A. gave help to Arbenz's enemies and brought about his downfall.

But, under Eisenhower, the 'good neighbour' policy began to be cautiously revived, and President Kennedy gave it an enormous stimulus by setting up the Alliance for Progress. Kennedy hoped to pour into Latin America twenty billion dollars' worth of aid to make possible economic and social reforms which those who received the aid had to promise to carry out. This programme, though huge, proved disappoint-ing, for Latin American problems were too enormous to be solved, even by a sum of this size. The early death of Kennedy helped to damage the programme and there was also confusion about how the aid should be given. Should it go to countries whose governments the U.S.A. disliked and, if not, would the poor in these countries be the chief sufferers? In the 1960's it became more difficult for the U.S.A. to be a 'good neighbour' as well as a stern opponent of Communism, for changes in governments in Latin America posed difficult problems. In Argentina, for instance, the armed forces were so alarmed by the giving of the vote to the former supporters of Peron, in 1962, that they intervened and altered the constitution to take away the vote from the groups that they did not trust. The U.S.A. disapproved of this and halted the flow of aid, but only for a short while. In Peru the U.S.A. took a similar step after the army had cancelled the 1962 elections because it did not approve of two of the candidates, but, once again, aid started to flow again after a little while. The U.S.A. had hoped all American countries would support its policy and would isolate a country where there were developments of which it did not approve, but in fact there was no real enthusiasm for such a policy and the U.S.A. soon felt embarrassed about its own action. When the army seized direct control of Peru in October, 1968, there was very little reaction from the U.S.A.

As the military seized power in state after state in the 1960's in Guatemala, Ecuador, and Honduras, so the U.S.A. seemed to have failed to fulfil Kennedy's hope that pouring out American aid would help establish moderate elected reforming governments who would be sufficiently popular to prevent Communism having any appeal. By 1965 the U.S.A. had reached the stage of being ready to intervene itself to keep out popular leaders of whom it did not approve. This was demonstrated in the Dominican Republic when Bosch, a reformer eager to undo all the harm done by the dictator Trujillo who had ruled the country for many years, went so fast that he offended the Church, upper classes, and much of the Army. The U.S. President, Johnson, was quick to recognise the new government which was forcibly put in power to replace Bosch in 1963, and, in 1965, when Bosch tried to stage a comeback with the help of some army units, U.S. marines rushed to the area to keep him out. Although U.S. intervention, carried out without consulting the Organisation of American States, clearly offended many Latin Americans, at least the U.S. leaders had the satisfaction of seeing the attraction of Castro's Cuba was fading. Administrative muddles, the failure of some industrial enterprises, the peasants' dislike of the way much of their farming was reorganised, together with Castro's harshness towards his critics in Cuba, all helped to disillusion the Latin Americans who had hoped for so much when Castro had first won power. Ernesto 'Che' Guevara, the Argentinian who had done so much to help Castro, quarrelled with him and

crossed to the mainland to try and stir up the poor to revolt in other
lands. But the determination of the U.S.A. to stamp out Communism
in Latin America caught up with Guevara. The U.S. trained army of
Bolivia succeeded in hunting him down and killing him.

f) Conclusion

The U.S.A. clearly showed that Latin American countries must take
account of its feelings about Communism when it intervened in the
Dominican Republic. Yet this was no solution to the long term problems
of Latin America. Bosch was popular because he represented the hopes
of people weary of poverty and poor government; his Communist
supporters were really very few in number. The aid sent into Latin
America, organisations like the Alliance for Progress, the inter-American
Development Bank, and the Latin American Free Trade Area, all these
could do little more than delay a worsening situation. Most of Latin
America remains in grave difficulty through two basic factors, economic
weakness and a continuing rapid rise in population. Economic difficulties are of long standing, because agriculture has remained backward
and designed to suit rich landlords who often did not even live on their
estates and who found human labour so cheap that they did not need to
care about modernisation. In Peru, for instance, haciendas, huge estates
in which the owners are all powerful, continue to exist. Other difficulties

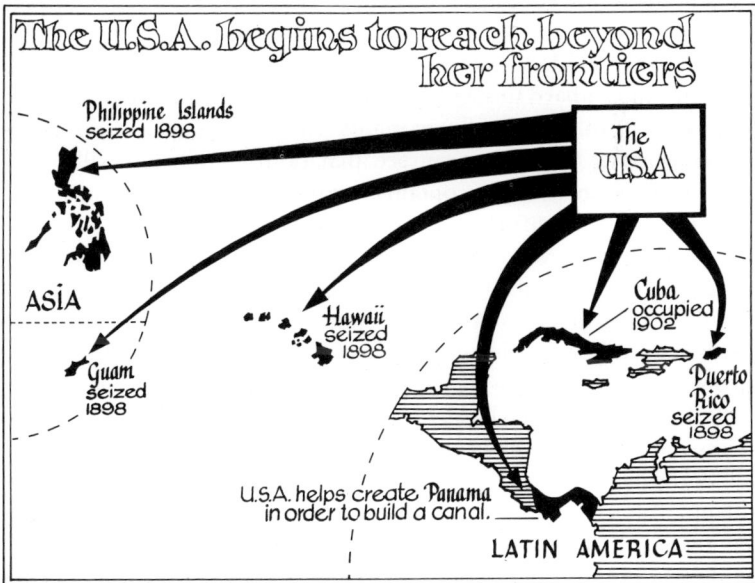

The U.S.A. begins to reach beyond her frontiers

Philippine Islands
seized 1898

The
U.S.A.

ASIA

Hawaii
seized
1898

Cuba
occupied
1902

Guam
seized
1898

Puerto
Rico
seized
1898

U.S.A. helps create Panama
in order to build a canal.

LATIN AMERICA

stem from the way some Latin American states depend so heavily on producing one item. Chile depends overmuch on copper. Social reforms by Allende's elected government stopped when Pinochet's soldiers seized power and ruled harshly. The danger of depending so heavily on a few items is all too clear, for a world slump in these items would prove ruinous for the countries concerned. Nor have Latin American states found it easy to develop their own industries. Their leaders have often made a safe income from the land and cared little about industries, whilst the existence of so many desperately poor people means that anyone trying to develop industries does not have a safe domestic market to use to build up prosperity. The Second World War and the Korean War did interrupt Latin America's normal imports sufficiently to help local industries a little, but the growth of these industries is still far too small to undo the huge degree of poverty.

Where progress is made in developing the economy it is soon cancelled out by the rise in population. People who are poor, often unable to even read or write, do not find it easy to understand a birth control campaign. Even when land reforms are carried out, the number of the peasants can mean that each has too small a piece of land to farm successfully. Many people leave instead for the cities only to find that work is almost impossible to obtain there. Some of the most magnificent cities, even Brasilia itself, are surrounded by ugly little ramshackle dwellings housing thousands of people and provided with no proper services of water and sewage disposal.

The kind of moderate government which the U.S.A. would like to see naturally finds it hard to survive in these conditions. Such a government usually needs to rely on a large middle class, and a well-to-do section of the working class who can see that cautious reforms will benefit them. Instead, many states contain a great mass of poor people, a small middle class, and an upper class determined to resist change for fear that it will lose everything. Harsh despots, like Duvalier of Haiti, represent this determination of the rich to cling on at all cost at their worst. Armies in Latin American states have only rarely fought one another or indeed outside enemies and have, instead, been much more involved in events inside their own lands. For many years, since officers came from the upper class, the armies opposed most popular movements, but recently they have changed a little as they have increased in size and taken in men from lower down the social scale. When Bosch attempted to return to power in the Dominican Republic, a section of the army led by Colonel Caomano supported him. If the upper class politicians are too unpopular and selfish, and popular movements are suspected by the U.S.A. of being pro-Communist, or reform too fast (like President Goulart in Brazil) then the armies see themselves as the only possible rulers, able to offer law and order, efficiency and some reforms. It is hardly surprising that, during the 1960's, in state after state the army has seized power; Latin America's political and economic problems are huge and it will be many years, if ever, before solutions are successfully applied.

The U.S.A.

a) The U.S.A. in 1900

The Expansion of the U.S.A.

In 1783 Britain had been forced to recognise the independence of a series of former colonies which were scattered along the eastern coast of North America. For nearly a century the U.S.A. made little impact on the affairs of other lands for she was absorbed with a westward expansion within North America, with colonising her own interior, as well as being distracted by a savage civil war between the states of North and South. But by the late nineteenth century this expansion was largely over and floods of immigrants had helped to fill the empty lands. Between 1820 and 1920 over thirty-five million people left Europe to make a new life in the U.S.A. Thus the U.S.A. began to look outwards, and in 1898 a reluctant President McKinley was swept by popular demand into fighting a war with Spain to help rebels in Cuba, to gain revenge for the blowing up of the U.S. warship *Maine* in Havana harbour and to satisfy American aggressive eagerness for war conquests. In fact the war with Spain was brief and easy, for the U.S. fleets of Admirals Dewey and Sampson were heavily superior to their Spanish opponents whom they easily destroyed and the U.S.A. was able to take Puerto Rico and the Philippines and to occupy Cuba until 1902. Thus, by 1900, one of the new features in the world was the readiness of the U.S.A. to look outwards beyond her shores. At first this was confined to the American continent, where the U.S.A. had long considered she had special rights, but eventually it led to U.S. intervention in Europe in two world wars.

The Government of the U.S.A.

The U.S.A. was formed by the needs of war against Britain and it remained a country in which the individual states kept a great deal of power and handed over as little as possible to the central federal government. Each state has its own governor, its assembly, its police and militia and its taxes with which it copes with far more work than do English local authorities. The federal government consists of a President and an elected assembly – Congress – which differs greatly from English central government. Whereas a British Prime Minister leads his party in elections, heads the government and is a member of parliament, the American president is chosen by elections that are quite separate from the elections to Congress. Each state selects a number of electors to vote for the President, the party that triumphs in a particular state naturally selects electors from its own party. Congress consists of two houses, the Senate which contains two senators from each state elected for six years, and the House of Representatives whose members are elected by the general public for a two year term of power. The President, is, therefore, not a member of Congress, and the ministers he chooses need not be Congressmen either: indeed, occasionally the majority party in Congress is not the party to which the President himself belongs. The basic laws of the American constitution were set down in writing and the Supreme Court, in addition to its normal legal duties, carefully examines all laws and denounces them if it considers they run counter to the constitution. American parties remain loose coalitions whose chief aim is power and who often contain differences of opinion far wider than those in British political parties. In 1900 both Republican and Democrat parties were divided into progressives, who wanted to see many reforms carried out, and conservatives opposed to increases in government interference in people's lives. The progressives in both parties were far closer to each other than to the conservatives within their own parties – though the Republicans often emphasised how much they were opposed to increased federal power, it was a Republican, Governor La Follette of Wisconsin, who was the most eminent progressive of the early twentieth century. Americans prided themselves on their democracy, were very ready to be suspicious of other forms of government, and were drawn into European affairs partly by a desire to defend democracy.

The American economy

Long before U.S. military power affected other lands, U.S. economic strength had been felt in other countries. Helped by the immigrants who provided the labour needed for an economic revolution, the U.S.A. pioneered many of the modern methods of mass production in industry by the use of large-scale power-driven machinery. The U.S.A. led the way in producing all sorts of new products, her large financial resources and her rich and powerful companies (for U.S. industry was dominated by a small group of massive corporations) were, by 1900, searching for outlets for their products as well as trying to secure supplies of raw materials for their industries. By this indirect means the U.S.A. had acquired great influence in other lands, especially in Latin America, whilst the competition of her products was already alarming the older industrialised countries of West Europe.

Her search for economic outlets, her military strength, and her feeling of wealth and confidence were all leading the U.S.A. to move away from her isolationism of the nineteenth century. This was a very slow process and not until 1941 did it really end, for many U.S. citizens believed it was wrong to interfere in the affairs of others, or believed that events outside the American continent were no concern of the U.S.A. It was only the Second World War and the following clash with Communism that finally destroyed these feelings.

b) The U.S.A. 1900–1918

The first U.S. experience of serious involvement in European affairs did not come until 1917 and was a brief experience that did much to save democracy in Europe, but, in the process, disillusioned many Americans. Yet this war greatly assisted the growth of U.S. power for, in battering away at one another, the leading European nations did great harm to their manpower, their economic resources, and their prestige, and from all this the U.S.A. profited.

Roosevelt and Taft

In 1900 McKinley was assassinated only six months after he had been re-elected President and therefore the Vice-President, Theodore Roosevelt, took over the supreme office. He dominated affairs until 1908 when he stood down and another Republican, Taft, headed the government until 1912.

Theodore Roosevelt was a very vigorous and capable man who had already led a colourful career in a variety of occupations as a writer, soldier, and rancher. He believed that he should try and use his position to improve life for ordinary people, to offer them (as he put it) 'a square deal'. One of the biggest obstacles to bringing the people a square deal was the power of the trusts, the massive corporations that tried to eliminate all rivals, and Roosevelt attempted to control the might of these trusts. He was not against businessmen as such, he simply believed that the men who ran the trusts had too much power over people's lives. In fact he was not able to do much at all. He managed to make coalmine owners settle a miners' strike and he managed to make the railway companies charge fairer rates instead of strongly favouring their big customers, but the trusts remained as mighty as ever. Perhaps his greatest achievement at home was to pass the Conservation Laws in an attempt to prevent the U.S.A.'s natural resources of land, forest, and mineral wealth from being used up in a shortsighted and careless manner.

These were also years of increasing interference in the affairs of other American countries following the victory over Spain, and led to U.S. Marines being landed in Santa Domingo, Haiti and Nicaragua. The U.S. held bases in Cuba and virtually ran the Cuban economy and it was U.S. support that enabled rebels in Panama to defy the government of Colombia, set up an independent Republic, and then grant the U.S.A. the right to cut a canal across Panama. American troops helped deal with the Boxer Rising in China and American 'open door' policy prevented the other powers from turning the areas they dominated in China into protectorates or even colonies. All these were signs of American confidence and power, and they were not always welcome signs, especially in Latin America, as we have seen, where the power of the 'Yanquis' came to be much resented.

Roosevelt represented the powerful section of U.S. opinion which believed that their country should take a bigger part in world affairs. He understood, more quickly than many of his fellow citizens, that so powerful a nation could not keep itself to itself in the twentieth century, could not expect its influence in the world to be simply to provide a good example of freedom and progress. He even extended his aims beyond the area immediately around the U.S.A. by sending a representative to the Algeciras Conference in 1906, where the U.S.A. exerted a moderately discreet influence against Germany. When the Russo-Japanese War ended it was the U.S.A. that offered to provide a meeting place and the means to end the conflict. After Roosevelt, Taft relapsed into a more cautious policy, dropping any attempt to interfere in European affairs. Roosevelt was, perhaps, something of a bully, a little too ready to believe that any cause he adopted was righteous as well as convenient. He certainly aroused suspicion in his own party and when he returned to politics from big game hunting, in 1912, his presence split the Republicans helping the Democrats to win victory.

Woodrow Wilson

A divided Republican leadership was defeated in the Presidential elections of 1912 by the Democrat, Thomas Woodrow Wilson, a serious, high minded man who disapproved of the aggressive policies of the Roosevelt-Taft period and hoped to introduce domestic reforms instead.

Looking gravely ill, ex-President Woodrow Wilson (left) rides beside his successor, Warren G. Harding after the latter's inauguration in 1921.

Wilson attempted to attack the growing problem of vast business monopolies in the U.S.A. as well as making a beginning in improving working conditions. After the very limited success of Theodore Roosevelt's 'Square Deal', Wilson offered, instead, policies which he called 'the new Freedom', designed to give ordinary people more opportunity to better themselves. He reduced customs duties, reformed banking, taxed high incomes and increased the rights of the trade unions. The power of the trusts was attacked and it was made easier for farmers to borrow money. Wilson would have liked to have done much more, but some of his proposals never became Law because the Senate successfully blocked

them. But, oddly, it was Wilson, re-elected as late as 1916 on his policy
of neutrality in foreign affairs, who drew the U.S.A. into the First World
War. American business and financial connections were already primarily
with the Allies, and the unrestricted German U-boat campaign of 1917
finally led a reluctant U.S.A. to declare war in April, 1917. Though
nearly one and a half million men eventually served in the war, the U.S.A.
was not really prepared and it took her a long time to build up General
Pershing's forces in France. Nevertheless this growing tide of men, plus
American wealth, finally solved what might otherwise have been a war
without a definite victory for one side. Wilson emphasised that the war
was fought to create a better world, to help democracy and to free all
peoples anxious to be rid of rule by foreigners. His ideas played a major
part in the peace conference, especially in bringing about the creation
of the League of Nations, yet he failed to carry his country with him.
In the 1918 Congressional elections his Republican opponents did well.
Wilson would not modify his uncompromising attitude about accepting
everything in the treaties and Congress therefore refused to give them
the necessary two-thirds majority vote. In despair at his failure, and
increasingly ill after a stroke in 1920, Wilson rapidly lost influence and
when his term of office ended the Republicans triumphed once more.

Though the U.S.A. once again returned to her old policy of isolation,
she was more influential in world affairs then she had been before. The
Allies, desperate for money and materials, had bought from U.S.
industry, borrowed from U.S. financiers, and had withdrawn loans they
had previously made to other lands, so the U.S.A. hastened to step in and
make new loans available. American industries boomed and prospered:
U.S. companies pioneered inventions like the telephone and the motor
car: in 1909 Henry Ford produced the famous Model T car which did so
much to make motoring cheaper. In 1914 Ford was already using the
modern assembly-line technique to assemble cars at his factory in
Detroit. The war led the U.S. government to interfere in the working
of the country's economy in order to co-ordinate the war effort by setting
up a War Industries Board and a Food Administration.

c) Between War and Depression

Republican leadership

From 1921 until 1932 Republican Presidents Harding, Coolidge and
Hoover attempted to follow policies that would please their supporters
in big business and keep the U.S.A. out of serious foreign entanglements.
Warren Harding, who replaced Wilson as President, was an impressive

looking man, but was weak, over-trusting in his friends and without political skill. His friends proved selfish and corrupt in their use of power and scandals began to be revealed; only Harding's death in 1923 stopped them. His successor was Calvin Coolidge, nick-named 'Silent Cal', because he rarely spoke; he was competent and honest and helped restore the Republican Party's good name. In 1928 Herbert C. Hoover replaced Coolidge as President and seemed an excellent choice since he had a fine record in running the war-time Food Administration and post-war aid to the poor in Europe. But, faced with a major economic crisis, Hoover proved too cautious and conventional and his political eminence was thus far briefer than many would have guessed when he was elected. In these post-war years the U.S.A. was also troubled by rather hysterical outbursts of hatred of Communism that really helped no-one except extremists like the members of the Ku Klux Klan which grew rapidly in the 1920's. This organisation with its secret rites and strange hooded uniform now preached hatred of Communism as well as the necessity of keeping negroes in the U.S.A. in an inferior position to the white man.

Prohibition

By 1920 a number of separate states had already made illegal the sale of intoxicating liquor. In that year, the U.S. constitution was amended (the eighteenth amendment) to extend this ban to the whole country, and Hoover's support for the ban helped him defeat his opponent, Alfred Smith, in the 1928 election, for Smith was a 'wet', who favoured an end to prohibition. In fact prohibition proved disastrously unworkable for alcohol was smuggled in from Canada or manufactured illegally and the chief result of prohibition was a rise in crime and a growth in organised gangsterism. Machine-guns and motor cars had already made U.S. gangsters more mobile and dangerous; they fought each other for control of territories in the big cities and they fought the police they had failed to bribe. Chicago became particularly notorious through the activities of gangsters like 'Legs' Diamond and Al Capone. Capone, son of an Italian immigrant, was the most famous of these gangsters, and at one time commanded a force of over 700. When he was eventually caught and convicted in 1931 through the efforts of Eliot Ness and his 'Untouchables' the crime for which he was punished was tax evasion because of the difficulty in proving his complicity in bootlegging. Prohibition was so clearly a failure that defeat had to be admitted and in December 1933 the eighteenth amendment to the constitution was scrapped.

P

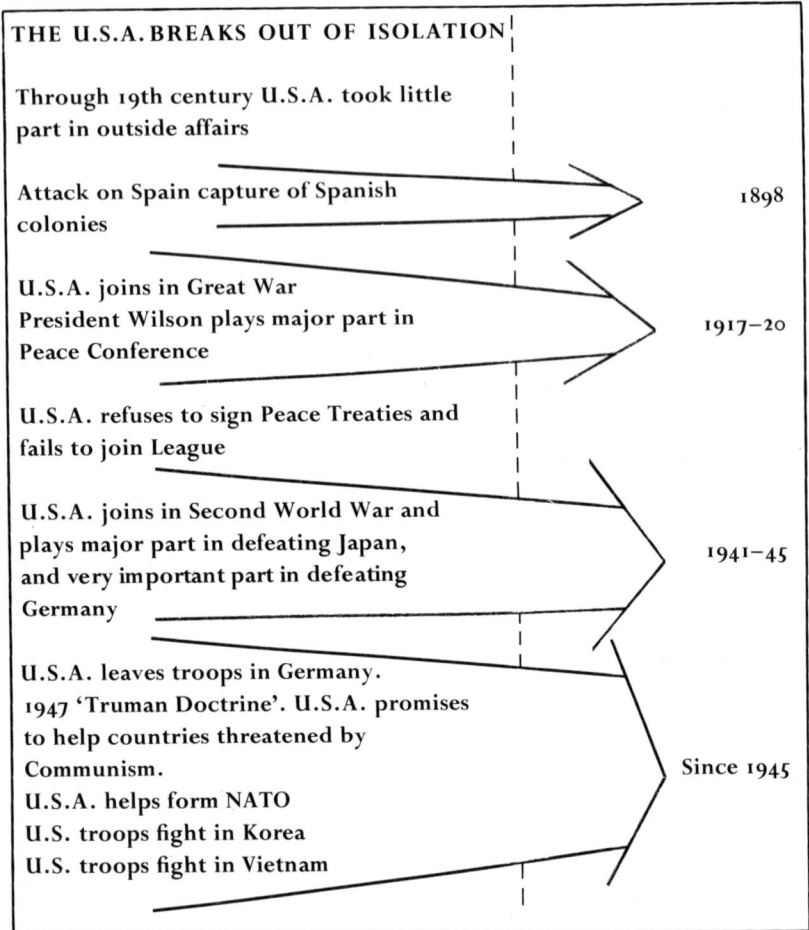

THE U.S.A. BREAKS OUT OF ISOLATION

Through 19th century U.S.A. took little
part in outside affairs

Attack on Spain capture of Spanish
colonies

1898

U.S.A. joins in Great War
President Wilson plays major part in
Peace Conference

1917–20

U.S.A. refuses to sign Peace Treaties and
fails to join League

U.S.A. joins in Second World War and
plays major part in defeating Japan,
and very important part in defeating
Germany

1941–45

U.S.A. leaves troops in Germany.
1947 'Truman Doctrine'. U.S.A. promises
to help countries threatened by
Communism.
U.S.A. helps form NATO
U.S. troops fight in Korea
U.S. troops fight in Vietnam

Since 1945

Prosperity

The Republicans prided themselves on being a businessman's government and soon repealed most of the legislation which had grown up
during the war to increase the power of the federal government. There
were tax cuts that favoured the wealthy: the large corporations
became larger, profits soared and dealing in stocks and shares
boomed, giving a general air of prosperity that greatly aided the
Republican Party. Between 1919 and 1929 industrial production
doubled, enterprises like Ford and Woolworths became interna-
tionally famous. The electricity industry expanded rapidly, plastics

industries appeared and through mass production methods, thousands of Americans were given the opportunity to own increasing numbers of 'gadgets' and labour-saving devices. The radio, the cinema, the growth of many sports, especially baseball, altered leisure habits for Americans at a moment when leisure time was increasing as machines took over more tasks from men and working hours became shorter. In fact this boom went too far and within the very success of this period were some of the reasons for later collapse.

Foreign policy

The success of the Republicans also represented the weariness many Americans felt with Wilson's high minded internationalism. The U.S.A. did not return wholly to isolation, but she was prepared to act in only the most cautious and limited fashion. Half-hearted intervention in the U.S.S.R. indicated U.S. hatred of Communism, but did not continue for long. The U.S.A. became involved in European affairs because the Republicans insisted that the money loaned to the Allies during the war must be repaid. Since there were high tariffs on foreign imports the Allies could not repay with goods and, unless Germany paid reparations, they could not pay in cash either. Thus the U.S.A. loaned the Germans money and, through the Dawes Plan and the Young Plan, helped re-organise reparations so that the U.S.A. could herself be repaid. This was not a great success, it made the Germans too dependent on American credit and it did not bring back more than a small percentage of U.S. loans. Eventually the U.S.A. faced the fact that the slump, rearmament, and then war meant that repayment would never be completed. In the Far East, too, heavy commitments were avoided and the U.S.A. contented herself with joining in the 1922 Washington Treaties to fix the relative size of U.S., British and Japanese fleets, and to join in a mutual guarantee of each other's rights.

d) The depression

The period of post-war prosperity was deceptive for within it there were areas of decaying industry and agriculture and the profits of prosperity went to too few citizens. U.S. industry and agriculture had, in fact, reached a stage where they were over-producing for the home market whilst the overseas markets were both uncertain and unreliable. Too much of the purchasing power of foreigners rested on credit which was partly provided by U.S. loans. In reply to the U.S. tariff system, other countries put up their own tariffs, whilst new competitors were appearing, especially in agriculture where Argentina, Canada and Australia all threatened the prosperity of U.S. farmers. U.S. finance was not as soundly based as it might have been. There were too many small banks, too much excitable speculation in stocks and shares and too much dependence on the feeling of confidence in a permanent boom.

It was on the Stock Exchange in 1929 that the depression began. The 'Wall Street Crash' was a collapse of confidence and a wave of panic that caused shares to drop and U.S. financiers to call in their loans. Unemployment rose, banks failed, the output of industry and agriculture fell until, by 1932, there were 14,000,000 unemployed with no system of national insurance to shield them from suffering. President Hoover put his faith in a cautious policy, hoping pre-slump conditions would return, so that, although he did introduce changes like the Federal Home Loan Bank and the Reconstruction Finance Company, the crisis continued. Above all, Hoover did nothing about the unemployed whom he felt were not the state's responsibility. The growing demand for more decisive action ended the post-war period of Republican power and let in a Democrat once more.

e) The New Deal

The Democrat who became President in 1932 was Franklin D. Roosevelt, the wealthy Governor of New York State and a distant cousin of Theodore Roosevelt. Roosevelt had risen rapidly to prominence in politics and had served in Wilson's government. A severe attack of poliomyelitis in 1921 had left him partially crippled. Yet Roosevelt had remained cheerful and hopeful through his suffering, took up every possible exercise to help recover his health and radiated confidence for his own and his country's future. His election compaign had been full of promises for vigorous changes (including repeal of prohibition) and had proved more persuasive than Hoover's platform that Roosevelt's proposals would make the government too strong and reduce the liberty of U.S. citizens. Roosevelt was skilful at finding impressive phrases to put over his ideas, it was one such phrase 'the New Deal' that became the popular description for his programme of reforms. His massive victory gave him the power he wanted and he promised the U.S.A. 'a Hundred Days' of furious reforms to deal with the crisis. Roosevelt's programme leaned heavily on the ideas of other men, like R. M. La Follette: it was a mixture of planning and of short term measures which had to be revised in the light of experience. He brought with him into government many able men from the universities, much as Kennedy was to do later.

The Reforms

A burst of government activity followed Roosevelt's election. Some government-controlled salaries were cut, aid was given to help save banks, a Civilian Construction Corps was created from young unemployed men. One of his most successful projects was the Tennessee Valley Authority, a corporation with power to revive a large area by building dams, providing electricity and improving the land. By the National Industrial Recovery Act codes of fair competition for prices, wages and conditions were laid down and firms that joined this scheme indicated this by displaying the Blue Eagle on their vehicles. In fact the N.I.R.A. became unpopular and the Supreme Court declared it was unconstitutional in 1935. A similar fate eventually befell the A.A.A. (the Agricultural Adjustment Act) which encouraged farmers to reduce production by providing them with subsidies instead. The money to finance the scheme was to be raised by a tax on food processing. But like the N.I.R.A. it helped reduce distress and marketing problems. Roosevelt helped the unions achieve a respectable position with a right to share in collective bargaining and he tackled unemployment by financing schemes of public works which helped provide the U.S.A. with roads, schools, hospitals and houses.

After something of a lull in 1934, a fresh spate of reforms burst out including devaluation, a reform of the stock exchange, further aid to house building, and the establishment of a federal commission to regulate the private companies that ran radio, telegraphs, and cables. But, above all, 1935 saw the introduction of the Social Security Act which created a federal system of old age pensions, unemployment insurance, maternity and child benefits – though not health insurance. The National Labour Relations Act helped unions by compelling employers to recognise them, and the Fair Labour Standards Act fixed maximum hours and minimum wages in a number of poorly paid occupations. It is not surprising that Roosevelt was re-elected in 1936 for he had not only introduced many beneficial reforms, he had shown great skill in explaining them, for instance by talks on the radio: his famous 'Fireside Chats.'

Opposition to the Reforms

Some politicians complained that Roosevelt was increasing federal power too much and interfering in the economy too vigorously, whereas others considered that he was not going rapidly enough. Such criticisms worried the President little, for although he was always very sensitive to public opinion and ready to respond to it, he knew what most people would accept better than his critics. But the opposition of the Supreme

Court was a different matter. The nine judges of the Supreme Court ruled that a number of the New Deal reforms were unconstitutional and Roosevelt made an unsuccessful attempt to reform the court and to bring in new and younger men. Fortunately the death or resignation of five of the members of the Court enabled Roosevelt to make new appointments.

The Success of the New Deal

Despite the many reforms there were still nine million unemployed in 1939, and there were still massive trusts and monopolies despite Roosevelt's attempts to break them up. But he did increase the power of the federal government, he did improve social security and his public works did improve the country.

f) Roosevelt's Foreign Policy

Roosevelt had been a vigorous supporter of President Wilson, whom he had served as Assistant Secretary of the Navy and his foreign policy bore the same marks of a desire for international peace and the spread of democracy. The U.S.A. withdrew further from her interference in Latin American states, but Roosevelt and Cordell Hull (his Secretary of State) could not carry Congress with them in their attitude to Europe. Congress insisted on the passing of two neutrality acts to try and isolate the U.S.A. from the tensions in Europe, insisting that foreign states buying American arms must pay cash; but Roosevelt's sympathies lay with Britain and France in their clash with Fascism. The Nazi conquest of France shook the U.S.A. and Roosevelt was able to provide growing aid for Britain, first in the shape of fifty old destroyers, sent in exchange for the use of British bases, later in the form of lend-lease, enabling Britain to obtain war supplies without paying cash. The U.S.A. also had to face up to the ambitions of the Japanese and their desire to take the European colonies in Asia, to which the U.S. forces were the chief threat. War was eventually forced on the U.S.A. in December 1941 by the Pearl Harbour attack and the German and Italian declarations of war, and this time the U.S.A. was better prepared than she had been in 1917. Conscription had been introduced in 1940 and American industries were vast and powerful and able to create the weapons of war, free from the aerial attack that Britain suffered. Roosevelt agreed to concentrate first on the war in Europe and American forces stood on the defensive in the Pacific whilst in North Africa and Europe they took the offensive. Roosevelt and Churchill met several times and developed an excellent relationship, the chief difference probably centred on their attitude to Stalin, of whom Churchill was far more suspicious than Roosevelt.

President Harry S. Truman (centre) with Churchill and Stalin at the Potsdam Conference in 1945.

But shortly after being re-elected in 1944 Roosevelt died (April 1945) and it was left to Harry Truman, the Vice President, to make the fateful decision to drop the atomic bombs on Japan and to participate in the creation of the U.N. Roosevelt had held office for a remarkably lengthy period and had faced major crises in domestic and foreign affairs which he had tackled with boldness and with energy. He had led the U.S.A. into an involvement in world affairs from which there was to be no turning back.

g) Post-War Problems

The U.S.A. emerged from the war strategically more powerful, her vast military forces guided by the Pentagon, nerve-centre of the Defence Forces, and she controlled a devastating new atomic weapon. In addition she had greater wealth and prestige than ever before. Her old competitors in Western Europe had suffered terribly during the war and American forces occupied Japan. Yet great problems faced the U.S.A. in foreign affairs, for as we have seen, Russia, too, had emerged with increased power and prestige, had extended her control over Eastern Europe, and was giving encouragement to the Communist Parties that were springing up in many parts of the world. U.S. rulers regarded Communism with fear and suspicion and one of their aims was to check its growth, if possible.

But there were other problems, too, for the war had helped raise the status of negroes (many served in the forces), negroes formed a growing proportion of the population, especially in areas outside their old centre in the South East. The U.S.A. still lacked social services comparable to those in much of Europe and, for a rich country, contained an alarming number of poor. Yet some politicians, especially the Southern Democrats, were opposed to negro equality and many were against federal action to improve welfare services. These were problems that continued to defy solution in the immediate post-war years.

President Truman

Harry Truman was a small town politician, unskilled in foreign affairs, who was regarded with some contempt both by New Deal Democrats, many of whom left the government, and by Republicans, who expected their candidate, Dewey, to win an easy victory in the 1948 Presidential elections. But in fact Truman displayed a tough shrewdness that confounded his opponents. He was ready to take difficult decisions such as the question of using the atomic bombs to defeat Japan and his sacking of General MacArthur during the Korean War. He tried to continue Roosevelt's domestic policy with the 'Fair Deal' programme of economic and social reforms, though Congress wrecked part of the programme including a scheme for national health insurance. By virtue of vigorous campaigning Truman defeated Dewey to the surprise of many – though not Truman himself. But his attempts to continue Roosevelt's policy of trying to improve the status of negroes was unsuccessful and he was also responsible for the Taft-Hartley Act which demanded non-Communist affidavits from union officials, banned union contributions to political funds, outlawed certain kinds of strikes and forbade closed shop policies by unions.

Truman's Foreign Policy

In China, U.S. policy failed to save the non-Communist forces from defeat with the result that the U.S.A. found itself faced by another hostile Communist power. Russia developed her own nuclear weapons and established a tight control over East Europe. Truman reacted by adopting more active U.S. policies. This was made clear as a general policy in 1947 when the Truman Doctrine proclaimed the readiness of the U.S.A. to help free peoples resist being subdued by armed minorities or outside pressure. The U.S.A. protected the non-Communist Chinese entrenched on Formosa; the U.S.A. played a key part in the air lift to Berlin; and the U.S.A. took over from Britain the burdens she could no longer afford of resisting Communism in Greece and Turkey. Truman also agreed to provide economic aid to Europe on the basis of the plan drawn up by his Secretary of State, George Marshall. As well, he sent military aid to form the backbone of NATO forces controlling Western Europe to deter the Russians from attacking. U.S. troops also went to Korea to halt Communism's spread South, and thus Truman had committed his country to a world-wide attempt to halt the spread of Communism.

President Eisenhower

Truman did not contest the 1952 election; instead Adlai Stevenson, the liberal minded Governor of Illinois, fought the campaign against the Republican candidate, General Eisenhower. Eisenhower's reputation as a soldier and as an honest, straightforward man, plus his promises to end the war in Korea and lower taxes, brought him victory in the election. He tended to distrust professional politicians and to promote businessmen instead, like Charles Erwin Wilson, President of General Motors, who became Secretary of Defence. Eisenhower did make some effort to reduce government economic controls and he lowered taxes on corporations; but he did not prove to be a skilful politician and he was forced to lean heavily on his very determined Secretary of State, John Foster Dulles. Increasing illness and the hostility of a Congress in which the Democrats won a majority marred Eisenhower's later years, and even though he defeated Stevenson again in 1956, his period in office was marked by few achievements at home and by a continuing crisis abroad. He died in April, 1969.

McCarthyism

In the post-war years, the U.S. distrust of Communism was aggravated by the frustrations of the quarrel with Russia and China which led to a mood of suspicion of all left-wingers. This mood was exploited by Joseph R. McCarthy, a Senator from Wisconsin, who, for a time, managed to suggest that the whole U.S. government was riddled with Communists. There had already been a few scares, notably in 1950 when a State Department Official, Alger Hiss, was condemned for passing secrets to the Russians, but McCarthy's accusations spread so widely that even Dean Acheson, who had served Truman as Secretary of State, was suspect. From 1950 until 1954, as chairman of a Senate Committee on Government operations, McCarthy conducted a policy of persecution which ruined several prominent men and helped foster a feeling of danger that led to laws requiring every Communist-front organisation to register with the Attorney General and forbade any member of a totalitarian society from entering the U.S.A. McCarthy was finally disgraced when a televised persecution, which involved Army personnel, showed up his bullying methods. Yet the episode did not end hysterical fear of Communism in the U.S.A., for other organisations, like the John Birch Society and the Minutemen, flourished on hatred of Communism. Politicians prepared to run a campaign based on a crude opposition of 'the free world' and Communism could be sure of many votes. Hatred of Communism led American policy into many blunders, such as aiding hated dictators like Batista in Cuba, and was prone to offend the less idealistic politicians of Europe who could see that Communist states were as tied by nationalism and their past as other countries.

Eisenhower's policies

The war in Korea was ended and big businessmen benefited from the favours shown them by the government. The rivalry with Russia led to continued increases in defence spending including the establishment of a National Aeronautics and Space Administration to direct space research. Eisenhower, too, continued the policy of trying to end discrimination against negroes. He used federal troops to enforce the 1954 Supreme Court ruling that segregation in schools must end, when this was defied in Little Rock, Arkansas, by Governor Faubus. Negro feeling was becoming more militant and was increasingly well organised by leaders like Martin Luther King. After Dulles had died in 1959, the tough hostility to Russia was modified a little and Eisenhower even met Khrushchev in 1959. A further meeting planned for the following year, was wrecked by the U2 affair when the Russians shot down an American U2 reconnaissance plane over Soviet territory. When Eisenhower's period of office ended, the Republicans chose Vice-President Nixon to run for office against the Democrats.

h) Kennedy and Johnson

The Democrat candidate was John F. Kennedy, a Senator from Massachusetts who was wealthy, liberal minded, and a very energetic politician of great charm and force. After a fierce campaign well organised by Kennedy's thirty-three year old brother, Robert, the Democrats secured a narrow victory over their Republican opponents. In his speech after the election, Kennedy spoke in terms reminiscent of those used by Roosevelt, urging the need for reforms and attracting to his government a host of intellectuals and experts.

Kennedy's Foreign Policy

The struggle with Communism continued and spread to Vietnam where U.S. military experts were sent to assist the South Vietnamese goverment against Communist attacks. It was in the Caribbean that the most striking events took place, both a failure (1961) when U.S. backed exiles failed to overthrow Castro, and a success in the following year when Kennedy stopped Russia from developing Cuba as a missile base by a blockade and stern threats to Russia. His success in 1962 helped to restore his popularity. After Castro's triumph in defeating the 1961 invasion, Russia had sent Cuba various kinds of aid including jet fighters and bombers and, most dangerous of all, ground-to-ground missiles. These missiles meant that the U.S.A. was threatened very seriously from a base close by, and when photographs proved the existence of these missiles beyond all doubt, Kennedy decided to act. The risks were huge, no less than the possibility of starting a nuclear war of untold destructive power. Kennedy's decision to block Russian ships taking more weapons to Cuba proved, however, to have been well judged, for the U.S.S.R. backed down, with a suitable show of bluster, and withdrew its missiles from Cuba. Kennedy believed that force alone was not enough to check Communism and tried to aid governments that promised real reforms which would benefit the mass of the people. U.S. aid poured into India and parts of Latin America and South-East Asia, whilst the arms race with Russia was brought a little nearer control by a treaty in 1963 (which Britain signed too) banning all nuclear tests above ground.

Home Affairs

Kennedy made a real effort to improve the position of negroes. He appointed negroes to senior posts, forced Southern universities to take in negroes and passed Civil Rights laws. But other parts of his 'New Frontier' policy ran into heavy opposition in Congress: yet another health insurance scheme failed, for instance. Kennedy's spectacular career was cut tragically short in November 1963 when, in Dallas, Texas, he was shot dead by an assassin. The Dallas police finally arrested a man named Lee Harvey Oswald and charged him with the President's assassination. While in police custody, Oswald was himself murdered by Jack Ruby, a local night club owner. Ruby died in turn shortly after from cancer. Despite various investigations and reports, the whole episode remains shrouded in mystery and confusion.

Johnson

The Vice-President, Lyndon B. Johnson, a Texan, succeeded Kennedy

President John F. Kennedy (left) with Vice-President, later President, Lyndon B. Johnson at a White House press conference in 1961.

and, in the elections of 1964, easily defeated the Republican candidate, Barry Goldwater. Johnson soon showed himself to be a skilful politician who, even if he lacked the style and intellectual appeal of John Kennedy, introduced a programme aimed at preventing the spread of Communism, easing poverty and ending negro segregation. A Civil Rights Act was passed to help negroes vote by making the completion of six years' schooling proof of literacy which was a necessary qualification. A full National Health Insurance scheme failed to gain support, but Lyndon Johnson did succeed in steering through a Medicare Act which gave free medical treatment to people over sixty-five.

Relations with Russia continued to improve slowly, but the war in Vietnam became increasingly more difficult as the U.S.A. was drawn into sending ground troops in ever growing numbers to prop up the South Vietnamese government, accompanied by bomber strikes launched against the North Vietnamese. The vision of a 'great society' began to fade under the growing burden of taxation needed to pay for the war and there was discontent with the war and conscription among young people. Negroes became increasingly intolerant of the continued subjugation under which they were forced to live and new leaders began to emerge who were far less moderate than Martin Luther King, who was assassinated in 1968. Prominent among the new leaders were Black Muslims like Malcolm X and supporters of the 'black power' movement of Stokeley Carmichael and Rap Brown.

A nation-wide opposition to Lyndon Johnson's policies persuaded him to declare, early in 1968, that he would not accept his party's nomination to stand again in the next presidential elections. The Republicans once again chose Richard Nixon as their candidate, but the Democrats were split between the supporters of Vice President Humphrey, Senator McCarthy and Robert Kennedy. But the number of candidates was tragically reduced when Robert Kennedy was assassinated by Sirhan Sirhan, a Jordanian, whilst celebrating a campaign success in California. The episode emphasised the high level of violence inherent in the U.S.A., a violence underlined by the ease with which Americans can purchase all sorts of firearms often without any form of control or restriction.*

It was the Republican candidate, Richard Nixon who was finally successful in the Presidential election in November, 1968. He was duly sworn into office on Monday, January 20, 1969. Nixon determined to prove himself as approachable as Kennedy had been and, on a 'whistle-stop' tour of Europe in February which took in Italy, Britain, Belgium, France and Germany, he went out of his way to meet ordinary members of the public.

The U.S.A. in the 1960's, whilst clearly the strongest and richest power in the world, with terrifying weapons, the ability to send men into space and a quantity and range of cheap, mass-produced goods which were the envy of much of the rest of the world, is also increasingly troubled by self doubts. A small minority of Americans prefer to reject the whole of society and take refuge in the dream world of drugs: rather more reject the war in Vietnam and the obsession with Communism. For the government it is difficult to withdraw from its commitments abroad and scale down the rising burden of paying for more and more expensive weapons in order to find the money and energy needed to tackle poverty inside the U.S.A. and, above all, the poverty of the negroes.

Nixon was easily re-elected in 1973. Helped by Secretary of State Kissinger, he made arrangements for the withdrawal of American troops from Vietnam and visited both Russia and China. Activity in foreign affairs could not save him from the disgrace of the Watergate scandal. A trial of Republicans who had tried to raid Democrat headquarters grew into an exposure of the whole of Nixon's government. In 1974 Nixon resigned, Vice President Ford replaced him, but only till 1976. The Democrat Jimmy Carter then defeated Ford in the Presidential elections.

9 | Asian Nationalism 1 – Japan and China

Japan

a) The Impact of the West on Japan in the nineteenth century

In the mid-nineteenth century when the Western powers began to put serious pressure on Japan to end the isolationist policy which had lasted since 1637, the Japanese government was already under severe strain from tensions within the country. From his palace in Kyoto, the Emperor had exercised little real power for centuries but had watched real authority being wielded from Yedo by a series of chief ministers. In the nineteenth century this position was controlled by the Tokugawa family who therefore held the position of *shogun* ('barbarian subduing general') and headed the government administration (the *bakufu*). Foreign influence had not been wholly excluded from the country, for a Dutch settlement had been tolerated near Nagasaki, but in principle the shoguns were attempting to maintain a feudal society free from Western influences.

Economic Changes

Several factors combined to make this an increasingly impossible aim. Economic development had already led to a growth in the numbers of merchants at Yedo and Osaka and a weakening of the economic power of the *samurai*, the warrior class. The Tokugawa shoguns were not popular with some of the other great ruling families (*daimyo*), especially restless were the Western clans of Satsuma, Choshu and Tosa, and these were the clans that had tended to benefit from the development of Japanese farming, cotton, silk, tobacco and sugar. In a mountainous country with poor communications, it was not easy for the bakufu to control the entire state and the local ties of people to the nearest daimyo tended to be more important than loyalty to the shogun. The inability of the government to provide stable economic conditions had already caused much discontent and there was an increasing tendency for the discontented to look to the emperor in Kyoto to rescue them from the rule of the shogunate.

Growing attacks on the shoguns

The shoguns themselves helped stimulate this threat to their own authority by encouraging both learned scholarships and the adoption of the Confucian religion (which stressed the duty of inferiors to superiors). The scholars who were thus assisted eventually began to question the legality of the shoguns' own position and to suggest that true loyalty was owed to the Emperor alone. These scholars assisted a revival of nationalism and of the distinctive Japanese religion of Shintoism, which took place against a background of mounting hostility to the shoguns' muddled and incompetent economic policy. The shoguns were thus ill placed to live up to their title of 'barbarian subduing' when the barbarians began to bully Japan into abandoning her isolationism.

Early Foreign Visitors

In the early nineteenth century British, Russian and United States vessels began to call at Japanese ports with increasing frequency, usually to ask for supplies. In 1853 Commodore Perry arrived with a polite ultimatum from the U.S. government, and a more brutal one from himself, that the U.S.A. expected trading relations to be agreed when Perry returned in one year. In 1854 Perry duly reappeared with a powerful squadron of war ships and the Japanese government did not feel sufficient confidence in its own military strength to deny American demands. Further concessions were soon being successfully sought by the Russian Admiral Putyatin, and the British Admiral Sterling.

The Fall of the Shoguns

The concessions were a sharp blow to Japanese national pride and prompted a fierce debate as to how Japan ought to react. The Japanese were an energetic and curious people, never too proud to learn from others and therefore more flexible in their response to the West than the more rigid and arrogant Chinese civilisation. The Choshu and Satsuma clans led those who wished to learn from the West and imitate its methods and were prepared to drop their rivalry to combine together against the shogun: Choshu forces, drilled and equipped on the European pattern overwhelmed the forces of Keiki, the last of the Tokugawa shoguns, and proclaimed, in 1868, the restoration to full power of the Emperor Meiji.

b) The Meiji Restoration

Reforms

The Emperor moved to Tokyo (as Yedo was re-named) and from there his ministers poured out a stream of legislation designed to modernise the country. Feudalism was abolished; internal customs duties were swept away; direct government intervention was used to stimulate railways, steamships, textiles, mining and chemicals. The armed forces were overhauled with the help of British naval experts and German army advisers, and guided by Japanese who had been abroad to study. In 1872 an ambitious programme of compulsory education was launched that soon made the Japanese the most literate people in Asia.

The rulers of Japan

This revolution was carried out, not by a democratic government, but by Samurai clan leaders like Okuma, Ito, Itagaki, Okuba and Inouye. The emphasis on industrialisation caused some distress among the peasantry and the over-large samurai class and risings by both groups had to be repressed. The only party politics that existed were tussles for control of power between the four leading clans. In 1899 Japan received a new constitution, framed by Prince Ito who borrowed his ideas chiefly from Germany. A Diet of two houses was formed, consisting of the House of Peers, and a House of Representatives chosen by substantial property owners (at first this amounted to only one per cent. of the population). Ministers did not have to be members of the Diet, and if the budget were rejected by the Diet, government would not be paralysed for the constitution prescribed that in this eventuality the previous year's budget would be carried out. In 1900 the constitution was modified as a result of pressure from the Choshu leader, Yamagata, whose clan, which dominated the army had been elated by the success of the war with China. Henceforth only generals on the active list could serve as Minister of War and Admirals on the active list as Navy Minister. This gave the armed forces great power over the government, enabling them to ruin cabinets they disliked and making the growth of peaceful democratic government more difficult.

Throughout this period, the Choshu and Satsuma clans dominated both government and armed forces, providing all but two of the Prime Ministers in the period to 1904. This helped to give unity to politics, and even as they aged the *genro* (elder statesmen) continued to control affairs, though not themselves in office. General Katsura, for instance, was Yamagata's nominee as Prime Minister, whilst Saionji co-operated

Russia

Sakhalin

China

HOKKAIDO

Vladivostok

Otaru

Sea of Japan

Sendai

Korea

HONSHU

Tokyo

Yokohama

Hiroshima

Kyoto

Shimonoseki

Osaka

SHIKOKU

Nagasaki

Pacific Ocean

KYUSHU

Japan

Q

with Ito. The Diet was frequently restless and clearly not wholly satisfied with this situation, but economic progress and two successful wars helped to justify it, whilst the Diet lacked the power to embarrass a determined government seriously.

c) Economic Progress up to 1914

Though the Japanese economy made most impressive strides forward, the extent of the progress prior to 1914 should not be over-emphasised. In 1914 fifty-seven per cent. of the population of 50 millions was still engaged in agriculture (in 1868 the proportion had been seventy per cent. out of a population of 33 millions). The bulk of heavy equipment was still being imported, much shipping was still built abroad, and half of the workers were in 'factories' with fewer than five employees. In order to pay for these imports there was an increasingly large debt owed to foreign capitalists, in 1914 it had reached 1300 million yen, whilst inflation proved to be a further apparently insoluble problem.

Yet these years laid the basis on which future success could be built, and good fortune rescued Japan from its debts and difficulties. In the twenty-five years up to 1914 total production and real incomes increased between eighty and one hundred per cent and the rising population could still be largely fed from domestic sources as a result of vastly improved farming techniques which boosted food production thirty-five to forty per cent. in the period 1894–1914. Japanese vessels were carrying half the country's overseas trade; Japanese cotton dominated the home market; new industries like chemicals and electricity were founded. To manage these growing concerns, large capitalist corporations, *zaibatsu*, emerged, backed by the state, the most important being Mitsubishi, Mitoni, Yasuda, and Sumitomo. The zaibatsu benefited from the government's policy of promoting industrial enterprises and then handing them over, very cheaply, to private companies. They received state subsidies (especially for ship-building) which helped them compete with the older industrial countries and were, therefore, closely linked with the ruling group. Ito, for example, was always identified with the interests of the Mitsui company.

d) Japan's Emergence as a Great Power

The unequal treaties with more powerful nations which had been forced on Japan were strongly resented in a country that had a strong sense of patriotism. In Africa the West had found only tribalism to overcome: in China they found an unpopular and decadent regime unable to rise to their challenge: but in Japan the West met a proud and determined people who were devoting their exceptional gifts to modernising their country and wished to be recognised as equals. Anti-foreign feeling was spurred on by patriotic societies, but the foreigners refused demands for the ending of the unequal treaties, asserting that the Japanese legal system was too inadequate to be trusted. Even reform of the legal system failed to induce the foreigners to negotiate new treaties, it became clear that a demonstration of effective military power was the best argument Japan could produce.

Events leading to War with Russia

In 1894 and 1895 Japan's prestige rose as a result of a successful war with China fought mainly in Korea where Japan had old ambitions. The Treaty of Shimonoseki gave Japan Formosa, the Pescadores, recognition of the independence of Korea, the Liaotung Peninsula on China's mainland, and an indemnity of 360 million yen. The gains benefited the Japanese economy, and the demonstration of the power of Japanese forces (further emphasised by the large part they played in putting down the Boxer Rising in China in 1900) impressed foreign nations and encouraged Japanese national pride. But although the unequal treaties were soon swept away, Japan received another blow when Russia, backed by Germany, and France, forced Japan to hand the Liaotung Peninsula back to China and then proceeded to take over the area herself. The build up of Russian troops in Manchuria, the extension of Russian interests into Korea and the rebuffs inflicted on Ito when he attempted to negotiate a settlement with Russia, all combined to make the Japanese feel that war with Russia was inevitable.

The War with Russia

The treaty of 1902 with Britain, which virtually guaranteed Japan a free hand in Korea and assured Japan that she would not have to fight France too, was also of important psychological significance since it indicated that a powerful Western nation was ready to treat Japan as an equal. Although Japan was eventually victorious in her battle with the Russians during 1904–5, waging the war threw a tremendous strain on both her economy and resources of manpower. Coupled with this the actual terms obtained in the Treaty of Portsmouth caused considerable indignation among some Japanese who thought the gains wholly inadequate. The genro, however, were united in support of the treaty, and Japan had to content herself with South Sakhalin, Port Arthur and 'influence' over

Korea which was gradually increased until the area was eventually annexed in 1910.

The areas gained in these wars were ruled efficiently, though the harsh military dominance of Korea did little to enhance Japan's hopes of winning the area's permanent support. The regions provided helpful sources of raw materials and markets for Japanese goods, in particular the government encouraged the development of sugar in Formosa. The war encouraged the formation of fanatical patriotic secret societies such as the Black Dragons and enhanced the prestige of the armed forces. This eventually led to a situation where the politicians could no longer exact obedience from the forces. Although few Japanese supported left-wing political parties, the victories provided the opportunity for the government to crush vigorously those who were radicals.

In 1912, the Emperor Meiji, who had presided over the emergence of Japan as a great nation, died. The Emperor's funeral was the opportunity for striking demonstrations of loyalty, of which the most extreme was the suicide of General Nogi, hero of the capture of Port Arthur, who revived the almost forgotten custom whereby the Emperor's servants followed their master into eternity. Meiji was succeeded by his third son, Yoshito Harunomiya, who became Emperor Taisho but he was so weak and ineffective that, by 1921, he was compelled to allow his son to rule as regent.

e) Japan and the First World War

Economic benefits

The war of 1914–18 proved to be of great value to Japan, benefiting her economy and giving her a free hand in China as her rivals in that country were preoccupied with the European conflict. The unfavourable balance of trade and massive debt were quickly cleared since the Allies placed large orders with Japanese firms and since neutrals increased their trade with Japan to compensate for the disruption of European trade. The Japanese merchant navy increased rapidly and by 1919 Japanese credit abroad equalled the debt she had owed in 1914.

Attacks on China

But the opportunity to increase her influence in China was seized with a vigour which offended both Britain and the U.S.A. At first Japan simply took over German concessions in Shantung, but then Foreign Minister Kato over-played his hand by issuing the Twenty-one Demands to China.

Japan asked for all German leaseholds in Shantung to be transferred to her, the extension of Japanese rights in Manchuria and the purchasing of at least half of China's war materials from Japan. She also demanded that the Chinese government should employ Japanese political, financial and military advisers and that Japanese police should share in the administration of important cities. Although the more extreme demands were eventually dropped, they nevertheless did harm to Japanese prestige, even though this might seem harsh to Japan since European behaviour in Africa and Asia had frequently been extremely unscrupulous.

Further opportunity to interfere on the mainland was provided by the Russian Bolshevik Revolution. Japanese troops were sent, ostensibly, to help in the rescue of the Czech Legion, in fact they stayed long after the Czechs had gone and the Kolchak regime had collapsed, and did not leave Eastern Siberia until 1922 and North Sakhalin till 1925.

At the peace conferences held after the war, Japan obtained Germany's rights in Shantung, two former German colonies on mandate and a permanent seat on the League Council. But Japan did not obtain the clear declaration of racial equality that both she and China had hoped for. Dislike of the Western powers persisted strongly in Japan, aggravated by the Western tendency to be condescending when dealing with Asians.

f) The Failure of Parliamentary Government

Post-war Japan

The defeat of Germany by the Western democracies encouraged those who wished to see parliamentary democracy flourish in Japan. The right-wing Terauchi government resigned, unable to cope with riots caused by rising rice prices and the new Prime Minister was Hata, the first commoner to hold this position (though he was rather more of a party boss than a democratic politician). The death of Yamagata in 1922 accelerated the declining influence of the Choshu clan on the army, whilst the behaviour and clothing of the Prince Regent, who modelled himself on the Prince of Wales, was another sign of the changing times. General Ugaki's cuts in military expenditure emphasised the apparent decline in the power and prestige of the armed forces. The zaibatsu backed politicians like Kato, Wakatsuki and Shidehara who seemed to be moving towards moderate liberalism, and so did the only surviving genro, Saionji, and the awarding of the franchise to all men over twenty-five years of age seemed to indicate that this policy was triumphing.

General Shunroku Hata, Japanese politician and a former Minister of War.

Growing Unrest

But there were other factors showing the huge obstacles to be surmounted if Japanese politicians were to create a stable parliamentary democracy. In September, 1923, great distress was caused by a huge earthquake in the Tokyo-Yokohama area which killed 100,000 people. By mid-1921 the war boom had collapsed and the discontent that unemployment provoked led to the passing of the Peace Preservation Law. Under this law anyone who formed or joined a society which had the object of changing the national way of life or the form of government, or denying the system of private ownership, could be imprisoned and, before long (by an amendment) even executed. The Washington Conference of 1921 pleased Japan by giving her security through the status quo agreement on naval bases in the East and by the 5:5:3 ratio of capital ship tonnage between Britain, the U.S.A. and Japan. But it also made Japan withdraw from Shantung and shortly afterwards the British yielded to American and Dominion pressure and refused to renew their treaty of alliance with Japan. In 1924 the U.S.A. further offended Japan by passing discriminating legislation against Asian immigrants. Japan had acquired a modern industrial system without a corresponding growth of liberalism for both tradition and circumstances combined to concentrate in a few hands control over wide sections of finance, commerce and industry. The agricultural areas remained basically conservative in outlook, whilst the paternalism of the zaibatsu (providing family allowances and retaining surplus labour) reduced the attractions of trade unions and moderate political parties. A series of arrests during 1928–30 decimated the left-wing and rendered it impotent to resist the growing militarism which soon destroyed the work of moderate politicians.

The Growth of Nationalism

An economic depression from 1927–31 increased discontent and, as in Germany, made people ready to welcome a vigorous nationalist appeal. Extreme political and economic ideas appeared and spread, especially among young army officers and civil servants who favoured, above all, the ideas of Kita Ikki. Ikki advocated a kind of Japanese fascism under which capitalists would hand over their power to the emperor and a form of state socialism would be established, run by a military dictatorship. The behaviour of the Diet presented an unsavoury spectacle of corruption and brawling which was a poor advertisement for parliamentary government to offset Kita Ikki's ideas.

The restless state of the Army

The moderate Hamaguchi government was ruined by the depression in which the silk trade, a secondary employment for nearly half the country's farmers, was especially badly hit. Rice crop failures led to famine, and all this discontent was bound to be reflected in the army which recruited its ordinary soldiers chiefly from the peasantry, and its officers from smaller landowners. In November, 1930, an attempt to murder Hamaguchi crippled him and caused his eventual death, and his successor, Wakatsuki, might well have suffered a similar fate if the army conspirators of the 'March Incident' had managed to persuade General Ugaki, Minister of War, to lead them. As it was, the would-be rebels went unpunished, as had earlier plotters who, in 1929, had assassinated a Chinese warlord as part of a plan to stage a coup in Mukden that had eventually failed. All the signs indicated that the restless armed forces were likely to take matters into their own hands and there was little the politicians could do about it.

g) Japan's Conquest of Manchuria

Japanese aggression in China was not simply caused by militarism and the fanaticism of the patriotic societies. Japan depended heavily on China for imports, indeed for the bulk of her lead, iron, aluminium, tin, petroleum, rubber, cotton and wool. The ability to pay for all these, and for the food imports made necessary by the continued growth in population, was badly damaged by the fall in the price of silk by one-third between 1925 and 1929. However, it was the military conquest which caught the world's attention, not the economic problems, and led many to condemn the Japanese government when, in fact, the Emperor, many intellectuals and politicians were against the army's actions. A resolute

Prime Minister like Inukai might have checked the army, but Inukai was assassinated: Yamagata might have held the army under firm control, but Yamagata was dead and the standard of army discipline declined: the Emperor Showa might have halted the army, but the politicians would not allow him to become involved in controversy.

The War in Manchuria

On the 18th September, 1931, the Japanese Kwangtung Army, based on Port Arthur, seized Mukden as a first step in its bid to win control of the whole of Manchuria and to halt the apparent success of Chiang Kai-shek in uniting China (a success for which the army tended to blame the 'good neighbour' policy towards China of Japan's Foreign Minister, Shidehara). News of the intended coup had reached Tokyo, but since Miriami, Minister of War, favoured the rebels, the government's attempts to halt the rising were ineffective. Japan's representative at the League of Nations accepted the League's resolution calling for withdrawal and thus earned Wakatsuki's government a reputation for deceit, since the army, far from withdrawing, extended its operations in Manchuria. In fact, Wakatsuki was both humiliated and embarrassed by his inability to halt the army and implement the League's resolution.

The Collapse of Moderate Government

After Wakatsuki, Inukai was the last Prime Minister to head a normal party government. A wave of emotional and extreme patriotism destroyed or thwarted the men who tried to maintain the supremacy of politicians over soldiers. The 'League of Blood' drew up a list of such moderates, with the intention of exterminating them, and Inukai figured prominently on that list. But though the League killed Inouye, a former finance minister, and Baron Dan, a Mitsui Director, Inukai himself was murdered not by the League, but by a group of young naval officers and army cadets who burst into the Prime Minister's residence and shot him. Admiral Saito took his place as Prime Minister, but real power lay with the leaders of the army faction known as *Koda-ha* who wished Japan to expand at the expense of Russia. Their rivals were the *Tosei-ha* who advocated friendship with Russia so that Japan could expand in South China.

Manchuria itself was soon conquered and, renamed Manchukuo, was governed by a puppet Chinese ruler, Pu Yi. The League of Nations adopted the Lytton Report which condemned Japanese action: the Japanese reply was to leave the League. The army's success made life hard for men of moderate views in Japan. Schools were ordered to devote more time to teaching Shinto and army training, and several liberal-minded university scholars like Professor Minobe were forced to resign. Within the government the two army factions fought for supremacy until, eventually, the Tosei-ha emerged triumphant. The Koda-ha lost ground through the illness and failure of some of its leaders and through being blamed for an army mutiny during which there was an attempt on the life of Admiral Okada (Prime Minister 1934–36). It was the Tosei-ha which dominated the Hirota government which took office in 1936, increased military expenditure by fifty per cent. and denounced the Washington Agreement and the London Disarmament Treaty.

Military success was coupled with economic recovery in which the possession of the rich resources of Manchuria proved very valuable. During 1930–36 Japanese exports almost doubled, increasing trade with South East Asia and China (at the expense of trade with the U.S.A. which declined) and helps show why the Tosei-ha considered their views to be in the interests of their country.

h) The extension of the War 1937–45

In 1937 a new Prime Minister, Prince Konoye, took office in an atmosphere of goodwill in which both politicians and soldiers expected much of him. In fact his few attempts to stand up to the army proved unsuccessful and the whole area of conflict in China soon widened. Japan signed the Anti-Comintern Pact in 1936, evidence of her hostility towards the Chinese Communists who were (officially at least) co-operating with Chiang Kai-shek against the invaders. Shanghai, Nanking, Canton and Hankow all fell rapidly to the Japanese in their bid to put such heavy pressure on Chiang that he would sue for peace. But although Chiang's resistance was small, he would not come to terms and the Japanese were forced to establish another puppet regime. This one, based on Nanking, was headed by a Kuomintang (Chinese National Party) deserter, Wang Ching Wei.

The news of the 1939 pact between Hitler and Stalin came as a shock to the Japanese who had not been consulted. They had regarded the Anti-Comintern Pact as directed against Russia, as well as against Chinese Communism and Japanese troops had been suffering in clashes with Zhukov's Russians on the frontier between North China and Russia. Japan was able to obtain her revenge on Hitler in 1941 when, although Germany urged Japan to attack Russia, the Japanese preferred to sign a neutrality pact and concentrate on their South-East Asia campaigns.

The defeats suffered in 1940 by the French and British offered opportunities for extending Japanese control into the valuable oil, rubber and mineral areas which the government could not resist. The war was fought by a mass national grouping of military and political elements led by Konoye that claimed it was going to establish a 'New Order' in the East. At first the Japanese were quite popular in the areas they freed from European rule, a Great East Asia Ministry was established in Tokyo and an East Asian Conference held in 1943 which adopted a charter pledging the participant countries to rid Asia of British and American influence. But the Japanese underestimated their enemies and ill-treated those who should have been their friends. After the shock of early defeats, the British showed great powers of recovery, and the U.S.A. demonstrated a fighting spirit that many Japanese had been confident she lacked. Japanese planning was inflexible – unable, for instance, to devise an effective convoy system that could check the Allied submarine campaign which was, by 1943, sinking far more ships than could be replaced by new building. The harshness of Japanese rule in the areas they had conquered (especially the brutality of the military police) lost them the goodwill they had at first experienced and partisan movements developed which were often Communist led. The rise of Asian Communism is one of the most important legacies of Japanese rule in Asia.

The entry into the war of Russia, the shipping losses, the effect of Allied bombing and finally the destruction by atomic bombs of Hiroshima and Nagasaki eventually led to a peace party, led by Togo and backed by the Emperor, agreeing to unconditional surrender. A final desperate bid by extremists to avert this failed. They planned to prevent the broadcast of the Emperor's recorded message of surrender, but were talked out of it by a general; four of the plotters committed suicide on the spot. Throughout the country a few groups of diehards committed suicide, one body of them seized a hill in Tokyo, and when attacked, blew themselves up with a hand-grenade.

i) Japan under Allied Occupation

Japan had never known occupation before and regarded with curiosity the Americans who formed the bulk of the occupation force. In theory, Japan was controlled by an eleven-nation Far East Commission in Washington, with a four-nation advisory council in Tokyo, but in fact it was controlled by General MacArthur, head of the S.C.A.P. (Supreme Command for Allied Powers) until he was dismissed in 1951 by President Truman.

War in the Pacific: U.S. Marines examine amtracks (ammunition tracks) and tanks bogged down on a beach on Iwo Jima after the Fourth Division fought their way ashore in March, 1945.

Changes in the Japanese Way of Life

S.C.A.P. initiated a series of reforms designed to transform Japan into a respectable peaceful liberal democracy. Women were given the vote, political prisoners freed, the Emperor renounced his 'divine status' and a constitution that was largely the work of MacArthur's staff laid down basic principles (like 'sovereignty of the People') which were revolutionary to the Japanese. The House of Peers was abolished and replaced by the House of Councillors elected by universal suffrage through a system whereby half of the members had to stand for re-election every three years. The Lower House had a maximum life of four years. Further safeguards against the re-emergence of military dominance included provisions that ministers must be members of the Diet, and that all members of the government must be civilians. In order to amend the constitution a two-thirds majority of the Diet and a favourable referendum of the people, were laid down as necessary. Article Nine of the constitution forbade Japan the possession of any armed forces, though the Americans later regretted this when they tried to develop Japan as an ally against Communism. But many Japanese did not agree with the

American politician, Nixon, when he declared in 1953 that Article Nine had been a mistake. Such people preferred to see their country follow a distinctive non-military line, avoiding excessive tension with such powerful close neighbours as China and Russia, and they disliked the devious method of obtaining Japanese armed forces by means of big increases in the police.

A variety of other reforms helped remodel Japan. A decentralised co-educational school system on the American pattern was organised: land reform was begun: a new judicial and administrative system was created: the zaibatsu were dissolved. Until 1948, however, economic recovery was slow, it was not easy to feed a population of 90 millions (swelled by Japanese repatriated home when Japan was deprived of her war conquests) and one of the features of life in post-war Japan was the train loads of foragers who poured out from towns to the countryside, searching for food. Left-wing parties and trade unions grew rapidly, but anti-Americanism was not strong for several years, despite MacArthur's rather vain and aloof attitude, despite too the fact that S.C.A.P. tended to be overhasty and clumsy in its reforms, sometimes destroying the good as well as the bad.

From 1945 until 1946 the veteran politician, Shidehara, served as Prime Minister. The following years until 1954 were dominated by Yoshida who held office for almost seven years within that period. S.C.A.P. was not altogether happy about the reliability of some politicians, even though post-war trials of war criminals had sentenced over 5,000 (executing over 500 of them) and even though the Emperor now seemed a tired middle-aged man to the Japanese, as he toured the country to exhort his people to accept defeat, 'to bear the unbearable'. Early in 1946 S.C.A.P. conducted a series of purges which affected about 200,000 people removing them from politics and excluding from the Diet all but forty-eight of its members.

Economic Recovery

After 1948 the Japanese economy began to expand more vigorously, helped by the Korean War which brought orders for war materials and money for U.S. bases in Japan. The economy was more diversified than in its pre-war days, less heavily dependent on textiles and included rapidly growing metal, chemical and engineering works. The Japanese proved particularly successful at ship-building and by the late 1950's were the world's leading shipbuilders. Amid this resurgence the old zaibatsu reappeared and 'purged' leaders also emerged once more in political life.

j) Modern Japan

The end of occupation

As economic conditions improved, so the occupation came to seem more irritating to the Japanese. The Americans were eager to end occupation and convert Japan into an ally in the clash with Communism. But attempts to hold a peace conference, in 1947–8, broke down and the U.S.A. tended to go its own way, encouraging Japanese autonomy and finally initiating a peace treaty in September, 1951. John Foster Dulles was given the task of convincing other states that a mild treaty would be the most satisfactory (Britain, Australia and New Zealand wanted various restrictions to be imposed). Russia and her allies refused to sign the treaty, but the U.S.A. proceeded to recognise Japanese independence on terms that deprived Japan of any claims to Formosa, Korea, the Pescadores, the Kuriles and South Sakhalin. Immediately afterwards the Americans and Japanese signed a security pact.

Anti-American feeling

But though the Occupation was technically over, many Japanese felt that it was still all too evident. American bases were scattered over Japanese soil and American servicemen were a common sight in Japanese cities. In May 1952, this feeling flared up into student rioting in which American cars were set on fire. The anti-American feeling was aggravated in 1954 when an American hydrogen bomb test in the Bikini area affected the crew of a Japanese fishing boat with radiation sickness. The ship's catch was condemned as dangerous, but since some of it had been sold there was a surge of panic in which fish sales slumped. However, this hostility was kept within bounds by the knowledge that Japan depended on the U.S.A. for defence, by the emergence of a strong, united China and by the expanding trade Japan was building up with the U.S.A. – partly to offset the small scale of the formerly massive trade with China.

Conservative control of Japan

On the whole it is the conservatives (the Liberal Democrat Party) who have dominated the politics of modern Japan. With the support of farmers who fear nationalisation and with the help of the expansion of the Japanese economy, the Liberal Democrats have been able to rule the country – to the indignation of the Left which claims that they are following a 'reverse course' (i.e. seeking to undo reforms).

In 1960 the security pact with the U.S.A. was renewed amid great

In commercial and industrial life the Japanese have become almost completely westernised. Only the Japanese trade signs in this photograph of a busy street scene in present day Tokyo immediately identify the location.

opposition in the Diet, huge hostile student rallies and violence provoked by small groups of the extreme Right. The Prime Minister, Ikeda, was attacked, but the most brutal event was the murder of Asanuma, secretary general of the Socialist Party, who was stabbed to death in the full view of an audience and of T.V. cameras. But the cautious moderation of Ikeda helped to damp down discontent and overcame the crisis. Signs of Westernisation have proliferated in Japan: T.V., large stores, even an addiction to golf; whilst the Crown Prince caused a stir by marrying a commoner in 1959. In 1964 Japan was honoured by the holding of the Olympic Games in Tokyo.

Though still a base for American aircraft and ships, Japan is a member of the U.N. and apparently determined to follow her own line of non-violence. The impressive performance of Japanese industry is a crucial factor in preserving stability, for the country supports a huge population. Japan's reaction to the impact of the West provides a striking contrast to the reaction of China, for Japan sought to borrow ideas from the West and has done so most successfully. But whilst it is relatively easy to borrow economic techniques, it is far more difficult to borrow political ideas and institutions and it remains to be seen whether the system of representative parliamentary government has struck deep roots in Japan. To Europeans, however, the Japanese have long been a nation to respect as an inventive, skilful people whose products rival those of Europe, and prove superior in many fields. Japanese motor cycles lead the world, Japanese cameras, television sets and motor cars achieve the highest standards, and Japanese shipbuilders often offer better terms than those of any other land.

China

a) The impact of the West on China

Though China is a vast country, much of it is composed of desert, mountains, and high plateaux and the population tends to be heavily concentrated in the rich river valleys with the result that ninety per cent. of the Chinese people live on only one-sixth of the land area. A civilisation had developed in the valleys when Western Europe was still living in barbarity and the Chinese with such an ancient and highly developed culture tended to be contemptuous of foreign 'barbarians' who came to their shores. China, 'the Middle Kingdom' considered itself the greatest power on earth, the only true civilisation, a country which had no need of trade with foreigners. There was no notion of equality with other states, China had no foreign relations but simply a 'Hall for the Governance of Barbarians' and a Board to fix the tribute to be paid by the barbarians.

Until the nineteenth century the West respected the huge centralised state of China: though it contained extremes of wealth and poverty so did Europe. But the industrial revolution, the growth in Europe's population, improved communications and methods of warfare all produced pressures to seek trade with China, together with the means to enforce this. China was ruled by the Manchus, the last of the twenty-five dynasties that governed the country (in contrast, Japan only ever had one dynasty). By the mid-nineteenth century Manchu rule had lost its early vigour and was put under some strain coping with the Chinese people's dislike of Manchu government, expressed through the growing number of secret societies which gained additional recruits from peasants ruined by the economic consequences of a rise in population.

European Attacks

An abrupt shock was inflicted on China by the military strength of the West, first demonstrated by the British in the Opium Wars which were ended in 1842 by the Treaty of Nanking. Britain acquired Hong Kong and forced the opening to trade of certain 'treaty ports', a policy which the French, Germans and Russians were quick to imitate. Control of a ring of important ports did not satisfy the Europeans, however: they moved inland seeking to establish spheres of influence, running railways and taking control of customs duties on the excuse that it was a guarantee against the loans they persuaded the Manchu rulers to accept.

The Failure of Reforms

Further weakened by the great Taiping Rebellion, the Manchus proved unable either to muster conservative forces effectively or to adopt the Western ideas which China had, for so long, scorned as contemptible. Soon China had to face an additional enemy, for Japan, which had eagerly copied the West, imitated Western imperialism too, overwhelmed China in a war, 1894–5, and extorted further concessions. This desperate situation in which control of the Chinese economy fell increasingly out of Chinese hands, in which Chinese were even kidnapped and sent abroad to work, prompted an attempt at desperate remedies in 1898. The new young Emperor instituted the 'Hundred Days of Reform' in which decrees abolished the old system of examination for choosing mandarins, established colleges and high schools, founded the Peking National University, reorganised the army on modern lines and gave all subjects the right to submit memorials to the throne.

But whereas this kind of policy had come early in Japan, and had triumphed, in China it came late and was thwarted by the Empress Dowager Tzu Hsi who had dominated government since 1860. Assisted by her favourite eunuch, Li Lien-ying, she proved too skilful and unscrupulous for the Emperor and his reforming advisers. Six leading reformers were executed, the Emperor was arrested and all that survived from the Hundred Days was Peking University. The Empress preferred to trust to the forces of conservatism, she allowed the Boxers to flourish (as did sympathetic governors like Yu Hsien in Shensi). The Boxer movement attracted many groups: those who hated foreigners; those motivated by social discontent; those of a Taoist religious inclination, who thought that the rituals associated with the 'Society of Harmonious Fists' (i.e. the Boxers) conferred invulnerability on them.

The Boxer Rising

But the Empress' policy proved hopelessly wrong for in 1900, helped by General Ting's Moslem troops, the Boxers rose in revolt against the foreigners and could not even capture the foreign legations in Peking. Although they destroyed such signs of the West as they could (both machinery and missionaries were common targets) the Boxers were easily defeated by a combined force of Western and Japanese troops who conducted a vicious punitive campaign and forced the Chinese government to accept the Boxer Protocol (1901). This awarded the foreigners an indemnity, gave them an extra-territorial area for their legations in Peking plus the right to keep troops there and the abolition of imperial examinations for five years so that the missionaries could increase their intellectual influence.

The Boxer Rising's defeat was a terrible humiliation for China and the Empress decided that a desperate attempt to reform China and copy the Western powers was the only way to stay in power. Between 1902 and 1908 the old entrance examination for the Civil Service was abolished, changes were made in the law, a national army was set up, new schools were established, and plans were drawn up to introduce elected assemblies to share in ruling the provinces and, eventually, a national parliament as well. A number of Chinese were sent overseas to study in the U.S.A., Japan, and West Europe so that they might learn the secrets of the success of these lands and bring the same benefits to China. But the reforms were too few, they were introduced far too late and they offered nothing to the peasants. The students who went abroad learned many things, but one of their clearest lessons was the need for a capable government in China, a need which the Manchus could no longer supply.

b) The end of Manchu rule

Thus the Boxer episode was a blow from which the Manchus never recovered. The Empress died in 1908 to be succeeded by a Regent, but greater power lay with the cunning Yuan Shih-kai who had built up a Model Army and encouraged some reforms. The example of Japan influenced many Chinese, some of whom went to Japan to study, among them Sun Yat-sen, founder of the Alliance Society which aimed to dethrone the Manchus, establish a republic, and carry out land reforms.

Few Chinese were willing to exert themselves to save the Manchus, so that although the anti-Manchu groups were far from united, it in fact proved easy to dislodge the boy Emperor Pu Yi. Allowing last minute reforms such as a revised legal code and a promise of parliamentary government were insufficient to dampen the anger of Chinese patriots, indignant at the way the foreigners were now starting to detach outer regions like Manchuria and Outer Mongolia. In 1911 the spark of revolt eventually came, a rising in Wuhan, which was crushed by Yuan Shih-kai. Having clearly shown the power of his army, Yuan did nothing further

R

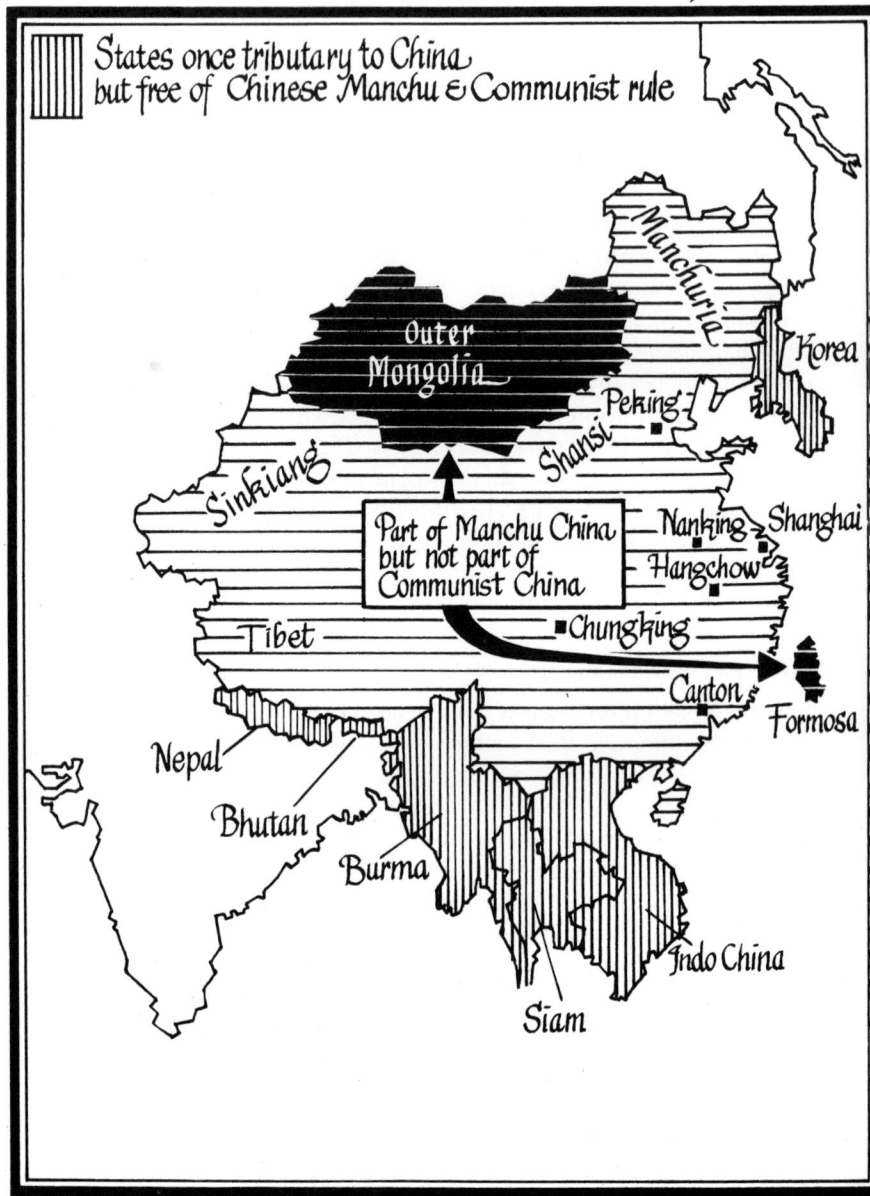

The Manchu Chinese Empire, 1911, & the Communist Empire

States once tributary to China but free of Chinese Manchu & Communist rule

Outer Mongolia

Manchuria

Korea

Peking

Shansi

Sinkiang

Nanking

Shanghai

Part of Manchu China but not part of Communist China

Hangchow

Tibet

Chungking

Canton

Formosa

Nepal

Bhutan

Burma

Indo China

Siam

to deal with revolts in south and west China inspired by the Wuhan rising. All over China the local population killed Manchu garrisons and soon centralised government was disintegrating. One of these rebel regimes was set up by Sun Yat-sen at Nanking. He declared that China was now a republic and that he was the President of it, though he also declared that he would resign if Yuan would compel the Manchus to abdicate. On February 12, 1912 the Manchu Emperor abdicated and Yuan was installed as President of the new republic of China.

c) Warlord rule

From 1911 until the eventual triumph of the Communists in 1949, no government effectively ruled China. Independent bodies of troops under local warlords formed constantly shifting and struggling alliances and no regime, not even Chiang Kai-shek's, could maintain itself without the aid of a warlord coalition. During this period China suffered not only from civil war, but also from determined Japanese aggression which the Chinese proved unable to halt. The miseries suffered by the Chinese during this period help explain why Mao Tse-tung's Communists, with their resolute hostility to landlords and to foreigners, were able to win such support from the peasantry.

The Fall of Yuan Shih-Kai

Until his death in 1916, Yuan remained the most prominent figure in China, but he could not control the warlords and resorted to the device of legalising their position by appointing them as governors. Yuan showed little sympathy for reformers like Sun who wanted drastic changes and a more democratic political structure. Helped by foreign loans he was able, for the moment, to thwart the reformers who had transformed Sun's party into the Kuomintang (National Party), he crushed their forces, declared the Kuomintang illegal, and dissolved parliament. His personal ambition became all too clear when, in December 1915, Yuan declared himself Emperor of China. This increasing arrogance proved his downfall, however, even his former supporters turned against him and so isolated him that in March, 1916, he hastily abdicated, leaving no tangible mark of his rule except a large quantity of porcelain, specially manufactured to commemorate the first year of his reign. Yuan died on June 6th, 1916, leaving a formidable record of treachery: he had betrayed the reforming Emperor Kuang Hsu to the Empress Dowager, the Manchus to the Republic, and finally the Republic itself.

It was during this period that the Japanese occupied German concessions in Shantung and pressed most of the Twenty-one Demands on China. The Versailles Conference after the First World War allowed the Japanese to stay in Shantung and brushed aside Chinese requests for the cancellation of the Twenty-one Demands. The Chinese reformers were increasingly disillusioned by the behaviour of the Western powers and began to look towards the new Communist government of Russia.

The Kuomintang Party, strengthened by students from Peking University, was still not powerful enough to menace the grip on the country held by the warlords. The warlords even competed with the Kuomintang for Russian weapons, realising that if they proclaimed a few revolutionary slogans they might receive weapons with which to continue their perpetual struggle with each other. Manchuria, encouraged by Japan, declared itself independent, and the rest of the warlords in the North were divided into two factions, the Anfu group and the Wu Pe'i fu group. Outer Mongolia also declared its independence, with the help of Russia, under a People's Revolutionary Government.

Sun Yat-sen

Although all the raw material of a revolution appeared to be present in China, the Kuomintang seemed to lack the ideas and organisation that could give it mass appeal. Their leader, Sun Yat-sen, the son of a poor farmer, had been educated (in missionary schools and at Hong Kong) to think well of West European democracies and hoped for aid from them. He was very disappointed to receive nothing and was driven, therefore, to turn to the Russian Communists for the skilled aid that he needed. In 1920 Sun had been able (through the protection of a local warlord) to establish himself in Canton. Though temporarily dislodged by a quarrel, Sun's National Government was back in Canton in 1923, helped by Russian missions led by Adolph Joffe and Michael Borodin. Since the Russians had advised the tiny Chinese Communist Party to co-operate with the Kuomintang, Soviet aid to Sun was thought to be in order. Chiang Kai-shek was sent to Moscow to study military science, and returned to found the Whampoa Academy where he was assisted by a Russian, Bluecher: meanwhile Sun had decided to proclaim his 'Three Principles' in a manner which identified his party with anti-imperialism and vigorous reform. The Three Principles were those of Nationalism, Democracy and the People's Livelihood which meant, basically, setting up in China a strong central government, educating the mass of the people so that they could take part in China's political life, and giving the land to those who cultivated it whilst allowing

General Chiang Kai-shek with one of his wives. A picture taken in the 1930s.

the state some control of industry. On the 12th March, 1925, Sun died, having never enjoyed much real power. The Kuomintang still needed warlord assistance, as Sun's Academy only produced officers. Much of Sun's life had been spent abroad in exile (in 1896 he had even been kidnapped in London and hidden for ten days in the Chinese legation), nor was he a great original thinker. But his determination and his opportunism, coupled with the increasing radicalism of his thought, made him a man that Chinese Communists like to remember as a fore-runner of modern China.

Early Chinese Communism

The Chinese Communist Party was officially founded on 1st July, 1921, on a boat anchored on a lake at Shaohsing. Its General Secretary was Ch'en Tu-hsiu, who had founded a revolutionary Marxist group in 1920 in Shanghai. Very little was known in China about the ideas of Communism until the October Revolution of 1917, but the strong opposition of Communists to imperialism was certainly very appealing to the Chinese, who had suffered far too much from foreign interference. Since the party was small, consisted mostly of intellectuals and had no military influence, it seemed sensible at first to join the Kuomintang – a policy which had Soviet support. Borodin and his Russian advisers helped the Chinese Communists grow in strength and influence until the more conservative Kuomintang members became alarmed. One of the more prominent Communists was Mao Tse-tung. Mao Tse-tung had had a difficult life almost since his birth in 1893. His father, a peasant farmer, was a stern master who made his son work hard in the fields and had no sympathy for Mao's ideas. He was sent to school in Hunan and to a Teachers' Training College in Changsha. It is clear he was both a clever and hard working student who cared deeply about the terrible confusion which existed in China and the misery in which most peasants lived. After working as a library assistant, Mao returned to Changsha as a teacher and spent much of his spare time in politics. He had studied the writings of Karl Marx for some time, and decided to set up a branch of the Party in Changsha; this work showed his skill as an organiser and agitator and he gained prominence in the small Chinese Communist Party. For the time being the Communists, mindful of their weakness, threw in their lot with the Kuomintang who provided them with the necessary protection. Following the death of Sun the Communists found their position less certain, for among those who aspired to leadership of the Kuomintang were men who hated the Communists.

d) The Rise of Chiang Kai-shek

After a period of some confusion within the party, Chiang Kai-shek emerged as the dominant figure in the Kuomintang. Chiang had trained as a soldier first in China, then in Tokyo, and had helped to drive the Manchus out of power. He was a devoted republican and, as commandant of the Whampoa Military Academy, commanded much respect and influence. He was assisted in his rise to power by the Russians, who thought he would hold the balance between the right and left-wing elements and that he could be kept under control by satisfying his lust for glory. Chiang became the Kuomintang commander-in-chief and was supplied with Soviet war materials. In fact the Russians made a grave miscalculation, and put the Chinese Communists at Chiang's mercy. Sun Yat-sen had been planning a northern campaign on which he planned to send Kuomintang forces to aid Chang Tso-lin, ruler of Manchuria, against a group of warlords. In 1926 Chiang began this Northern campaign, still supplied with aid by Stalin who saw the Northern warlords as agents of imperialism. This campaign went well, Chiang's forces took Nanking, dominated the middle and lower Yangtze and enabled the Kuomintang government to move to Wuhan and then to Nanking. The vital port of Shanghai was taken, and Chiang's position was further aided by the death of Chang Tso-lin (killed by explosions which blew up his train) and the accession to power of Chang Hsueh-liang, 'the Young Marshal', who declared he would support the Kuomintang.

Chiang's attack on the Communists

Chiang was now in a strong position to deal with the Communists who had been causing him increasing alarm by organising discontented peasantry and encouraging the restless workers of Hankow. Despite assurances from the Russians that a bourgeois revolution was all the Communists were trying to bring about, Chiang decided to strike at the Communists and their left-wing Kuomintang allies. All Chiang's connections were with conservative elements, and the loans he obtained from Shanghai bankers freed him from heavy reliance on the Russians for aid. On 12th April, 1927, the Communists in Shanghai were massacred. Local warlords in many other regions followed this example and killed such Communists as they could catch. A switch in policy by Stalin failed to save the situation and the Soviet advisers were expelled from the country. Stalin encouraged the setting up of Chinese Soviets, but an attack on Swatow failed, the 'Autumn Harvest' uprising was crushed (Mao was blamed for this and dismissed from the C.C.P. Politburo) and finally a desperate rising in Canton which gave the Communists control of the city for two days was suppressed. The Communist Party seemed shattered beyond recovery.

e) The revival of the Communist Party

Chiang Kai-shek had triumphed but he was still far from being the effective ruler of China. For want of an adequate alternative he still adhered to Sun's Three Principles, but as he had become increasingly conservative in outlook, he did nothing to bring about the enactment of the principles of democracy and the People's Livelihood. Although he did much to rid China of her unequal treaties with foreign powers, his efforts to give material form to Nationalism were weak. The main enemy was Japan, but Chiang's resistance to Japanese demands was feeble, he clearly rated exterminating the Communists as his highest priority. He also had to cope with intrigues against him within the Kuomintang and with rebellions by warlords such as the Kwangsi group, and Feng Yu-hsiang (a general who took up Christianity with such fervour that he insisted all his army be converted and baptised them with a fire hose). The Communists refused to be crushed and staged insurrections which gave them temporary control of some towns. Poverty-stricken China was overburdened with troops, at least $2\frac{1}{2}$ millions of them, and Chiang seemed all too much like just another warlord unworthy of popular support, even though he displayed great skill at dividing and overcoming his enemies. Chiang's reforms, such as they were, brought benefits to the well-to-do, not the peasantry. He improved transport, education and hospitals, but did not attempt to tackle the land question and preferred to allow the landlords to continue to extract huge rents from the peasantry. Chiang's rule relied chiefly on force, censorship, and secret police, so that though most Chinese knew nothing of Karl Marx and his ideas, they did know that Chiang's rule was not worth fighting for. The Communists, on the other hand, made increasing efforts to appeal to the peasantry: when they won control of a village they gave the land to the peasants, cancelled the peasants' debts, and set up a peasants' association to manage village affairs. The Red Army's discipline was far stricter than that of other armies in China, including Chiang's, and this too helped win respect for the Communists.

Japan's attacks on China

The Japanese attack on Manchuria in 1931 put an end to Chiang's hopes of success, for as anti-Japanese feeling rose in China, so it became more difficult for him to justify his policy of concentrating on exterminating the Communists. The loss of Manchuria deprived China of valuable resources, thirty per cent. of her coal, seventy-one per cent. of her iron ore, and twenty per cent. of her electricity. Mongol nationalism revived, Sinkiang looked to Russia rather than Nanking, and by 1934 Chiang controlled only about half of the old Manchu Empire. The only spirited resistance to the Japanese was led by Ma Chan-Shan who not only fought bravely, but also 'defected' to the Japanese, became

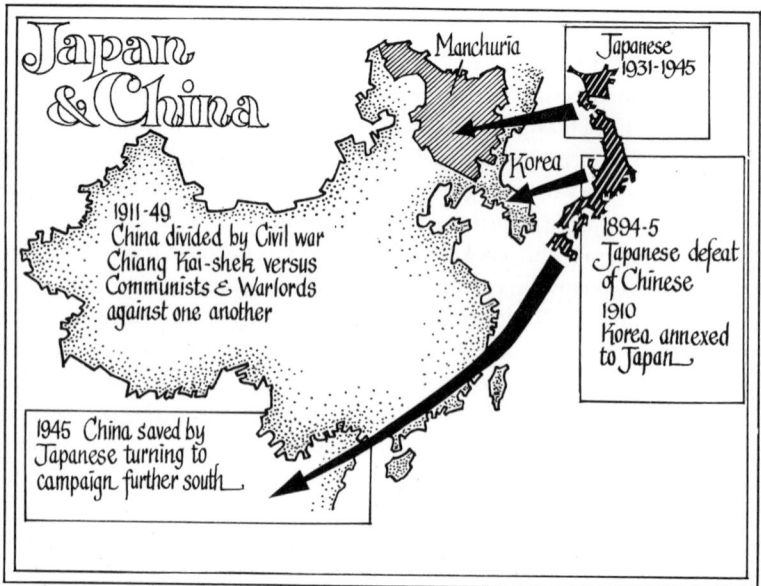

Japan & China

Manchuria

Korea

Japanese 1931-1945

1911-49
China divided by Civil war
Chiang Kai-shek versus
Communists & Warlords
against one another

1894-5
Japanese defeat
of Chinese
1910
Korea annexed
to Japan

1945 China saved by
Japanese turning to
campaign further south

Minister of War in Manchukuo and then escaped with a truck convoy of useful supplies. The Japanese resurrected Pu Yi, to be nominal head of their Manchukuo government (Pu Yi's curious career led, later, to imprisonment by the Communists and eventual release as a reformed man who regretted his past behaviour).

The 'Red Army' Appears

The Communists were led by two separate groups. Officially their leaders were the Central Committee and the Politburo living in secret in Shanghai but more effective power was exercised by Mao Tse-tung and by Chu Teh who led the Red Army. The Red Army was recruited largely from peasantry; following 1931 its ranks were swelled by men made desperate by a terrible famine, which killed thousands and left many more destitute. Consisting of about 10,000 men, the army lived a hard existence in Ching Kangshan, was forced to fight frequent battles and only able to raise money by ransoms and forced levies. But at least they became hardened to suffering and their leaders saw clearly the need to appeal primarily to the poor peasantry. In 1929 the Red Army shifted its base to South Kiangsi and by 1931 its leaders were linked more clearly with the Party's official leadership. A meeting in November at Juichen elected Mao as Chairman of the Central Executive Committee of the Party. Under his guidance the area controlled by the Red Army was subjected to reforms in which confiscated land, taken from landlords and rich peasants, was redistributed among poorer peasants. These peasants were also vigorously instructed in Mao's version of Communism. By now Mao had come to realise that he must concentrate on the countryside, and not the towns. This was a break with orthodox Marxism which maintained that only the urban proletariat were a truly revolutionary force, and it was a break with Comintern policy. But Mao had reached this conclusion after the hard experience of seeing the failure of Communist attempts to seize and hold towns supposed to be ripe for revolt. His tactics eventually proved successful because there was so much discontent to exploit. The prevalence of banditry, the growth of anti-warlord and anti-foreign secret societies like the Red Spears (in 1928 it was estimated that 730,000 peasants north of the Yangtze belonged to secret societies), the decay of industry, the restlessness of intellectuals, and Chiang's failure to find a successful political philosophy to replace the old Confucian religion, all show why the Communist appeal could be so strong. Communism offered real reforms, resolute hostility to warlords and foreigners, and a simple striking political philosophy.

f) The Long March

Chiang was now assisted by German military advisers, who had replaced the Russians. But his initial attempts to finish off the Communists failed and he decided to try a new strategy. In 1933 Chiang's forces abandoned direct attacks on the Communist strongholds in favour of a policy of encirclement which ringed the Communist held areas with block houses and fortifications and then enforced an economic blockade.

By October 1934 it was clear to the Communists that they would have to break out and seek a more distant stronghold. About 90,000 Communists pushed through Chiang's defences and embarked on an astonishing 6,000-mile-long march which took them over twelve provinces, eighteen mountain ranges and twenty-four rivers, and involved fighting several pitched battles. The 'Long March' lasted just over a year, the losses sustained by the Communists were huge, but eventually Mao led 20,000 followers to a resting place in Shensi Province where they linked up with Communist partisans and were safe for the moment.

This apparent triumph for Chiang was marred by the fact that from 1935 onwards the Japanese became increasingly aggressive and extended their control over more of China. Officially both Chiang and the Communists were at war with the Japanese, but in fact Chiang refused all Communist offers of alliance against the common enemy until he was kidnapped by Chang Hsueh-liang and virtually forced to negotiate an alliance in December 1936 (Chang later paid for his presumption by being seized, and has spent the rest of his life as Chiang's prisoner). Communist garrison areas were recognised around Shensi, Kansu, and Ningsia and the Red Army was reorganised into the Eighth Route Army, commanded by Chu Teh who was assisted by P'eng Te-huai, Ho Lung, Lin Piao and Lui Po-ch'eng. The government of the area to which the Long March had brought Mao was reorganised. There were reforms of land tenure and a pyramid of people's councils in which no administrative organ could have more than one third Communist members was set up.

g) The War with Japan, 1936–45

Help for the Chinese in the widening conflict with Japan came primarily from the Soviet Union. The U.S.A. delivered nominal protests, but did little more. Stalin had reason to fear Japanese aggression; faced with the Fascist threat in West Europe, he struggled to avoid the nightmare of a war on two fronts. Russian munitions, aircraft, pilots and military advisers (including Zhukov and Chuikov) were sent to aid the Nationalist

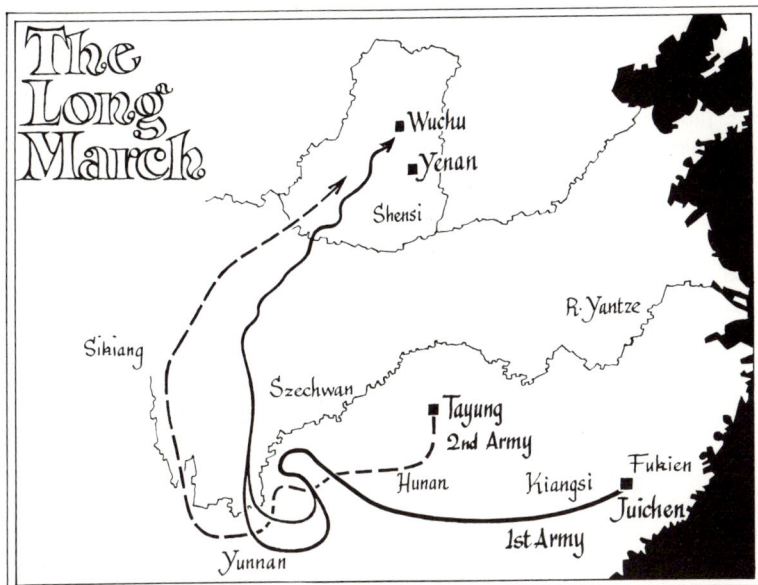

The Long March

Wuchu
Yenan
Shensi
R. Yantze
Sikiang
Szechwan
Tayung
2nd Army
Hunan
Kiangsi
Fukien
Juichen
1st Army
Yunnan

and Communist forces. Chiang made little effective use of these forces, he still lacked heavy artillery, and his commanders were inexperienced in modern warfare and tended to follow the traditional warlord strategy of aiming, chiefly, at the avoidance of heavy losses.

The Japanese campaigns, therefore, followed a pattern of almost unbroken success, taking Shanghai, Nanking and Hankow, and cutting off the Chinese forces from the main seaports. Supplies from abroad could now only come via a single rail link through French Indo-China, or from Russia by an arduous overland motor route. Chiang despite his defeats, refused to accept the harsh peace terms dictated by the Japanese, and the Japanese were pushed into the expedient of establishing a puppet regime in Nanking.

China gained new allies when Japan attacked the European colonies and assaulted U.S. forces too. Now it was the U.S.A.'s turn to send supplies to Chiang, and General Stilwell's turn to attempt to modernise Chinese fighting methods. Stilwell had no more success than Zhukov had met with, nor would Chiang put his American weapons to serious use against the Japanese, he preferred to watch the 'barbarians' fighting each other and concentrated his efforts on pushing Russian influence out of Sinkiang. In 1943 Chiang conferred with Roosevelt and Churchill at a conference held in Cairo, and extracted from them the promise of the return to China of Manchuria, Formosa, and the Pescadores.

The Communists received none of this flow of American aid and their relations with the Kuomintang worsened as it became clear that Chiang was husbanding his forces with a view to striking at those of Mao when the Japanese had left China. Mao busied himself in educating his followers, organising intense small discussion groups and, in February 1942, launching the 'ideological remoulding movement'. Communist troops clashed with the Japanese in guerrilla operations which won them prestige and experience in flexible fighting methods. The Japanese struggle to hold their early conquests in South East Asia left Chiang and Mao to skirmish with one another; Chiang annihilated a remnant of the Communist army which he had ordered away from Shanghai, and a Communist-aided peasant revolt in Honan butchered Kuomintang forces. U.S. attempts to patch up the quarrel were led by Major General Hurley, but met with no success. Thus, even before the war with Japan was over, Communists and Kuomintang were preparing to fight for the control of China, and the control of the Japanese-held areas became a vital point of dispute between them.

h) The Defeat of Chiang Kai-shek

Chiang's forces had a five-to-one superiority over the Communists, a monopoly of the best equipment and U.S. aid, that made nonsense of any American claim to be impartial. The Communist lead in the race for the control of towns was offset by the Americans who airlifted three of Chiang's armies to key points, provided ships to move his troops, and used U.S. marines to hold crucial areas like Tientsin and the Kailan coal mines. MacArthur's Order No. One which designated Chiang as the authority for accepting the surrender of Japanese in China increased the Kuomintang's claims to be the sole legitimate government. After the failure of General Marshall's efforts to bring the war to an end in January 1946 – Chiang would not recognise the truce he arranged – U.S. aid continued to pour into China as part of the developing American policy of resisting Communists. Lend lease, financial credits, payments for the use of war facilities in China, all aided Chiang Kai-shek.

Yet Chiang did not use this aid properly. By rejecting Stilwell's reforms he had missed the chance of having his army modernised at American expense, his strategy remained rigid and unable to cope with the more mobile and flexible Communist methods. Above all the inefficiency and corruption of Kuomintang leaders did great harm to their cause. The greed and selfishness of Kuomintang political and military leaders led to trouble in Manchuria and Formosa especially. Much of the U.S. aid simply went to officials, or even rotted away, unused. The Communists obtained many of their weapons from the Kuomintang forces which showed little spirit and often deserted in large numbers. None of this kind of behaviour was likely to impress the Chinese people, and the government offended still more of them when, in December 1947, it outlawed the Democratic League, a movement with strong backing from scholars and intellectuals.

Mao did not receive large-scale aid from Stalin, who showed little faith in the eventual victory of the Chinese Communists, but he did acquire Japanese weapons in Manchuria which Soviet forces turned over to him. Manchuria was the scene of repeated clashes between the two sides in which Chiang's forces, at first, triumphed, but were unable to pin down and destroy sizeable Communist forces. Teh's soldiers proved adept at avoiding serious defeat, and at attacking the weak points in an enemy whom they forced to over-extend his lines. In 1947 the Communist P.L.A. (People's Liberation Army) conducted successful operations in Manchuria and North China and soon controlled much of the countryside, though not the towns. During 1948 these operations continued, the Communists felt strong enough to risk a major clash and in the battle of Tsinan destroyed 80,000 of Chiang's troops. Chiang decided, too late, to evacuate Manchuria and only a few thousand of his troops escaped; the rest surrendered, were defeated, or simply defected to the P.L.A.

Communist operations extended into central China where their general, Ch'en Yi, launched his army, half a million strong, into battle with a Kuomintang Army of similar size at Hwai-Hai. This vast clash of military might lasted two months and resulted in huge losses on the Kuomintang side, including the destruction of all their American equipped divisions. In the Kuomintang-held towns the economic situation deteriorated since the Communist control of the countryside meant the cutting off of food supplies. The war came to a rapid end in 1949 with General Fu Tso-yi's capitulation in Peking giving Mao control of North China. Nanking fell in April, all Sinkiang in September and Chiang fled with some followers to eventual refuge in Formosa. The victorious Communists proclaimed the establishment of the Central People's Government on the 1st October, 1949, in Peking.

i) The Chinese Communist Government

Mao Tse-tung had developed his own distinctive pattern of thought, stated in works like *On Protracted War*, and *On the New Democracy*; he had certainly no intention of blindly copying Russia. There were to be four classes of people in China, (Confucian China had contained four classes of subject) workers, peasants, petty bourgeoisie, and national bourgeoisie. Landlords, capitalists and Kuomintang reactionaries were deliberately excluded. The Chinese were more tolerant of non-Communists than the Russian Bolsheviks had been, partly from necessity, partly as a result of the special pattern of Chinese thought which believed in the existence of a universal truth that embraced many ideologies. Since most Kuomintang members stayed in China the Communists reorganised them through the Kuomintang Revolutionary Committee. The Democratic League was allowed to exist, though weakened by having its functions limited (chiefly to education) and by being divided into separate categories. The trade unions, the Students Federation, the Federation of Democratic Youth, were all controlled by the state.

Mao held advantages which Lenin had not possessed when he seized power. The Chinese Communists controlled an army of nearly five million men, they were already experienced in ruling the areas they had controlled for many years and they were led by men who had worked together for a long time – Mao Tse-tung, Chu Teh, and Chou En-lai (now premier of the Central People's Government). The country was divided into six military districts each controlled by a general responsible for law and order, the whole structure being led by a People's Revolutionary Military Council whose chairman was Mao. In 1954 the Communists felt more secure and adopted a new constitution which included a Congress which was to meet yearly but was too large to be an effective instrument of government. Effective power was held by a Standing Committee, a State Council, and a Supreme State Conference where the heads of the various state bodies could meet and co-ordinate their work. Below the National Congress lay a structure of Congresses at provincial and local levels, but at every level a Communist Party organisation made sure that the assembly was controlled by the right people.

j) Domestic Reforms – Agriculture

The Communists launched intensive campaigns against the evil legacies of Kuomintang rule – corruption, bribery, tax evasion, fraud and profiteering. The usual policy of anti-landlordism was pursued: according to the reform laws of June 1950, the land and stock of landlords was to be confiscated and the landlords permitted an equal share in the redistribution of their former property so that they might 'reform themselves through labour'. Some landlords were tried by people's tribunals and suffered various punishments. The peasants were also encouraged to form mutual aid teams (to assist each other in busy times) and agricultural producers' co-operatives in which the land was pooled and held in joint ownership. Through these mutual aid teams and the co-operatives, the Chinese leaders hoped to develop habits of sharing and working together that would make the peasantry see the benefits of co-operation and would make them more ready to accept the next step. By 1956 ninety per cent. of the peasantry were part of co-operative organisations, but most of these bodies were semi-private in nature, and the quantity of production was inadequate for the needs of a growing population, especially since a greater proportion of this population was engaged on industrial work. In 1958, therefore, as part of the 'great Leap Forward' whereby China aimed at a massive increase in industrial production (despite a fall in Soviet aid) it was also planned to establish agricultural communes which, it was hoped, would produce more food-stuffs, partly by being larger units and partly by making more efficient use of labour. The communes included nurseries, so that women's labour could be used, and communal dormitories and mess halls. The 740,000 agricultural producers' co-operatives were turned into 26,425 com-munes in which devoted party workers sought to introduce better farming methods. During slack periods this huge labour force was set to work on other projects such as the construction of irrigation works. Just as Stalin had to withdraw from his policy of total collectivisation, so the Chinese found it necessary to do the same. The Wuhan Resolu-tion (December 1958) proposed that the peasants' homes, savings and patches of land be returned to them, that they need not use the mess halls, and that they need no longer be expected to carry out industrial work too. Within the authority of the commune, production brigades were organised and within each brigade, production teams were allowed an increasing degree of responsibility and incentive. Agriculture has expanded far more slowly than the Communists first hoped, it has become clear that good land is already being farmed and that it is very difficult to exploit effectively the huge waste areas. Since the population has continued to rise the Chinese Government has realised the likelihood of a worsening situation and in 1958 launched a birth control campaign.

Despite the need for more caution, the 26,000 communes remain the basic unit of government in the countryside. By grouping together several villages to form a commune the government created regions which were big enough to attempt a variety of activities. The communes cope with local social and welfare work, they are able to develop small industries, build schools and hospitals and use labour far more efficiently

Chairman Mao Tse-tung (left) with Soviet Premier Nikita Khrushchev and President Liu Shao chi (third from left) watch the Tenth Anniversary (of the Communist régime in China) Parade in Peking.

than the old village unit could ever do. Communist China has suffered unpleasant food shortages but it has freed China from the famines that were so frequent in earlier days.

k) Domestic reforms – Industry and Trade

At first industrial expansion was very slow and concentrated on limited exploitation of mineral resources, and even this depended on Soviet skill and capital. In 1953 the first Five Year Plan was launched in a bid to speed up industrialisation and helped by increased Russian aid, symbolised by the visit of Bulganin and Khrushchev to Peking in 1954. Over six-and-a-half thousand Chinese students went to Russia to acquire scientific and technical training in a bid to break with the traditional Chinese education in the humanities and bureaucracy. Mao estimated in 1956 that three Five Year Plans would enable China to achieve industrialisation, but his plans were hampered by lack of capital, which had to be borrowed or squeezed out of agriculture, and by the rising population. Poor planning, an inadequate communications system and a lack of specialists also hindered progress. The hostility of the U.S.A. and U.S. influence in Japan deprived China of sources of supply and of markets forcing her into increasing dependence on the Communist block. In 1950 twenty-six per cent. of Chinese trade was with this group, in 1954 it had risen to eighty per cent.

The 'Hundred Flowers'

The 1955 Bandung Conference marked a shift in Chinese policy and trade developed once more outside the Communist block. Within China there was a counterpart to this thaw when, in 1956, Mao allowed criticisms of the government when he declared 'Let a Hundred Flowers Bloom and a Hundred Schools of Thought Contend'. This criticism grew to such intensity that Mao realised that this was no way out of China's difficulties, reversed his policy and launched a campaign against ideas which were 'poisonous weeds'. Not till 1960 did the Party relax again and this time in a much more circumspect manner.

The 'Great Leap Forward'

A deterioration in relations with Russia after 1957 meant that offers of Soviet aid began to slacken, and it was in this critical situation that the Chinese attempted a forced programme of industrialisation, the 'Great Leap Forward' of 1958. Ambitious production targets were set for the various industries and a campaign begun to encourage the setting up of 'backyard' steel furnaces. By October it was reported that 600,000 of these were in operation. By the end of the year Party leaders were boasting of great successes and were claiming that China would reach the final stage of Communism before Russia. During 1959 it became increasingly evident that these boasts were unjustified, the steel produced by the backyard furnaces proved useless and the failure of agricultural reforms forced China to enter the world market in 1961 to buy grain. China desperately needed Russian aid, but the new rulers of Russia refused to underwrite the large-scale growth of Chinese industry and population and insisted on being paid for all they conceded, in current Chinese deliveries of goods. China lost the bulk of its Russian technicians and advisers – there may have been 10,000 of them – who returned home by the trainload; trade between the two countries declined so that Chinese trade with the Communist block was $100 million less in 1960 than in

1959. The priorities of the Great Leap Forward were reversed in 1962 when Chou En-lai declared that encouragement must be given to agriculture, light industry and heavy industry – in that order.

However, despite the failure of the Party to achieve an over-ambitious programme, the real successes of Communist rule in China must not be underestimated. Communist rule has proved far more effective than that of the Manchus or the Kuomintang and China has no tradition of western democracy that might make people restless. Western visitors are consistently impressed by the cleanliness and good order of the country and the hard working nature of its people. The educational programme of developing primary schools, middle schools, and universities had drastically reduced illiteracy, whilst preventing too wide a gulf opening between intellectuals and the rest of the population by forcing students and professional people to work for a time in fields and factories. No doubt there are many unsatisfactory features in life in China, and much poverty, but the situation has to be viewed against the earlier background of Western oppression, warlordism, and civil war.

Freedom in China is not the freedom of France or Britain, but at least there is less disorder than under the warlords, no more foreign interference, far less disease, a position of equality with men for Chinese women (who had been near slaves under the Manchus). China has become one of the healthiest lands in Asia, the attacks on diseases, on filth and vermin, and on inadequate medical care, have brought great benefits to the Chinese people. To have introduced compulsory primary schooling (1962) and done so much to reduce illiteracy among adults is also an achievement of enormous importance which could only have been managed by a strong central government.

l) The Cultural Revolution

In September 1966 new upheavals began in China, sparked off by Mao himself, in which some leaders made a determined effort to try and prevent their country from becoming as cautious as Russia and as full of middle class experts with growing wealth and fewer contacts with ordinary people. Defence Minister Lin Piao was prominent in this movement and thousands of Red Guards, who were mostly young people, were mobilised to see that Mao's thoughts were studied by all classes. Leaders who disliked this 'cultural revolution' were denounced – even though one of them was President Liu Shao Chi – and sometimes ill-treated, but occasionally the Red Guards ran into opposition from workers and from local army commanders. In the outer regions of China, especially, the movement met with very limited success, yet it represents a most amazing effort to keep the revolution alive, to prevent China from settling down into the class-ridden moderate Western-type society that Mao has encouraged his people to despise. For over two years the differences between Chinese leaders continued to trouble the country. In October, 1968, Liu Shao Chi was pushed out of power by his rivals who claimed he was, like Russia's Khrushchev, far too reluctant to continue to try and develop the revolution in China.

m) Early Foreign Policy

It was inevitable that, at first, Chinese Communist foreign policy should be closely linked to Russia's, for Russia was the source of economic aid and Russian strength was a guarantee of Chinese safety. The treaty of alliance between the two countries, signed in 1950, covered political, economic, and military matters. 'Mopping up' operations in areas like Hainan and the Chusan islands occupied the first year of Communist rule, and then the Chinese turned their attention to areas which had once been part of Manchu China, but were now independent. Outer Mongolia had Russian support; Formosa, Quemoy and Matsu were areas of increasing interest to the U.S.A., so the Chinese Government concentrated on the most vulnerable remaining area, Tibet.

Tibet

In declaring that they would 'liberate' Tibet, the Communists were following the same policy as Chiang, who had already been training the Panchon Lama to serve as China's puppet ruler. In October 1950 the Chinese Red Army under Liu Po-ch'eng began to occupy Tibet; Tibet protested to the United Nations but the U.N. were powerless to stop the Chinese over-running the country. A surrender agreement negotiated in 1951 gave China control of Tibetan foreign and military affairs. But the influx of Chinese immigrants following the conquest led to a minor tribal revolt in 1956 and repeated outbreaks of disturbance in the following years until, in March 1959, the revolt spread to Lhasa itself. The Dalai Lama fled to India whilst the Khampa tribe and armed monks put up a gallant but hopeless fight against the Chinese who could rapidly move up troops on the new roads they had built into Tibet. The Chinese were left in a stronger position by their suppression of the revolt – a factor of great political significance to India. China could now bring pressure to bear on the border states of Nepal, Bhuku and Sikkim. The Chinese would not recognise the validity of the 1914

McMahon Line as a frontier in this area; they claimed 40,000 square miles of Indian territory and had already nibbled away some of this by building the Yehchung-Gartok road across part of Ladakh.

n) The Korean War

North Korean Attack

Korea had always been an area of interest to China, and the Chinese Communists made clear their support of the North Korean Communist regime which had been established, under Russian protection, north of the 38th parallel. South Korea was ruled by Syngman Rhee's government, with American aid; it seemed weak and unstable, the country was short of industry and harassed by land-hungry peasantry who disliked the U.S. stress on preservation of private property. The weakness of the South, and the success of Communism in China encouraged the North Korean government to order their troops to invade the South in June 1950. The U.N. Security Council unanimously condemned this action during the absence of the Russian delegate who was protesting at the U.N.'s failure to recognise and admit China. American forces, with the help of Britain, the Commonwealth and Turkey, were rushed to South Korea and under the command of MacArthur, broke out of the small area around Pusan – which by August had been all that was left of Rhee's state.

The U.N. Counter-attack

U.N. forces advanced rapidly north by land and, via a landing at Inchon, by sea. MacArthur's forces crossed the 38th Parallel in pursuit, despite Chinese warnings, and a crisis was reached when the U.N. forces reached the Yalu River (the Korean-Chinese border) and MacArthur planned to cross it. Chinese 'volunteers' began to join the North Koreans and pushed U.N. forces south, capturing Seoul from them. MacArthur planned to resist this not only with conventional counter-attacks but also by striking at bases in China and by encouraging Chiang to launch an invasion from Formosa. President Truman decided that his general had exceeded his orders, dismissed him and installed General Ridgeway in his place, with orders to follow a less risky policy.

Heavy and indecisive fighting continued until, on July 26th, 1953, a truce was agreed after long and bitter negotiations had gone on for over two years. The truce line has since marked the frontier between North and South Korea. The Chinese Communists won great prestige in Asia by the success of their forces against an enemy with superior equipment

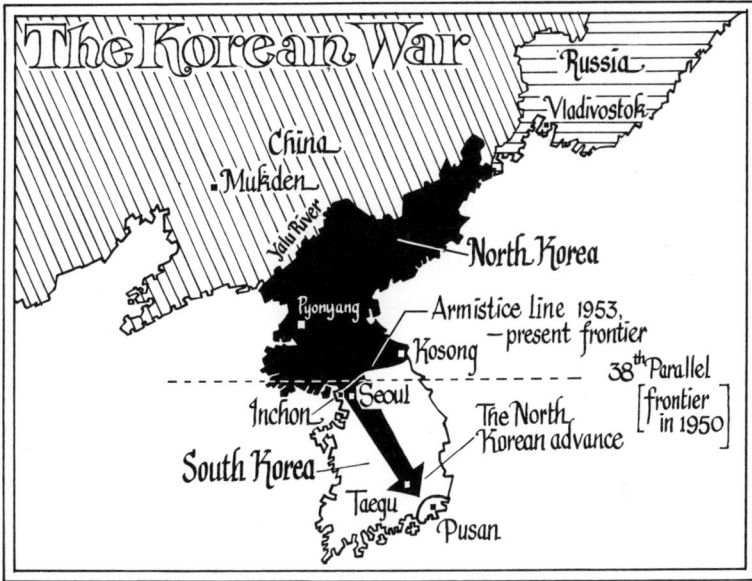

The Korean War map showing Russia, Vladivostok, China, Mukden, Yalu River, North Korea, Pyongyang, Armistice line 1953, – present frontier, Kosong, 38th Parallel [frontier in 1950], Inchon, Seoul, The North Korean advance, South Korea, Taegu, Pusan.

and almost complete air supremacy. They had shown how their disciplined, determined ground forces, prepared to dig in, could hold their own against a technically superior enemy.

o) Later Foreign Policy

The Korean War not only demonstrated the undoubted efficiency of China's Red Army but also taught the U.S. government a grim lesson. As a result, America was determined not to allow the Chinese to extend their sphere of influence; they did this by means of S.E.A.T.O. (the South East Asia Treaty Organisation) founded in September 1954 and actively aiding Chiang Kai-shek. The Bandung Conference, April, 1955, in which China and twenty-eight Afro-Asian states held discussions and declared the need for economic co-operation and respect for national sovereignty, proved a short-lived aberration from the hardening Chinese policy towards the U.S.A. But attempts to recover Taiwan (Formosa) would have to overcome U.S. opposition, and even Quemoy and Matsu could not be taken, despite heavy shelling of the islands in 1958. This crisis passed when the U.S.A. agreed to stop the bombardment.

India

China's relations with her other Asian neighbours have tended to worsen.

In 1958 she annoyed several countries by dumping cut price goods on the Asian market. Her good relations with India (embodied in a 1954 agreement on the Five Principles of co-existence) were soured by the development of military highways on India's borders. In 1959 China accused India of supporting the Tibetan revolt and in October, 1962, invaded India and defeated the Indian forces which attempted to stem the attack. Having demonstrated their superiority, the Chinese forces withdrew from most of their conquests, but tension between the two countries remains and was underlined by China's support of Pakistan in the 1965 war between India and Pakistan.

Russia

During the conflict with India, Russian sympathy and supplies went to India, not China. This was indicative of the way relations between the two countries had worsened since the death of Stalin. The Russians refused to follow the kind of aggressive policy advocated by the Chinese, refused to agree that the West was only 'a paper tiger', refused to use her I.C.B.M.'s in an offensive capacity and refused to help China to become a nuclear power. China has had to struggle down this path alone and in October 1964 managed to explode a simple nuclear device. In 1967 the Chinese successfully tested a hydrogen bomb, whilst there is also clear evidence that China is fast developing a missile system to provide the means for delivering these terrifying bombs. This is an immense achievement in view of the hostile attitude of Russia. In 1960 Russian technical experts left China, taking their plans with them, and other forms of aid dwindled away. A weak China suited Russia best: Stalin had never really had to face this problem, but his successors could not escape the serious difficulties posed by a neighbour with a long, common frontier with Russia, growing power, and a real feeling that some of the frontier lands dominated by Russia were rightfully China's. Since China could not compete economically with Russia, she sought to compete ideologically. Mao's Marxism was put forward as the most appropriate form of revolutionary thinking for Asian countries – a challenge that Russia had to resist. The Russians were derided as 'revisionists' – often indirectly through attacks on the Yugoslavs – and the Russians replied by declaring 'only madmen and maniacs can call for another war'. A crisis of ill-feeling was reached at Communist Party conferences held in 1960, but the Chinese found few allies other than the Albanians. China rejoiced at the fall from power, in 1964, of Khrushchev, only to find that his successors followed an equally firm policy with considerable skill. In 1966 both Cuba and Indonesia denounced Chinese activities in their countries and expelled Chinese representatives. 1976 saw considerable changes in China. First Chou en Lai then Mao himself died. China's new leaders were cautious men who disapproved of the radical activities of the group led by Mao's widow and suppressed them.

The reactions of China and Japan to the West have differed greatly. Japan's success in borrowing technical discoveries far exceeded China's, but China has adapted Western political philosophy to suit her own needs and developed a society which is more distinctively her own than Japan's. In both states, traditional societies were already under stress before the impact of the West brought about their final overthrow. Both have ancient traditions of unity and culture that make them eager to assert themselves as the equals of Russia and the Western powers. But both have to cope with the strain on resources of rising population, China supports over 700 million people, and Japan over 95 million, and even the Chinese, who once argued this was an asset, are realising the crisis which it could provoke.

American Marines advancing through the outskirts of Inchon following Allied landings during the Korean War.

10 | Asian Nationalism 2 – India and S.E. Asia

India

a) The Background

THE LAND: India is a vast subcontinent in which there are tremendous geographical variations extending from mountain areas to deserts and swamps. It contains a wide range of mineral resources including coal, iron, bauxite, copper and salt; but agriculture is hampered by the very limited rainfall which is usually confined to a summer monsoon of six to eight weeks which can not always be relied upon to provide sufficient water.

THE PEOPLE: The people who inhabit India are as varied as the land; there are differences in appearance, tradition, religion and language which point towards the danger that modern India may split apart into several states. The division of India and Pakistan already shows the danger, but there are other signs, too, that the wide differences between peoples threatens unity. Language is, particularly, a problem, for though the major language is Hindi, there are so many groups with other languages (e.g. the Tamil-speaking peoples in the Madras area) that to insist on one official language is to ask for trouble. Though speaking English is a blow to national pride, at least it does not benefit one area rather than another. A degree of unity is provided by the Hindu faith, to which most Indians belong. There are Christians, Buddhists, and Moslems, but the Hindu beliefs, rituals and sacred books have played a major part in creating the character of India, and, in particular, in helping to develop tolerance and an acceptance of fate. The Hindu religion stresses the need to accept the position into which one is born, even if it is one of poverty, for it is not possible to move from one group, or caste, to another, during one's life; but only in the rebirth in which Hindus believe. Thus a Brahmin, a member of the highest caste, may be reborn as a member of a lower order, perhaps an 'untouchable', the lowest order, or even some kind of animal. Hindus also venerate cows and will not kill them, a belief that has great importance in modern India's economy.

Colonialism

Civilisation developed early in India, on the River Indus, and the series of conquerors who have swept over the country have, on the whole, not greatly affected the Hindu Indians. The Moslem conquerors, who created the Moghul Empire which was overthrown by the British, failed to convert many Hindus, though the presence of scattered Moslem communities of soldiers and administrators all over India left a serious problem for the future. In the eighteenth century it was the British who emerged as the dominant Europeans in India, not the Portuguese or French, who also had settlements there; but the British, too, were received with calm, for their interest was in trade and political control, not in disturbing the social and religious situation. British rule helped to unite India, whether it was in directly controlled regions, or in regions still ruled by princes, but under British protection. The building of roads and railways, the development of schools and the growth of trade, encouraged a minority of Indians to think nationally and to learn English themselves for the benefit of their own careers.

b) Imperial India

Under its Viceroy, Lord Curzon, British India in 1900 seemed immensely impressive and valuable. The frontiers had been settled by a series of wars which had established British control in Burma, defeated the troublesome states on the outer fringes of India and held back the challenge of Russia. Indian trade flowed in the vast fleets of merchant steamships, using the Suez Canal for their voyage to Europe, and bringing to Britain all sorts of valuable materials whilst taking in return British manufactures to the vast Indian market. Railways and roads crossed the country, linking up regions as never before; British administration brought to India an unusual degree of peace and considerable religious tolerance since the upset of a mutiny in the Indian army in 1857 had warned the English to be more sensitive to Indian feeling. The Indian Civil Service, recruited by examination, included Indians as well as Englishmen, and Indians possessed a minor share in government by the India Councils Act, 1892, which enabled them to play a small part in the legislative councils that existed in the different provinces and the central government.

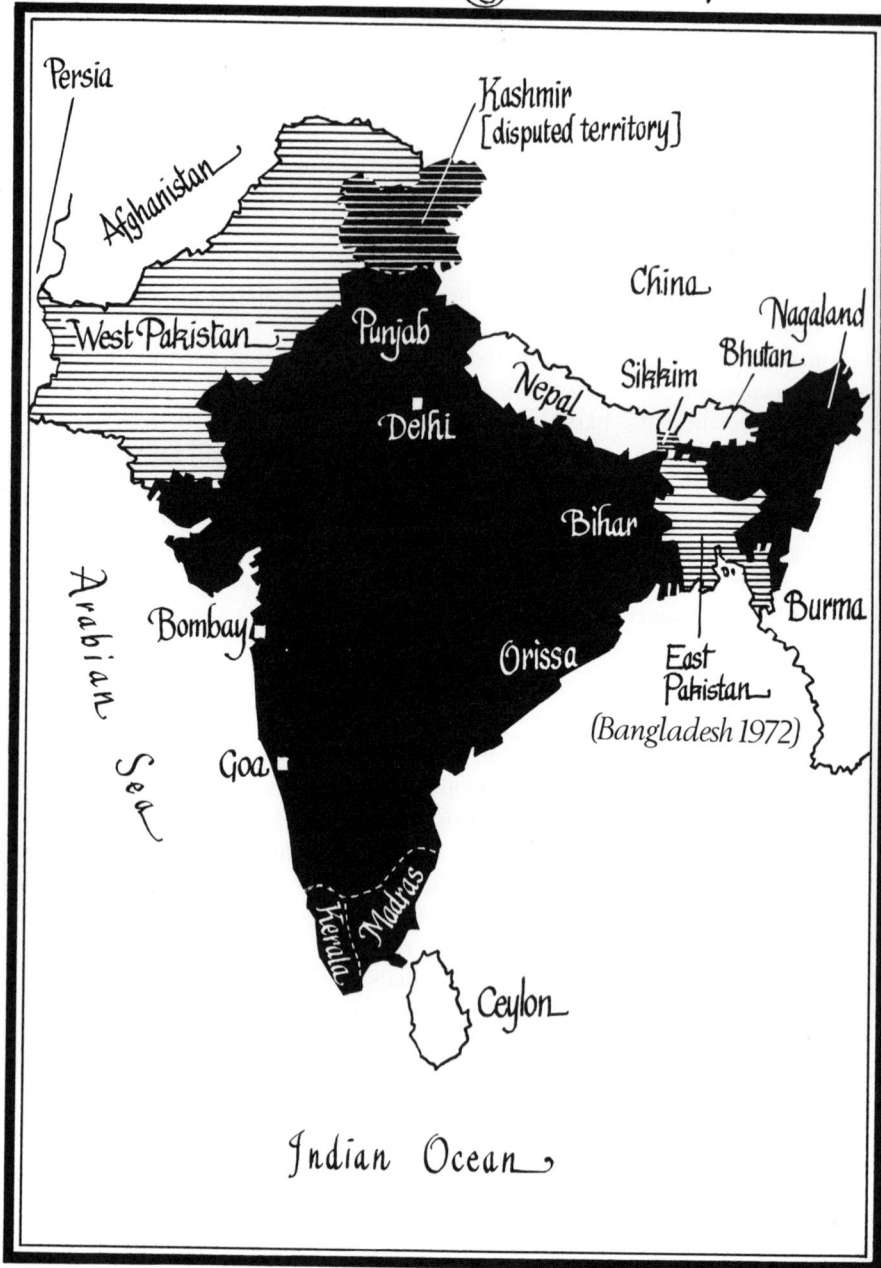

India & her neighbours

Persia

Afghanistan

Kashmir
[disputed territory]

China

Nagaland

West Pakistan

Punjab

Sikkim

Bhutan

Nepal

Delhi

Bihar

Burma

Arabian Sea

Bombay

Orissa

East Pakistan
(Bangladesh 1972)

Goa

Kerala

Madras

Ceylon

Indian Ocean

The Congress Party

This happy picture was far from acceptable to many Indians. In 1885 the Indian National Congress held its first meeting in Bombay, formed from middle class Indians led by Krishna Gokhale and B. G. Tilak who, having received the benefits of higher education, felt frustrated at the very tiny opportunities allowed them by the government. The arrogance of many Englishmen in India towards the Indians infuriated a middle class who were now spread throughout India and felt not only that they were denied a proper share in government, but also that Britain was using India unfairly to exploit her resources and crush Indian industries which might rival Britain's. The cotton industry had especially suffered from the competition of Lancashire cotton. Curzon's vain and arrogant manner did not help. He certainly introduced many useful reforms, but he also annoyed the Bengalis by dividing their province into two and by tightening government control over education. Curzon's policy helped unite the middle class behind the Congress Party and made the British government realise it must allow more reforms.

Concessions to India

John Morley, the British minister responsible for India, and Lord Minto, the Viceroy, attempted to reduce the growing trouble in India by an act of 1909, allowing Indians to become members of the executive councils which assisted governors in ruling the provinces, and increased the Legislative Council (which assisted the Viceroy) to sixty members, twenty-two of whom were elected. Minto, and then Hardinge, worked hard to win Indian goodwill. Gokhale was consulted about reforms, Curzon's division of Bengal was scrapped (1911), the capital was moved to Delhi, and King George V visited India. The atmosphere improved, though a sign of future trouble was that special provision was made for Moslem representation in the 1909 act.

The Moslem League

At first Moslem leaders had co-operated in the Congress Movement, but they became increasingly dissatisfied at the attitude of the Hindu Congress majority towards the question of a special place for Moslems in the new India they were trying to create. In 1906, led by Mohammed Ali Jinnah, a Bombay lawyer, the Moslems formed a league to fight for the interests of the people of their faith. The rather scornful attitude of Congress leaders towards this League annoyed its leaders, enabled them to build up the League, and eventually made them decide that an independent state for Moslems would have to be formed from British India.

c) The decline of Imperial India

The First World War

Most colonial areas were strongly affected by this conflict and India was no exception. Already the success of Japan was encouraging Indian leaders to regard the British with less respect, now the long and terrible war in Europe was a further blow to British prestige. Moreover, the war saw the emergence of Communist Russia, a country committed to helping 'suppressed peoples' and to ending colonialism, and the U.S.A. which, similarly, criticised colonialism. Indian leaders pressed for greater power only to be told they must wait; Indian soldiers fought in the war and saw Europe at its worst while Indian Moslems felt strongly that the harsh treatment of their fellow Moslems in Turkey in the peace treaties was most unjust. Clearly more concessions would have to be given to India, but these were given in a slow and grudging manner which caused offence, whilst a new leader brought greater power to the Congress party and turned it from a middle class minority movement into a movement with mass support.

Mahatma Gandhi

The new leader was a lawyer who had spent much time helping the Indian community in South Africa and now returned to India. Gandhi was physically an unimpressive man, small, slight and bespectacled, yet with a great intensity of belief and courage. He also had the knack of appealing to ordinary people. His ideas were developed from a mixture of Hindu, Christian and Western sources but they all revolved around the need to create a united country in which poverty and class distinction would be reduced and people would work in village communities. He wore the clothes of a peasant, welcomed the untouchables (the lowest caste) as his equals, and developed the technique of non-violent protest. Under Gandhi, Indians protested not by rioting but by refusing to work, or by fasting, a method the British found impossible to deal with. He turned disputes into clear moral issues of right and wrong that were far more simple and more serious than the squabbling of the Congress leaders over minor points.

The Montagu-Chelmsford Reforms

A report produced in 1918 by the British government outlined reforms that were eventually put into force in 1921. Three of the Viceroy's Executive Council were to be Indians, and in the provinces the system of 'dyarchy' (double government) would allow power to be shared between the governor of each province and his officials, and ministers responsible to elected legislative councils. Some aspects of government, such as the police, law and land revenue were controlled by the British governor, but other matters, for example education and health, were managed by the Indian ministers. There was a national legislative assembly of two houses with a majority of elected members. The vote was given to Indians who owned property and paid income tax or land tax, creating an electorate of some five million voters for provincial legislative councils; one million fewer could vote for the Upper House, the Council of State, which represented rich landowners.

But there was so great a gap between the report and the implementation of the reforms that Indians became restless and the government's proposal to allow judges, not juries, to decide political cases, caused such anger that rioting began. A major incident occurred at Amritsar in 1919 when 379 peaceful demonstrators were killed and many more wounded, when General Dyer opened fire on a prohibited meeting. Gandhi's policy of non-violent resistance proved so troublesome that the government imprisoned him, but it was also forced to try new concessions to recover Indian goodwill. With Gandhi in prison Congress dithered as to whether or not to contest elections and the movement seemed in danger of splitting.

The Act of 1935

A new viceroy, Lord Irwin, (1926–31) made strenuous efforts that, for a time, reduced the disturbances that Gandhi had inspired on his release from prison by refusing to pay the salt tax. The largely Conservative government of 1935 granted further power to Indians – despite objections from Winston Churchill – with the aim of creating a system of federal government that would satisfy Indians and yet not lead to a very radical government in India. The dyarchy system was abandoned, instead the governments of the provinces were responsible to their increased electorates. But the areas still ruled by princes presented a problem that was tackled very cautiously in the hope that the princes would co-operate. In fact, they did not, and their conservative attitude, plus the failure of the act to take any notice of the Hindu-Moslem clash, helped

to spoil the reform which was clearly a major move towards the creation
of an independent dominion of India.

d) The Coming of Independence

The Second World War

As before the First World War, there was a period of reasonable calm
ruined by a conflict. The war shook British prestige again, especially
since Japan, an Asian power, achieved successes that brought her troops
up to India's frontiers. Indian demands for dominion status met with
delay from Britain, indeed some Indians were now so bitter, that led
by S. G. Bose, they fought for the Japanese.

The Moslem-Hindu Problem

By 1940 the Moslem League was a formidable force which had declared
its aim was to found an independent state, and the hostility of Congress
and League ruined all efforts of the Viceroy, Lord Wavell, to form a
national administration in India. Moslems were especially numerous
in East Bengal, Sind and the Punjab, but there were many small groups
scattered in Hindu areas just as there were Hindu minorities in Moslem
areas. Their quarrel worsened just as the British, now ruled by a Labour
Government, were deciding their colonial rule of India must be ended
as soon as possible. Gandhi himself felt very strongly that the unity of
India was vital, yet the refusal of Jinnah and his followers to offer any
compromise obstructed all Gandhi's hopes and wrecked the provisional
plan drawn up for independence by a British Mission. Jinnah's reply to
the scheme for a united independent India with a weak central government was to call a Direct Action Day on which Moslems demonstrated
and rioted.

Independence

Since calling Indian leaders to London to settle their country's future
had failed, the British government declared its intention to grant independence by the summer of 1947 at the latest, in the hope that this
would force the Indian leaders to reach a realistic solution. A new
viceroy, Mountbatten, was sent out to supervise the end of imperial
India. It was proposed that two separate states would have to be
established – Pakistan and India – formed from provinces whose legisla-
tives would vote to decide which state to join. Where there were large
numbers of Hindus and Moslems as in the Punjab and Bengal, a

Mahatma Gandhi addresses a crowd of followers and disciples after evening prayer in Bombay.

boundary commission would settle a division of the area. Congress leaders were compelled to see there was really no alternative, despite Gandhi's hostility to a divided India, but independence on August 15, 1947, came as a near catastrophe as Moslems and Hindus fought one another, the Sikhs of the Punjab tried to resist the division of their state, and refugees poured from India into Pakistan and Pakistan into India. Terrible slaughters occurred in the chaos and panic, the refugee problem reached a monumental proportion as over eleven million people were involved. Both Delhi and Calcutta were the scenes of frightening violence. Gandhi made a bid to end the bitterness by going to Delhi to appeal for moderate treatment of Moslems, and suffered the fate of assassination for his boldness. On the 30th January, 1948, Gandhi was shot by a Hindu fanatic, an event that shook all India and helped discredit the extremists who had caused so much trouble.

e) Nehru's India

Nehru

Jawaharlal Nehru, independent India's first Prime Minister, had been Gandhi's lieutenant for many years and combined the appeal of this connection with his reputation as a left-wing Congress leader who attracted the radicals. Unlike Gandhi, Nehru wished to see India advance as an industrial power with a central government strong enough to destroy the power of privileged groups and achieve justice for Indians. Nehru's ideas were a mixture of Marxism and Western democratic thinking: he believed the state should act to improve people's welfare, yet he did not believe in using the state for harsh bullying methods of government – India was to be a democracy in which parties could compete for votes.

The Indian Government

Nehru had to face the problem that a number of the states ruled by princes were not enthusiastic about joining the new democratic government. Most princes were bought off with pensions and privileges but the Nawab of Jungagadh, a Moslem ruling a Hindu state, attempted to declare for Pakistan and Nehru sent in troops, organised a plebiscite, and accepted the resulting overwhelming vote for union with India. Hyderabad, too, proved difficult as the ruler attempted to go his own way, but technical excuses were found for intervening and merging the area into India. Both these areas were very vulnerable, but it was Kashmir on the frontier between India and Pakistan which posed the greatest difficulties and was finally referred to the United Nations for settlement. Having destroyed the political power of the princes, Nehru insisted on a form of government similar to Britain's in which ministers were responsible to an assembly (*Lok Sabha*) whose members were elected by the votes of all adult Indians. There was also an upper house (*Rajya Sabha*) to represent the different states. Congress was so dominant that, at first, there was little in the way of real party conflict; clashes occurred within the Congress Party rather than outside it, but Nehru's ability and unchallengeable prestige avoided too much bitterness. A charter guaranteeing fundamental rights to all Indians, and a federal court, and the declaration that India was a republic, though still within the Commonwealth, completed the constitution. On the whole government worked well, for Indians trained in the old Civil Service provided a source of skill and many politicians had experience of running provincial government.

The Economic Problem

India's vast population (the 1961 census recorded 434 million) increased rapidly as a result of a falling death rate since many of the worst diseases were much reduced in severity. Eighty per cent. of this population were village dwellers living on the meagre returns of tiny farms and very vulnerable to natural hazards, especially the failure of the monsoons. Nehru was determined to improve living standards, yet the rise in population more than tended to offset improvements, whilst the permanent problem of trying to find capital to invest in power, irrigation and industry meant that money had either to be borrowed from abroad, or squeezed out of India itself. Agricultural methods were primitive and poor, and as families increased farm sizes fell, the typical farm is now under five acres. People with no land poured into the swelling towns only to find no work and no homes, so that vast numbers of people living on the pavements have become a feature of Indian cities.

The Five Year Plans

One answer attempted by the Government was to copy Russian methods and plan for certain improvements over a limited period. The first Five Year Plan attempted to improve agriculture, the second, beginning in 1956, concentrated on industry, and the third, 1961–6, endeavoured to help both agriculture and industry. Many successes can be pointed out, the first Five Year Plan increased overall agricultural production by eighteen per cent., for instance, and Nehru's schemes for a 'mixed' economy in which some industries were state-owned and some privately owned were developed. But the overall result was depressingly unsatisfactory – prices rose, much of such profits as emerged went to the rich and peasants often remained heavily in debt to money lenders. Foreign loans have often been used for attempting to cope with hunger, not for investing in improvements. The need to re-arm to face China and Pakistan diverted money and some industries, e.g. jute, were severely harmed by the partition of India. The constant problem of a rising population has not yet been solved by the government's birth control programme.

Famine

The failure of monsoons demonstrates, repeatedly, how desperate is the plight of many Indians. The Hindu faith, with its veneration of the cow, provided another difficulty which Nehru failed to conquer, for the slaughter of cows is violently opposed by devout Hindus and Nehru dared not tackle the difficulty, even though it is reckoned that India contains well over 220 million cattle, half of which are not productive. Aid to purchase food has been provided by many states, especially by the U.S.A., as well as by international relief organisations, yet thousands

T

Independent India's first Prime Minister, Jawaharlal Nehru, with his daughter Mrs. Gandhi (right) and his deputy, Ali Mohammed (left).

of Indians continue to starve and even die of hunger, often accepting their fate with a calmness which reflects the strength of their religion.

Goa

French controlled towns were readily handed over to India, but Portugal refused to hand over Goa and eventually the Indian government seized the town in an act of violence that, though understandable, caused considerable annoyance in other lands. Nehru took great interest in foreign affairs. He refused to tie his country to either the U.S.A. or Russia, preferring instead to be non-aligned, judging each issue on its rights and wrongs. Few states were more critical of the British and French attack on Egypt in 1956 than India, and it was therefore a sharp blow to Indian prestige when Nehru used force in Goa in 1961.

Kashmir

Nehru preferred to use India's limited resources for peace not war, but armed forces were necessary since India's relations with Pakistan were so poor. There were quarrels about compensation for refugees who had moved from one state to the other in 1948 and about the way India used for irrigation rivers which eventually flowed into Pakistan, where the water was also desperately needed.

But it was Kashmir that was the cause of fighting, for though the bulk of the population of this state was Moslem, India claimed the area as hers because of the strategic importance of the region, the richness of the vale of Kashmir, and, above all, because the ruler of Kashmir had declared he would unite his state to India. The Hindu ruler of Kashmir, faced with attacks from Pathan tribesmen from Pakistan who objected to his persecuting the Moslem refugees who had poured in, called upon India for aid and in return for the services of the Indian army, united his state to India. Indecisive fighting between India and Pakistan followed until the U.N. arranged a truce. Nehru avoided suggestions of a plebiscite and refused the idea of partition, insisting that India was a non-religious state and that the presence of large numbers of Moslems in Kashmir was irrelevant.

The War with China

Nehru and Krishna Menon (the Defence Minister) believed in friendly relations with China and India was one of the first states to recognise China's Communist government. The two states signed a friendly agreement by which both accepted the 'Five Principles' which involved not using force against one another and respecting each other's territories. When China seized Tibet, and quelled a revolt, causing the Dalai Lama to flee to India in 1959, the Indians became alarmed, but did little except protest mildly. But China claimed that Indian frontier areas were rightly hers, and that India had aided the Tibetan rebels: probably the Chinese were also concerned in demonstrating the superiority of their Communist ideals over India's democracy. In 1962 a Chinese attack easily routed Indian troops and might well have achieved further success if the Chinese had not been content to withdraw and secure the frontier areas they had taken. Krishna Menon was ruined and soon replaced by Chavan and Nehru's non-alignment policy was shattered. Britain, the U.S.A. and Russia all showed sympathy with India, whilst China replied by backing Pakistan against India at every opportunity.

Nehru died on the 27the May, 1964, at the age of 74, leaving no one of comparable stature to succeed him. The problems he faced were so vast that it is difficult to criticise him, but Nehru was reluctant to be very positive, to be bold and take risks. He understood the problems of India all too well, but believed far too strongly in the methods of persuasion and peaceful progress to be ruthless in his attempts to solve them.

f) India since Nehru

Congress Party's Decline

Nehru was succeeded by Lal Bahadur Shastri, a moderate figure whose selection was designed to avoid offending either wing of the Congress Party. When Shastri died, Mrs. Indira Gandhi became P.M. in February, 1966. But the danger of the decline of the Congress party with Nehru's death was all too clear. On the right were parties like the Suntantra Party, attractive to the well-to-do, and on the left the growing Communist Party which, for a time, ruled the province of Kerala, and appealed to the young and to all those who believe India's problems need forceful handling. Congress Party bosses have been increasingly accused of corruption, and Mrs. Gandhi wearied of overhauling India by slow democratic methods. During 1975-6 she greatly increased her personal authority and clamped down on critics in press and politics.

The difficulties of unity

The vast size of India together with its peoples of many faiths continued to produce problems. In January 1965 Hindi replaced English as India's official language, only to meet a burst of violent opposition by the many non-Hindi speaking groups, and especially from the people of Madras. The riots and disturbances became so great that the government had to make many concessions including the right of each state to have its own state language and the assurance that no-one applying for an official post would be penalised for an inability to speak Hindi.

The threat that parts of India might break away has been stressed by the rebellion of the Nagas, a Christian hill-people living near the Burmese border who have steadily resisted the Indian army's efforts to crush their armed demand for a special position in India in which they can manage their own affairs.

India contains several religions and Indian rulers have always attempted to stress that India is a secular state not a state committed to one particular religion, like Pakistan. But this has been hard to maintain under pressure from Hindu enthusiasts who want their veneration of the cow made a general law in which the slaughter of cows would be totally banned. Nehru had refused this demand, but in November 1967 it came

Mrs. Indira Gandhi, who succeeded Lal Shastri as Prime Minister in February 1966, distributes food and milk to children during a visit to the drought affected areas of Orissa in May of that year.

again with new vigour as Hindu leaders feared the government would encourage cow slaughter. This agitation, too, led to rioting and was important enough to force changes in the cabinet.

FAMINE: The problem Nehru never solved also baffled Shastri and Mrs. Gandhi. In 1965 the failure of the monsoon caused a famine affecting nearly 50 million people in Orissa in the following year and was then aggravated by the partial failure of the 1966 monsoon, too, causing great suffering in Bihar. Once more foreign aid was needed to save thousands of Indians from death, and even foreign aid has not wholly ended the recurring food crises.

KASHMIR: In September, 1965, the question of Kashmir's future, which had never been clearly settled to the satisfaction of both sides, once more led to an outbreak of fighting. This war caused distress to most of the countries of the world except China who strongly backed Pakistan and, at one time, seemed likely to enter the war herself, so strong were Chinese threats that India had violated the border with China. The support given to India by other countries and China's own domestic problems enabled India to reject China's ultimatum and stand firm, but both India and Pakistan were probably glad to use the chance offered by Kosygin, the Russian leader, to negotiate an end to the Kashmir war. In January, 1966, Shastri and Ayub Khan (the general who had made himself leader of Pakistan in 1958) met at Tashkent and worked out the Tashkent Declaration, under Kosygin's guidance, in which they agreed to pull back their armies and renounce the use of force. To two countries with so many domestic problems, the war was a tragedy of great proportions, yet hostile feelings between the two sides remain. In 1971–2 India and Pakistan clashed once more. India backed the people of East Pakistan who were fighting to establish their own state. The successful rebels set up the new country of Bangladesh. Desperate poverty has afflicted Bangladesh since its creation. Defeat ruined Pakistan's military government. So poor and so overpopulated a region as the Indian subcontinent can ill afford to squander scarce resources in conflicts.

South East Asia

a) Colonial control of the Area

Scattered European colonies appeared in South East Asia as early as the beginning of the sixteenth century when Portugal was the leading colonial power in the East Indies, and British influence began to creep into Burma and especially into Malaya with the establishment of a colony at Singapore by Stamford Raffles in 1819. Even so, it was not until the later nineteenth century that colonial control really spread over the region, directly affecting all of it with the exception of Siam which was only indirectly influenced. The area contained rich resources of spices, rice, oil and timber, rubber and tin which was attractive to the expanding economies of European nations. It was an area consisting of warring kingdoms, not greatly advanced in military skill, which were too divided to resist the pressure of the powerful forces of European nations.

British Colonies

Singapore was ideally situated on important trade routes, attracted Chinese merchants and by 1900 was a large and flourishing centre. Britain had, by 1900, extended her control over the states lying to the north and in 1896 had organised these states into a Federation with a capital at Kuala Lumpur. Though most inhabitants were Malays there was also an Indian community and increasing numbers of Chinese were drawn to the area by the prospect of trade and business opportunities. Thus British control certainly helped expand Malaya's economy, especially in rubber (introduced from Brazil by an Englishman) and tin, but it also created racial problems. Farther north the British had also taken control of Burma by 1900. This had been achieved in two stages and had involved difficult wars, but the rice and teak of the area were thought to be worth the struggle. Rangoon was developed, and Burma ruled as part of British India. Finally, Britain had established control over North Borneo in the shape of one area ruled by the British North Borneo Company from the 1880s and Sarawak and Brunei as protectorates ruled by a remarkable dynasty of 'white rajas', descendants of an Englishman, James Brooke, who brought law and order to his rather piratical region.

DUTCH COLONIES: The Dutch colonies (which correspond to modern Indonesia) were of long standing, but by 1900 the Dutch were showing greater interest in exploiting the area, and in extending their control fully over the many scattered islands of the region.

FRENCH COLONIES: The French conquest of Indo-China came in the later nineteenth century, beginning in 1858, affecting Vietnam in the 1880s and spreading into Laos and Cambodia in the 1890s. The French followed their usual policy of trying to integrate the area as a part of France, spreading French culture and the French language, as well as trying to exploit the area's resources which were rather limited, consisting chiefly of rice. Between the French and British colonies lay Siam (Thailand) acting as a kind of buffer state; during the 1870s its rulers displayed considerable skill in modernising their country, influenced a great deal by Britain. Bangkok grew in size; tin and rice were developed.

U.S. COLONIES: Winning the war with Spain in 1898 made the U.S. a colonial power too. Though the war was brief, the Americans were not completely out of trouble when victory was declared, for the Filipinos, to whose aid the Americans had originally come, bravely resisted U.S. forces until 1902 when they were forced to admit defeat.

Tiny Portuguese and German colonies were also to be found in the area, but it was the British, French and Dutch who made the greatest impact. The Europeans greatly altered the region, opening it up by building roads and railways, developing steamship trading from rapidly growing ports, and searching out and exploiting the raw materials of the area. Most of the prosperity thus developed in a region was not, however, shared by the original inhabitants, rather it went into the pockets of Chinese settlers who had moved into the area eager to share in the trade, or went to Europeans. By their conquest, the Europeans discredited the traditional rulers of the area, weakened their authority and thus paved the way for new forms of government, but little was done to help the local inhabitants to become administrators themselves. The peoples of South East Asia were accustomed to being ruled despotically and this tradition was continued by the colonial powers, so that when colonialism finally ended, serious problems arose, in many areas, of finding acceptable stable governments.

b) The Decline of Colonialism

As in other parts of the world, colonial control was severely damaged by the furious wars waged among the colonial powers themselves in 1914–18 and 1939–45. The rise of Communist Russia was, similarly, a factor of extreme importance as it encouraged the growth of Communist parties in the area. But South East Asia was also especially affected by two other factors, the rise of Japan and her conquest of the area and the success of Communist China in freeing herself from colonial influence. The European powers were weakened and disgraced by their wars with each other, but the success of Japan in her war with Russia in 1904–5 proved that an Asian people could stand up to Europeans and defeat them, and in 1942 the inhabitants of South East Asia were ready to welcome the Japanese as liberators. In fact Japanese rule proved cruel and harsh, it disappointed local leaders who had been ready to help the Japanese, and thus made Communism more attractive. Communist parties were present in South East Asia well before the Second World War, the P.K.I. was established in Indonesia in 1920, but this war greatly assisted them, for the Communists were able to come forward as nationalists in the fight against Japan (for which they often received Western military equipment) and were thus well placed to bid for power in 1945. The success of Russia in defeating Hitler, and the conquest of China by Mao Tse-tung's forces, both increased Communist prestige in South East Asia.

Against these disturbing forces the Europeans were able to offer little to win local favour, French rule in Indo-China was increasingly unpopular, seeming only to benefit the landlord class. An outward

S.E. Asia in 1900

China

British India

Burma

Siam

Indo China

Hong Kong [British]

Macao [Portuguese]

Philippines

Malaya

Singapore

Brunei

Sarawak

N. Borneo

Borneo

Sumatra

Celebes

Java

Dutch

British

French

U.S.

German

appearance of power was given to Bao Dai, the ruler of Vietnam from 1925, but in fact all his efforts at reform were thwarted by local French officials. Dutch rule in Indonesia did begin to make an effort to follow a 'new course' after 1901 but it consisted chiefly of providing welfare services, not in sharing power and helping the people towards independence. Burma was greatly affected by the rise of the Congress Party in India and managed to win similar concessions such as dyarchy in 1923 and a separate system of government in 1935, but felt far from satisfied by this. The U.S.A. was probably the least happy as a colonial power and promised the Philippines independence, a promise which was finally honoured in 1945.

Thus, by 1945, South East Asia was in an explosive state. Recently conquered by Japan, influenced strongly by many Communist parties and resenting the attempt of the former colonial powers to return, the area was ripe for revolt. Rapid economic progress had come to the area, rubber exports in Malaya, for instance, rose from 200 tons in 1905 to 700,000 tons in 1948, yet it had come without a parallel growth in education or government and its benefits spread to few local people. To the poor peasantry, whose standard of living was menaced by the rise in population. Communism seemed no worse than the colonial or Japanese rule they had already experienced.

c) The Coming of Independence

In the ten years following the end of the Second World War, independence came to the states of South East Asia, but it was not, usually, a happy experience, for it involved fighting with colonial powers in Indo-China and Indonesia, fighting between competing local groups in many areas, and a misery and instability that has still by no means disappeared.

Independence in British Areas

Though Britain had not thought in terms of early independence for Burma, the success of the Congress Party in India, coupled with Japan seizing Burma from Britain in 1942, led to a Burmese demand for independence which the British government did not feel able to resist. In 1947 independence was granted and U Nu's government decided that they did not wish to retain any contacts with Britain and Burma therefore left the Commonwealth.

Malaya obtained independence less rapidly. It consisted of nine states ruled by sultans, plus Penang and Malacca, organised in a federation in which the central government was firmly in British hands. The Japanese had been driven out of the area, but there remained the problem of local Communists who had been resisting Japan and now turned their weapons on the British. This state of emergency was successfully dealt with in two ways. Military operations, ably conducted by General Templer, were launched against the Communists. These would have proved useless however, without a political programme to win over the local population and prevent the Communists appearing as nationalists too. Fortunately for Britain, Malaya produced an outstanding moderate leader, Tunku Abdul Rahman, who co-operated in drawing up a constitution that gave independence in 1957 and led to elections in 1959 in which Tunku Abdul Rahman's Alliance Party won a clear victory. By 1960 the emergency was over, the policy of methodically clearing villages of Communists and protecting them had worked, and Malaya's chief problem now was her vast Chinese population whom the Malays regarded with suspicion. Much of this Chinese population was crowded into Singapore which developed separately and tried to match Malaya's independence by acquiring self-government. Not until 1959 did Singapore win control of its own affairs and then it was the left-wing People's Action Party led by Lee Kuan Yew which triumphed and formed a government. Yet it seemed sensible to Britain to link Singapore to Malaya, and in 1963 (Sept.) the state of Malaysia was created by which the joining of Singapore to Malaya was offset by the addition of the British territories of North Borneo, except for Brunei. Britain hoped she had thereby created a state large and prosperous enough to withstand pressure from Communism and from Indonesia.

Independence in French Areas

The French returned to Indo-China after Japan had been defeated to find a very difficult situation in which it was hard to re-establish control. In Vietnam a Communist organisation, the Viet Minh, had been formed in 1941 under the leadership of Ho Chi Minh and with an army ably led by General Giap. The Viet Minh had fought the Japanese, now they demanded independence, and Ho compelled the luckless ruler of Vietnam, Bao Dai, to hand over power to him. Since the French would not agree to an independent North Vietnam, fighting began in 1946 in which Giap soon showed himself a master of the Chinese Communist tactics of avoiding pitched battles unless you are very strong, controlling the countryside, and finding supplies and recruits by persuasion and terror. The best French general, Lattre de Tassigny, who defeated Giap in 1951 at Vinh Yen, fell ill and his replacements were less successful in planning strategy. In 1954, in an attempt to keep the troubles of

Vietnam from spreading too seriously to Laos, the French decided to try and hold a highly vulnerable fortress, Dien Bien Phu. Giap's large army had artillery and broke through French defences, capturing the fort. The French empire was in ruins, for there was also trouble in other areas, especially in Laos where the Communist-inspired Pathet Lao forces were increasingly active. The French had never succeeded in winning real local backing, despite restoring Bao Dai as nominal ruler of the area, and without local goodwill, superiority of equipment meant little. Much of this material was American, for in Indo-China the U.S.A. was drawn increasingly into the problem of resisting the spread of Communism, a serious difficulty since the Americans also wished to appear to be opposed to colonialism.

At first the U.S.A. had opposed the return of France to the area, and even showed sympathy to the Viet Minh, but as the war with Communism became more difficult, and especially after Communism established itself in China, the U.S. was sucked into the Indo-China area in an effort to halt the spread of Communism.

But Mendès-France, the French P.M., was determined to be free of the burden and a conference at Geneva in 1954 gave independence to Cambodia, gave independence to Laos on the understanding that the Pathet Lao withdrew to the North, and divided Vietnam along the 17th parallel on the understanding that elections would be held in 1956 to re-unite the Viet Minh-controlled North to the South. The Geneva Conference freed France of her troubles but left the area in turmoil, with traditional governments weak and discredited, yet no real local alternative other than Communism to which the U.S.A. was strongly opposed.

Independence in Indonesia

Like the French, the Dutch attempted to re-possess their former colonies in South East Asia after the war and, like the French, found that the Japanese conquest of the area had totally altered the situation. Indonesia had already contained parties hostile to the Dutch before the war, the Communist P.K.I. party, established in 1920, and Sukarno's P.N.I., the Indonesian National Party. Sukarno had been one of many Indonesians who welcomed the Japanese and co-operated with them only to become disillusioned by Japanese cruelty. With Japan's defeat, Sukarno attempted to declare Indonesia independent, the Dutch attempted to reconquer the area, and a war developed which lasted until 1949 when pressure on Holland from other lands, especially the U.S.A., plus the difficulty of conquering so vast an area of scattered islands, compelled the Dutch to admit defeat.

S.E.Asia today

China

Pakistan

India

Burma

Laos

N.Vietnam.

Hanoi

Formosa

Thailand

Communist controlled

Neutralist

Cambodia

S.Vietnam

Philippines

Saigon

Vigorous Communist activity

Malaysia

Brunei

Singapore

Sumatra

Borneo

Java

Indonesia

d) The Problems of Independence

A rapidly growing population, the discrediting of old rulers, the pressure of China and the interest of the U.S.A. in checking Communism, have all made life very difficult for the peoples of South East Asia. The American desire to see Communism held back has only been really successful in areas where the local peoples have been ready to follow an able non-Communist leader of their own, otherwise it has been very difficult to find stable governments. In the Philippines, independent since 1945, such a leader emerged. Magsaysay defeated the Communist Huks and carried out reforms that reduced the old evils of over-powerful harsh landlordism, and his death in 1957 was a real blow. Similarly in Malaya Tunku Abdul Rahman, and in Singapore Lee Kuan Yew, have provided skilful non-Communist leadership. But in Indonesia, Laos and Vietnam there has been persistent trouble which has not been helped by the very hard line taken by American policy. Under Dulles it was held that neutralists were as good as Communists and that it was necessary to stand firm lest a 'domino effect' occur in which the falling to Communism of one state would cause the next to fall too and lead to a chain reaction across South East Asia and perhaps into India.

Nor has the western type of democracy found it easy to flourish in the area, for the peoples have been used to despotic native rulers and then foreign colonial rule. The French and Dutch, especially, did little to train local peoples to take over the running of government. Thus the army has emerged as a force in politics in South East Asia as in some other areas; containing as it does many well-educated men, it offers hope of unity, and it is the only means of ruling when democracy has failed. In Burma, General Ne Win took power from the Socialists in 1958 and again in 1962, and in Indonesia the army has taken control too. Such leaders are not necessarily pro-American – Burma has never been sympathetic to the West since independence, and in Cambodia Prince Sihanouk has shown a tendency to look to China in preference to the U.S.A. The American attempt to create an alliance of states, S.E.A.T.O., to block China in South East Asia has not found much sympathy in the area outside Thailand and the Philippines and the European areas like Australia and New Zealand.

The Problem of Laos

Here the American hostility to neutrals proved most unsuccessful, for U.S. aid flowed to General Phoumi Nosavan, the strongman in Prince Boun Oum's government, yet he could not defeat the Communists led by Prince Souphannouvong and he was so unpopular that the neutralist forces of Kong Lae co-operated with the Communist Pathet Lao to defeat Phoumi Nosavan. By 1962 the right wing pro-U.S. forces had been crushed, whilst the decision of a 1961–2 conference to form a government of all three groups led by the neutralist Prince Souvanna Phouma had not produced stability and by 1963 had broken down with renewed outbreaks of fighting. Communist success in South Vietnam in 1973 led to the fall of Laos and (1975) Cambodia too to the Communist backed forces.

The Vietnam Problem

In South Vietnam the U.S. found a local strong man, Ngo Dinh Diem who deposed Bao Dai and became President, to whom it gave increasing support in the shape of equipment and military advisers. Diem's rule was a family despotism in which his brother Nhu and Madam Nhu were especially prominent. In 1963 Diem also ran into trouble from non-Communists, the powerful local Buddhists disliked the Catholic Diem family and many of their policies and demonstrated against the government to the extent of a number of them committing suicide by burning themselves to death. In November, 1963, Diem was murdered and during the next year there was a succession of unstable military regimes until eventually Air Marshal Ky emerged as the dominant leader. Through all these troubles war had been raging between South Vietnamese forces and local Communists, the Vietcong, who were aided by units from North Vietnam. America was dragged into sending more and more aid and, when superior equipment failed to bring victory, began to build up the ground forces of General Westmoreland and use air power to strike at North Vietnam itself as well as Vietcong areas. Despite efforts to create 'safe' villages as the British did in Malaya, the Americans have not found victory possible since the Vietcong are so hard to detect and local leadership has not won the renown of Ho Chi Minh's Northern Government. Air power involving extensive use of helicopters, and chemicals to destroy the jungle foliage, has led to errors in which innocent South Vietnamese have perished and has involved heavy U.S. losses over North Vietnam where the government uses Russian missiles to shoot down U.S. aircraft. With the Americans refusing to admit defeat, with the South Vietnamese government needing U.S. aid to survive, and with North Vietnam refusing terms which involve the permanent division of Vietnam, an endless war seems to stretch ahead and has aroused bitter divisions within the U.S.A. itself. Not until 1968 did any kind of negotiation begin. Then discussions began very cautiously and suspiciously in Paris where the North Vietnamese and

Vietcong representatives agreed to meet the representatives of the U.S.A. and of President Thieu's South Vietnamese government. President Nixon wearied of the failure of costly efforts to crush Communist forces in South Vietnam. He determined to pull out U.S. forces and their departure in 1973 was rapidly followed by a Communist capture of power in South Vietnam.

The Indonesian Problem

President Sukarno's troubles did not end with the winning of independence for he had to extend his control over outer islands, and in the Celebes and Sumatra there were rebels who resisted until 1958. Sukarno claimed West New Guinea from the Dutch and managed to add that to his vast state of 100 million people, but after this success things went badly. Democracy did not work well and in 1955 Sukarno abolished the constitution and substituted his system of 'guided democracy' which virtually meant dictatorship. Within his government the Communists, led by Aidit, gained increasing influence and in 1961 Sukarno recognised Communism as one of the three major forces in politics (the others being nationalism and religion). Sukarno's foreign policy reflected this more extreme line too, for in 1963 he declared that Indonesia would crush Malaysia, which he denounced as a power propped up by Britain and

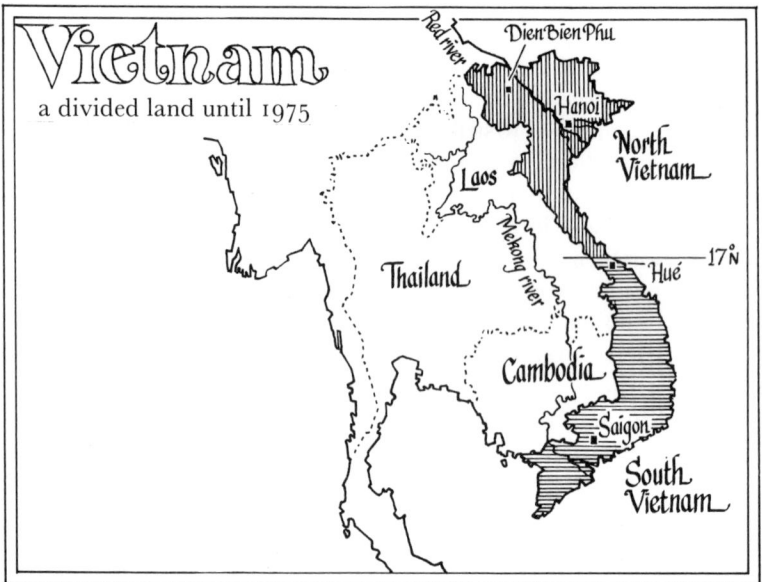

Vietnam
a divided land until 1975

owning lands that were properly Indonesian. In January 1966 Indonesia even left the U.N. But in Indonesia Communism increasingly meant China, and the large Chinese minority in Indonesia were not popular. Nor did the policy of confrontation with Malaysia prove very successful, for British units in North Borneo had considerable success in dealing with attacks whilst a worsening economic situation in which prices and unemployment soared made this war seem foolish. On October 1st, 1965, the Communists made a bid for power which failed (though they killed six generals) and this triggered off troubles in which Chinese were persecuted, Communists hunted down and killed and the Communist Party banned. Sukarno's power was reduced as a group of soldiers led by General Suharto gained power. In June 1966 the policy of confrontation was ended, in September Indonesia rejoined the U.N. and Sukarno struggled in vain to hold on to power that was now slipping away from him. Finally, in February, 1967, General Suharto pushed Sukarno and his grandiose schemes out of power completely and Indonesia settled down to tackle the huge problem of poverty.

U

11 | African and Arab Nationalism

Colonial Africa

a) The Colonisation of Africa

The continent of Africa is vast, it is bigger than either the U.S.S.R. or North America, and it is inhabited by peoples who are as varied in appearance, character, and tradition as the peoples of Europe. There had been European colonies for several centuries scattered along the African coastline and acting chiefly as trading bases, but in the late nineteenth century most of the interior of Africa was colonised so rapidly that this period is usually described as 'the scramble' for Africa. By 1914 only Abyssinia lay outside European domination, and even here there had been a European attempt at conquest. This conquest was possible since European military methods were vastly superior to those of the African peoples; it was also caused partly by the desire of European nations to find bigger markets for their products, and to secure control over sources of raw materials. But basically it was caused by a desire for prestige, a desire that led Italy to attempt twice to take the poor country of Abyssinia, and to conquer the largely desert area of Tripoli. Africans were the helpless victims of European greed and ambition.

The conquests were preceded by a period of exploration, in which travellers like Mungo Park, Burton, Dr. Livingston and Stanley penetrated the interior of the continent by following river routes. The conquest was achieved at considerable cost to the African tribes who offered resistance, but the competing European nations largely managed to avoid conflict with one another. West Africa was soon mainly French, with the exception of a series of coastal areas that were British and were hastily extended inland when the French conquest became a threat. In the 1800s Germany entered the race and secured Togoland, the Cameroons, South West Africa and Tanganyika as a result of peaceful bargaining. In East Africa Britain extended her influence south from Egypt (this caused a clash with the French at Fashoda) and north from the Cape of Good Hope. The British in South Africa had to fight their most bitter war against Europeans, the Boers, who were descendants of the original Dutch colonists from whom Britain had captured the Cape, and who had left the Cape to escape British rule and find new homes farther north in the Transvaal and the Orange Free State. The British, too, expanded to the north by occupying Natal and Rhodesia, which was the creation of the great Cecil Rhodes, a man who wished to see the whole of Africa from the Cape to Cairo in British hands. The Boers were defeated by 1902, after a surprisingly lengthy and very bitter war, and Britain further secured her hold in the area by occupying Uganda and Kenya, and by taking Zanzibar as the result of an agreement in 1890 with Germany.

Italy acquired Eritrea and part of Somaliland as well as Tripoli, but her empire was one of the least economically useful, certainly less profitable than the Congo which King Leopold II of Belgium gained as his private property, and exploited ruthlessly until conditions became so scandalous that in 1908 the Belgian Government took control. Older imperial possessions held by Portugal remained in Portuguese hands, and Spain, too, occupied small regions of Africa. The colonisation had been sudden and easy, and its impact on the African peoples was overwhelming.

b) The African Colonies, 1900–1918

It did not prove very difficult to keep control of the newly-won colonies, for though there were rebellions, European weapons, especially the machine-gun, were sufficient to give the small European forces superiority. A revolt by the Herero people in South West Africa in 1904 was dealt with so brutally by the Germans that two-thirds of the Herero died. However, European governments did little, directly, beyond keeping law and order, and often allowed chartered companies to control colonies; European countries did not, at this time, have a strong sense of responsibility towards the peoples they had conquered, hence most energy went into the economic exploitation of useful products. In areas that Europeans found pleasant to inhabit as well as profitable to own, numbers of white settlers arrived; in Rhodesia there were 10,000 of them by 1914, and in Uganda and Kenya white people also gathered in sizeable numbers; Portuguese settlers came in greater numbers to their ancient colonies, Germans settled in Tanganyika, and Indians were attracted to East Africa by opportunities as traders and skilled workers.

The building of railways and the use of steamships on rivers helped to open up the interior of the continent and put more pressure on the old tribal system. This pressure was increased by Christian missionaries who established village schools where their teachings helped educate Africans in the European ways and beliefs. Some tribes suffered punishment for their resistance to Europeans, but others prospered from European patronage – the Swahili people, for instance.

During the first World War there was little fighting in Africa for most German colonies were weak, hard to defend, and easily captured, though in East Africa General Von Lettow-Vorbeck's forces could not be rounded up and eliminated. The victors shared out Germany's colonies, the Cameroons and Togoland were divided between Britain and France, Britain gained Tanganyika, and South Africa gained South West Africa.

c) Colonial Development, 1918–1939

A stronger feeling of responsibility for the welfare of the colonies was clear after 1918. The system of holding the former German colonies as mandates was proof of the feeling that something should be done to improve conditions in the African colonies. By now the colonial governments felt secure, home governments had founded special colonial ministries, and more money was available from the higher taxation system developed during the war. But it was also increasingly clear that the future of African states depended on the size of its white population. Few Europeans settled in West Africa since the climate was inhospitable, thus traditional tribal systems survived and were sometimes even used as a system of local government. In East Africa and South Africa the sizeable white minorities had upset the tribal system and demanded greater power for themselves. South Africa already had such a system of white rule, and in 1923 the 33,000 whites of Southern Rhodesia were given control over their domestic policies. The European impact could also be seen in the systems of elementary and (occasionally) secondary schools developed in British colonies for Africans. From these schools were to emerge Africans who were to challenge British control. In seeking to improve their colonies, the British were training men like Nkrumah and Banda who were later to organise the downfall of British rule.

The French empire was governed in a more centralised and uniform manner than the British African Empire and attempted to make prosperous Africans, citizens of France. The French used state schools, rather than the missionary schools common in British areas, and had some success in passing on to African leaders ideas of French culture and the French language. The Portuguese and Spaniards showed little desire

Colonial Africa in 1914

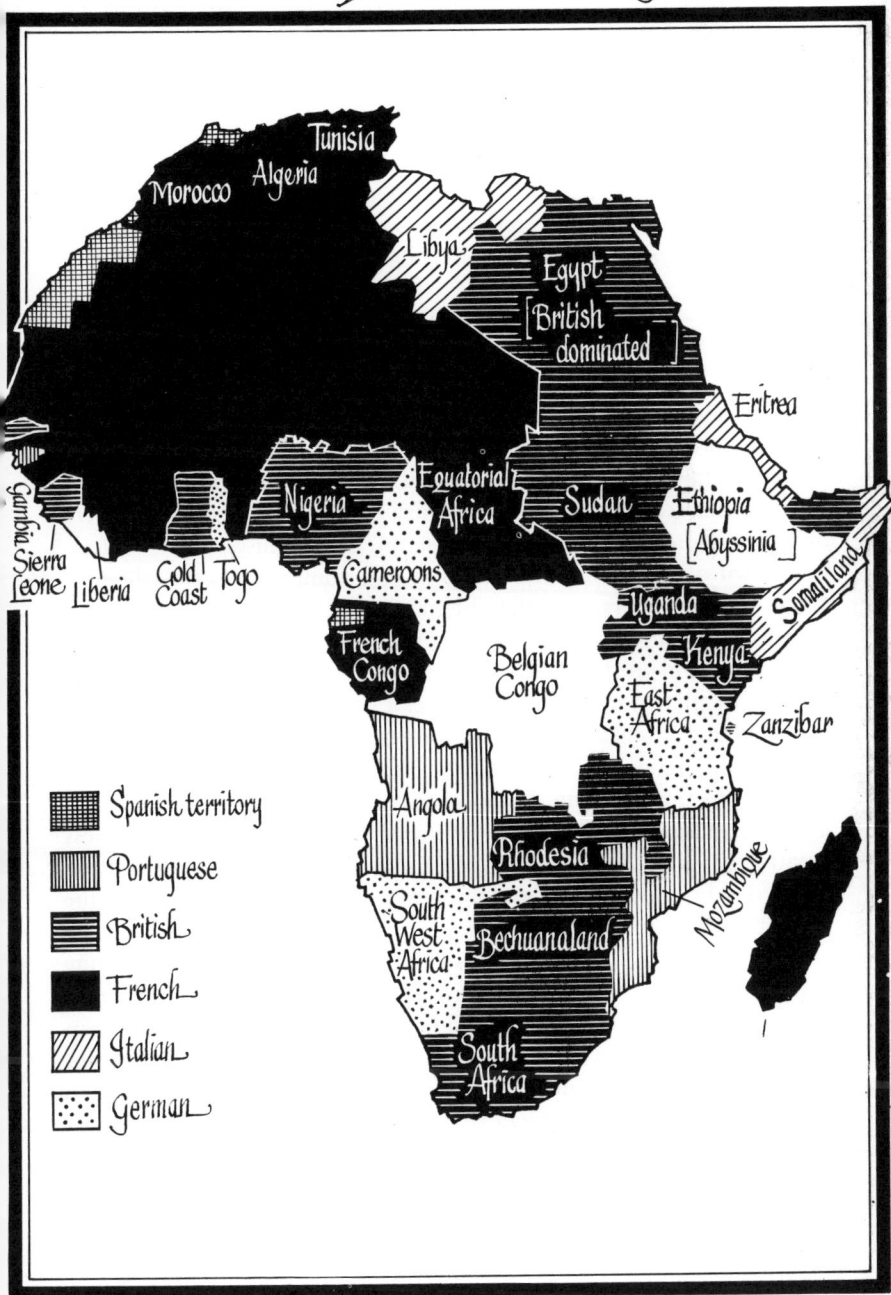

Morocco
Algeria
Tunisia
Libya
Egypt [British dominated]
Eritrea
Gambia
Sierra Leone
Liberia
Gold Coast
Togo
Nigeria
Equatorial Africa
Sudan
Ethiopia [Abyssinia]
Somaliland
Cameroons
Uganda
Kenya
French Congo
Belgian Congo
East Africa
Zanzibar
Angola
Rhodesia
Mozambique
South West Africa
Bechuanaland
South Africa

Spanish territory

Portuguese

British

French

Italian

German

to raise African living standards in their areas, and the Belgians, too, did not seriously attempt to train Africans to hold responsible positions. In general, the Europeans continued to deny senior positions to the Africans. The attack of Mussolini on Abyssinia, the one really independent African state, increased African hostility to Europeans in 1936. But Africans were still not well organised, nor were they well led, and they found it hard to challenge seriously European control. Leaders like Azikiwe, who copied European ideas and wanted to build nations, not tribes, were hampered by the poverty and ignorance of their peoples.

d) South Africa

The dominance of Europeans was most obvious here. In 1902 the Treaty of Vereeniging had concluded the Boer War with promises of self government to the Boer areas. In 1906 and 1907 this was granted, and in 1910 the British Government agreed to the creation of the Union of South Africa from the Boer and English colonies. Since the Boers were the more numerous they found themselves, only eight years after defeat, in control of far more land than they had dominated before the war. Moreover, the Boers tended to be more hostile to sharing power and wealth with Africans than the English, and disliked rules implying equality such as the system in the Cape whereby Africans and coloureds (people of mixed African and European descent) could vote as equals provided they reached certain minimum standards. The British protectorates of Basutoland, Bechuanaland and Swaziland, in or near South Africa, were free of this problem, but were poor areas likely to fall under the influence of South Africa with her mineral resources and farming, unless greatly helped by Britain. When the Union was formed, no African was allowed to become an M.P. and resentment was shown by Africans in the formation of their own movement, the National Congress.

From 1910 laws were introduced, gradually at first, to confirm white control and restrict the Africans. In 1913 the Natives' Land Act forbade Africans from obtaining land outside the areas which the government had decided to define as African areas. Even men like Botha and Smuts who seemed liberal in international affairs, and had supported Britain in the Great War to the extent of crushing a pro-German Boer Movement, were far from liberal in internal affairs. Yet even so, some white South Africans felt their government was too moderate, and supported General Hertzog's Afrikaner National Party which stressed the need to separate European and African peoples in order to preserve white supremacy. In 1934 this group merged with Smuts' party to form the

United Party, after an economic crisis had forced greater co-operation on the political parties. The influence of Hertzog's group can be seen in laws which were now enacted, such as the 1936 Natives' Representation Act which ended the system of allowing qualified Africans to register as voters in the Cape. This blow finally destroyed the hopes of moderate African leaders who had hoped to reform the South African government by co-operation and caution.

But the principle of separating peoples – apartheid, as it was called – was very difficult to work in practice. Areas reserved for Africans were too small and poor to support the African people: in 1913 they held seven per cent. of the land – yet formed seventy-five per cent. of the population. As industry grew in South Africa, so Africans were needed to work in towns and cities outside their reserves.

Thus apartheid did not become a reality and the government had to make sure, through laws and the use of police, that Africans were prevented from striking and demonstrating against their poor wages and inferior conditions. Africans outside the reserves had to have permits and were compelled to produce passes to justify their presence outside their areas. Yet Africans were not militant, partly because the government was strong and efficient, and partly because African living standards were better than those in states farther north. The noisiest nationalism came from Afrikaners, especially the followers of Dr. Malan, who stressed their non-English origins and their hostility to the mixing of different races. This apartheid system was extended into South Africa's mandate, South West Africa, which provided cheap farms for white settlers.

e) The Weakening of Colonialism

In 1939 Europeans dominated the whole of Africa either in states run by white settlers, or in states run by European colonial departments or, in the case of the state of Liberia (formed from freed slaves) indirectly through the all-powerful position of the Firestone Rubber Company. Though Africans shared in local administration in some British colonies, this did not satisfy the growing numbers of Africans educated in European-run schools. The Second World War did much to damage the prestige of the colonial powers in Africa and the two clearest victors, the U.S.A. and Russia, were both hostile to colonial rule in Africa. Also, many Africans served in the war and returned home, afterwards, more resentful at poor conditions there, after being well paid and cared for in the Forces.

Despite growing African restlessness, the post-war years were a time of economic progress in which more aid was provided, public works were begun (like the hydro-electric schemes at Kariba and Volta) and agriculture and industry both progressed. University colleges were established to which Africans could go at Ibadan, Khartoum, Achimoto, Makerere, Salisbury and Fourah Bay; these, like the schools, were bound to produce Africans resentful of European domination.

Independent Africa

a) The Difficulties facing African Nationalism

The movements against white colonial rule were increasingly modern nationalist movements and not simply tribal activities seeking to return to pre-colonial days. But it was not easy for African nationalists to organise united movements among tribes that often had a tradition of hostility to one another but which now inhabited the same colony. The nationalist leaders had to work in areas whose frontiers had been drawn up to suit European colonisers; these frontiers often cut across tribal lands and frequently lacked any natural geographical unity. At the same time, African leaders had to try and rid their countries of European rule and build among their own peoples a feeling that they were all part of the same state, members of a nation as well as a tribe. In areas where there were large white minorities there was the problem of the hostility of these settlers, which was far more determined than the resistance of the governments of European states. Yet, oddly, where there was little resistance it was difficult to build an African movement, as Congo leaders found, for common resistance to white rule helped bind Africans together. In some parts of Africa, the nationalists have still not thrown off white control, for where real determination has been shown, as in Angola or South Africa, the superiority of white military methods has been too much for African resistance. The African leaders lacked the advantages of Chinese and Japanese leaders, of being able to appeal to ancient traditions of greatness and civilisation to give a feeling of pride and unity to their peoples. There is evidence of quite complex civilisation in parts of Nigeria, Southern Rhodesia and East Africa and some African leaders have made much of this, but it does not form a strong enough tradition to be effective. The high rate of illiteracy and widespread poverty have added to the difficulties of creating efficient African political organisations.

Some inspiration has been found by Africans' leaders in Ethiopia (Abyssinia) which was only briefly held by Europeans and further encouragement has come from abroad from Africans now living in the

Independent Africa

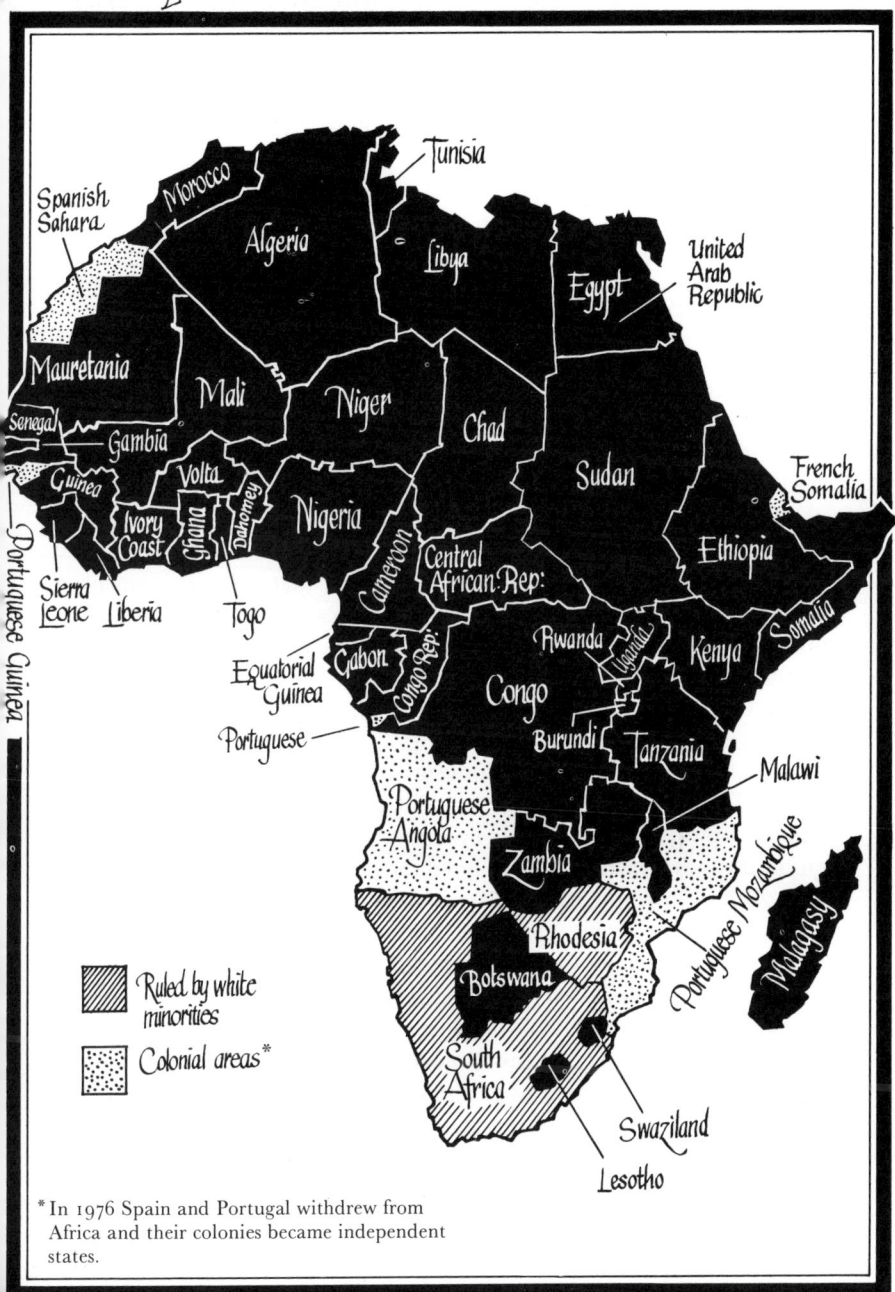

Spanish Sahara

Morocco

Tunisia

Algeria

Libya

Egypt

United Arab Republic

Mauretania

Mali

Niger

Chad

Sudan

French Somalia

Senegal

Gambia

Guinea

Volta

Nigeria

Cameroon

Central African Rep.

Ethiopia

Somalia

Ivory Coast

Ghana

Dahomey

Portuguese Guinea

Sierra Leone

Liberia

Togo

Equatorial Guinea

Gabon

Congo Rep.

Rwanda

Uganda

Kenya

Congo

Burundi

Tanzania

Portuguese

Malawi

Portuguese Angola

Zambia

Portuguese Mozambique

Malagasy

Rhodesia

Botswana

South Africa

Swaziland

Lesotho

Ruled by white minorities

Colonial areas*

*In 1976 Spain and Portugal withdrew from Africa and their colonies became independent states.

West Indies and the U.S.A. and from Africans receiving higher education overseas. Early movements for African freedom and unity started abroad, for example Aurelius Garvey proclaimed a Negro Empire from New York and announced that he himself was president of Africa. African lawyers, doctors and teachers living abroad began the Nigerian Democratic Party, and William Du Bois established the National Association for the Advancement of Coloured Peoples and inspired a series of Pan African Congresses which met outside Africa.

b) Independence in West Africa

Nkrumah's rise to power

British control over Nigeria, the Gold Coast, Sierra Leone and Gambia consisted of managing the administration and the economy, not attempting to settle permanently. Such a system was more easily ended than one where there were white settlers with permanent homes to defend, and it was West Africa, then, that set the pace for the end of colonial rule. In the Gold Coast, a prosperous area by African standards, Nkrumah's Convention People's Party provided a pattern that other movements were to copy. Kwame Nkrumah had been educated at a mission school and a secondary school and, for a time, was himself a teacher. He studied at Lincoln University in the U.S.A. and helped to organise the Pan African Congress held in Manchester in 1945 and here met other leaders, including Jomo Kenyatta from Kenya. Older African leaders had founded the United Gold Coast Convention and they invited Nkrumah to become their General Secretary. Nkrumah made this movement far more popular by founding district branches and by organising violent demonstrations in which he exploited the discontent of ex-soldiers and the growth of unemployment. His activities led to his being imprisoned and pushed out of his party for being too extreme. He therefore established in 1949 the Convention People's Party and was once more arrested for organising strikes and demonstrations. However, the British government showed little desire for a lengthy bitter struggle and accepted the reforms suggested by the Coussey Committee which proposed universal suffrage, an African Legislative Assembly, and an Executive council with eight of its eleven members elected from the Assembly. The C.P.P. did so well in the 1951 elections, winning thirty-four of the thirty-eight constituencies, that Nkrumah was released from prison and agreed to form a government. For six years Nkrumah and the British Governor, Arden-Clarke, co-operated successfully and in 1957 the Gold Coast became the independent state of Ghana.

Nkrumah's rule

Nkrumah devoted considerable time and energy to trying to make Ghana the leader of a movement for African unity. The conference of African states which he organised in 1958 at Accra was marred by the suspicions of the French African areas and of Europeans and Nigeria. Nkrumah's policies also included the stressing of his own prestige and importance in order to try and provide a centre of unity for his state. He attempted to eliminate political rivals, hamper trade unions, and weaken the authority of tribal chiefs and he allowed rather dubious trials to be held to deal with his enemies. All these policies were unpopular and in February, 1966, while Nkrumah was absent in China, an army coup took place that established a military council led by General Ankrah in control of the government. Nkrumah was not permitted to return home, many of his followers were punished, and the new government concentrated on less spectacular policies of domestic reform. Many signs of the corruption and greed of those who ruled Ghana with Nkrumah were brought to light by the men who succeeded him, but Nkrumah's task had not been easy and a fall in the world price of cocoa, Ghana's main export, had increased his problems by reducing the revenue he desperately needed to improve Ghana. His C.P.P. had been strong in the coastal areas, but inland it met with far more opposition from tribal chiefs. Nkrumah paid the price for trying to unite his country's people too rapidly and for trying to do it by hoping that he could make all of Ghana look up to him as a great leader.

Nigeria

Nigeria has suffered from more difficulties than Ghana, largely because of its huge size. It was formed in 1914 by Lord Lugard, a British administrator who joined together the large, poor, and Moslem north with the Yoruba-inhabited west and the Ibo-dominated east. The different traditions of the areas led many to agree with Dr. Azikiwe that Nigeria should have a strong federal structure, and some attempt was made to allow for this when independence was granted in 1960. The first Prime Minister of the newly independent state was the quiet and courteous Sir Abubakar Talawa Balewa who came from the north, and followed policies that avoided Nkrumah's flamboyance. But tensions between the different peoples increased and in January, 1966, the Prime Minister was murdered in a plot born in the eastern area that led, eventually, to a military government led by General Ironsi, which tried to emphasise the unity of Nigeria. This attempt to create greater unity

International observers interview an Ibo refugee who has just returned to the liberated areas in Federal hands.

failed. Ironsi died later the same year during a series of massacres in which Ibo people who had left their area to live in other regions suffered particularly. A new military administration took office, relations between regions became distant and suspicious, and led before long to a savage civil war. The Ibo people attempted to proclaim that their region was to become an independent country, the state of Biafra. The region was only a small part of Nigeria but it contained rich oil deposits, and General Gowon's Federal Government refused to agree to the independence of Biafra. With weapons from such contrasting sources as Britain and the U.S.S.R., the Nigerian army pressed forward against the small Biafran Army and forced it to retreat. This civil war brought the most terrible suffering, civilians forced to flee from their homes were reduced to such misery that thousands died of starvation whilst their leaders argued about how they should be supplied with food by relief organisations like the Red Cross. Discussions between the two sides failed to bring a settlement and the war dragged on, made more lengthy as the expected Federal victory was delayed by the arrival of French weapons to help the Biafrans. Finally, in January 1970, the Biafran leader General Ojukwu, perhaps sensing the near collapse of his army, left the country. Within days Biafra had capitulated to the Federal Government, and the war was over. Although this terrible war was clearly partly caused by old tribal rivalries, it was also bound up with the effect on Africa of being occupied by Europeans. Nigeria was created by the British out of an area that was not already a natural unit, whilst British rule was too brief to bind together different tribes in either common loyalty to or hatred of their British masters.

Sierra Leone

In 1961 Sierra Leone, formed from freed slaves and dominated by the descendants of these slaves, the Creoles, gained independence. Like Gambia (independent in 1965) Sierra Leone is small and, like Ghana and Nigeria, its government has fallen into the hands of soldiers after elections in 1967 had produced an embarrassing situation in which the defeated Prime Minister, Sir Albert Margai, refused to recognise that he had been beaten. This growth of military power is not surprising in view of the fact that the army officers are often the most well-educated section of the community and the one group most likely to hold together states that threaten to split apart. Britain's attempt to export her parliamentary system to her colonies has not really suited their needs, for they lack the prospects, stability and readiness to compromise which makes the parliamentary system work.

French Areas

French West Africa was inevitably affected by events in British West Africa, and by events in other parts of the French Empire, notably in Indo-China where the French were defeated. The influence of the French system of centralised government affected some African leaders, so that they tended to divide into those who followed Sekou Toure of Guinea and wanted a series of free states, and those who followed Leopold Senghor and Felix Houphouet-Boigny, the leaders of the *Rassemblement Democratique Africain* who wanted to try and avoid the splitting of French West Africa into a series of states which would all be weak. In 1956 the French Socialist Government led by Mollet agreed to establish African cabinets in each of the eight French provinces, elected by universal suffrage, and in 1958 de Gaulle offered the African provinces membership of a French Community or full independence and a total break with France. Toure refused to follow the other states in joining the

Community, he was thus forced to look for aid from other sources and turned to Russia. However, this breach was partially healed by 1962, by which time Madagascar too was independent. Economic and cultural ties still bind the former French colonies to France itself.

c) Independence in East Africa

The British belief that there was less need for early independence in East Africa because the tribes there were poorer than those in West Africa was sharply jolted by a rebellion in Kenya by some of the Kikuyu. This land-hungry people staged a rising in 1952 which involved secret religious ceremonies and came to be known as the Mau Mau rising. Kikuyu leaders like Kenyatta were arrested and harsh methods were used by British forces to put down the rebellion, though the bulk of the people who suffered from it were African not European. Altogether during the Mau Mau troubles 8,000 Africans died whilst only sixty-eight Europeans lost their lives. Britain was, however, much more ready by 1956 to plan independence for Kenya, Uganda and Tanganyika, despite the alarm of the white minorities living there. Kenya itself became independent in 1963, though some difficulty arose from the fear of other tribes that the Kikuyu would dominate them, but this was, surprisingly, two years after Tanganyika's independence. Tanganyika owed its success to the speed and skill with which a large movement, T.A.N.U., was built up by Julius Nyerere, an ex-school teacher and graduate of Edinburgh University. The stability and moderation of Nyerere's government was upset by army mutinies in 1964 and by the effect of a Communist revolt in nearby Zanzibar against the Arab rulers of the island. British troops were called in to put down the risings and Zanzibar was now linked to Tanganyika to form Tanzania. But Nyerere clearly felt the need to adopt a more left-wing position and became much more bold and extreme in his speeches.

Uganda was granted independence in 1962 after Milton Obote's Uganda People's Congress had allied with the royalist Buganda Kabaka Yekka Party. One of the main problems in Uganda was the privileged position occupied by the Kingdom of Buganda and in 1966 Obote tried to solve this problem forcibly by abolishing Buganda's privileged position and forcing the Kabaka, its ruler, to flee. In 1971 a soldier, Idi Amin, seized control of Uganda.

The Rhodesian Problem

The Central African Federation of Rhodesia and Nyasaland posed even more serious problems, for a large white population regarded the area as their home and were unwilling to grant equality to the Africans. At first Britain attempted a compromise, the 'multi-racial' society, in which limited concessions to Africans were granted. The region seemed a natural economic unit for it contained copper, coal, tobacco and other industries, and its economic growth was rapid. The Kariba Dam was built to provide cheap hydro-electric power from the Zambesi and the Federal Government, led by Sir Roy Welensky, seemed hopeful of great progress. But Nyasaland was never satisfied with the system and led by Dr. Hastings Banda its people were soon expressing dissatisfaction in demonstrations, strikes and riots. Nyasaland was poorer than Rhodesia, felt neglected, and resented white control of the Federation. Macmillan, the British Prime Minister, and Macleod, the Colonial Secretary, decided that the multi-racial experiment was not likely to be a success and the Federation was dissolved. In 1963 Nyasaland became the independent state of Malawi and in the following year, Kaunda became Prime Minister of Zambia (formed from the former colony of Northern Rhodesia). Southern Rhodesia with its relatively large and long established white ruling minority, remained theoretically a British Colony. The European Rhodesians now began to demand dominion status, following lengthy discussions with the British government, a new constitution was introduced in December 1961. It allowed for minority African representation, but because of its limitations was violently opposed by African leaders. The principle African opposition party, Z.A.P.U., was banned and its leaders placed under restriction. The moderate P.M. Field was replaced in 1964 by Ian Smith. Lengthy negotiations followed, during which the Rhodesians lost patience with Britain and threatened to make a unilateral declaration of independence (U.D.I.). On November 11th, Smith announced that Southern Rhodesia was now an independent dominion within the Commonwealth. The British government immediately declared this move illegal and applied sanctions, but refused to use force to deal with a rebellion that was backed by 250,000 whites. The four million Africans made little trouble since their leaders had already been confined, or exiled, and they themselves were vulnerable to pressure on their jobs. An economic war developed, as Britain attempted to cut off trade to Rhodesia, backed by the U.N. in April 1966. Sanctions on Rhodesia damaged her chances of selling tobacco, but no stranglehold was possible since, though the outlet through Portuguese Mozambique could be blockaded, the outlet through South Africa could not, and Britain was unwilling to risk a clash with South Africa. Britain's caution offended many African states; some threatened to leave the Commonwealth; some broke off diplomatic relations; but the

British Premier Harold Wilson (left) shakes hands with Rhodesian Premier Ian Smith at the end of a fruitless meeting on the Rhodesian independence crisis in October, 1965.

military weakness of the African states made action by them unthinkable. Further attempts at a negotiated ending to the rebellion by meetings between Smith and Wilson aboard a cruiser, H.M.S. *Tiger*, were a failure and so were discussions in 1968, in Gibraltar. Rhodesia was increasingly drawn towards South Africa, despite the distrust the English inhabitants of Rhodesia held for the Afrikaans rulers of South Africa. The final split came on 2 March 1970 when Ian Smith announced that Rhodesia would become an independent republic from that date. In 1976 South African and U.S. pressure led to fresh talks between Britain, Ian Smith and nationalist leaders.

d) The Congo

Belgium had devoted little money and energy in developing the Congo in ways that would help it achieve stability as an independent state. Independence was granted in 1960 after a period of trouble in which African tribal rivalries were far more prominent than hostility to Belgian rule. The Belgians shrank from the prospect of having to deal with uprisings and bloodshed and decided to withdraw despite the fact that African political organisation was poor and based on a tribal rather than a Congolese framework. Until the 1950s, the Belgians had thought of the vast African area they ruled merely as an area with economic assets useful to Belgium. They had not attempted to develop the area as a united political and administrative region in a way which would accustom the many different tribes to working with one another. Patrice Lumumba was one of the few Congolese to see the need for a national party. No sense of unity could be developed from a common struggle by Africans against Belgian rule: the Belgians would not even permit a five year transition period which African leaders were quite ready to accept. The 1960 elections were thus the first national elections ever held in the Congo and no clear cut results emerged. Lumumba managed to form a government and Kasavubu became President of the new republic, but army mutinies and tribal rivalries led to a collapse of law and order aggravated by the separation from the Congo of Katanga. Katanga was the wealthiest part of the Congo and the whole state badly needed its resources and revenues, but Tshombe, supported by the *Union Minière* which controlled the copper mines, insisted on independence. The difficulties facing Lumumba were, therefore, enormous. He was trying to run a state which had little sense of being a unity; he was trying to run it, moreover, with very few assistants capable of skilled administration and with negligible help from the Belgians. Lumumba led the *Mouvement National Congolais*, the main party that tried to work on a national basis, but countless numbers of Congolese preferred to think in terms of their own region, not on the Congo as a whole. Nor could Lumumba rely upon the armed forces to help him rule the country. Only two days after independence there were widespread mutinies in the army led by soldiers who expected independence to bring prompt increases in pay and rapid promotion. In Katanga, on the other hand, law and order seemed effective and Tshombe made much of this fact to win sympathy in European lands. In fact he owed much of his success to the support he received from the Belgians who provided him with administrators and helped run the mines. The Katangese share of the profits from the mines enabled Tshombe to hire mercenary soldiers who could bring more skill to the leadership of his army than the Congolese government could find for its own forces. Lumumba appealed to the U.N. and then to Russia before he himself was swept aside by the Congolese army under Colonel Mobutu and by Kasavubu and the politicians who disliked the strong centralised government Lumumba was trying to create.

In response to appeals from Kasavubu and Lumumba the United Nations sent technical experts and soldiers to help run the Congo more successfully, to try and deal with those areas that were trying to break away, and to endeavour to stop individual countries from using the Congo's troubles to their own advantage. To some extent

v

the U.N. forces did well in this crisis for they managed to force the Belgians to leave the Congo, they put a stop to Russia's attempt at intervention, and they helped to keep the Congo's economy going. But the breakaway state of Katanga could only be brought to heel by the use of force, much as the U.N. Secretary General, Hammarskjold, hated this, and even when it had been re-united to the Congo Katanga continued to prove a difficult problem. Hammerskjöld died in an air crash whilst on his way to meet Tshombe to try and work out a settlement. By this time Lumumba, too, was dead, murdered by Tshombe's troops. The U.N. lacked the money to stay in the Congo and as U.N. forces left, so civil war returned. Neither Tshombe (who returned to head the Congolese government for a while) nor Kasavubu were able to bring peace to their troubled land. Instead, white mercenaries were called in to strengthen Colonel Mobutu's Congolese army, and this proved a very successful move. The various tribes attempting to resist the central government were steadily defeated. This success increased the prestige of Mobutu so that in November, 1965, he decided to take over the government himself and drive out of office President Kasavubu, who had managed to cling on for so long. The Congo remained an exceedingly difficult area to govern, especially for a government so short of skilled manpower, but at least a more peaceful period followed the 1965 change of government.

e) South Africa

In South Africa, the volume of legislation aimed at creating apartheid increased as post-war South Africa continued to be governed by the National Party whose members believed in both white racialism and Afrikaner nationalism. In 1960 South Africa became a Republic, and in 1961 it left the Commonwealth before the pressure of other states could produce its expulsion. For much of the time Dr. H. F. Verwoerd was Prime Minister, and under him the device of calling opponents of the government Communists gave them power to arrest and imprison without trial and to keep people confined to their homes by house arrest. In 1953 the Bantu Education Act, the work of Verwoerd, removed control of African education from missionary schools to make sure that the Bantu were not given 'the wrong type of education'. In 1960 African discontent was shown by demonstrations at Sharpeville against the Pass laws which controlled the movement about the country of Africans. The demonstrations were marked by police brutality when the police opened fire on the demonstrators killing and wounding many of them.

It was not easy to oppose the government, particularly since South African prosperity boomed; the limited number of white liberals were harassed very effectively; the African leaders were imprisoned whether moderate, like Chief Luthuli, or more militant like Nelson Mandela. The South African government was efficient and determined: not even the murder of Verwoerd in 1966 and his replacement by B. J. Vorster made any difference to this.

APARTHEID LAWS: Among the laws hampering non-whites were the Group Areas Act (1950) dividing cities into racial zones; the Bantu Authorities Act (1951) increasing the power of the chiefs; the Natives' Resettlement Act (1954) which removed 70,000 Africans from the middle of Johannesburg; the Natives' Law Amendment Act making even social evenings between blacks and whites a punishable offence. In 1963 Transkei, the first of the Bantustans (areas where limited self-government was allowed the Africans) was created but, like other similar designated areas, was inadequate and overcrowded. With the continued growth of industry and the need for African labour, the Government cannot fully enforce a separation of the races.

The control of South Africa over the former mandate, South West Africa, was challenged by Ethiopia and Liberia in a lawsuit before the International Court which failed by one vote. The three British protectorates in or near South Africa have also been increasingly tied to South Africa by their poverty and her strength. Basutoland has become the independent state of Lesotho, and Bechuanaland the independent state of Botswana, yet they, like Swaziland, continue to need their South African links.

f) Portuguese Colonies

Portugal clung to her African colonies until 1974. Then revolution in Portugal itself ended the country's dictatorship and the Portuguese pulled out of their colonies. Mozambique and Angola both became independent, though the latter suffered a civil war eventually won by the Communist backed M.P.L.A. helped by Cuban troops.

The areas of Africa still dominated by whites cannot be freed by African states while they themselves are militarily weak and occupied with the development of their own education, industry and agriculture. The 'white' areas stress that they are a bulwark against Communism, despite the fact that Communism has made surprisingly little progress in Africa, and they are often the wealthiest areas – certainly South Africa and Southern Rhodesia enjoy a prosperity not enjoyed by the rest of Africa. All too often the economy of African states depends heavily on one product, such as copper in Zambia and cotton in Uganda, whilst a rapid population growth makes greater prosperity even more difficult to achieve. With these problems, plus the instability of governments in some regions, jealousies between states and the constant battle to create a sense of national unity, it is hard for the independent African countries to do more than pass resolutions at their Organisations for African Unity denouncing the white-controlled areas.

g) Conclusion

In 1945 Africa contained a mere three fully independent states, Ethiopia, Liberia and South Africa. In twenty years this situation changed rapidly as the British, French and Belgians withdrew as rulers of much of Africa. Such sudden change in so short a time was bound to create problems and the new states of Africa found themselves to be particularly weak. In developing their governments and their economies the problems of lack of skilled manpower and of capital meant that foreign aid was necessary, yet foreign aid all too often implied taking sides in the quarrels of the outside world. The Russians took a vigorous interest in African affairs, offered money and technical skill and were less suspicious than the Western powers of the position of neutrality in the cold war preferred by most African states. Even the Chinese interested themselves in African affairs, sending Chou En-lai on a tour of African states in 1963–4, offering to train soldiers to throw off foreign oppression in states still without independence and welcoming African leaders in China itself. However, in comparison with Russia and the West, Chinese aid is minimal and therefore Chinese influence is very limited. But the Chinese can appeal to the Africans as their allies in the battle to reduce the power of white people.

The problems of developing countries whose boundaries are usually artificial ones inherited from colonial rulers have driven most governments in Africa in the same direction. Strong government has come to mean single-party government, even military government, since a strong single party with an able leader (like Kenyatta or Nyerere) seems the only way to hold the country together. To many people in the West the result looks suspiciously like harsh rule and the denying of freedom but the situation in Africa cannot be compared to the situation in Britain or France. Most opposition parties in Western democracies work peacefully, accepting many of the things that the ruling party accept too. In most African states opposition is all too often tribal, or religious or local separatism completely opposed to the existence of the state. To find a suitable form of government that will bring peace, order and a chance of economic progress is a battle that all African leaders have had to fight. It is perhaps, surprising that most have done so well and that major disasters have been limited to Nigeria and the Congo. All have been short of administrators, economic specialists, scientists, teachers and doctors: the boundaries between them could well have been the source of violent quarrels. Problems of poverty, ignorance, tribal rivalries, and disease have been tackled, often with United Nations' aid. An enormous amount remains to be done but the part played by African states in world affairs is bound to be one of growing importance.

Arab Nationalism

a) Colonial Control of Arab Lands

The Arab peoples inhabit an extensive area which stretches from the northern coast of Africa into the Middle East northwards to the frontiers of Turkey and east and south down the shores of the Red Sea. A common language and the Moslem faith are unifying features among these peoples, but poor communications and the difficulties of living in areas where mountains and desert occupy so much of the land have prevented the permanent creation of effective unity. Instead the Arabs fell victims to Turkish conquerors (in the sixteenth century) and in 1900 Arab areas of Syria, Iraq, Jordan, Saudi Arabia, Palestine and the Lebanon were all part of the Turkish Empire. The Arab areas of North Africa fell into European hands during the nineteenth century. The French began a conquest of Algeria in 1830 and captured Tunis in 1881 whilst Britain took over increasing control of Egypt in order to protect the Suez Canal (the vital route to British India). In 1898 British control was extended farther south by the victory of Kitchener's army at the battle of Omdurman in the Sudan. Libya was seized by Italy in 1911 and complete European control of North Africa was finally secured by the conquest of Morocco by France and Spain. The Arab peoples were, on the whole, poor and badly organised, though they did manage to put up a stiff fight in Morocco that lasted for several years.

The Europeans treated their conquests in different ways but rarely in a very progressive spirit. Britain was content to administer her lands, but France poured in settlers, especially into Algeria, and Italy was wholly preoccupied with the difficult task of subduing the nomadic peoples of Libya in a struggle that lasted until 1931.

The Middle East

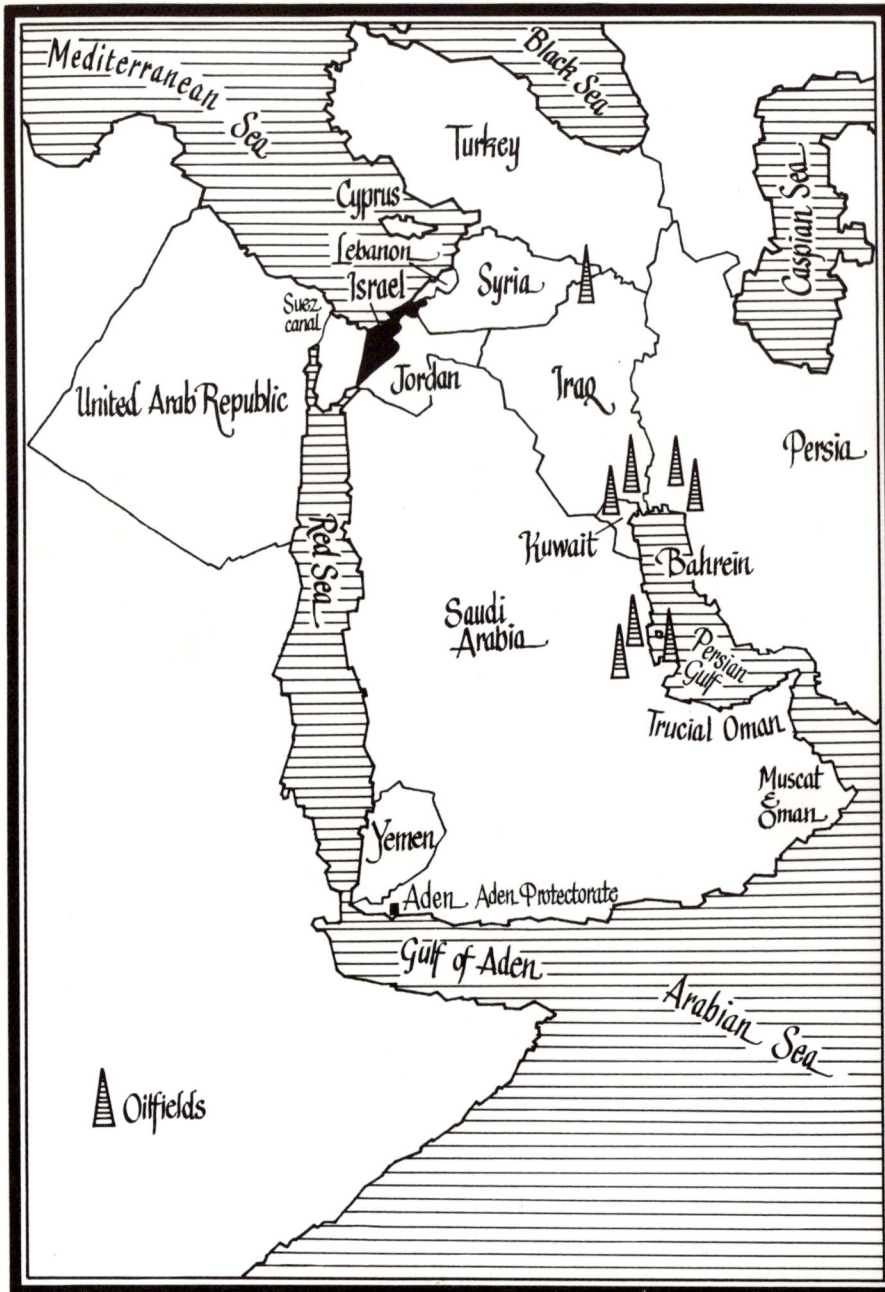

Mediterranean Sea

Black Sea

Turkey

Cyprus

Lebanon

Israel

Suez canal

Syria

Caspian Sea

United Arab Republic

Jordan

Iraq

Persia

Red Sea

Kuwait

Bahrein

Saudi Arabia

Persian Gulf

Trucial Oman

Muscat & Oman

Yemen

Aden   Aden Protectorate

Gulf of Aden

Arabian Sea

△ Oilfields

The First World War

The entry of Turkey into this war as an ally of the Central Powers gave Britain the excuse to declare a protectorate over Egypt and develop Egypt as a base for military operations. To assist her in her war efforts Britain appealed to the Arabs to rise in revolt against the Turks and, in the McMahon letters, offered vague promises for future independence to Arabs living in the Turkish Empire. Helped by T. E. Lawrence and led by the Hashemite prince, Hussein, and his sons, Faisal and Abdullah, the Arabs greatly assisted General Allenby's campaigns which drove the Turks out of the Middle East. But, in the desperation of war, Britain was rather too ready with promises that were contradictory, for she also negotiated the Sykes-Picot agreement (whereby France was to be allowed a share in controlling the Lebanon and Syria) as well as issuing the Balfour Declaration in 1917.

The Balfour Declaration

The British government was ill-informed about conditions in the Middle East and seems to have thought that most Arab peoples were nomadic Bedouin. The Balfour Declaration stated that the British government sympathised with the Jewish desire to establish a national home in Palestine and was ready to help; this was a major factor in creating one of the greatest problems of the Middle East, the clash of Arab and Jew. The British did not create Zionism, the strong desire of the Jews to return to the home from which they had been dislodged nearly two thousand years earlier, but they did make it possible for Jews to go in increasing numbers to settle in Palestine.

b) The decline of Colonialism in the Middle East

Egypt

Egypt contained a considerable number of nationalists by 1918. With its tradition of independence stemming from the early nineteenth century, its large population, flourishing towns, and intellectual leadership, Egypt was more restless under colonial rule than other states and became so troublesome to Britain that the British decided to concede independence. But the desire to maintain troops to guard the Suez Canal was seen by Britain as an essential part of any settlement, and no Egyptian leaders would risk unpopularity by signing such a settlement. In 1922 the British therefore issued their own, one-sided declaration that Egypt was independent and was to be a constitutional monarchy with safeguards for

British interests in the area, only to find that the Egyptians would not co-operate. It was Mussolini's aggression in Abyssinia that shook Egyptians sufficiently to persuade them to agree to a settlement in 1936 whereby Britain was allowed to maintain up to 10,000 troops in the Canal Zone for twenty years. Egypt's monarchy was given considerable power and an unhappy period of squabbling followed during which the monarchists and the Wafd Party tussled for supremacy and neither introduced the social reforms Egypt so badly needed.

The British Mandates

To the fury of the Arabs, they were not granted independence when Turkey was defeated in 1918, but were parcelled out between Britain and France. Britain founded states for Hussein's sons – Faisal was established in Iraq and Abdullah in Transjordan – but now there was a new problem, Palestine. As more and more Jews poured in, especially after Nazi persecution began in Germany, so the Arab population of the area became rapidly more alarmed. Iraq was granted independence in 1930 but, again, as in Egypt, British influence remained in the shape of bases, whilst Transjordan had to await the end of the Second World War before it was recognised as independent. Britain had squandered opportunities to create goodwill by her slowness in reaching a settlement which did justice to Arab nationalism, and by insisting on maintaining military rights that continued to cause offence. This interference was worst in Jordan for not only were there British bases, there was also the Arab Legion, led by Sir John Glubb and aided by British money.

The French Mandates

The Lebanon and Syria were split off from the other areas which Hussein and Faisal had hoped to see united as one large independent Arab state, and France proceeded to rule them with so little regard for Arab feeling that a revolt broke out, first led by Faisal whom the French expelled, and then widened in 1925 in protest at French attempts to split up Syria into weak units. The area never really settled down, there was fighting there between Vichy French and Free French forces and even an attempt by the French to re-impose their authority after the Second World War which collapsed under Arab hostility and the opposition of France's allies. Probably the French were fearful that the example of a successful revolt in Syria might affect their other possessions in North Africa and thus tried to adopt stern tactics.

The Middle East reached independence in turmoil and confusion.

European states maintained bases in the areas they left; the new rulers were rarely enlightened enough to introduce social reforms, despite the growing revenue that poured into many from the exploitation of oil. Rivalries between Arab states, especially the Hashemite kingdoms of Iraq and Jordan, and Ibn Saud's kingdom of Saudi Arabia, were exceeded only by the common Arab alarm at the continued growth of a Jewish community in their midst.

c) The Decline of Colonialism in North Africa

Tunis and Morocco

These two areas were less vigorously settled and controlled by the French than Algeria; their rulers, they Bey and the Sultan, continued in power and in both there grew up nationalist parties eager to be rid of French control. The Second World War struck hard at French prestige and encouraged the Arab leaders – the Sultan Mohammed V himself in Morocco, and Habib Bourguiba in Tunis. The French became so heavily involved in trying to control Algeria they were forced to admit defeat to Algeria's neighbours and allow independence to both in 1956, but even then ill-feeling persisted, aggravated by the French retention of Bizerta as a naval base in Tunis until 1962.

Algeria

Over a million French settlers eventually gathered in Algeria where they took most of the best land and occupied most of the best positions (to the indignation of Moslem leaders). The Algerians despaired of achieving independence by negotiation and formed the F.L.N. (*Front de Liberation Nationale*) which sought independence by violence. From 1954 until 1962 a savage war raged during which massive French armies were poured into Algeria and yet were unable to win final victory. It was de Gaulle, the leader from whom the French settlers had expected a tougher war policy, who had the courage to end the war with negotiations at Evian. Again, independence in French North Africa as in the French and British Middle East left behind it many reasons for Arabs to dislike the West.

Libya

The Italian colony in North Africa was captured during the Second World War by Britain, but creating a new state from it was not easy for there were great differences between Idris and his Bedouin followers and the coastal peoples. Not until 1951 was a new and independent state created, helped by the discovery of oil within its frontiers. Italy's other colonies met varying fates: Eritrea became part of Ethiopia; Somaliland was ruled as a United Nations' trust territory by Italy until 1960 when it became an independent state, leaving French Somaliland as the only colonial area in the region.

d) The Independent Arab States

Many vast difficulties faced the areas the Europeans had been forced to leave and not all Arabs were in agreement as to the correct solution to these problems. Some wished to renounce the West and all its ways and the Moslem Brotherhood, based in Syria and ready to use violence, represented this feeling at its most extreme. Others preferred to copy the West and seek to industrialise their lands and free their peoples from traditional restrictions. But some of the Arab states were soon dragged into the clash of Russia and the U.S.A. for their region lay in a vital strategic area and included vast supplies of oil. To the rivalries of Arab states, and of Arabs and Israel, was added the rivalry of states favouring Russia and those sympathising with the West. Money spent on armaments meant money diverted from the enormous tasks of coping with rising population, poor arid soil, a difficult climate and illiteracy and backwardness. With so many tensions, the yearning for Arab unity achieved little reality, despite the creation of an Arab League in 1944.

Egypt

The failure of the Arab peoples to prevent the creation of Israel in 1948 disgraced their rulers and led to another upsurge of hatred of the foreigners, especially the British, who had helped to cause the problem of Palestine. In 1951 Farouk, the selfish and incompetent King of Egypt, allowed a policy of harassing the British in the canal zone to begin. Farouk had no reason to like the British for they had forced him to widen his government during the war by taking in members of the Wafd Party; but if he thought that harassing Britain would make him popular he was wrong. Modern-minded army leaders had come, like the mass of the Egyptian people, to loathe Farouk and in July, 1952, the army seized power and Farouk was expelled. At the head of the rebellion stood General Neguib, but he began to have doubts about whether the army should remain in power and he was replaced by the more energetic and determined Colonel Nasser who, in 1954, became President.

The army leaders who had seized power were able to negotiate agreements with Britain whereby the Sudan was to be allowed to decide its own future and the British forces were to leave the canal zone to return only if one of the Arab League were attacked. In fact the Sudan, which Nasser confidently expected to join Egypt, eventually decided on independence though its history was troubled by quarrels between the north and south and by an army seizure of power 1958–64. Britain and the U.S.A. hoped the settlement with Egypt would mean that Egypt would now feel herself able to join the Western powers in opposing the U.S.S.R. But the Egyptians preferred not to be tied to either side in the cold war, and Nasser was especially offended by the Baghdad Pact, the military alliance which the Western powers were building as a barrier to the entry of Russia into the Middle East. Iraq, who joined the Baghdad Pact, was ruled by a monarch hated by the Egyptian leaders, thus the end of the direct quarrel with Britain did not end Egypt's suspicion of Britain and her allies.

Nasser combined a programme of social reform with a vigorous foreign policy designed to make him the leader to whom all Arabs would look for guidance. His success was reflected in elections in the Sudan which brought to power a pro-Nasser Party and helped the Sudan to obtain independence from Britain in 1956. A programme of reforms improved education, abolished titles, attacked corruption, redistributed land and restricted the maximum size of farms. Industrial development was encouraged and labour laws protected the position of workers in Egypt's industries. Nasser pinned great hopes on the building of the Aswan High Dam to create a huge lake on the River Nile that would provide water for irrigation and hydro-electric power too. But his foreign policy and domestic policy could not be separated, and on 19th July 1956 the American loan to finance the dam was withdrawn on the excuse that Egypt could not pay the interest charges, but also because Nasser's insistence on being independent had led him to purchase Czech weapons. Nasser replied by nationalising the Suez Canal on the 26th July, intending to use the canal revenue to finance the dam. This move was attacked by Britain and France who objected to the canal being nationalised and who co-operated with Israel in a brief war. U.N. pressure halted the European powers and though Nasser's forces were defeated by the Israelis, he emerged well since the canal remained in Egyptian hands (and was very efficiently run) and Russian aid replaced American. But his attempt to become the leader of all Arabs in the Middle East made disappointing progress. In 1958 the United Arab Republic linked Syria to Egypt, only to split up in 1961, Nasser proving unable to control the Baath Socialist Party which dominated Syrian politics. Despite defeat in the 1967 war with Israel, Nasser was sufficiently popular to remain president until his death in 1970. He was succeeded by President Sadat.

Jordan and Iraq

The monarchies in the Middle East were also divided by the hostility between the two Hashemite kings and the ruling family of Saudi Arabia. All three inclined towards Britain and the U.S.A.; Iraq, for instance, joined Britain, Persia, Turkey and Pakistan in the Baghdad Pact in 1955. But in 1958 King Faisal II of Iraq and his pro-Western chief minister, Nuri-es-Said, were murdered by rebels who proceeded to seize power and establish a republic led by a soldier, Kassem. Iraq's economic resources are stronger than those of many other Arab states, and include fertile land and oil, but the political stability which would best help progress has not come. In 1963 Kassem was killed in another army revolt that placed Field Marshal Aref at the head of the government. Aref died in 1966 and was succeeded by his brother, who was then deposed in 1968. The various leaders of the republic of Iraq have also had to struggle with the problem of the Kurds, a people living within Iraq's frontiers who have persisted in demanding special rights despite all the efforts of the army to crush them. Iraq is not wholly free to decide policy, her oil is piped through Syria which makes her very vulnerable to the rather violent rulers of Syria.

The other branch of the Hashemite family that controlled Jordan has managed to cling on to power. To the poor land of Transjordan was added, in 1948, a section of Palestine containing Arabs of a more advanced political character lacking the traditional loyalty to the king of the tribes of Transjordan. Abdullah of Jordan was assassinated in 1951, but Hussein, his grandson, who became king, showed skill in modifying his policies in order to survive. In 1955 he dismissed the British officers who led his army, in order to free himself of the accusation that he was a mere agent of Britain; then, in 1957, he had to use his loyal tribesmen to put down a pro-Egyptian rising by the more advanced Arabs in the west of his kingdom. Jordan suffered particularly heavily in the Israeli attack of 1967 for Hussein's forces were soundly beaten and the western area of his kingdom, including part of Jerusalem, was lost to Israel. Hussein's land is not rich, he has been frequently criticised by Arabs in Syria and Egypt for not being sufficiently hostile to the West and yet bold action to demonstrate his loyalty to the Arab cause against Israel has cost his country a terrible price.

Saudi Arabia

The kingdom of Saudi Arabia was created in 1925 by Ibn Saud when he ejected Hussein, the head of the Hashemite family, from there. It has remained a backward state although it contains vast resources of oil which meant that growing revenue was available for reforms. For decades depressingly little was done and this led King Saud to be eventually pushed out of power in 1964 by his brother, Faisal, who was more determined to modernise the state. Saudi Arabia is, therefore, a despotism with the difficult problem of trying to modernise itself without a political revolution, yet other Arab states, especially Egypt, dislike the monarchy of Saudi Arabia and would be only too pleased to see it overthrown.

Around the fringe of Saudi Arabia lie a number of small states, some poor and backward, others like Kuwait rich through the discovery of oil. In all these states the same problem faces the sheikhs who rule them: how to modernise their lands without bringing about their own downfall. Before them they have the warning of the Yemen, where there has been civil war since 1962 between the royalists (backed by Saudi Arabia and controlling the countryside) and the republicans (backed by Egypt and controlling the towns). In 1965 Nasser and Faisal (the King of Saudi Arabia) negotiated an agreement to end the Yemen civil war; both sides agreed to pull back from the area and the tension between the two states relaxed for a while. Close to the Yemen is the town of Aden, developed by Britain first as a base on the route to India, then as an oil refinery and as a Middle East headquarters for British troops. Since 1958, it had become a growing source of anxiety and expense as British troops were faced with attacks from Arab nationalists. The British plan of 1962 to link Aden to surrounding areas in a federation strong enough to stand up to Egyptian pressure proved impossible to achieve since so wide a gulf exists between the nationalists of Aden and the sheikhs of the rural areas nearby. Clashes between Arabs and British forces led the British Labour government to decide to withdraw from Aden in 1967 as part of its policy of reducing British forces outside Europe.

Algeria

Independent Morocco and Tunis have proved much less restless than independent Algeria. The moderation of Hassan II of Morocco and Bourguiba of Tunis has been annoying to the nationalists of Egypt; there was even a break in diplomatic relations for a time between Tunis and Egypt. But Algeria has emerged as a nationalist state rivalling Egypt as a leader of Arabs who wish to be rid of monarchies and proclaim their determination to eliminate Israel. By the time of the granting of independence the old F.L.N. leader, Ferhat Abbas, had been replaced by Ben Bella and his more extreme followers, who were so determined to unite their state that they caused a civil war. The Kabylia area broke into revolt against the central government and the disgrace which fell on Ben Bella encouraged the army chief, Boumedienne, to seize power himself in 1962. Boumedienne began cautiously, but growing confidence has encouraged him to take a more prominent part in Arab politics, denouncing Israel and the West as frequently as Nasser.

e) The Problem of Israel

Though divided on many other matters, the Arab states are, at least in theory, agreed that they wish to see Israel eliminated. On the whole Jews living in Arab lands were treated with toleration before 1914, probably with more toleration than Jews found they received in European states. A small community of Jews remained in Palestine despite the expulsion from their homeland of the mass of the Jewish people by the Romans in A.D. 21. During the following centuries they were joined by other families returning from exile, but their numbers remained too few to give serious cause for alarm to the Arabs. In the later nineteenth century however a Zionist movement developed in the U.S.A. and Europe, bent on recovering full control of Palestine and sympathetically supported by British and U.S. leaders. The Balfour Declaration and the Nazi persecution both contributed in causing a big increase of Jewish immigrants into the British mandate of Palestine. The British government clung to its mistaken belief that Jews and Arabs could live contentedly together, but the Jews aimed at establishing an independent home of their own and the Arabs of Palestine were afraid they would soon be outnumbered. A Royal Commission was sent out which decided that the partition of Palestine between Jews and Arabs was the only solution, a solution naturally resented by the Arabs.

The problem that Britain had done so much to create, she soon found herself helpless to solve and her chief ally, the U.S.A., urged Britain to let into Palestine far more Jews than the British government had come to think was reasonable. As the British remained in Palestine, uncertain as to what to do, the Jews next turned their attention to pushing out the British so that they could turn the Jewish-occupied area into an independent state. Extremists among the Jews began to use violence which led to a series of tragedies, the worst was the blowing up of the King David Hotel in Jerusalem, causing the death of ninety-one people. Britain determined to be rid of the problem and attempted to

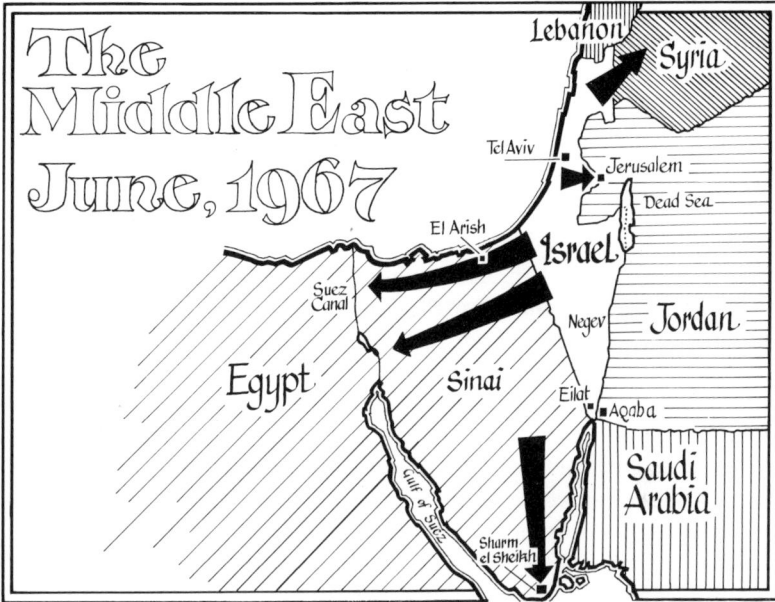

place it in the United Nations' lap. The U.N. came up with a highly complex plan for the partition of Palestine which was quickly rejected by the Arabs. In 1948 the British government decided to leave Palestine, regardless of the consequences and the Israeli leader, Ben-Gurion, promptly declared the existence of an independent state. Although the Arab states were totally opposed to this development, there was little they could do. The armies of the Arab League were poorly led and poorly equipped and the forces from different Arab states co-operated very badly. The Israeli army on the other hand was well armed and organised, many of its men had fought with the British during the Second World War, and, as a result, were experienced soldiers. The United Nations sent out Bernadotte in an attempt to end the conflict but Bernadotte was murdered by Jewish extremists and the truce he had just patched up died with him. By 1948 the Arabs had to admit defeat, though they refused to recognise the existence of Israel. The existence of Israel has prolonged Arab dislike of Britain and has upset Arab states themselves, for the defeat of 1948 was followed by upheavals in Arab states where the unsuccessful governments were swept away by dissatisfied nationalists. Yet in 1956 the Arabs were defeated again, caught unprepared by a sudden Israeli attack led by General Dayan which destroyed much of Egypt's Russian equipment before it could ever be used. The Israeli victory enabled them to open the port of Eilat on to the Red Sea which broke the economic war the Arab states had been waging on Israel. This Israeli victory owed much to the British and French, whose forces attacked Egypt; indeed the support of British bombers with the ability to destroy Egyptian airfields was a vital part of the Israeli campaign and freed them from a very real menace.

The conflicts of 1967–1973

Border incidents and threats marked the next few years; the Syrians were particularly prominent in these for Syria housed many of the several hundred thousand Arab refugees pushed out of Israel when it was created. These refugees were encouraged to think only in terms of returning to their divided homeland, no attempt was made to find them places and work in other Arab states. Israel herself proved very skilful at making the best of a poor area, helped by aid from American Jews and German reparations for Nazi crimes against Jews. Industry and agriculture prospered, Tel Aviv became a flourishing centre, and vital new villages, the Kibbutzim, ran communal agriculture. Yet much had to be spent on defence, the Israelis were especially alarmed by the missiles Nasser acquired and by the West German scientists working in Egypt. In spring 1967, new pressure was put on Israel when Nasser insisted that U.N. forces move from the Egyptian-Israeli border and the straits of Tiran (Israel's outlet to the Red Sea) should be closed to Israeli trade. After some delay the P.M., Eshkol, launched the Israeli forces in a highly successful six-day war that had been carefully planned by General Rabin and won astonishing success in the air and in armoured battles. Once again the Arab forces did not seem to be ready and did not co-operate with each other so that the Israelis were able to capture Jordan's area of Jerusalem, seize the straits of Tiran, drive across the Sinai Desert as far as the Suez Canal, and attack Syrian forces, pushing them back from their mountain defences. No peace settlement followed this victory, however, for Israel would not give up her conquests without effective guarantees of her trade and her safety and the Arabs could not bring themselves to recognise Israel as a permanent neighbour. Once more thousands of miserable Arab refugees poured from their homes, many of them crossing into Jordan which could ill afford to support them. In 1973 a new Arab assault on Israel brought Arab forces early successes. Israel recovered, but only at serious cost. Oil producing Arab states entered the fray by cutting off supplies from states supplying Israel. This new menace has made Israel's position even more uncertain. In 1974 Yitzhak Rabin replaced Mrs. Golda Meir as Prime

Minister; both leaders have been very determined to keep U.S. weapons.

f) Persia

The ancient state of Persia (known nowadays as Iran) lies within the vital oil-producing area of the Middle East and is an important key to the rivalry of the West and the U.S.S.R. within this area. During the twentieth century the British and Russians had both attempted to extend their control over the area, the result being a series of uneasy compromises like the division of the area during the Second World War. The rich oil resources of Iran were controlled by the Anglo-Iranian Oil Company in which the British government held a considerable number of shares. After 1945 this question of the control of the oil industry became increasingly important, for Iran needed more revenue to improve the country. Eventually in 1951 Dr. Musaddiq nationalised the oil industry, supported by rich landowners, nationalists, Communists, and religious fanatics, all of whom hated the British. But, backed by the U.S.A., the British successfully blocked Iran's attempt to run the oil industry for her own benefit, for Britain feared that a display of weakness here would damage her whole Middle Eastern position. The U.S.A. suspected Musaddiq of being a Communist (certainly he was driven by necessity to look to Moscow for help) and the result was that Musaddiq was pushed out of office in 1953 by the army. A new agreement was worked out which recognised the nationalisation of Iranian oil, gave Britain compensation, and created a new body to manage the industry in which the British share was smaller. Fifty per cent. of the profits from oil went to the Iranian government and helped the Shah, who was soon in full control of his country's government, to introduce a cautious programme of land reform and other changes. Such reforms are desperately needed – Persia, like Jordan and Saudi Arabia, is one of the few remaining areas in the Middle East where a traditional ruler is trying to maintain his authority and yet introduce sufficient changes to avert the kind of political upheaval experienced by Egypt, Syria, and Iraq.

12 | Canada, Australia and New Zealand

Introduction

During the enormous changes which transformed the British Empire and Commonwealth in the twentieth century, events in Asia and Africa tended to attract most attention. It was in these areas that the British government struggled to cope with the increasingly costly and difficult problems of non-Europeans seeking to be free from European rule and, sometimes, trying to create a nation where none had been before. Asian and African states, once free of British rule, transformed the Commonwealth into an organisation embracing many races.

Yet the developments that took place in the older, largely European-inhabited states in the Commonwealth were of major importance too. Britain owed a great deal to the support of Canada, Australia and New Zealand during the two world wars. Whereas in the non-European areas of the empire, most people were eager to be rid of British control, in the older Dominions there were many eager to maintain close ties with Britain, eager to remain monarchies when new Dominions hastened to become republics. The older Dominions were sharply jolted by Britain's attempt in 1962 to join the European Common Market – it seemed to some in the Dominions as if Britain were trying to break away from her own Commonwealth. In fact this application merely emphasised one of the vital developments of the twentieth century: Australia, Canada and New Zealand had matured into wealthy independent countries with their own special problems whilst Britain's position in the world had declined. The Great War demonstrated that the older Dominions must try and reduce their economies' close ties with Britain, whilst the Second World War showed that they could not even depend on Britain for military protection. In both respects Australia, Canada and New Zealand found themselves drawn, often reluctantly, towards the U.S.A.

By the time the Great War began, all three states were in full control of their affairs at home but all had their foreign policies managed by Britain. When Britain went to war in 1914 her Dominions were automatically involved. But, by 1939, Britain's declaration did not automatically carry

Australia, Canada and New Zealand into the conflict as well; their support here was entirely voluntary. At home all three states had economic difficulties in 1900 which they had gone some way to overcome by the 1960s; indeed, they developed into countries able to offer their inhabitants a higher standard of living than could be found in the mother country, Britain.

But although there are similarities in the development of all the countries, in their struggles to mature and to become less dependent on exporting large quantities of primary products, there are also major differences.

Canada

a) Canada Before 1914

Background

The most immediately obvious impression of Canada gained by looking at a map is its huge size. Canada fronts onto three oceans, the Pacific, Arctic and Atlantic; it stretches close to Asia on the one hand and, by way of Greenland, across to Scandinavia on the other. Yet the country's population is small (around twenty millions in the 1960s) and these people are concentrated in small areas, particularly in the south. Canada is not an easy country to live in, for its winters are long and severe, and its northern areas are mountainous and bleak. These problems of size and climate do much to explain the difficulties Canada has faced during her history. Her small population in relation to her southern neighbour, the U.S.A., makes Canada fear she will be too easily dominated by the U.S.A. Her scattered communities inhabit areas that look most naturally to the south, towards nearby areas in the U.S.A., not east or west to their fellow Canadian communities. The communities living on the west coast, the east coast and the Great Lakes – St. Lawrence River area, are all readily drawn into contact with nearby southern, U.S. areas, closely similar to their own. Canada is not a natural geographical unit and one of her abiding worries in the twentieth century is whether she is truly a nation with a special character of her own.

The Pre-European Canadians – Indians and Eskimos – were (and are) few in number. Early European settlers in Canada were French and, though conquered by Britain in 1763, remained (through their Catholic faith, their special schools, laws and language) a quite distinct community of people. British settlers were not numerous until the end of the War of American Independence when colonists loyal to Britain fled north from the States. During the nineteenth century their number was swelled by immigrants from Europe, not all of whom were British, who came to Canada to seek adventure, freedom and an opportunity for a better life. These settlers gathered in quite separate communities, some many hundreds of miles apart, and each managed their own domestic affairs. Not until 1867 did a number of these communities join together to form the Dominion of Canada and these merely included Quebec, Ontario, Nova Scotia and New Brunswick. From the vast lands farther north new provinces were created and in 1871 British Columbia joined the federation, but one of the oldest settlements in the area, Newfoundland, did not finally decide to join until 1949.

Canada's government

In setting up the new federal government in 1876 to manage affairs inside Canada, the Canadians were influenced partly by Britain's system of government and partly by the U.S.A. From Britain Canada copied the principle of cabinet government by men who were members of parliament. The U.S.A., like Canada, was a federation of several states but the recent civil war in the U.S.A. alarmed Canadian leaders into believing that it was dangerous to have a weak federal government which could be defied by separate states even to the extent of war. Instead of leaving the federal government with a few stated powers, the Canadians decided to follow the opposite policy. It was the provincial governments who had their powers defined, all the remaining powers of government lay with the federal authority. This federal government consisted of two assemblies. One assembly, the Senate, represented the different provinces and its members were appointed for life. Its power was not great, however; during the twentieth century its position deteriorated until it was almost ridiculous, yet to reform it might be to strengthen it so that it might seriously clash with the House of Commons, whilst to abolish it altogether might offend provincial feeling by sweeping away the organisation aimed at representing the provinces. Ministers were normally members of the other assembly, the House of Commons, which was elected on the basis of representing the majority of the population.

Canada's economy

Canada's early settlers developed her furs, fisheries and timber trade and though other sources of wealth were developed in the nineteenth century, these too were mostly agricultural, the most important being wheat. Railways linked the different parts of Canada more closely than ever before: in 1885 the Trans Canada Railway made possible a complete east-west crossing of the country. In the 1890s a rise in the world prices of raw materials helped Canada recover from her economic depression, together with mineral discoveries of which the most famous was the discovery of gold in the Yukon. The industries which began to grow, helped by British and U.S. capital, still made only a small difference to the fact that the Canadian economy depended so heavily on producing a few items.

The pre-war government

For fifteen years from 1896 the government of Canada was headed by the Liberal Party, led by Sir Wilfred Laurier, a skilful French-Canadian politician who hoped to encourage more friendly co-operation between English- and French-speaking Canadians. This was no easy task for the French Canadians, cut off for so long from France itself and less sympathetic to Britain than English-speaking Canadians, disliked a number of government actions. They felt little interest in the Boer War, whereas many English-speaking Canadians volunteered for service to help Britain; they disliked the small navy that Laurier had been persuaded into planning to provide for Canada. For some time a quarrel with the U.S.A. over a strip of territory claimed both by the U.S. state of Alaska and by British Columbia, helped unite all Canadians: but when the U.S.A. was eventually victorious many felt Britain had not supported Canada sufficiently and Laurier set up a Department of External Affairs as a cautious move towards the time when Canada would manage her own foreign policy.

As the years passed, Laurier was increasingly attacked as being too sympathetic to the U.S.A. More and more trade flowed between the countries, and greater co-operation between them was inevitable. Yet so many Canadians were so sensitive to the idea that the U.S.A. was trying to control them completely that moves towards co-operation were likely to be misinterpreted. In 1909 Laurier joined with the U.S.A. to establish an International Joint Commission to control the boundary waters between the two countries and in 1911 he negotiated an agreement to encourage trade between the U.S.A. and Canada by allowing free trade in natural products and in some manufactured products too.

For this latter agreement in particular the Liberals were sharply attacked, and in 1911 they were defeated by the Conservatives led by

Robert Borden. However, Borden was no more successful than Laurier had been and an economic depression in 1913 made his popularity dwindle.

b) The First World War

There was no strong and widespread resentment in Canada in 1914 at being pulled automatically into the Great War. Canadians readily volunteered for service overseas and Canada's industries and agriculture worked hard to provide the allies with necessities. Canada suffered heavy casualties for a country with a small population and the length and burden of the war encouraged the demand that Canadians should have more control over matters which directly concerned them. When Lloyd George became Prime Minister he agreed that Canadian troops should have their own commander and that Canada's Prime Minister should join the Imperial War Cabinet. In the peace negotiations after the war, Canada was separately represented; at least the war had finally established Canadian control of her own foreign affairs.

But war brought problems too. English-speaking Canadians had felt more concerned about the struggle in Europe and had volunteered for service overseas more readily than the French Canadians. When the government decided that conscription was necessary and, after an election, enforced it, there was great resentment among the French Canadians of Quebec. These settlers were a minority in their own land and for many years had been accustomed to thinking chiefly in terms of Canada alone, not in terms of Canada as part of a wider British Empire. Accusations and misunderstandings therefore grew in intensity between the two groups as a result of the war.

The Great War had a marked effect on Canada's economy, too, and led to an increase in government intervention in economic affairs. The federal government took over a number of railways and joined them into the Canadian National Railway: industries were stimulated too. As in Britain, the war raised the importance of women in the economy and led to their being given the right to vote. Canada was a little irritated to see so much attention falling on the U.S.A. for her part in the war when Canada's losses had been just as heavy and her ability to afford them was much less. But at least the Great War made it clear Canada was going to decide her own future; it emphasised the need for Canadians to concern themselves with their position as a separate country in North America, not simply as a part of the British Empire.

c) Between the Wars

Post-War Canada

This independence of mind soon showed itself in Canada's determination to avoid becoming heavily entangled in foreign difficulties, and her very unenthusiastic attitude to the League of Nations (in marked contrast to her later support of the United Nations). Canadian leaders emphasised how safe their country was, how free from the serious menaces that troubled Europe. In fact it would not have been easy for a vigorous policy to have been pursued, for Mackenzie King's Liberals, elected to power in 1921, lacked a clear overall majority in the Commons. Mackenzie King had succeeded Laurier on his death in 1919 and soon showed himself to be a very cautious politician determined to avoid giving offence to the French Canadians or the more pro-British Canadians. In 1926 he joined other Dominion leaders in discussions with Balfour, the British statesman, which resulted in the British government accepting Balfour's principle that the Dominions were completely independent states, equal with Britain, and united with her in common allegiance to the Crown. This principle, formally set down in 1931 in the Statute of Westminster, probably meant more to Canada than to Australia and New Zealand (who were far less enthusiastic) though it really made no serious changes in fact to a situation of independence already clear in 1918.

Canada enjoyed prosperity after the Great War but it rested on foundations that were far from secure. She still depended too heavily on the export of a few primary products and the Liberal government made little effort to do anything about this. Faced with conservative opponents and a Progressive Party backed by the farmers of Ontario and the West, Mackenzie King spoke of policies in only the vaguest of terms.

Depression

The Liberals were slow to act when there were increasing pointers that the period of prosperity was over. They preferred to hope that the rise in unemployment and the fall in price of the goods Canada exported was merely temporary; when, instead, the troubles increased, the Liberals suffered defeat in the 1930 elections. The victors were the Conservatives, led by R. B. Bennett, who promised Canadians a strenuous effort to sell Canada's goods overseas, tariffs to protect Canada's industries from foreign rivals, and help to provincial governments struggling to cope with the huge numbers of unemployed. Bennett was rather unfortunate, however, for the depression worsened, dragging Canada with it, and a solution seemed impossible. Nor was Bennett personally very popular; he was a wealthy lawyer with a rather aloof manner and very little political experience. His attempts to help Canada by trying to increase trade with Britain at the Ottawa Conference, and by heavily taxing U.S. imports, brought small benefits. Not until 1935, shortly before a general election, did he produce a bold scheme and by then it was too late. His ideas, borrowed from President Roosevelt, were dependent on a major programme of government intervention to find jobs and help for the unemployed, to stimulate industry and agriculture and to control hours and conditions of work.

Bennett was defeated by Mackenzie King in 1935, but discontent in the country also showed itself in the rapid growth of a socialist party (the Co-operative Commonwealth Federation) and of the Social Credit Party. This latter group blamed the depression on the banks and the financial system of the western world, and though some of its ideas were peculiar it managed to win control of the province of Alberta. Mackenzie King was helped by some of Bennett's measures which now began to take effect, especially those aimed at improving trade with the U.S.A. Many of Bennett's plans were, however, killed off when the Liberals decided to check on their legality and the British Privy Council eventually ruled that they were not an acceptable increase in federal power. The severity of the depression decreased, but Canada had still not really escaped from it when the Second World War began.

Foreign Policy

Realising the importance to her of both the U.S.A. and Britain, Canada attempted to remain on good terms with both and mediate between them if they seemed likely to differ. With the rise of Fascism and Nazism in

Europe, a heated argument developed in the country as to what Canada should do. Some argued for open and vigorous support of Britain, while others preferred to cling on to isolation. The latter group consisted mainly of those who held vivid memories of the Great War and who preferred in future to keep out of European affairs, and many French Canadians who continued to believe that Canada must think, above all, of herself. Mackenzie King needed the support of both sides to remain in power, and though he personally felt that Canada would back Britain in the event of war, he kept his belief to himself and avoided any kind of commitment. Yet when war broke out in Europe, Canada's own declaration of war on Germany came only one week after Britain's and aroused little indignation since the government promised not to introduce conscription.

d) The Second World War

The general support of Canadians for Mackenzie King's declaration of war showed that in fact he had been right. Canada still felt ties and responsibilities towards Britain that led her to declare war whilst the U.S.A. remained neutral. Canadians alarmed by their country's economic dependence on the U.S.A. and by U.S. influence through radio, cinema and magazines, had the reassurance of seeing that their country was not yet completely tied.

Canadian soldiers crossed over to Britain, R.A.F. crews came to train in Canada, but Canada was not really organised for war and reorganising herself was, at first, expensive. She was forced to buy costly U.S. equipment to develop her war industries and it was fortunate that the friendly relationship between Canada's Prime Minister and the U.S.A.'s President led to an agreement which lessened this burden. The U.S.A. began to build up war industries too, and the two countries agreed not to compete with each other: each produced certain agreed items and this led to U.S. purchases from Canada as well as Canadian purchases from the U.S.A. Canada also found the means for a programme of aid called Mutual Aid to help sustain Britain and her allies. The war led to the establishment of another link with the U.S.A., the Permanent Defence Board consisting of representatives from both countries who worked out joint advice to offer to their leaders. In the actual conflict, however, Canadian forces tended to concentrate on the areas that mattered most to Britain; the fighting in the Pacific was not regarded with the same seriousness as it was in the U.S.A.

Unfortunately the war led, once again, to a quarrel centering on the question of conscription. In 1942 the government felt so concerned about the war situation, it asked the people of Canada to release it from its promise not to introduce conscription. In a referendum, held to allow all voters to express their opinion, sixty-four per cent. of those who voted agreed that the government should be so released and consequently conscription was brought in. But the minority who opposed conscription was of considerable size; in Quebec province the number of opponents of conscription was as high as seventy-two per cent. At first the dispute was not serious, for the limited areas of fighting meant that there was no need for conscripted men to be sent abroad and the opposition to conscripted men serving in Canada itself was small. But the Allied invasion of Normandy meant that many more soldiers were needed and conscripted men had to be sent overseas. The hostility towards the government felt by the province of Quebec showed up clearly in Quebec provincial elections in 1944 for Maurice Duplessis' Union National won office and proceeded to resist any attempts by the federal government to increase its power at the expense of the provinces.

When the war ended Canada had become the world's fourth strongest military power and had developed a more varied and prod' 've economy to cope with war needs. The war re-emphasised the incre.singly close links, both military and economic, between Canada and the U.S.A.

e) Post- War Canada

Liberal rule 1945–1957

Led by Mackenzie King until 1948, and then by St. Laurent, the Liberals appeared to be permanently in power in Canada. Their leaders were capable ministers and they were supported by able colleagues; the opposition to them was divided between Conservatives, Social Credit members and the Co-operative Commonwealth Party. Although the Liberals did not always win a clear overall majority of the votes cast in an election, their majority in the House of Commons seemed unshakeable.

The post-war situation led the Liberals to concentrate on two main aspects of foreign policy; support for N.A.T.O. and support for the United Nations. Canada was one of the most enthusiastic founders of the United Nations, she placed great importance on events at the U.N. and contributed both money and men to serve in the U.N. peace-keeping force. Canadian delegates at the U.N. spoke calmly and sensibly, suggested moderate and practical policies, deliberately avoiding the excitable emotions shown by the representatives of many other nations. The U.N., like N.A.T.O., provided Canada with a way to emphasise her independence of the U.S.A.

But closer co-operation with the U.S.A. was inevitable in the post-war situation in which Canadians could no longer claim to be far from any danger of war. In 1957 the two countries went as far as to join their air defences to form the North American Air Defence Command. Like the U.S.A., Canada was alarmed by the way Russia established a close control over Eastern Europe. Both St. Laurent and Lester Pearson (who succeeded St. Laurent as Minister for External Affairs when the former became Prime Minister) spoke vigorously of the need for Canada to abandon her pre-war attitude of detachment, and join in the defence of the Western World from Stalin's Communism. By helping to found N.A.T.O. Canada contributed to this defence and kept up her ties with Europe and the U.S.A. The Korean War compelled Canada to take more interest in the Far East, but though Canadian troops went out there, Canada refused to agree with all the U.S.A.'s actions in the area, criticised some of them as being too rash, and caused some alarm to the U.S.A. by her readiness to export her large wheat crop to Communist states in Asia. In the American continent too, Canada insisted on not simply following obediently behind the U.S.A. and refused to join the U.S.-led Organisation of American States.

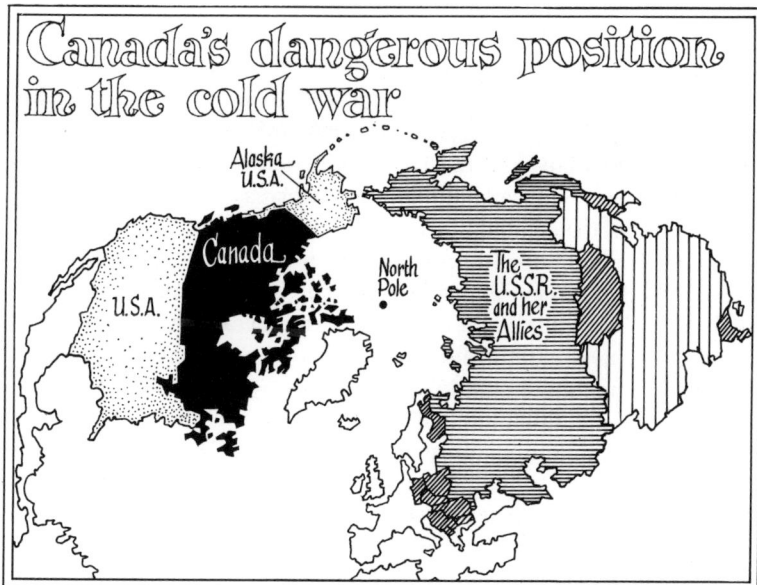

Canada's dangerous position in the cold war

The defeat of the Liberals

Yet it was partly due to charges of being too much in favour of the U.S.A. that the Liberals were eventually forced out of power. The Conservative Party complained of the way St. Laurent criticised Britain for her 1956 Suez action and deplored the ruthless manner in which the Liberals pushed through Parliament a bill to allow a U.S. company (helped by a large Canadian loan) to take natural gas supplies from the Canadian provinces of Alberta and Saskatchewan through a pipeline down into the U.S.A. Rumours spread that Canadian-U.S. efforts to build a radar screen around North America to give early warning of enemy attack would lead to U.S. control of northern Canada. Perhaps, also, there was a feeling that the Liberals had been in power for long enough and it was time for a change. Certainly the 1957 election jolted the Liberals for voters chose fewer Liberals than Conservatives.

Conservative rule, 1957–1963

Although John Diefenbaker's Progressive Conservatives had done well, they failed to obtain a clear majority over all other groups combined. This unsatisfactory situation was ended in 1958 for a new election gave Diefenbaker's party a clear overall majority in the House of Commons and reduced Liberal representation to a mere forty-nine.

The Conservatives had been in opposition for so long they naturally lacked experience in federal government and the times were full of troubles including differences with the U.S.A., disappointment in the hope of closer ties with Britain, a growth in unemployment and an increase in restlessness among French Canadians. The U.S. spy plane shot down by the Russians and the U.S. supported attempts to invade Cuba (the 'Bay of Pigs' incident) did much to increase Canadian criticisms of the U.S.A. Yet Diefenbaker's strongly proclaimed affection for Britain was jolted by the British application to join the European Common Market; Diefenbaker's grumbles did not please Britain either. His relationship with President Kennedy (who became very popular in Canada) was never good and occasionally became a serious problem for two countries so closely linked in so many ways. Canada's economic troubles led to an open and embarrassing quarrel between the government and the governor of the Bank of Canada. Eventually some of Diefenbaker's own party became so discontented they staged a vain attempt to compel their leader to stand down.

Many of Diefenbaker's troubles were far from being of his own creation, his Liberal successors battled with the economic and defence questions too, and also had to cope with the French Canadian problem. There were enough criticisms however to cause a sharp drop in Conservative representations in the 1962 elections so that, once again, smaller parties held the balance between the two major ones. Diefenbaker struggled on until a new election in 1963 finally brought the Liberals, now led by Lester Pearson, back into power. In his last months in office Diefenbaker had cut imports and government expenditure in an effort to deal with Canada's economic difficulties, and had worried inconclusively about whether Canada should fit nuclear warheads to her U.S.A.-supplied rockets.

f) Conclusion

The French Canadian problem

From 1963 until 1968 Lester Pearson led the Liberals in power, developing better relations with the U.S.A. and accepting the nuclear warheads that had so worried Diefenbaker. Quebec continued to be a problem as the French Canadians complained they were not being fairly and adequately treated, and that special attention should be given to the distinctive way of life they had developed. There was even a movement demanding that Quebec should become completely independent, encouraged by the support given to the movement by the French President, de Gaulle, during a visit to Quebec in 1967. Lester Pearson's successor, Trudeau, himself a French Canadian, hoped to have more success in tackling this problem.

Relations with the U.S.A.

The fear of being wholly dominated, and even swallowed up by the U.S.A., is a persistent theme in Canadian history. The U.S.A. has more capital invested in Canada than in any other country; Canada is the U.S.A.'s biggest foreign market and in return supplies the U.S.A. with vital raw materials. Around sixty-five per cent. of Canada's economy is owned by U.S. companies, and some industries like cars, electrical goods and rubber are wholly U.S. dominated. The discovery in Canada of new wealth, like petroleum, natural gas, uranium, asbestos and vast iron ore deposits, has only added to the problem, for U.S. capital has been needed to exploit these finds and the U.S.A. is their biggest purchaser. All this U.S. activity looms large in the thoughts of Canadians; in the U.S.A., with its huge population and many diversified interests, it does not dominate thinking and Canada tends to be taken for granted in too many ways. U.S. influence is seen in radio and T.V.

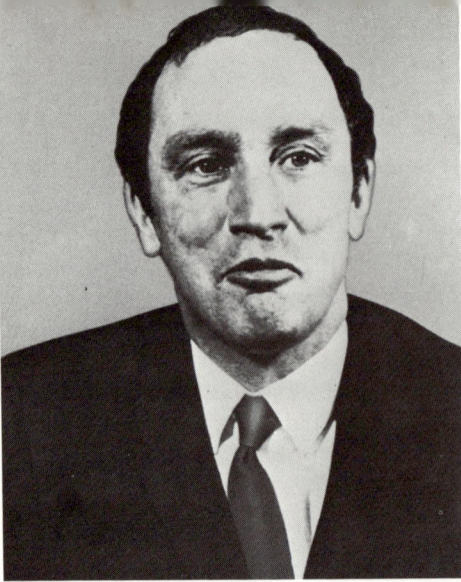

Pierre Trudeau, who succeeded Lester Pearson as Prime Minister of Canada in July, 1968.

programmes, books and magazines, and the games Canadians play; indeed one of Canada's concerns is whether she is a distinctive country at all, and not just a pale reflection of the U.S.A. The development of communications like the Trans Canada Highway of 1962 and the St. Lawrence Seaway of 1959 do not solve the problem that many Canadians naturally tend to look south to the U.S.A. rather than east or west to their fellow Canadians.

U.S. influence has helped to continue Canada's dependence on the export of raw materials, for the U.S.A. herself tends to have large resources for processing these goods. Helped by protective tariffs and backed by a government Department of Industry, Canada's industries have grown, but are still small in relation to her production of primary goods. Even so, Canadians today enjoy one of the highest standards of living in the world, the problems of the 20 million inhabitants of this vast land, though serious, seem small indeed compared to the problems of over-crowded Asian and Latin American states.

Australia

a) Australia before 1914

Background

Like Canada, Australia is an enormous country with a small population concentrated in a few limited areas because much of the country is not readily inhabitable. As in Canada too the European settlers who came to Australia found a fairly small native population which was backward in comparison with themselves. But whereas the Indians and Eskimos in Canada are as numerous now as in the days when Europeans first came, the aborigines of Australia have dwindled in numbers. Like Canada, Australia's early economic development was closely tied to producing primary agricultural products – in Australia's case the chief export was of wool. Indeed, the creation of huge sheep farms was one of the main reasons why the aborigines were driven from their lands.

But, unlike Canada, many of the early European settlers who came to Australia were convicts, shipped out from Britain and who, having served their sentences, remained in the country. This policy of transporting convicts began to dwindle after 1830 and transportation to Western Australia finally ended in 1840. Australia's population was swelled by the coming of free settlers, hoping to make their fortune. In 1851 the number of adventurers sharply increased for Edward Hargraves found gold; sailors deserted from their ships, shopworkers and office workers left their desks and counters to join the rush to discover more of the precious metal. The population of New South Wales, where the gold strikes were made, rose sharply. In 1883 the Broken Hill Proprietary Company was formed to mine silver; copper was found in Tasmania, and still more emigrants were attracted from Britain by the hope of prosperity. But agriculture remained the most important activity. The development of steamship services and of refrigeration enabled Australian farmers to export all sorts of new farm products in addition to wool, whilst more advanced farming methods copied from the U.S.A. helped Australians to produce more.

Although towns and cities grew, and railways were built to link them together, the different settlements in Australia were so widely scattered that a series of separate colonial governments grew up in Australia instead of one single central administration. Frequently these governments squabbled with each other, and petty differences and restrictions grew up (like a change in railway gauge from New South Wales to Victoria) that made many feel a central federal government would be very beneficial.

The growth of Australia in the nineteenth century brought problems as well as prosperity. A rush to buy land in the 1880s went too far and led to bankruptcies. The growth of the working class led to the growth of trade unions who demanded better conditions and clashed with the unco-operative employers. In 1890 strikes that began on the dockside went on for five years and spread to bring in sheep shearers and miners too. The unions were eventually defeated, and this encouraged them to take more interest in politics, and, in particular, in the new Labour Party.

The establishment of the Commonwealth of Australia

The move towards unity was encouraged by a growth in nationalism in Australia, by the feeding that immigration by Asians must be resisted; other Europeans (the French in New Caledonia, the Germans in New Guinea) pressed in around Australia. Negotiations between the different colonies dragged on between 1897 and 1900, with New South Wales proving particularly difficult to please. But the advantages of co-operation and better organisation were clear, and able leaders like Edmund Barton and Alfred Deakin were eventually successful in obtaining the establishment of a federal government. By an act 'to constitute the Commonwealth of Australia' in 1900, the British Parliament confirmed Australia's actions and thus emerged a central government formed from the leaders of the biggest party in the Senate (which gave equal representation to the states) and the House of Representatives (elected on a population basis). A Governor-General was appointed to represent the Crown. The new federal government was weak, however, for the states proved reluctant to part with much control over their affairs and insisted on keeping in their own hands control of education, health, income tax, and many other matters of immediate importance in most people's lives. Control of foreign policy remained firmly in the hands of the British government. The early party organisations were weak too; the Labour Party developed an efficient organisation most rapidly, driving the Liberals and Conservatives to copy it. The first federal government was Liberal, led by Barton and Deakin, and with some sympathetic support from Labour.

'White' Australia

In some respects, the parties were in agreement and in no issue was this agreement more closely aligned than in the question of immigration. It was felt that immigration into Australia must be firmly controlled. The policy of keeping Australia 'White' meant excluding Asians and encouraging the entry of Europeans; a policy that was aimed at keeping up workers' living standards by excluding Asians used to much poorer conditions, whilst also maintaining a racial unity that would prevent quarrels between people of different races from troubling the country. People who arrived in Australia were given a fifty-word dictation test in a European language and this had the effect of keeping out almost all Asians.

The Harvester Judgement

As part of the policy of increasing Australia's wealth and raising living standards, the Liberals developed industry and tried to shelter it by means of tariffs. Taxes could also be used to persuade employers to pay adequate wages. For instance, employers who could show that they were paying fair wages could escape a duty on agricultural machinery. In fact the Australian High Court denounced this latter action, but it did lead to great interest in what was exactly a fair wage, and to a definition of this by Justice Henry Higgins president of the newly established Commonwealth Court of Conciliation and Arbitration. Higgins was considering the wages being paid at a harvester factory (1907), and his attempt to define in some detail what made up a basic wage adequate for a man's needs in a civilised community had considerable influence throughout the country.

Labour in Power

Though the Labour Party gained effective control of the federal government in 1910, with Andrew Fisher as P.M., its actions showed that men of other parties had no need to fear that it would adopt revolutionary policies. The party had support from unions and from the Roman Catholic Church. Many Irish had emigrated to Australia, bringing their Catholic faith with them, and tended to feel that the Liberals and Conservatives were Protestant parties. Labour introduced pensions for invalids and maternity allowances, but it was only following the Liberals, who had introduced invalid and old age pensions in 1908, and like the Liberals, it limited payment of these benefits to Australians of British origin who had been in the country for many years. A Commonwealth Bank was established and a moderate tax on landowners who failed to work their land properly completed the Labour Party's cautious reforms.

b) The First World War

Australia's support for Britain had been shown by her co-operative attitude during the Boer War, and in 1914 too, Australians were eager to come to Britain's aid. Volunteeers served in the terrible Gallipoli campaign and on the Western Front, and their courage and energy made them very popular with British generals. Australian ships were in action too; it was an Australian cruiser, the *Sydney*, which sank the famous German commerce raider, the *Emden*. Australia's industries, hitherto very small, were encouraged by the circumstances of the war to grow in size. In 1915 the Broken Hill Proprietary Company opened an iron and steel works at Newcastle, the beginning of an important industry. The chemical industry, the production of sugar, and improved agricultural output, were all assisted by the war. The federal government had to act more and more as a result of the conflict, taking powers to fix prices, create state control of marketing some items, and purchasing ships.

But the war led to ill-feeling too. The cost of living outpaced the rise in wages and increased restlessness among workers. But the biggest storm of all was stirred up by W. M. Hughes, Leader of the Labour Party and Prime Minister in 1915. Hughes, born in Montgomeryshire in 1864 and educated to be a school teacher, emigrated to Australia where he held jobs that varied from stone-breaker and seaman, to drover, pantry-man, and actor. Though small and partially deaf, Hughes was a fiery, cunning, and skilful politician who was able to dominate his colleagues. His outlook on life was rather sour and bitter, and his manner of speaking could be savage and offensive to colleagues as well as opponents. A visit to Britain and a tour of the Western Front filled Hughes with confidence in himself as a popular orator, and a burning determination to increase Australia's war effort by introducing conscription. But a referendum in October 1916 to find out whether this was what Australia wanted led to Hughes' conscription proposal being defeated. He persisted in seeking it however, his party expelled him, and followed by a small group of supporters he resigned from office. This split in the Labour Party brought about its downfall and Hughes returned to power, now leader of the National Party formed from his Labour supporters and the Liberal Party. Once again he raised the question of conscription and by now he had stirred up violent feelings on the subject. Some people, especially soldiers, cheered Hughes' violent speeches and hailed him as 'the Little Digger', a great patriot; others turned out to jeer him and, if possible, to pelt him with eggs and tomatoes. In great disappointment Hughes had to see, once again, his conscription plan defeated in a popular vote.

But Hughes was a bustling irrepressible figure much in evidence as the war continued, and even more so at the following peace conference. He obtained the former German colony of New Guinea and thwarted an attempt to allow people of any race or nationality to emigrate to former German colonies. The 'white Australia' policy was not to be dented by any such roundabout method. The war had brought Australia the same independence as it brought Canada, including control of foreign policy, and had emphasised the need for Australia to try and develop her own industries. But it did not lead to the emergence of a vigorous and separate foreign policy. Canadians might worry about what to do if Britain went to war again; Australians continued to accept the need to follow Britain's lead and trust in the protection of the Royal Navy.

c) Australia Between the Wars

The defeat of Hughes

By 1920 Hughes was beginning to lose his dominance in politics. This was partly because in Australia, as in Canada, the post-war years saw the rise of a party backed by farmers which became a formidable third force in politics. This party, the Country Party, objected to the dictatorial way in which Hughes managed the government and its objections became very serious for Hughes when elections made the Country Party's support necessary if the National Party were to stay in power. The result was seen in 1923, for Hughes was compelled to resign and to see his place taken by a Cambridge-educated, well-to-do lawyer, Stanley Melbourne Bruce. There could have been no greater contrast than between these two leaders; on the one hand Hughes, a self-made man, cunning, even ruthless, and adept at mob oratory; on the other hand Bruce, distinguished, aloof, clad in English-style clothes and affecting English manners and speech.

Bruce in power

Increased government activity engendered by the Great War continued for some years afterwards. A fixed retail price for sugar, subsidies to the canned fruit industry, help for butter exporters, irrigation works like the Hume River Reservoir on the River Murray to benefit fruit and sugar growers, and more road building, all furnish proof of the attempt by Bruce's government to improve Australia. In 1927 the Duke of York visited Australia to open the newly completed federal capital of Canberra, specially built to avoid quarrels between the capitals of the different provinces as to who should house the federal government. But Bruce had also to cope with strikes by seamen and waterfront workers and his attempt to be tough with them helped cause his downfall. His enemies were gleefully urged on by Hughes, who saw himself revenged, though he was not rewarded by his former colleagues with a position in the new Labour government that took office in 1929.

The depression

Led by James Scullin, the Labour Party gained power only to find itself,

like the British Labour Party, faced with all the problems of a world slump. The price of goods exported by Australia fell sharply and credit to develop her industries became impossible to obtain. Unemployment rose to twenty-nine per cent. of the work force, compelling the government to introduce a dole to help the unemployed buy necessities. As in other countries, argument raged as to what should be done and (again as in many other countries) the government failed to tackle the problem with a bold solution. A plan was drawn up by E. G. Theodore, the Commonwealth Treasurer, to deal with the slump which had the necessary boldness and daring, but the hostility of the Senate, the Commonwealth Bank and trading banks, and the Loan Council (created in 1927 to manage public borrowing), meant that it was impossible for Scullin to enforce it. In any case his chief concern was increasingly the need to hold together the splintering Labour Party in which one group led by the vigorous bullying figure of J. T. Lang, leader of the New South Wales government, battled with another led by the cautious and respectable Joseph Lyons.

Thus the actual policy followed, based on the lofty advice of a Bank of England official Sir Otto Niemeyer, consisted of cutting federal and state expenditure by twenty per cent. as well as reducing rates of interest and increasing taxation. In 1932 Scullin was ousted by Lyons, who had left the Labour Party and joined the opposition to form the United Australia Party, but policy changed little. The hounding of Communists, which Hughes had made almost an Australian tradition, continued under Lyons, but failed to divert public attention from the fact that the depression was slow to lift and that schemes of imperial preference for Australia's goods were not a sufficient solution. But at least the slump made industry more efficient, lowered costs, and made it clear to Australia how necessary it was that she should make more goods at home.

The depression also killed off Bruce's plans for a bigger navy and a new air force. The cancellations caused little stir for Australians took far more interest in the development of their own country than in foreign affairs. Indeed, so limited was Australia's desire to make clear her full independence from Britain that it was not until ten years after it had been passed that Australia bothered to endorse the Statute of Westminster. The distant menace of Japan would be dealt with, it was hoped, by Australian support for Britain and, particularly, by the base at Singapore.

d) The Second World War

The Great War had helped show Australians that they must not become overdependent on British markets and British industry and Australia had come to develop industry of her own and traded more widely. From the Second World War, Australians learnt that they could not rely on Britain for protection and security, and this encouraged a move towards the U.S.A. instead.

Menzies as Prime Minister

Australia entered the war under a new leader, Robert Gordon Menzies, a lawyer who had been Attorney General in Lyons' ministry and, at the age of forty-four, succeeded Lyons as Prime Minister and leader of the United Australia Party. Menzies had had an outstanding career as a scholar and a lawyer and had great charm and wit; but he was also scornful of those he disliked, not all of whom were in the ranks of the Opposition. Menzies had a very deep respect and admiration for Britain, her institutions, people and civilisation, and he had no hesitation in leading his country into the conflict when Britain herself declared war. His chief opponents, the Labour Party led by John Curtin, likewise supported the declaration of war, and Australian troops were soon in action in North Africa, the Middle East and Crete, whilst Australian warships helped defeat the Italian navy in the Mediterranean. But Menzies had to work with a very slender majority. He was absorbed in the war and in provincial politics rather than in keeping his colleagues happy, and the number of those dissatisfied with his leadership and offended by his sharp comments grew until they forced him to resign. His successor Arthur Fadden of the Country Party needed the support of two independent members to stay in power, soon lost this support, and was himself forced to resign shortly after Menzies' own fall.

The Japanese entry into the war

Late in 1941, the Governor-General invited John Curtin to form a government. Curtin accepted the invitation, eager to improve conditions in Australia, and backed by able men like Herbert Vere Evatt and Joseph Chifley. All their reform plans had to be hastily pushed into the background, for the Japanese decision to strike southwards totally altered Australia's viewpoint of the war. The Japanese onslaught was sudden and rapid, overwhelming the base at Singapore from which Australia had hoped to obtain protection, and trapping large numbers of British and Australian troops. At sea, too, Japanese warships backed by aircraft swept aside British opposition and rushed south, hopping from island to island, ever closer to Australia itself. John Curtin accepted that this was a new war and that Britain could not save Australia, but his insistence on this, and on the need for Australian forces bound for Burma to return home, offended more traditionally minded politicians who still looked to Britain for their safety. Yet with Japanese aircraft bombing Darwin, Japanese submarines damaging Australian coastal shipping and Japanese troops in New Guinea, Curtin could hardly be said to have been wrong. It was only the U.S.A. who could supply the large forces needed to halt the Japanese and Australia had to look to her, not Britain, for rescue. The battle of the Coral Sea saved north Australia and Australian troops were soon harassing the Japanese and defeating them at Milne Bay. The long war to drive the Japanese back absorbed Australia's resources and her attention, yet she still found men to help in campaigns in the Mediterranean.

Though the war was expensive, two-thirds of the cost was found from taxation and the rest came from domestic loans. As in 1914–18, the war increased the power of the federal government giving it control of income tax and reducing the states to depending on grants issued by the federal government. In 1943 the government introduced improved benefits paid for unemployment and sickness, pensions for the old and the widowed, and maternity allowances. Before the war had ended, Curtin died, to be replaced by Chifley. Like Curtin, Chifley was a man of Catholic-Irish origins; he had worked his way up from being a railwayman and union politician until he headed an able Labour ministry that continued to control federal government for some time after the war.

e) Post-War Australia

After 1945 Australia was forced to come to terms with her special problems of being a nation of Europeans situated in the Pacific, no longer

John Curtin who was Labour Prime Minister of Australia from October, 1941 to July, 1945.

protected by being part of the British Commonwealth, still with a population that was small in comparison to Asian nations, and heavily dependent on exports. Some comfort came from a pact with New Zealand and some from British troops stationed in the Far East, but New Zealand was a small country and British troops began to pull out of the area. Britain's 1962 application to join the European Common Market emphasised the dangers of being too dependent on Britain economically. Even a Premier as sympathetic to Britain as Menzies could not hide this. Just as Australian politicians and economists had to look hard at their nation's position in the world, so Australian painters and writers came to examine, both critically and affectionately, the special features of their own land, history and people.

Labour rule 1945–9

Labour, too, was forced to concern itself with how it wanted Australia to develop, and whether its system of war-time controls was intended to be a step along the road towards socialism. If the Labour Party was concerned with cautious, moderate reforms, and not with trying to make Australia a fully socialist state, then the problem remained as to whether war-time controls should be retained. Criticisms of Labour's continuance of war-time controls were levelled frequently by the revived Liberal Party, led by Menzies. Labour policies extending controls were limited and included clearly beneficial activities like the development of Qantas, a state airline for overseas services. Hydro electric schemes – the most famous being the Snowy Mountains Scheme – were also of real benefit to the country. The government encouraged immigrants from Europe, including many of non-British origin, to strengthen and enrich Australia.

John Grey Gorton, who succeeded as Prime Minister of Australia in 1968 on the death of Harold Holt. He was re-elected in 1969.

But in 1949 the Labour Party was finally ousted from power. Apart from criticisms of its controls it also suffered from a wave of strikes which it did not know whether to handle sympathetically or firmly oppose. The party was also divided as to whether it ought to recognise Communist China, and its many differences provided a ready target for Menzies which he fully exploited.

Menzies' return to power

Menzies' promises of fewer controls, less planning and a firm line in dealing with Communists brought him success in the 1949 elections and led to his party remaining so long in government as to seem almost permanent. When eventually he gave up the office of Prime Minister in 1965 it was because he was retiring to make way for Harold Holt, not because he had been defeated by Labour opponents who were, all too often, divided among themselves. Some Australians felt that Menzies was too devoted to Britain (he was the only Commonwealth leader to give sympathetic backing to Britain's 1956 Suez operation) at a time when Britain's position and power had diminished, and she was busy with drawing from Asia and trying to strengthen her ties with Europe. Others held that he was too obsessed with Communism; his attempt to suppress the Australian Communist Party was defeated in a popular vote in 1951. But his government supported his policy of joining those seeking to halt the spread of Communism in Asia, which meant particularly supporting the U.S.A. Australia joined the South East Asian Treaty Organisation, sent troops to Korea, and later sent small numbers of forces to support the U.S.A. in Vietnam.

The prosperity of Australia helped Menzies retain power and made possible the Colombo Plan, in which Australia took a leading part with other nations, to find money to aid poorer Asian states. It also enabled him to follow his policy of stressing the need for freedom of the individual to make arrangements for his own welfare, rather than providing a large state welfare system. Australia's welfare schemes are far more limited than those in many European states (including Britain herself); there is no equivalent of the National Health Service, for example. Yet with a generally favourable climate and a high standard of living helped by the discovery of new minerals, including uranium, and growing trade with the U.S.A., many Australians feel that their country has no need to make elaborate arrangements for problems of poverty and sickness which are less prevalent in Australia than in Europe.

Labour, led by Gough Whitlam, recovered office from 1972 till 1975 and tried to free Australian foreign policy from close dependence on the U.S.A.

New Zealand

New Zealand in the nineteenth century

It was not until 1840 that New Zealand was declared a British possession, although British traders, settlers, and missionaries had been coming to the country for some time. Britain felt it necessary to take this step in an attempt to bring law and order to a rather wild group of European inhabitants, and to try and control the clashes which were becoming increasingly frequent between the Europeans and the Maori people who already inhabited New Zealand.

The main cause of the squabble was a simple one – the European settlers wanted land for their farms and settlements and the Maoris did not want to part with it. Some Europeans, especially the missionaries, tried to persuade the British government that the right policy was to recognise the independence of the native rulers and interfere with them as little as possible. But the government proved neither able nor willing to follow this line; instead the Maoris were persuaded to sign a treaty

Richard John Seddon, Prime Minister of New Zealand from 1893–1906, laid the pattern for much of New Zealand's advanced social legislation.

recognising Queen Victoria as their ruler. The promises they were given in return were not kept, as the pressure from settlers for Maori land was too great. Eventually the occasional clashes developed into serious fighting in the late 1850s and throughout the 1860s. Fighting in which at first the Maoris did very well although they were eventually defeated. After their defeat the Maoris lost much of their land, their numbers decreased and they drew back from their contacts with the Western way of life.

The victorious settlers did not prosper easily at first; only sheep farming seemed to pay. The government of the country was uncertain, some wished to join Australia, some wanted New Zealand to keep the separate provincial governments that had grown up after 1852, and others hoped that New Zealand would acquire a central government of her own. It was this latter group that eventually triumphed, exploiting the fact that New Zealand was not a huge country like Australia, and the provincial governments had not been a success. A central government was able to find money to improve the country as the provincial councils could not; roads, railways and bridges were built, new settlers were attracted and more efficient farming methods adopted. The system of Provincial Councils was eventually scrapped in 1876.

The Liberal success of 1890

In 1890 the close group of conservative-minded men who had controlled New Zealand's government were pushed out of power and replaced by a Liberal ministry led by John Ballance that was more ready to change the country. Groups who had felt they were not being fairly treated joined together to elect the Liberals who therefore represented the hopes of town workers, and of farmers who were eager to break the barrier of huge estates which prevented them from obtaining more land. In order to bring about changes the Liberals were prepared to use the power of the state in a vigorous way that was unusual in most countries at this time, but both Ballance and his successor, Richard Seddon (Ballance died in 1893), pushed on with determination to put their country, in many ways, well in advance of most other states in the world.

Liberal reforms

By means of taxation the Liberals hoped to raise money to finance changes and, at the same time, make life so costly for the owners of large undeveloped estates that these estates would be broken up. Backed by loans from overseas, the Liberals found money to establish many small farmers on the land, helped by a general rise in world food prices which made farming more profitable. Regulations controlling working hours and conditions in factories, a labour code, and a system of compulsory state arbitration to settle quarrels in industry were all designed to reward workers for their support. By 1890 New Zealand already had the secret ballot and had given the right to vote to all male adult citizens. Seddon gave women the vote in 1893, long before they gained it in Britain itself. In 1898 the government brought in old age pensions and in 1903 provided free places in secondary schools – again, pioneering reforms. Seddon, or 'King Dick' as he was popularly known, died in 1906 and was succeeded by Sir Joseph Ward, previously Postmaster General. But Ward did not have Seddon's drive and the Liberals seemed to relax; their support from workers tended to filter off to the growing Labour Party, and the farmers' votes were won, with increasing success, by the Political Reform League. In 1912 the Liberals were finally toppled from power and in their place a more conservative government, the Political Reform League, took office.

Reform Rule

The Reform ministry, determined to put the interests of farmers first, was led by William F. Massey, who was himself a farmer from Auckland. The lack of a clear overall majority made it difficult for him to govern effectively; he was faced with the growing violence of workers' organisations complaining of the way wages lagged behind prices despite the arbitration system; finally the outbreak of war in 1914 came to dominate all other issues. New Zealanders responded to the war out of all pro-

Peter Fraser, war-time Premier of New Zealand, succeeded Michael Savage in 1940. He died in 1950.

Rt. Hon. K. J. Holyoake, who was re-elected Prime Minister of New Zealand in November, 1969 for his fourth term of office.

portion to their small numbers. Over 100,000 troops served overseas and the casualty figures of 58,000 (17,000 dead) meant that one in seventeen of the population was affected. At Gallipoli and on the Western Front the New Zealanders fought alongside the Australian troops, yet despite the terrible suffering in which they were involved, New Zealanders remained more determinedly pro-British than any other Commonwealth country. Massey denied that the war left the Dominions as fully independent sovereign states; he had little time for the League of Nations; he criticised Balfour's report stating that the Dominions were Britain's independent equals (indeed the Statute of Westminster itself was not formally adopted by New Zealand until 1947). When Lloyd George involved Britain in the Chanak crisis and war with Turkey seemed likely, one of the few states to offer promptly support to Britain was New Zealand.

Helped by post-war prosperity the Reform Party ruled until 1928. Massey had died in 1925 and was followed as Premier by J. Gordon Coates. Despite its name, it carried out few reforms, though it did bring in family allowances and also set up Meat and Dairy Boards. Its successor in power was the United (formerly Liberal) Party, but the new Ministry needed Labour support to stay in office, the Prime Minister was unwell and the ability of his cabinet was not impressive. The world economic depression, therefore, found New Zealand ill-prepared, with a large national debt, heavily dependent on selling abroad the products of farming whose value was now falling sharply.

The depression

The suffering brought about by the depression helped to develop in New

Zealand what the Great War had not – a feeling of nationalism. It also had political effects in that it pushed together the Reform and United Parties to form a National Government, whilst helping the growth of the Labour Party, which seemed to offer better solutions to the crisis than could be found by Coates, Minister for Unemployment and Finance, and the dominant figure in the National Government. New Zealand farmers tended to operate on a small scale and thus lacked the resources to tide them over a bad patch, so that they felt particularly strongly the inability of Britain to absorb endless quantities of New Zealand wool, wheat, meat, and dairy produce. Indeed, Britain began to introduce protection for her own farmers, an action which was bound to hurt New Zealand. The Labour Party made use of the growth in hostility towards a government that tried to do little more than balance its budget, and widened its appeal to the workers by offering farmers a guaranteed price for their goods. In 1935, led by Michael J. Savage, Labour efforts were duly rewarded by election to office.

Labour in power

The entry into power of Savage's ministry brought with it a more vigorous attitude in dealing with the depression. Wage cuts were stopped, a forty-hour week introduced, industry encouraged, and a system for marketing goods in an efficient manner within the country was brought in. A policy of public works improved the country and provided extra jobs, a health scheme was organised, and state housing developed to be available at low rents. By means of negotiated agreements with Britain the government guaranteed the sale of much New Zealand produce in the British market.

With the beginning of the war in 1939 the rise in demand for New Zealand's goods finally ended the depression, though the war also brought home to New Zealand the menace of Japan that threatened Australia too. The Labour Party had taken a more lively interest in foreign policy than its predecessors, but this interest centred on the League rather than on independent foreign policy. Despite the entry of Japan, New Zealand forces fighting in the war remained primarily involved in the Mediterranean area, not the Pacific. However the war did emphasise to New Zealand how vulnerable she was if she depended on British protection alone.

Modern New Zealand

Michael Savage died in 1940 and was succeeded by Peter Fraser. Under

A view of New Zealand's Parliament Buildings at Wellington.

Fraser the Labour Party continued to rule New Zealand until 1949 when it was defeated by Sidney Holland's National Party which offered, as did Menzies' Liberals in Australia, fewer controls and more competition. Post-war New Zealand has enjoyed prosperity, but this still depends very heavily on selling farm produce to Britain and Britain's attempts to join the European Common Market were probably more worrying for New Zealand than for any other Commonwealth country. Like Australia, New Zealand has had to concern herself with her Asian neighbours and has drawn closer to the U.S.A. – sending troops to Vietnam, for example. The prosperity enjoyed by New Zealand – which has greatly benefited the Maori people too – has been useful in bringing stability and in attracting immigrants; it has also meant that the New Zealand of the 1960s seems far more conservative and cautious than the New Zealand of 1900.

Norman Kirk led Labour to victory in 1972. Although he died in 1974, Labour remained in power till 1976. Under Labour, New Zealand began to follow policies more independent of the U.S.A.

Conclusion

The first half of the twentieth century contained changes in the pattern of life for millions of people that involved political, social and economic upheaval. In some ways the world of the 1960s appears very different in the decline of colonialism or the rise of Communism for instance – but in other ways old problems not merely remain but assume larger and more terrifying proportions. The problem of warfare is a striking example of this and the problem of poverty has, too, in some ways become more explosive.

a) The Decline of Colonialism

In 1900 the world was dominated by Europe either directly in colonies, or indirectly through European economic power. By 1969 this situation had changed drastically, few colonies remained in European hands and Europe's economic dominance was diminished by that of non-European powers like the U.S.A. and Japan. Yet colonialism had transformed the areas it affected, altering frontiers, spreading Western methods of government, warfare and economic organisation as well as Western ideas. The colonial powers destroyed the power of the traditional rulers of the areas they conquered and thus created political confusion and instability, a situation which tends to lead to military leaders seizing power.

b) The Growing Unity of Mankind

A revolution in transport has vastly reduced the isolation from each other of the different peoples of the world. To the railways and steamships of the nineteenth century have been added the aircraft and motor vehicles of the twentieth century. During the present century the two major wars have been world wars, and the weapons developed during and after these conflicts have also made men increasingly conscious of the inter-dependence of different peoples. A war in which nuclear weapons are used will affect civilians as well as soldiers, the innocent as well as the guilty. The need to control war in view of the rapid growth in the destructive power of weapons helps explain the emergence first of the League of Nations, and secondly of the United Nations.

c) The Changing Balance of Power

By 1969 the U.S.A. had finally emerged from its semi-isolation of 1900 to take a vital part in political, economic and military affairs all over the world. China, divided and at the mercy of the West in 1900, has now found new strength and unity under Communism, is acquiring all the weapons of a modern state, and is bound to be of major importance in world affairs. Russia, too, had gained in importance under Communist leadership, becoming richer and stronger, no longer the ramshackle backward power that Japan had defeated so heavily in 1904–5. Britain, France and Germany, so dominant in 1900, have declined in importance to second-rate powers lacking the size and resources of the U.S.A. and the U.S.S.R. and, in Germany's case, being split into two separate states. The dominant powers in 1900 were led by monarchs, emperors, or respectable middle-class politicians. By 1970 two major powers, Russia and China, and many minor ones, were ruled by Communists, members of a party that in 1900 had been a nuisance but not a major menace. Yet the world has not split into a simple division of Communist and non-Communist, for the Communists are divided between the Chinese and Russian sections, and many new African and Asian states have insisted on not joining sides in this clash.

d) The Problem of Poverty

Few non-Western states except Japan have managed to achieve a rate of economic growth to match their growth in population and the gulf between rich and poor is tending to widen, not narrow. Difficulties in Asia, Africa and Latin America come sometimes from lack of resources, often from lack of capital, skill and education, but above all, from the growth in population. Studies of world population in 1900 put the figure at around 1,500 million; by 1955 this had risen to 2,500 million, and a United Nations estimate for 1975 puts the figure at 4,000 million. Yet this growth has tended to come in areas where there is already pressure, like Egypt and India, and generally is far greater in the non-industrial areas than in the more advanced states. The populations of Europe and North America increased rapidly in the nineteenth and early twentieth centuries but emigration and industrial expansion enabled these areas to cope with the problem and even grow richer. But the techniques of dealing with the major diseases (that helped keep numbers down) developed in Europe and North America have been applied in other parts of the world too. Here, then, life expectancy has increased, yet there has not been an adequate growth of the economy to cope with this increased population. Western nations have a high level of education and have understood the problem and adopted birth control programmes. Japan has coped with the problem by allowing and even

A view from City Hill in Canberra, Australia's national capital. In the foreground is the Canberra Theatre Centre and behind, office buildings and the City Square fountain.

encouraging abortion. But in other lands tradition and religious beliefs coupled with ignorance and backwardness make the introduction of birth control programmes difficult. The result is that the lands which are most in need of birth control have least success in adopting it. Short of capital and overwhelmed with surplus labour the governments of countries like India are faced with an almost impossible task if they are to raise the standard of living of their peoples. Without doubt the major problem in world affairs in the remaining decades of the twentieth century must be the steadily rising population.

e) The problems raised by industrialisation

Whilst the poor countries of the world struggle to build up industries that will help to support their growing populations, the richer countries are adding to the future problems of the world by the very fact that they have developed industries on such a large scale. The processes of industry involve digging up or otherwise obtaining raw materials, processing them, and marketing an end product. All these processes raise problems which must be faced in the future – essential raw materials are rapidly being exhausted, the industries carrying out the processing produce harmful waste material, and some of industries' products may have harmful effects. The waste of industrial society helps to pollute the atmosphere and the waters, its discarded products like old cars, cans, bottles etc., pile up in huge and ugly heaps. Some of the products

Y

produced by industry directly harm human beings, drugs like thalido-mide for example; others have an indirect effect, like the chemical sprays (particularly pesticides) used on crops. Industries carry out limited tests on their products, but their long-term indirect effects are impossible to assess and many people prefer to hope blindly that if a problem should emerge in the next ten or twenty years, a solution will also have been found by then. A small beginning of looking serious-ly at the long-term results of modern industrialisation has been made by United Nations specialists but most people are too concerned with immediate results to allow seriously for effects that may not be felt for a generation or more. In any case it would be a mistake to believe that developing modern industries and living in modern cities will solve the problems of mankind. The strains, illnesses and suicides of people living in the cities of the most highly developed industrial areas are a sufficient warning against being too optimistic. The modern industrial revolution, pioneered by Britain, has harmful consequences that stretch beyond the wretched housing and working conditions of the early nineteenth century.

Problems to Discuss

1. Is it fair to blame the terrible suffering endured by soldiers during the Great War on the incompetence of their military leaders?

2. Do you see Stalin's rule in Russia as a necessary stage of suffering through which Russia had to go or as something both evil and unnecessary?

3. Explain why the United States' twentieth century foreign policy has changed so much from isolationism to intervention.

4. Why were Mussolini and Hitler so popular in their own countries for so long? Do you think they deserved this popularity?

5. Britain and France had won the Great War, yet after 1918 they suffered from increasing doubts and weaknesses. Why do you think this happened?

6. Compare the effect of the two world wars on the position in the world of Europe and the U.S.A.

7. How far was Hitler responsible for his own defeat in the Second World War?

8. In what ways would it be fair to argue that the United Nations is a big step forward from the League of Nations?

9. Compare the problems facing modern China and India and the ways in which these two countries are trying to solve these.

10. Why did the British and French empires dwindle so rapidly after 1945?

11. Both China and Japan were strongly affected by the impact on them of the West. Why did they react in such different ways?

12. Do you agree that the Arab-Israeli problem is so difficult to solve because 'both sides are right'?

13. Why do you think so many states in Africa have become dictatorships of armed forces?

14. Why has West Europe made more progress towards unity since 1945 than at any other time in the twentieth century?

15. What difficulties hold back the countries of Latin America from

occupying a more powerful and influential position in the world?

16. Why have some East European states been more successful than others in defying the power of Russia since 1948?

17. Why were U.S. forces so successful against the powerful state of Japan and yet faced with so many difficulties in the weaker countries of Korea and Vietnam?

18. Why has there come to be so wide a gap in wealth and power between the 'developed' and 'underdeveloped' nations of the world?

19. Does a study of the twentieth century lead you to agree with the opinion that 'it would be better for mankind if nationalism were abolished'?

20. Examine the way Communism has changed during its development from 1900 to the present day. Do you think the countries where Communists have won power have benefited from this?

Glossary

E.A.M. –	The National Liberation Front. A Greek Communist movement linked closely with E.L.A.S., the Communist People's Liberation Army.
E.D.E.S. –	The non-Communist Greek movement called the National Democratic Greek Union.
F.A.O. –	Food and Agriculture Organisation.
G.A.T.T. –	General Agreement on Trade and Tariffs.
G.D.R. –	German Democratic Republic.
I.C.A.O. –	International Civil Aviation Organisation.
I.L.O. –	International Labour Organisation.
M.L.F. –	Multilateral Force.
M.R.P. –	*Mouvement Républicain Populaire*
T.A.N.U. –	Tanganyika African National Union.
U.N.E.S.C.O. –	United Nations' Educational, Scientific and Cultural Organisation.
U.N.I.C.E.F. –	United Nations' Children's Emergency Fund.
W.H.O. –	World Health Organisation.

Index

Acknowledgements

The author and publishers are grateful to the following for permission to reproduce copyright photographs:

The Associated Press Ltd., pages 123, 189, 201, 206, 342.
Australian News and Information Bureau, Office of the High Commissioner for Australia, pages 348, 351, 352, 361.
Camera Press Ltd., pages 21, 37, 41, 44, 47, 54, 95, 186, 204, 264.
Federal Republic of Nigeria, Ministry of Information, page 308.
The High Commissioner for New Zealand, pages 354, 356, 358.
Imperial War Museum, pages 26, 31, 131, 136, 137, 139, 143, 144, 147, 156, 176, 271.
Keystone Press Agency Ltd., pages 87, 152, 166, 168, 171, 223, 228, 238, 243, 246, 279.
Radio Times Hulton Picture Library, pages 72, 82, 106, 111, 117, 253, 334.
Topix (Thomas Newspapers Ltd), pages 120, 282.
United Press International (U.K.) Ltd., Frontispiece and pages 15, 52, 57, 69, 198, 215, 285, 312.